THE AMERICAN LEONARDO

Addison Gallery of American Art, Phillips Academy, Andover, Mass.

SELF–PORTRAIT

By Morse — About 1814

Painted in London, when, as he said, his face approached the "hatchet class."

THE AMERICAN LEONARDO

A Life of

SAMUEL F. B. MORSE

BY

CARLETON MABEE

With an Introduction by ALLAN NEVINS

1944 ALFRED · A · KNOPF NEW YORK

THIS BOOK HAS BEEN PRODUCED
IN FULL COMPLIANCE
WITH ALL GOVERNMENT REGULATIONS
FOR THE CONSERVATION OF PAPER, METAL,
AND OTHER ESSENTIAL MATERIALS

Published simultaneously in Canada by The Ryerson Press

Manufactured in the United States of America

PUBLISHED FEBRUARY 1, 1943
SECOND PRINTING, MAY 1944

TO

MY GRANDFATHER

Charles Neander Bentley

[1854-1942]

A

NEW ENGLANDER

WHO UNDERSTOOD MORSE

INTRODUCTION

The life of Samuel F. B. Morse is one of the most interesting in American history; a life fascinating partly because of the versatility of his undertakings, partly because of the rich interest of his mind and character.

Morse crowded four careers into an ordinary lifetime – that of an artist; that of an inventor or at least combiner and promoter of inventions; that of a man of business; and that of a politician. All four careers were full of struggle, controversy, and misfortune, but in three of them he achieved a distinguished success. Had he never touched a piece of mechanism he would be remembered as an eminent portrait-painter and the founder of the National Academy of Design. Had he never lifted a painter's brush, he would still be famous as the chief figure among the varied group of Americans who made the electromagnetic telegraph a success. While some inventors of his time, like that tragic figure Charles Goodyear, gained nothing but debts from their enterprises, Morse amassed a comfortable fortune long before he closed his days. His energy, impetuosity, and somewhat prejudiced strength of conviction carried him also into public affairs; and if here his chief allegiances were unfortunate and his labors barren, he was at any rate an unflinching exponent of what he believed to be the truth. When he died, men thought of him almost exclusively as an inventor; the telegraph operators of the country had already raised his statue in Central Park, and Congress honored him for his work in the furtherance of communication. But it is now possible to see that he had a memorable influence on several sides of our national culture.

This stalwart, manly, intensely earnest figure might seem to those who follow only the external events of his life a typical man of action, always pioneering, always organizing, and, it must be added, always battling something or somebody. But he was a good deal more than that. He was a man of a rich inner nature as well: a student, a devout churchman, an artist of sensitive heart as well as eye, and even something of a poet. It is evident that he had inherited both a practical set of traits from his mother, who came of a seafaring and mercantile family, and a philosophical and artistic set of traits from his father, the distinguished clergyman, philanthropist, pamphleteer, and geographer. Morse displayed at all times the nervous, irritable nature of the artist, eagerly responsive to his environment. He wrote verse, he showed in his various love affairs (down to that idyllic second marriage with a beautiful deaf cousin twenty-six years his junior) a susceptible heart, and in every undertaking he was sanguine and ardent. Probably his very combativeness sprang from his sensitiveness and impetuosity. He was quick to defend his own ideas in art, politics, sociology, and science, while he was sometimes excessively anxious to see that his achievements received not less than proper credit. At times he asserted altogether too much, making claims that proved untenable. Yet after all he was essentially a modest man. He wrote to his wife, after a reception in Washington, of the blushes of "your *modest* husband," and when he made a speech at a London dinner in his honor it was to emphasize the simultaneity of invention and wave aside any special crown. "Man is but an instrument of good if he will fulfill his mission; He that uses the instrument ought to have the chief honour, and He thus indicates his purpose to have it. It is surely sufficient honour for any man that he is a co-laborer in any secondary capacity to which he may be appointed by such a hand in a great benefaction to the world."

It is clear that his greatest enthusiasm in life was for art. His happiest years were those of his early struggles and aspirations, when he was studying in London under Allston, showing *The Judgment of Jupiter* at the Royal Academy, wandering from Boston to Charleston to paint portraits, and returning to Paris and Italy for more study. In this work really lay his heart. When he took up the labors of a daguerreotypist, it was chiefly because he thought they might be of profit to him in his artistic career. When he, Leonard D. Gale, Alfred Vail, and others had made the telegraph an unquestioned success, he would have been glad to sell his share of his patent to the government for a mere hundred thousand dollars; for this sum would have given him a competence and enabled him to return to his easel. Even later he played with the idea of reverting to art. At fifty-five, when superintendent of the Washington-Baltimore telegraph and immersed in details of business, a last opportunity seemed about to open before him. Inman's panel in the Capitol rotunda had never been completed; some of the most eminent men in the land, feeling the injustice which years earlier had deprived Morse of a share in this work, strove to have the empty space assigned to him; and he knew that, thanks to Amos Kendall, the telegraph could now stand alone. But Congress voted to give the commission to a young wire-puller who had enlisted the politicians. Morse accepted the verdict; he turned back to business, abandoning the thought of art forever.

Yet we need not regret the dualism of his career. It is probably a fact that he had reached the utmost height that he could achieve in art when he turned his back on it; that great as his attachment for it was, he had exhausted his possibilities there. His contribution to the telegraph was worth far more than a dozen panels in that rotunda at which few Washington tourists even glance – far more than a score of additional portraits. Various writers have contested Morse's title to the position of a great inventor, calling him rather an ingenious welder of other men's ideas and a gifted promoter of the result. He of course did not originate the idea of the use of electromagnetism in telegraphy, and simply made himself ridiculous when he so asserted. But it seems clear that the Morse code was truly Morse's, and not Alfred Vail's. It is unquestionably true that the relay device which opened a second circuit automatically when one did not suffice was Morse's conception. And beyond doubt Morse's indomitable work in making the telegraph known to scientists, to Congress, to the general public, and to financiers, in laboring against innumerable obstacles to gain for it a fair trial, was indispensable to its early success. There are few more heroic stories than that of his incessant struggles between 1838, when the message: "Attention, the Universe, by kingdoms right wheel," was sent through ten miles of wire, and 1844, when in Washington he telegraphed the words: "What hath God wrought!" to Vail in Baltimore.

Morse was more of an artist than Robert Fulton, who also painted; he was more of an experimenter and business man than Audubon, who combined painting with scientific inquiry. He had a mind that was constantly busy with inquiry and quick in relating seemingly diverse facts. As his friend William Cullen Bryant pointed out when both men had attained old age, even as a youthful painter he had experimented assiduously in materials, color-combinations, and lighting effects. His mind then "was strongly impelled to analyze the processes of his art – to give them a certain scientific precision, to reduce them to fixed rules, to refer effects to clearly defined causes, so as to put it in the power of the artist to produce them at pleasure and with certainty." When he took up daguerreotypy, it was to experiment with and improve it. He was one of the first to apply the microscope to photographs. He laid what he thought the first submarine telegraph – though two Britons had actually preceded him. And he was also a born organizer. Just as when a mere youth he was patenting a fire-engine pump and constructing a marble-cutting machine, so when barely settled in New York after his art studies abroad he was organizing an anti-Catholic and anti-alien campaign. Not so well known as the story of his work in helping organize the National Academy of Design is that of his share in launching the *Journal of Commerce*, for which he wrote the prospectus and to which he probably gave its name. He was no tyro in the art of organization when the telegraph captured his enthusiasm.

Not the least interesting part of Morse's life is the endless succession of controversies in which he was engaged. They were an integral part of his career, for they grew naturally out of his intense convictions, impulsive temperament, and indefatigable energy. His deep conservatism on most points was a natural inheritance from that staunch Calvinist and Federalist, old Jedidiah Morse. It was natural for him to feel a strong antipathy for Unitarianism on one side, Catholicism (whose seamy aspect he had studied in Rome) on the other; natural for him, in spite of his Jacksonian Democracy, to be a lover of the social order of his youth. Out of all this stemmed his hatred for abolitionism, with its Unitarian connections and its upsetting radicalism; and the natural sequel was his Copperhead attitude in the Civil War. Like so many stern Calvinists, he obviously found a moral exhilaration in his incessant battles. In art he fought Trumbull and the American Academy, in religion Channing and all his followers, in public morals the theater and lottery, in politics the

Irish. He went through the Civil War years assailing the "usurpations" of the Lincoln administration. His quarrels with partners and associates were of a type common in the history of invention, vividly recalling those of Richard Arkwright; and in most of them he was in the right. The one highly deplorable controversy of his lifetime, in which he was quite unforgivably wrong, was that with Joseph Henry, a scientist as gentle as he was great, whose friendship and aid had been invaluable to Morse. But no career as active as Morse's, no temperament so kinetic, is without its grave errors. Most of his quarrels were but illustrations of the defects of his fine qualities.

Morse was something better than a great inventor; he was one of the great representative Americans of his time, a leader in many activities, and a man who enriched the national culture in various ways. The story of his life has been told before, but never told with satisfying fullness or comprehension. It is fortunate that the materials for a complete biography have fallen into the hands of a student so industrious and keen-sighted, and a writer so gifted, as Mr. Mabee.

Allan Nevins

PREFACE

COLLECTING Morsiana has been a glorious chase up and down the Eastern seaboard. I have walked under an elevated railroad along the once elm-shaded street on which Morse was born, and kicked the cinders on the site of the meeting house in which he was christened. In New Hampshire I have followed him to the house where he courted a dark Concord beauty, and along the Souhegan River valley where he drove in a gig on his honeymoon. Between Concord, New Hampshire, and Johns Island, South Carolina, I have found his paintings in the proud possession of families for which he painted them, and not a few times I have heard the whisper that some day he will be known as the Stuart of his generation. My quest has led me to St. Michael's Alley, Charleston, where he slept on the floor of his studio-bedroom, and to his splendid later home overlooking the Hudson, where his granddaughter, Leila Livingston Morse, guided me about; it has led me to a white frame factory in Morristown, New Jersey, where he and his partners once labored over wires, batteries, and magnets, while the world, so far as it bothered, jeered at them; it has taken me to the United States Capitol to find the rooms where he first exhibited his telegraph to unbelieving congressmen and finally sent the resounding message: "What hath God wrought!" The stage on which Morse moved gradually took form in my mind as I gathered materials.

Using the materials has proved scarcely less exciting than discovering them. It has led me to question several of the standard legends about Morse, as, for example, that the message: "Attention, the Universe," was the first to be sent in Morse code; that when the telegraph bill was before Congress, Morse insisted that Congressman Smith should resign from his seat if he was to become a telegraph partner; and that Annie Ellsworth was the first to inform him of the passage of his telegraph bill. It was exhilarating to learn, what seems never to have been told, that before he revolutionized journalism with his invention, he was a founder of a great city newspaper, the New York *Journal of Commerce*. Plowing through old newspapers one day, I thought I had made another discovery when I read an editor's announcement that he had just seen the first daguerreotype ever taken in America, one made by Morse. After turning a few more crumbling pages, however, I found that Morse had written to the editor confessing that he had missed the honor by a few days. Oh, the pitfalls that await the writer who does not turn a few more pages!

In 1932 as part of the nationwide celebration of the hundredth anniversary of Morse's *Sully* voyage, when the Metropolitan Museum of Art, New York City, arranged an exhibition of Morse paintings, Harry B. Wehle, the museum's curator of painting, issued a list of Morse's paintings. In the preparation of this biography I have found information to supplement Mr. Wehle's work. I have not included it here because I expect it will be separately issued.

From the beginning this work has been a co-operative undertaking. Allan Nevins of Columbia University first suggested it to me, and has helped it along its way by advice on materials, by criticism of the manuscript, and especially by confidence in me, without which, indeed, I might well have faltered long ago. It was he who introduced me to Leila Livingston Morse of New York. With her almost limitless enthusiasm, with her access to Morse letters, diaries, photographs, and paintings which otherwise would have been inaccessible to me, and at the same time with her insistence that she would not influence my criticism of her grandfather, she has made the collection of materials for this biography much more efficient and delightful than it otherwise would have been. Among all the persons to whom I owe thanks (I name some of them in the Acknowledgments), Professor Nevins and Miss Morse deserve to be named first.

In large part this is Morse's book, the record of how he felt when he ran for mayor of New York, knelt in St. Peter's, met rival telegraphers, passed slave girls on the Charleston Battery, painted President Monroe, saw Mrs. Siddons at Covent Garden, or received the bows of Napoleon III.

But this is not only Morse's book, if for no other reason than that

Morse changed his conception of himself. At one time, for instance, he conceived of his future as bound up with his painting; at another he hoped that he would never be remembered as a painter. He forced me to choose between different judgments that he made of himself, and thus to take the right of judgment from him. While I have avoided making a pat appraisal of him, preferring to leave that for the pleasure of the reader, the mere acts of selection necessary to reduce a book to a convenient size are personal judgments. If to know such of my preconceptions as are pertinent here is useful to the reader, he is welcome to them. In politics I prefer the tradition of Jeffersonianism; in church government, congregationalism. Believing that creativity is very nearly an end in itself, I think that Morse was fully realizing himself when he was creating in the medium of brushes, pens, cameras, machines, or men. Yet I would distinguish among his various bents not only by how they stirred his soul but by their utility to society. Since material progress is not an end in itself, I believe inventions may or may not be useful. Already the telegraph and the wireless telegraph which sprang from it have been used both to benefit and to harm society. Whether in the long run they are to be used primarily to satiate our senses and chain our minds to the interests of power, class, nation, or race, or whether they are to be used to break the barriers that divide us and to free our spirits is one way, I believe, of stating the riddle of modern history. The final significance of Morse will not be known until we resolve that riddle.

This book too is a record of the judgments of Morse's fellows: those he painted, those who traced future telegraph lines on the map with him, those who hated him as a snob, a bigot, a charlatan avid for fame, or those who loved him as an enthusiast, a creator of beauty in a world of ugliness, a doer in a world of inertia.

Above all, this book is intended as a vigorous affirmation that Morse should be known as more than a telegrapher. If his friend Dunlap was the American Vasari, then Morse was the American Leonardo. As such he should be known not only as an inventor, but also as an artist, promoter, controversialist, and man of faith.

C. M.

Lewiston, Maine *Summer 1942*

CONTENTS

Contents

ILLUSTRATIONS

THE AMERICAN LEONARDO

CHAPTER *i*

Below Breed's Hill

LIKE millions of Americans, Samuel Finley Breese Morse was born on a small-town main street in a rented house.

Yet a learned historian soon called upon him to muse whether he would some day have the sagacity of a Jewish rabbi, the profundity of a Calvin, or the sublimity of a Homer. A college president held him in his arms and, after the manner of the Hebrew patriarchs, gave him a solemn blessing. Presently a Greek scholar, who had been Postmaster General, sent his parents "something to make Master a frock." [1]

His cradle was not only an aristocracy of intellect, but an aristocracy of position too. The houses near his, like boxes of two or three stories, with doorways, windows, and even chimneys regularly spaced, were as sternly unpretentious as the New Englanders who lived in them. Down toward the town square the houses were still essentially wooden boxes, but they were more gracefully decorated in the Georgian manner. They had elegant pilasters, Ionic porches, or felicitous window casings; they had boxed flowers set about the narrow spaces between the houses and street fences. In these houses the father of Finley was a familiar guest, for he was a man of position, the town pastor. He often called at the handsomest house in town, Miss Russell's, where Finley soon became acquainted with the pantry; he often called on Nathaniel Gorham, who as president of the Continental Congress had revealed the inner thoughts of not a few revolutionary gentlemen when he attempted to interest the brother of the King of Prussia in becoming the king of the United States.

Charlestown was as much a citadel of Federalism as Boston, the city that was only a few minutes' walk across the Charles River bridge. As Americans, Charlestown gentlemen boasted of independence, but as Federalists, like their pastor Morse, they favored the recent enemy, Britain, over the recent ally, France. The substantial citizens, those who frequented the society of the town pastor, blamed the coming of the American Revolution more on American hot-heads than on the British. It was the democratic hot-heads, many believed, who had brought on the battle that had raged on Bunker Hill and along the ridge to the higher Breed's Hill, just above their houses.

The British had spared few of their houses, not excepting that of Nancy Shepherd, Finley's nurse, nor the old meeting house on the square. One of Finley's earliest recollections was his walks on the hills when nurse Nancy told him over and over again how the redcoats had burned the town below. When the enemy had been driven out, Charlestown quickly rebuilt. The first house to go up again was the one where the Morse baby first lay.* The most prominent new building, the meeting house, was now behind the square on Town Hill. Its tower, designed by Charles Bulfinch, gracefully proclaimed to town, harbor, and Boston that Charlestown had come through its ordeal by fire with fresh courage and faith.

Pastor Jedidiah Morse had not been long in town when his first son, Finley, was born. When the young cleric first came to the meeting house, the only one in town, there was already a split between the orthodox and liberals of the congregation.

At his installation – it was at the same hour of the same day on which Washington was inaugurated first President of the United States – the parishioners peered at him from their boxed pews. He was only twenty-eight years of age, but his long head, his sharp features, his slim body in black robe and white neckbands, and his inclination to the serious made him appear responsible enough. They expected their pastors to be learned persons. Beginning in 1632 their church had installed five graduates of the University of Cambridge in the old country. Shortly after one of them, John Harvard, had

* The house was torn down only in 1928. The site, on Main Street near Wood, is now occupied by the Snappy Dress Shoppe. A plaque commemorates Morse's birth.

concluded his ministry, the church began to draw its pastors from the college which bore his name in the Cambridge only three miles away. The series of Harvard pastors was broken only by the installation of one from Oxford and now of Jedidiah Morse from Yale. Surely Jedidiah was a learned man. They knew he was already an accomplished geographer, the author of the first geography ever printed in America. They had heard him preach as a supply. They knew he had held brief pastorates in his home state, Connecticut, and also in Georgia. They had liked him and chosen him unanimously. They hoped he would heal the dissension in their congregation.

As the young cleric listened to the installation sermon of Jeremy Belknap, historian and pastor of the Boston Federal Street Church, he was aware of how much the Boston pastor had done to bring him to Charlestown. While he was coddling along the publication of his first full American geography, Jedidiah had been candidating in a New York Presbyterian church. One of its leaders, the scholarly Postmaster General Hazard, had taken kindly to him. It was through the Postmaster General that he had come to know the Reverend Mr. Belknap. When Belknap had asked Hazard how he liked the preaching of the young geographer-parson, the Postmaster General had replied: "I like him; and indeed, *so far,* he proves very acceptable to our people in general. He composes well, has many new and striking ideas, and there is something pleasing in his manner. He wants animation, but probably will have more of it after he has been longer in the ministry, and . . . when he is more weaned from his manuscript; for you must know it is not the *fashion* among us for ministers to read *all* their sermons, as in New England. . . . In his doctrines, he is strictly Calvinistical. As a *man,* I am charmed with him. He is judicious and sensible, decent and modest in his deportment, a chearful companion, who prettily supports the dignity of the clergyman in the midst of friendly affability."[2] Morse had soon learned, however, that Hazard's church had decided not to invite him to remain as pastor. Hazard had advised him, as a friend, that his geography took too much time from his theology. And he had known that it was the Reverend Mr. Belknap who had sent him, through Hazard, the invitation to supply in the Congregational establishment of Charlestown.

His friend Belknap was addressing the meeting on the responsibilities of the ministry. Belknap was mindful of the minatory liberal-orthodox divisions within the congregation as he said: "To insist much on controversial points, may serve to feed a party-spirit; but it is not good for the use of edifying." [3]

The new pastor little heeded Belknap's advice either on controversy in the church or on the propriety of arriving in Charlestown with a wife. At Postmaster General Hazard's home in New York Jedidiah had first met the girl he hoped to marry. Hazard had studied under her grandfather, Dr. Samuel Finley, the Calvinist president of the College of New Jersey, later Princeton University. After the death of President Finley, the president's son-in-law, Judge Breese of Shrewsbury, New Jersey, and his daughter Elizabeth were often guests at Hazard's New York home.

Elizabeth came by the vivacity that charmed the young cleric not only through her mother but also through her father. Her paternal great-grandmother came across the Atlantic alone, fleeing from what she regarded as the persecution of her parents. And she was not the only bold Breese. In Trinity Churchyard, at the end of Wall Street near where Elizabeth herself was born, her grandfather left an epitaph that has ever since been attesting to his spirit:

> SIDNEY BREESE
> JUNE 9th 1767, MADE BY
> HIMSELF. HA! SIDNEY,
> SIDNEY, LYEST THOU HERE!
> I HERE LYE
> TILL TIME IS FLOWN
> TO ITS EXTREMITY!

When the body of the virile Sidney was placed under the stone he had prepared, his widow continued the already traditional Breese vigor by herself becoming a New York merchant and importer. Her son Samuel, the father of Elizabeth, was the founder of Shrewsbury, which he named for the town his ancestors had come from in England. Now he was a judge and postmaster of the little town, hearty and buoyant, accustomed to handsome living. Young

Parson Jedidiah, in his trips to near-by Elizabethtown to consult his geography-printer, contrived occasionally to go on down the coast to Shrewsbury to see Judge Breese's daughter. He may have meant to include himself among the "genteel" New Yorkers whom he described in his well-known *Gazetteer* as coming down to the resort town of Shrewsbury for "health and pleasure."[4]

Postmaster General Hazard knew that young Morse wished to marry Elizabeth. He wrote to Belknap that the new pastor would be likely to bring a wife along when he came to Charlestown to settle. Belknap dropped the news to one of the congregation. "In a day or two," he wrote Hazard, "it was all over Charlestown; and the girls who had been setting their caps for him are chagrined, while some of the elders of the land are really enquiring how, when, and where the house shall be got. I suppose it would be something to Mr. Morse's advantage, in point of *bands and handkerchiefs,* if this report could be contradicted; but, if it cannot, O how heavy will be the disappointment! When a young clergyman settles in such a town as Charlestown, there is as much looking out for him as there is for a 1000 dollar prize in a lottery; and, though they know that but one can have him, yet who knows but *I* may be that one. . . . Do tell Morse, if he is not *too far gone,* that it will be much in favour of his popularity, and something in his pocket, if he can come to Charlestown with his neck clear of that fatal noose."[5] In reply Hazard could only promise: "His Reverence will be on" to settle, "*single.*" "Further, this deponent saith not."[6]

He was still single on the day of his installation, but the following month he went to Shrewsbury to marry Elizabeth. "A valuable young woman, and I believe truly pious," was Hazard's judgment of her.[7] And in June when Mr. and Mrs. Belknap met the bride at a Boston dinner party, Belknap was pleased with her. She was pretty. She called at the Belknaps' and presently with Mrs. Belknap was shopping about Boston.

Despite Belknap's prediction that the pastor's having a wife would chill the generosity of the twelve single women and forty widows of the church, the parish gladly assisted the Morses in furnishing their house. The pastor could easily be grateful for their gifts, for his annual salary at first was only twenty cords of wood, $570, and the use of the parsonage. Moreover, his parishioners expected hospitality from their pastor. In time they found it. They used to say he didn't keep a tavern, but he did keep a public house.

The pastor played the part of a gentleman whether he received his comfortable parishioners dressed in his long red gown and seated in his upstairs parsonage study, or faced the congregation in black robe and gloves and powdered wig, or prayed with the rejected of men in the state prison. His dress was tidy, his manners gentle, his voice persuasive. Yet he could heartily condemn wrong. If his violent sick headaches reminded him that he had not inherited his forebears' whole vigor of body (one of his grandmothers numbered three hundred and nineteen descendants before she died), surely something of their vigor persisted in his tongue and brain. When he was convinced that international Masonry was a menace, that French Jacobinic liberalism was threatening American order, that Unitarian doctrines were undermining the stability of the state-supported church, he flung out against them. While he had the support of the Charlestown people in much of his righteous fury, even when he did not he continued his course beyond the bounds of the safety of his position. And he was as hearty in his sympathy as in his wrath. Mrs. Morse learned to check his impulsive generosity to the Negroes of Charlestown, to the Indians of the hinterland, or to immigrants who knew him as Dr. Morse, Edinburgh LL.D., and author of geographies that had beckoned them to America.

While Mrs. Morse was more cautious, she too was often intense, sure of her judgment, confident in the recurring task of distinguishing right from wrong. Though pious, she showed her Breese impetuosity by sometimes breaking through the weight of formalism. She was willing to dress in lace and puffed skirts; occasionally she would crown her powdered curls with feathers and pearl beads; but she relished especially the unfamiliar freedom of wearing calico dresses when she called on the ladies of the congregation. Her manners were graceful, her conversation animated, her will strong. When a new white, square parsonage was built on Town Hill next the church, it was she and not her husband who determined just where the doors and cupboards would be. Unafraid of questioning her husband's decisions, and even tending to pout a little when they did not suit her, she opened the way for her children to have uncommon independence of mind. She contributed a relieving sparkle to the intensity of her husband's conferences with fellow pastors or scholars; with parishioners in trouble; with promoters of a navy yard for Charlestown, or a canal to join the Charles and the Merrimac, the first canal in the country, or missions to remote settlements in Maine.

The Morses had ministered to the people of Charlestown for nearly two years when their first-born son came to them, on April 27, 1791. He was born within sight of Boston, where Franklin, with whom his name was often to be coupled, was born, and within a year of Franklin's death. It was the mother who was favored in the choice of names with which his father loaded him in the Town Hill meeting house the next Sabbath. Samuel Finley the parents named him after her maternal grandfather, the Princeton scholar. And Breese they added, her family name. When the Reverend Mr. Belknap notified Hazard that the poor baby had almost as many names as a Spanish ambassador, the Postmaster General replied in pretended affront. If the parents were so faint-hearted about the prospect of future progeny as their choice of names would indicate, he said, they should add the names of Belknap and Hazard at once. The baby came to style himself Samuel Finley Breese Morse, but the family soon chose to call him Finley.

The parents were pleased with the kindly attention to their son from Belknap, Dr. Witherspoon of Princeton, and Postmaster General Hazard. They were so full of pride that it frightened them. Should they find so much joy in love of their son? In a world of sin was it right for servants of the Lord to care so much for any soul, even their son? The father spoke his fear to friends. Hazard replied: "Do you have an high opinion of Master Finley? How little do single & newly-married men know of the feelings of a father. Go on & love your boy." [1]

The parents soon forgot their fear of loving too freely. When within five years there were two other sons, the only others of their eleven children to survive infancy, they could only speak of Finley, Sidney Edwards (Finley at first called him Edud, then Edwards, and finally Sidney), and Richard as the "dear boys." They were glad their lads were hearty, playful, and humorous like Grandpa Breese. When the mother was away on one of her "sacrifice visits" to her parents, one of the boys would sleep with his father. As soon as he wakened in the morning the boy would demand, to his father's delight: "Come, Papa, now talk about Mama." [8] From Shrewsbury the plain-spoken mother wrote many letters to her husband in warm affection, execrably punctuated. If no one had taken the trouble to teach grammar to the granddaughter of the president of Princeton, it was too late now, even if she was married to a scholar. She had enough to keep her busy as it was. Her ignorance could only be kept secret by reminding the family, as she often forcefully did, to be sure not to leave her letters exposed on the parlor table. From Shrewsbury she would write Mr. Morse, as she took care to call her husband, her concern for all the household, for the "dear boys," for nurse Nancy, and for coachman Prince: "I hope you found the Dear Boys Well and that you did not forget to carry them something for their good behaviour, I hope Nancy is well give a great deal of love to her & tell her not to forget to love the dear Boys and to kiss them every Morning and Night for Mama. I am much pleased with the good account She gives of them I never Doubted her Sincere love for them but am more than ever convinced of it. Remember me to Prince also and tell him that I need not *tell* him to have his Chaise harness Barn Cellar & yard in good order for us for he will do that of *course*. I need not ask my good Husband to kiss the Dear Children for me for he will do *that* of course." [9] Papa Morse no longer hesitated to join in the morning rite of kissing his "dear boys."

CHAPTER *ii*

Hare and Tortoise

THE CHILD Finley first gave earnest of being father to the painter Morse, as the painter himself remembered it, at the age of four. In those days he toddled from the new parsonage on Town Hill past the meeting house and a few hundred yards beyond the shadow of the Bulfinch steeple to Old Ma'am Rand's school. Being an invalid, Miss Rand influenced her young charges by the use of a rattan. One day Finley scratched a pin portrait of her on a chest of drawers. Not being flattered by the portrait, Ma'am Rand pinned the artist to her dress the better to control him. He wriggled free, carrying part of her dress with him into a distant corner. Even there the ubiquitous rattan found him.[1] From the blows of Old Ma'am Rand to the final blow of his painting career, the rejection of his proposed commission to decorate the rotunda of the national Capitol, he found cause to ponder the reception accorded his artistry.

He grew capricious and shifting. Moods passed over him as lightly as the shadows of the Town Hill elms.

He was disposed to be vacillating, his father warned. Attend to one thing at a time; " hurry, bustle, and agitation are the never-failing symptoms of a weak and frivolous mind." [2]

He was quite unlike brother Sidney. Their father once took the two boys on his knees to tell them so. Neither was as he ought to be. Finley was a hare, too quick; Sidney a tortoise, too stubborn. The names clung. Even after the Hare had far outrun the Tortoise in public acclaim, the brothers affectionately signed their letters with drawings of a hare or a tortoise.

The parents' Puritan faith in the reforming power of education led them to send Finley away to school at the age of seven.[3] The Phillips family had established an academy only twenty-two miles north of Boston in Andover, to promote "true Piety and Virtue." The founders were all Calvinists. The first principal had been Eliphalet Pearson, the staunch friend of Pastor Morse; he was to be

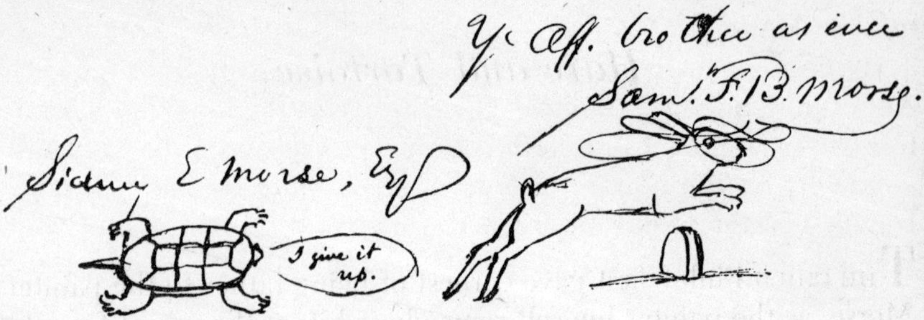

the subject of one of Finley's finest portraits. For several years Finley's father had been an academy trustee.

Shortly after Finley entered the preparatory school of the academy,[4] his father represented the Phillips Academy trustees at the annual exhibition in "a large and elegant building," as he described it, "on a delightful eminence."[5] It was then characteristic of the exhibitions at Andover for the students to "construe and parse," declame, sing sacred choruses, and hear such solos as "Oh, dear, what can the matter be?" The trustees were complaining that the exercises were too theatrical.

The author of school geographies did his part to solemnize the occasion. After the honest flattery of telling the boys that they were in the richest and perhaps the most respectable school in the country, he charged them with a terrible responsibility. Here, he said, "you are now laying a foundation . . . for both worlds. The character and habits you are now forming . . . will be likely to continue through this life, and to determine your future everlasting condition."[6]

Was he thinking of Finley? The only official Andover Academy record for him now extant is eight demerits in spelling and eighteen for whispering[7] – not an encouraging report for a worried father.

The parents tried to steady him. They sent him a copy of the exhibition address and asked him to memorize it.[8] They offered rewards for "improvements": books, cakes and "Pyes" that his mother hoped would "eat very good," [9] more frequent visits to Charlestown, and happier receptions when he did come home. They increased his disciplinary duties by requesting him to account for his pocket money, keep a daily journal, read the Bible and pray morning and evening, write a Sunday letter on the sermons, and reread their letters constantly.

He needed steadying. It is said he once ran away from school.* At best his studying was fitful. Once he was at the top of his class; a few weeks later he was described by his tutor as "regardless of truth – idle – & at the bottom of your class." [10] He soon found needed friends in Samuel Barrell of Charlestown and brother Sidney. But when Finley, aged eleven, and Sidney, aged eight, entered the academy proper in the same year and Sidney soon won the praise of the instructors for his perseverance, the Tortoise's presence was not soothing to the Hare.

From the first summer there was the consolation of blackberries. He wrote his papa: "I have as many blackberries as I want I go and pick them myself." [11] As he grew older, there was the additional joy of reading books not on the required lists. His reading of Plutarch's *Lives* is said to have moved him, at least temporarily, to ambition. Because it had had a great effect on her when a child, his mother asked Dr. Morse to send him Janeway's *Token for Children.* When it was read aloud, Dr. Morse observed with pleasure that Sidney "retired by himself of his own accord to say his prayers"; [12] perhaps Finley read it in one of his moments of desperate resolution to reform. Other relief the crotchety lad found in drawing and painting. From the medium of a chest of drawers he had now moved on to a drawing book and even ivory. Dr. Morse was sufficiently pleased with his painting to send a specimen to the lad's grandfather with

* In *Letters*, I, 3, the editor comments that Finley may have run away, and later writers have magnified that careful comment into the statement that he did. The story is doubtful. Oliver Brown of Charlestown, a student at Phillips Academy, had a tutorial responsibility over Finley in 1799. In his letter to Dr. Morse, June 15, 1799, YC, he expresses his sorrow at "the sudden call of Finley from the Academy." Nothing in the letter would indicate that he was called for any other than family reasons. But the "Finley" of this letter may not be Dr. Morse's son at all. In a letter of John Rogers to Dr. Morse, July 18, 1799, YC, appears the story that Dr. Morse had sent "Master Finley" home in disgrace to his mother at Brunswick. This letter probably refers to Samuel Finley, a New Jersey relative, who stayed briefly in Charlestown.

the explanation: "he is self taught – has had no instructions."[13] And more than the freedom of painting without guidance, there were the glorious whirls of the "federal balloon," the current fandango, and in season skating or splashing along the banks of the wooded Shawsheen.

Having already lost her sixth child, Mother Morse was well aware of the power of death. The sudden death of a Boston girl prompted her to warn her sons. "She ate her dinner perfectly well and was dead in five minutes after her name was Ann Hinkley. You see my dear boys . . . the Importance of being always prepared for *death*. . . . We cannot be *too soon* or *too well* prepared for that all-important moment as this is what we are sent into this world *for*. The main business of life is to prepare for death."[14]

Despite the cheer of blackberries, "federal balloons," "drum fiddle guns," or painting books, at sober moments Finley accepted his duty of preparing for death. While temporarily at home in the parsonage during his final year at the academy, he wrote to Sidney and Richard, now both at Andover: "I now write you again to inform you that Mama had a baby, but it was born dead & has just been buried, now you have three brothers & three sisters in heaven and I hope you & I will meet them there at our death. It is uncertain when we shall die, but we ought to be prepared for it, & I hope you & I shall."[15]

Through the many years before the three brothers died, they all continued to prepare for the end according to the tradition of the family faith.

Their father was becoming known about Boston as a champion of Calvinism. As an overseer of Harvard, Dr. Morse, with the former Andover principal, Pearson, now a professor at Harvard, led the fight to keep Harvard safe for orthodoxy. During Finley's last year at Andover, Morse and Pearson made a mighty effort to prevent the election of "Unitarian" Henry Ware to a professorship of theology. The liberals insisted that the qualification for a teacher of religion was not his creed but his good life. To the orthodox this was simply irreligion. Pastor Morse saw the issue as a terrible one. He wrote to a friend: "I fear and deprecate a revolution in our university more

Courtesy, Mrs. Russell Colgate

JEDIDIAH MORSE

By Morse

The artist's father.

Addison Gallery of American Art, Phillips Academy, Andover, Mass.

ELIPHALET PEARSON

By Morse 1817

Professor at Harvard and Andover.

than a political revolution. I pray God in mercy, to prevent both."[16] At the meeting of the overseers on the election of Ware, he insisted that the professorship had been founded expressly for a person of "soundness and orthodoxy" and that therefore the purpose of the founder would be defeated unless the professor were a Calvinist. Ware was elected; Harvard became increasingly liberal, and when the liberals within Congregationalism withdrew to form the Unitarian denomination, Harvard became eventually associated with it. So it was that Finley did not attend the college for which most Andover students were destined.

"It must be mortifying to Morse, Pearson, & men of their stamp, that they can rule at Cambridge no longer,"[17] wrote a liberal observer. It was. Pearson left Harvard and, zealously aided by Morse, fostered the founding of an orthodox seminary associated with Phillips Academy. Their purpose was partly to provide a stay against Harvard and partly to supply the need, never before met in America, for a systematic course of study directed to the training of clergymen. Through a long series of maneuvers Pearson, Morse, and other Old Calvinist leaders drew into their plan the Hopkinsians, a more extreme orthodox group, and secured the aid of the Phillipses. When Dr. Morse wrote his friend, President Dwight of the still orthodox Yale, inviting him to preach at the opening of the new seminary, he added triumphantly: "The camp of the enemy is alarmed, they are awake, and every engine of opposition is in requisition."[18] Dr. Morse was seldom happier than when he knew his opponents felt his blows.

Finley did not attend the new Andover Theological Seminary, though at one time he expected to and though his brothers eventually did. By the year it opened he was already safely at Yale.

"Dr. Dwight president of Yale College being here I was examined with S. B. Barrel and my brother Edwards to enter that College & entered."[19] It was simple enough to make the notation of acceptance in his diary, but it had not been easy staying home for months tending the cow, piling wood in the kitchen for Nancy, carrying across the toll bridge to Boston the proof for the latest edition of the geography, continuing his drawing, and at the same time reviewing his

Æneid, Sallust, *Græca Minora,* and Greek Testament for Dr. Dwight. Now that he was finally accepted, the family sent him off with the admonition to be satisfied for once.

At the age of fourteen he set out alone for New Haven. On the third evening the stage left him in Hartford at an inn opposite the State House. On the fifth day he entered New Haven as darkness was beginning to obscure the Green.

Immediately he was dissatisfied; he was longing to be living in the college, in one of the two parallelograms that squatted athwart the Green. Living in town did not seem to bring him any closer to the essence of Yale than living at home.

While he pleaded with his father for permission to live in college he could at least study collegiate ways. He took to gunning in the fields about New Haven until his parents forbade his "foolish whim." His brown coat for every day and his blue coat for Sabbaths were not enough; he now demanded a "tight body'd coat" for dress affairs. He dreamed of living in college with a "chum" and having in their room brandy, wine, and segars. His studies languished.

In the winter the long-awaited letter of assent came from Charlestown. He carried it joyfully to college officials. The president and tutor in conference found Finley to have an "aversion to study." Unfortunately the tutor conveyed their discovery directly to Dr. Morse, Yale 1783 and Yale tutor 1786. "He writes, at times, decently in Homer," the tutor explained, "but in Horace he has been of late quite deficient. He appears disposed to study no more than what is absolutely necessary; and I am extremely apprehensive, were he in college with his present habits, that he would in a short time sink to the bottom of his class. I have frequently conversed with Dr. D. respecting your son. . . . We cannot help feeling extremely apprehensive that his aversion to study is unconquerable, & that his admission into college at any period would not be attended with consequences which would conduce in any considerable degree either to his usefulness or his happiness." [20]

The Hare continued his wavering course. He began to enjoy his own grace and suavity. He acquired a taste for idle, gay companions and fashionable amusements. While the laws of "Pope" Dwight forbade attendance in town at establishments where dancing, card-playing, wine-drinking, or dramatic performances were in order, the college rules were broken not seldom by Finley, doubtless, among many. Just walking was no amusement to him at all. In spite of his resolve against it, the passion for gunning seized him again. And he had a whim for bad books.

At Beers and Howe, booksellers, where he had been charging up against his father a variety of items, such as a penknife, a leaf chair, and skates, he chanced one day upon a set of Montaigne's essays. Boldly he wrote his father why he had bought the ungodly volumes. "The reason they are so cheap," he explained, "is because they are wicked & bad books for me or any body else to read. I got them because they were cheap & have exchanged them for a handsome English edition of Gil Blas, price $4.50." [21]

Dr. Morse, being already the author of geographies, gazetteers, a biography of Washington, a history of New England, and dozens of pamphlets, was disturbed that his son did not know the value of books. Montaigne is unfit, he wrote the boy, and the *Gil Blas* unnecessary. All the books just bought were to be returned, he directed. "Messrs. B.[eers] & Howe will readily take them if they are not injured (as I presume they cannot be), because I requested them not to have an acc.t with you or to let you have books but by order of Mr. Twining [then his tutor] or myself." Because Beers and Howe were his agents for selling geographies in New Haven, Dr. Morse had conveniently directed them to supply Finley's demands. But now the son had proved to have a lack of Yankee acumen. He could neither buy nor barter soundly. You have not learned, wrote Dr. Morse, something that "is very important to your happiness & usefulness, & that is the *value of property*." [22]

As during Andover days, his parents encouraged him to know his own folly, his "disposition to change" and "natural volatility," and to comfort them by resolving to overcome it. He did so resolve; but his letters were read with parental wisdom. His parents knew too much about such of his fellows as the diarist who concluded after a week's notations that he spent in study each day only three and three-quarters hours. Finley's parents used quotations from his resolutions to preface their letters of reproof.

There was hope of improvement after sober brother Sidney Edwards joined him in the fall of 1807. But when a revival under a local preacher produced a period of "seriousness" at Yale and the mother rejoiced that both boys were in New Haven rather than "at Cambridge, in the midst of all their wicked tricks," [23] it was Sidney who went to Dr. Dwight to discuss regeneration. When the tutors spoke well of both boys, it was only Sidney whom the parents urged to try for prizes. The Tortoise placed the Hare under increasing compulsion; the Hare did now choose a steadier course, but his goal could not be the goal of the Tortoise.

When not joining his fellows in the agreeable Yale "tricks," Finley did apply himself to an occasional lecture. There were three professors at Yale all together; all were friends of Dr. Morse. From Professors Jeremiah Day, later Yale president, and Benjamin Silliman, later illustrious as the editor of the only scientific journal in America, Finley heard lectures on electricity. The subject was new to him, tangible, yet mysterious. In his classes in natural philosophy Professor Day lectured on the proposition that if the electric "circuit be interrupted, the fluid will become visible, and when it passes it will leave an impression upon any intermediate body." Before the class he experimented with the proposition in two ways. With the room darkened he had the "fluid" passed through a chain, and called attention to the visibility of the "fluid" between the links of the chain. Again, placing several folds of paper in the chain in the path of the current, he commented on the perforation that was made through the paper. The presence of the "fluid" in any part of the circuit could be easily detected.[24]

Finley was impressed. In the winter of his junior year he wrote home: "My studies are at present, *Optics* in *philosophy, Dialling*, Homer, beside disputing, composing, attending lectures &c. &c. all whh I find very interesting, and especially Mr. Day's lectures who is now lecturing on Electricity." [25] A week later he was still marveling. The whole of Mr. Day's class, joining hands in a circle, received a simultaneous shock with noisy repercussions. Finley had never received an electric shock before. It seemed to him as if someone had struck a light blow across his arms.

One vacation that year Finley assisted Tutor Sereno Dwight in experiments on electricity in the "Philosophical Chamber." It was probably during the same year too that he sat before Professor Silliman when, like a child with an enigmatic toy, he took apart the simple batteries that then excited curiosity, the batteries of Volta and Cruikshanks. For it was during that year that Finley constructed models of them for his own amusement.[26]

While the brief lectures on electricity might incite him to study, it was a non-collegiate pursuit that claimed his devotion. In his dormitory room Geography, as his fellows called him, had excellent facilities for amusing the amiable students who visited him. One wall he had covered with a line and color extravaganza that he dubbed "Freshman Climbing the Hill of Science"; it portrayed humble youths crawling upward on hands and knees toward the pinnacle of knowledge. He may also have entertained with caricatures. According to a legend, one of his caricatures of a professor was seized and taken to Dr. Dwight. The president's reproof could not move him to penitence, but his remark: "Morse, you are no painter; this is a rude attempt, a complete failure," brought him to tears. As an instance of his passion for his art the story rings true; Morse himself denied the tale altogether, but his denial had not yet caught up with it fifty years after his death.[27]

During his first two years in college he did little or nothing with his brush. Then in his junior year he found not only the release in painting that he had already known, but also the joy of recognition.

Freshman Zedekiah Barstow, admiring the paintings in his room one day, asked: "Why can you not paint my likeness?"

The immediate reply was: "I will do it." The portrait that presently appeared under the hand of the confident youth astonished the subject with its accuracy.[28] Although Finley would take no pay for this painting, his reputation spread and he discovered an easy source for pocket money. At the close of his junior year he had a regular scale of prices: one dollar for a simple profile and five dollars for a miniature on ivory.

Before he left college he had done a profile of Professor Kingsley and reported him pleased with it, and ivory miniatures of Miss Leffingwell of New Haven, of Joseph Dulles, a fellow student, portrayed as sadly wise beyond his years, and of his own suave self. They asked him to paint a "mourning piece" for Madam Phillips of Andover, and his first group, the whole family posed about a table at home, with the father's tool, a globe, prominently in view.

Even with the excitement of constructing batteries and surprising his fellow students with the skill of his brush, Geography was restless. In July of his junior year, feeling languid and heavy, weary of discipline, he indulged in the futile gesture of threatening to run home long before the end of the term. In reply Mrs. Morse spread Finley's shame before the eyes of his younger brother by writing both the Hare and the Tortoise:

Charlestown, July 26, 1808

Dear Boys

We received Finleys letter. . . . I could not but be *pained* to perceive by it that he still retains that disposition to change which I had fondly hoped he was geting the better of. . . . You can never study here, you have always said that this place was the worst you ever knew, for any such purpose, as we have so much company, and so many Interruptions, of course you would be running about, in quest of company, and rather than have none would take up with such as would be your ruin for both worlds, for soul & for body[,] for I know of none that I think it likely that you would associate with who would not be likely to have this affect on you. Wonder not therefore, my son, at the extream solicitude, of an Affectionate Mother . . . think my dear boy of the length of time your coming home now would oblige you to stay here, in *Idleness, & of course in Sin. . . .*

Be . . . manly and philosophick and prepare yourselves for to rough it as you go through life. . . .

Your Affectionate Mother
E. A. Morse [29]

Finley was the family bad boy. While he muddled through his studies his brothers were brilliant scholars, at home in pious and classical studies, as they were to be all their lives. They found that their duty and inclination coincided, but he sought lasting satisfaction outside the scholastic routine. During his last year at Yale he was convinced he had found it in painting.

Two months before leaving New Haven he had a plan for his future. He had met Washington Allston and instantly worshipped him. In his abject devotion Finley was not alone. When Allston was studying in Rome, Coleridge found himself more drawn to him than to anyone else save the Wordsworths. In Rome also Washington Irving was so blown from his moorings by the force of Allston's imagination and verve that he declared himself ready to desert literature to follow him. He was considered the greatest American

U. S. National Museum, Washington

FAMILY GROUP

By Morse — About 1810

This unfinished watercolor, his first attempt at painting a group, Morse presented to his nurse Nancy, and she to Charlestown friends. Many years later Morse found the likenesses of his father and mother and Richard (extreme right) satisfactory, but his own (to his father's left) and Sidney's disagreeable.

painter of his generation. Though like most of his contemporary artists he had long lived abroad to escape the paucity of American art patronage, Allston had returned to America briefly to visit his mother's people in South Carolina and then to go to Boston to marry the girl to whom he had been engaged for the eleven years since he had been a radiant student at Harvard.

Finley knew that Allston was soon going back to England. He wrote home: " I still think that I was made for a painter; and I would be obliged to you to make such arrangements with Mr. Alston for my studying with him as you shall think expedient: I should desire to study with him during the winter, and as he expects to return to England in the spring I should admire to be able to go with him." [30]

The reply was cryptic. " Your Mama & I have been thinking & planning for you. I shall disclose to you our plan when I see you. Till then suspend your mind." [31] It was only a few days before commencement when he finally knew his parents' plan. With immense dignity, as if he had as much bargaining power in the matter as they, he wrote that he had decided to accept their plan of making him a book clerk to atone for all the anxiety he had caused them, adding: " I am so low in spirits that I could almost cry." [32]

He floated through his last few weeks at Yale by " waiting on " Jeannette Hart of Saybrook, one of the famous sisters known as " the beautiful Miss Harts." Those who knew them said it was impossible to distinguish which of them excelled in chiseling of features, clearness of complexion, richness of brown, curling hair, or brilliance of large, dark eyes. At a gala wedding in New Haven that summer one of the sisters married a young Episcopal cleric whom Morse came to know, Samuel F. Jarvis of New York. Another sister was soon to marry Commodore Hull, then the hero of the *Constitution*'s victory over the *Guerrière*, whom Morse also came to know. And Jeannette came near enough to marrying Finley for her sister Mrs. Jarvis to warn him not to exact a promise of marriage from a girl with no knowledge of the world. The ecstatic evenings that the pair spent together, reading to each other and strolling about the town, have been thinned in the Hart family records to the " tradition " that Jeannette became engaged to a " young artist, who afterwards, in another field, became one of the most distinguished men our country has produced." [33]

As he left New Haven, Finley hastily arranged to pay part of his forty-two- or forty-three-dollar debt to the buttery – for pastry, oysters, segars, and the like – by taking an ivory likeness of the student who served as butler, Asahel Nettleton. For that miniature at least he wangled a price of seven dollars. But, as it was, he had debts amounting to over a hundred dollars still outstanding when he left New Haven. It was a surprise to some of his creditors when eventually they were paid.

He quit Yale, as he had Phillips Academy, without leaving behind an official record of distinction. In his wildest brooding over his miniatures he could hardly have imagined that more than a hundred years later he would be ranked in the records of these institutions, themselves among the most distinguished in the nation, as among their most distinguished alumni. Recent Phillips Andover records notice that among Andover graduates only Morse and Oliver Wendell Holmes have been commemorated in the Hall of Fame. Yale records of graduates of his period rank him with five persons, three of whom became his friends: Benjamin Silliman, James G. Percival, Lyman Beecher, John C. Calhoun, and James Fenimore Cooper.[34]

CHAPTER *iii*

Rebellious Son

DUTIFULLY Finley returned to Charlestown to continue in the uncongenial world of books. Following parental directions he clerked for Daniel Mallory, one of Dr. Morse's publishers, near Scollay Square in the heart of Boston's book trade. Dreary duty held him from nine to twelve thirty and from three to sunset. At one he attended lectures on anatomy to help him in his painting. Going home in the evening, he could easily stop on Court Street at Allston's studio for a breath of warm encouragement from the master he adored. Then in the parsonage across the Charles River bridge he could "improve" his evenings in a room over the kitchen specially fitted up for him. There by the light of his new lamp, one of the six-dollar "patent lamps, those with glass chimneys," his friends watched him painting a landscape. Even when they declared it "proper handsome,"[1] he was not content; ambition was driving him to more persistence than Yale discipline could. In a few months the unwilling parents knew that their boy's heart was not in the quill that they put in his hand by day, but in the brush that he took in his hand by night.

For the few, at least, painting was an acceptable calling in the Boston of 1810. John Singleton Copley had first made it so. Living in dignified affluence on Beacon Hill, Copley had painted prominent Bostonians in the brilliant period preceding the Revolution; more recently he was continuing his sedate life in London, along with Benjamin West of Philadelphia giving American-born painters distinction in England. Gilbert Stuart was still blithely running in and out of the homes of Boston's bigwigs and wits. A dimmer figure in retrospect but in his time scarcely less sparkling was Allston. It was the sister of William Ellery Channing of the Federal Street Church that Allston had come to Boston to marry. The Channing family stood well among Bostonians of caste. Since Unitarians and Trinitarians had not yet divided the church, with Dr. Channing a leader of one camp and Dr. Morse of the other, Dr. Morse knew Channing pleasantly and still thought a relative of the Channings a safe associate for his son, if indeed any artist could be.

It was Stuart and Allston who finally secured to Finley the possession of his brush. Two of his paintings he showed them: his landscape, now lost, and *The Landing of the Pilgrims.* Finley's variety of Pilgrim was jaunty, with a feather in his tri-cornered cap, dazzling colors in his belt, a sword at his side. The drawing was poor, the colors pleasing, the movement convincing. When Stuart and Allston approved, Dr. Morse made a decision.

As he dreamed of the coming days when he would be a painter of mighty stature, Finley conceded that his parents would have contributed to his growth. His future biographer would not be able to charge his parents, he thought, with being so given to preaching, missions, tracts, and books that they held their son to their own ways. They had watched his every capricious inclination, waiting for him to find himself. Now vacillations were over; he had made his choice and they had been convinced by the good judges Allston and Stuart that his choice was sufficiently wise to be tolerated.

They knew there was little Finley could accomplish in painting without study abroad. With " sacrifice of feeling (not a small one)," and a great " pecuniary exertion," they arranged to place him under the care of Allston, urging him to consecrate his art " to the glory of God and the best good of his fellow men." [2] At last Finley was to become one of those favored persons who find their satisfaction in their work.

At the same time that Finley knew his fond wish would be fulfilled, his brothers were disappointed with paltry honors at Yale. He wrote them soothingly: " But then consider where poor I should come. Think of this, Rich.d, and *don't hang yourself."* As if to remind them that even the student who receives no honors may have his triumphs after college, he added complacently: " I have left M.r

Mallory's store and am helping Papa in the Geog.y. Shall remain at home till the latter part of next summer & then shall go to *London* with Mr. Alston. I wish Edwards would begin to bottle his cider & have it ready for me – 3 barrels will be enough."[3]

On July 15, 1811, the good ship *Lydia,* sails taut before the wind, moved easily through the Narrows. Finley was glad enough to be out of New York, an insipid city compared with Philadelphia or Boston, he had thought, in spite of an agreeable visit with the Allstons and their friend Washington Irving. Uncertainty touched him lightly as he watched his native shores retreat. A youth of twenty, he was to try his strength on English shores, where those of his profession were indeed mighty. But other art students who had made this voyage had triumphed: West, Charles Wilson Peale, Copley, Stuart, Trumbull, Allston. He persuaded himself that he was in good spirits. Without effort he could turn his attention to what was about him. He found delight in repeating a toast made by one of the company who thought he was a writer of renown: "The cocks proclaim the morn, and the ducks quack the roast."[4] Morse explored its mumbo-jumbo possibilities to the full. At the least likely moment he would repeat it and burst into laughter. Before the end of the voyage the whole company was shouting: "The cocks proclaim the morn."

Twenty-two days on the sea left him three shades darker and without the recollection of one disagreeable circumstance on the crossing. At Liverpool the ship was greeted by hundreds of people waiting for news of the threatening war with America. Except that the crotchety Liverpool mayor would give them only a ten days' permit for the ride to London, Morse and the Allstons were not inconvenienced because they came from an annoying little nation across Britain's seas. Indeed, Morse found the customs inspector genial. When he first went ashore Morse carried under his hat and in his pocket part of the generous supply of segars he had brought along to comfort his exile. He had made eight or nine such runs past the customs when his trunk, still holding some segars, was sent ashore for examination. The inspector came upon the segars. "I told him they were only for my own smoking," Finley wrote to Charlestown, "and there were so few that they were not worth seizing. 'Oh,' says he, 'I shan't touch them; I won't know they are here,' and then shut down the trunk again. As he smoked, I gave him a couple of dozen for his kindness." [5]

As he sat down to write his first letter home from London, he imagined his mother across the sea wishing she could hear of his arrival. At the close of his letter he wrote: "I wish that in an instant I could communicate the information: but three thousand miles are not passed over in an instant, and we must wait four long weeks before we can hear from each other."

On rereading the letter many years later, Morse wrote in the margin: "Longing for a telegraph even in this letter." [6]

To be in the artist quarter he took rooms at No. 4 Buckingham Place, Fitzroy Square. To the north was Regent Park, and to the south Oxford Street, the throbbing thoroughfare to the West End. By making slight variations in his walks out to dinner, in a few days he was familiar with the streets in between. Near him lived Charles B. King, an American artist friend of Allston. On London Street was the Allstons'; on Newman Street, Benjamin West's extensive establishment where American artists had long been generously received; near-by Berners and Queene Anne were the streets where Coleridge and Turner were soon to be living.

Allston introduced him to West, the Pennsylvania-born president of the Royal Academy. It was an important meeting to Morse, for West's kindness had become almost necessary to an American artist in London. When Joshua Reynolds died in 1792, West had become president of the academy. But beginning well before then a long stream of American painters had passed under his influence, including Matthew Pratt, William Dunlap, Charles Wilson Peale, Robert Fulton, Ralph Earle, Gilbert Stuart, John Trumbull, Washington Allston, Edward Malbone, Thomas Sully, Rembrandt Peale, and Charles B. King. Hardly an American painter of first rank in 1811 or for a generation after was not indebted to the great master. For the past thirty-five years they had found him quietly painting in his Newman Street home, as Leigh Hunt said, "happy, for he thought himself immortal." [7]

In the famous mansion Morse walked through the long gallery that faced the inner court. He passed nearly two hundred of West's sketches along the wall and wondered at West's vitality. When he

National Academy of Design, New York

SELF–PORTRAIT

By Morse 1808 or 1809

Miniature on ivory painted at Yale.

finally saw his host he was still wondering; he seemed far younger than his seventy-odd years.

West received him amiably. He soon had Morse feeling that he was letting him into a secret by showing him what he said he had not shown to anyone else, a sketch for a new composition, *Christ before Pilate*. It was to be one of his enormous paintings, of the kind that Stuart called "a ten acre canvas."

Under Allston's kindly directions, often received over an afternoon segar at Morse's rooms, Morse prepared to enter the academy school. He was thankful for his study of anatomy in Boston because the academy had strict requirements for knowledge of the figure. From classical sculpture he drew with what were new tools for him, black and white chalk. With a little practice he felt confident enough to begin drawing the figure of a gladiator to submit to academy officials. When he had been in London only three weeks it was finished. Allston declared that it was better than two thirds of those generally offered, but that it was defective in the handling of the chalks; West, that it was an extraordinary work, indicating talent, and also lack of knowledge of the art.[8] He began again, this time from what he thought the most difficult of all statues to draw, Laocoön. By early November his sketch of it had admitted him to the academy school. He began to paint in the evenings at the academy rooms in Somerset House, facing the Thames, continuing to work in his own rooms during the day. He tried not only historical subjects but portraits and landscapes as well. Following his generous custom, West lent Morse a copy he had made of a Van Dyck portrait; from it Morse made a copy which Allston told him was just a hundred times better than he expected. Presently he had completed one landscape and begun another, a sunrise scene. With soaring hopes he wrote home: "I am pursuing my studies with increased enthusiasm, and hope, before the three years are out, to relieve you from further expense on my account. Mr. Allston encourages me to think thus from the rapid improvement he says I have made. You may rest assured I shall use all my endeavors to do it as soon as may be."[9]

That autumn his eyes were wide open as he went about the city. On a four-mile walk to Hackney he joined a crowd of three hundred thousand, the largest in which he had ever been, to marvel at "the ascension of a Mr. Sadler and other gentlemen in a balloon"; [10] at St. Bartholomew's Fair he was giddy watching boxes, holding five or six people, swoop through the air in a semicircle; in the galleries of the British Institution he was astounded to discover ladies as well as gentlemen at their easels; when he saw the marbles recently brought from Athens by Lord Elgin to his house in Piccadilly, he thought all sculpture since the Greek inferior; in his exhilaration from the blazing lights and gay music of Vauxhall Gardens he concluded that here was the answer to the Eastern Sage's quest for happiness!

Both in his painting and in his knocking about London he was often alone that fall, but in December Charles Leslie came to join him in both. Like Morse, Leslie from childhood had shown talent in drawing and had been placed in a book shop against his inclination. He had haunted Philadelphia theaters, Charles Wilson Peale's famous museum, and the friendly studios of Thomas Sully, until his employer, discovering that he had made an excellent drawing of the English actor George Frederick Cooke, raised a subscription to send him to Europe for two years' study.

With letters from Sully to West and Charles B. King, Leslie went to London and settled in the usual artist habitat about Fitzroy Square. His first few days satisfied his intoxicating anticipations of the city he had learned so much about from Philadelphia gossips, but a few days later he was ill and his rooms seemed desolate.

Discovering suddenly that Morse "felt very much as I did," [11] Leslie agreed to live with him. On Great Titchfield Street they took rooms which the artist-inventor Robert Fulton is said to have occupied before them. There they were soon painting each other, each at his own window, Leslie as a Spaniard and Morse as a Scot. Morse found Leslie an agreeable companion; he thought him as good a painter as himself, though Leslie was three years younger. "I find his thoughts of art agree perfectly with my own," Morse wrote. "He is enthusiastic and so am I, and we have not time, scarcely, to think of anything else; everything we do has a reference to art, and all our plans are for our mutual advancement in it." [12] Soon Leslie was in the Royal Academy school and together they were painting at Somerset House in the evening, and at their rooms or occasionally at the British Museum during the day.

Allston called on them daily. He impressed them with his love for the color of the Venetian school, especially of Veronese; Morse was ever after a lover of richness of color. But Allston was not always a gentle master. Morse found him trying at the end of a hard day's work when he said: "Very bad, sir; that is not flesh, it is mud, sir; it is painted with brick dust and clay." [13] With quick dismay Morse was sometimes ready, quite unlike Leslie, to dash his palette through his painting. But in a moment Allston could cool his heat by taking his brush, showing him how to put in a few flesh tones here, a few grays there.

Tea, coffee, and Madeira, novel-reading, and musical entertainment, probably on the piano, which survives only in King's phrase: "music by Morse," were features of the evenings at their rooms. As Morse said of his friends: "We meet by turn at each other's rooms and converse and laugh." [12] Besides the familiar figures of Allston and King, their companions included the ardent artist and literary protagonist Benjamin R. Haydon; a facetious pair, pianist Collard, and portrait-painter Lonsdale; the poet Coleridge; and John Howard Payne, the American actor who had just outgrown his boyish charm.

When Allston had first met and painted Coleridge in Rome, they had immediately recognized each other as kin; it was Allston who brought the poet into the circle. Now Morse and Leslie came close enough to Coleridge to try to guide his surging moods.

On one of his visits to their rooms Coleridge entered faltering and gloomy. "I was just wishing to see you," said Morse. "Leslie and myself have had a dispute about certain lines of beauty; which is right?" Coleridge remaining silent, the two painters artfully argued between themselves until they roused him from lethargy. Once launched, Coleridge easily soared above the understanding of the more stable youths.[14]

Morse long remembered hearing Coleridge "improvise, for half an hour, in blank verse, what he stated to be a strange dream." [14] Full of imaginative figures, it captivated Morse. But his recollection that part of the monologue later appeared in *The Rime of the Ancient Mariner* indicates that Morse was not among Coleridge's faithful public, for that weird poem had been written a dozen years before Morse knew him.

Leslie had quite as much passion for the theater as he did for his chosen profession. It may have been under his influence that Morse began to attend the theater and join in the stage gossip of his companions. His first reference to theater-going in letters home is a cautious one: "Our amusements are walking, *occasionally* attending the theatres."[12] A few weeks later, after seeing *The Gamesters,* he hazarded a description of it to his parents: "At Covent Garden there is the best acting in the world. . . . Mrs. Siddons is the first tragic actress, perhaps, that ever lived. She is now advanced in life and is about to retire from the stage; on the 29th of this month she makes her last appearance. I must say I admire her acting very much; she is rather corpulent, but has a remarkably fine face. . . . At the close of the play, when she utters an hysteric laugh for joy that her husband was not a murderer, there were different ladies in the boxes who actually went into hysterics and were obliged to be carried out of the theatre. This I think is a proof of good acting. Mrs. Siddons is a woman of irreproachable character and moves in the first circles; the stage will never again see her equal."[15]

Both he and Leslie painted their friend John Howard Payne, the former in his character as Zaphna in *Mahomet,* and the latter in the character in which he first made his devastating sweep of the American stage, Young Norval in *Douglas.* Morse believed the erratic youth was of sound character. When he wrote his parents that he was acquainted with him his mother replied that they too had found him "unexceptionable" when they had traveled eleven days in his company coming north from Charleston one time, but she warned against any acquaintance with actors "as it will, sooner or later, have a most corrupting effect on the morals. . . . I hope you do not attend the theatre, as I have ever considered it a most bewitching amusement, and ruinous both to soul and body."[16]

With Leslie, Morse often went to Covent Garden; he saw Coleridge's *Remorse* on its second or third performance, in a box with the author, Lamb, Allston, King, and Leslie. He himself wrote a farce and sent it under an assumed name to a comedian whom he much admired, Charles Mathews, but apparently he received no reply. Yet neither then nor at any time in his life was he unsuspicious of the enervating influence of the theater. Leslie, for all his palpable purity and enthusiasm, could not set him directly against his parents on this score. His break from his parents was to be neither merely over his amusements nor incidental to his youth; it was to be fundamental to his political career.

England in 1811 had less than its usual little amiability for Americans. As if it were not enough for Britons that on the Continent Napoleon was encroaching upon markets they held sacred to themselves, across the Atlantic President Madison's Democratic administration was continuing to restrict British trade. As a New Englander of respectable family, however, Morse had a Federalist's aversion to the American embargo. His pro-English inclination, wisely used, might smooth his path to English welcome.

On his second day in London he had announced his ready judgment of the effect of the embargo: if continued, he expected England would collapse. In the face of predictions of war he had stood by the conviction that the English desired adjustment with America. They were as much opposed to war, he wrote, "as the better part of the American people,"[17] among whom doubtless he intended to include his parents. As he had read newspaper accounts of rioting and explored the city for himself, however, he had found increasing cause for alarm. He slept with pistols under his bed.

Shortly after Leslie arrived, in January 1812, Morse had written his trusting parents the surprising news: "Federalists are certainly wrong in very many things."[18] He was shying from the Federalism that was the safe approach to English hosts.

In April Morse was yet more firm against the Federalist sympathy with England rather than France. He wrote home without temporizing: "You may depend on it England has injured us sorely, and our Non-Intercourse is a just retaliation for those wrongs. Perhaps you will believe what is said in some of the Federal papers, that that measure has no effect on this country. You may be assured the effects are great and severe; I am myself an eyewitness of the effects; the country is in a state of rebellion from literal starvation. . . . Troops are in motion all over the country, and but last week measures were adopted by Parliament to prevent this metropolis from rising to rebellion. . . . Now when you consider that I came to this country prejudiced against our government and its measures, and that I can have no bad motive in telling you these facts, you will not think hard of me when I say that I hope that our Non-Intercourse Law will be enforced with all its rigour. . . . Some of you at home, I suppose, will call me a democrat, but facts are stubborn things, and I can't deny the truth of what I see every day before my eyes. A man to judge properly of his country must, like judging of a picture, view it at a distance."[19] By not denying he could be called a Democratic Republican he made his somersault all too clear to his parents.

Before receiving a reply to his declaration of rebellion Morse had time to write of events moving swiftly toward war. He went to the Parliament buildings and saw crowds rallying around the slogan: "Peace or the Head of the Regent"; later he heard Prime Minister Perceval's assassin cheered to the gallows with cries of "God bless you." Just four days before the offensive orders in council were withdrawn by Britain he expected war. Unless the withdrawal should come, he now wanted it. He had abounding confidence in American strength. Every American who understood affairs believed, he thought, that as soon as America declared war Britain would sue for peace. He still refused to trim his words to please his parents. He poured out to them his shame that Federalist editors could support Britain in every move; it was these editors who had induced the British ministers to continue the orders in council by giving them the vain hope that Federalists could compel the rest of America to their belief.

There was as yet no telegraph to send to America instant word that the orders in council were withdrawn on June 16. Blind to England's concession, therefore, Congress declared war two days later. To the mother in Federalist New England the rulers of her wretched country made unnecessary war against the people who were doing more to spread the gospel than any other people on earth. The father wrote of the glorious majority of 244 that the anti-war Federalists achieved in the Massachusetts House soon after the war began. But their son was in a different mood. Hearing a gentleman at a chop house urge that Britain blockade the American coast with five or six frigates, he made the impertinent comment: "*What a pity this man couldn't be in Parliament*"; and hearing another propose sending twenty thousand men to take possession of New York and overawe the country, replied: "*What a dust I make, says the fly.*"[20] The parents continued to flood their son with earnest counsel. They thought they understood, as he did not, the worldly necessities of his position: wisdom taught that an aspiring artist anywhere should leave politics to politicians; in an enemy country, wisdom demanded it. His mother amused him when she wrote that next to changing his religion she despised a man most for changing his politics. He professed to understand just how his good mother felt. Before he came to England he too had thought Federalists infallible. Now he knew better. He was growing free of the weight of his parents and their friends of the New England hierarchy. After she had endured his saucy replies for three years his mother wrote valiantly that she expected to continue to advise him " with the greatest plainness " the rest of her life. When he disagreed, she expected him to convey the difference to her " in the most delicate and gentlemanly manner." [21]

It was the father's darling hope that Finley was rebellious only because in want of correct facts; if so, sober friends might check his defection to Democracy and the Jacobinic dangers with which it was associated in Dr. Morse's mind. Ever since the " Reverend Granny," as Democratic opponents dubbed him, had sent his son away to Andover, he had been anxious for him to have the right friends. He had approved of Allston; he accepted Charles B. King, for when King returned to Philadelphia, he chose him to do his portrait; when he met Leslie's people he found them agreeable. He disapproved of Payne and perhaps of Coleridge, but in neither instance could it have been in the interests of Finley's political soundness. In the early 1790's Dr. Morse might have winced at the like of Coleridge, the pantisocrat, dreaming over his plan for an egalitarian utopia in Pennsylvania. But by 1811 he and the other romantic Lake poets, whom Morse may also have casually known, were eating better, dressing better, accepting orthodox religious forms; no longer to be feared as Jacobins, they were employing their divine arts in the cause of patriotic England.

Moreover, Dr. Morse had tried to introduce his son to Englishmen who might be expected positively to encourage sound morals and politics in a friend's son. Finley met many of these associates of his father: William Wilberforce and Henry Thornton, members of Parliament, George Burder, editor of the London *Evangelical Magazine*, Zachary Macaulay, editor of the *Christian Observer*, Charles

Taylor, bookseller, Henry Bromfield, American-born merchant, and Dr. John Lettsom, eccentric physician and littérateur. Except for the last, who was a Quaker, they were all known to Dr. Morse through their endeavors in the Sunday-school movement, the British and Foreign Bible Society, the London Missionary Society, or similar groups. It was especially into the godly Clapham Sect, which Wilberforce led, that Dr. Morse successfully introduced his son.

Already known for his sponsorship of the act of 1807 to suppress the British slave trade, Wilberforce was the keeper of England's conscience. His early years were linked with those of William Pitt the younger. As wealthy young parliamentarians they had run about London together, gambling, dancing, theater-going, supping in the best Tory company. While remaining friends, they had been drawn apart by the one becoming a conservative Prime Minister and the other passing through a profound spiritual experience from which he emerged a sober Evangelical of the John Newton or Hannah More school. Radicals who were demanding that the common people be given the right to vote feared Wilberforce's piety as a mask for his distrust of democrats. High Church Tories abhorred his Evangelicism and suspected Jacobinic tendencies in his preferences for mild parliamentary reform. Remaining in the Establishment, he nevertheless received the homage of Methodists and other dissenters for aiding in securing their toleration.

It was not until his second winter abroad that Morse began to frequent the homes of the Claphamites. It was too late to keep him a Federalist, but his degradation might be mitigated.

Morse understood that he was invited to dine at the town house of Thornton, one of the Clapham Sect, only out of respect to his father. The Tory banker seemed pleasant enough. At his table that evening were Morse, Wilberforce, and a son of the James Stephen who had written the orders in council for Perceval. The talk turned inevitably to the war. Thornton asked Morse whether the war would have been prevented if the orders had been repealed a month or two sooner. It would, Morse replied.

That answer pleased Wilberforce. Turning to Stephen, he asked: "Do you hear that, Mr. Stephen? I always told you so." [22]

Within a week he had dined at Wilberforce's, and in another week he reached the very citadel of the sect. Thornton invited him for a day or two to his Clapham seat, seven miles from the street where Leslie and Morse roomed. It may have been the sumptuous house that induced Morse to see himself as an intruding American endured by English hosts. Such coldness he did not know in America. He met it now with growing resentment. It bothered him at Thornton's, but he was too assertive to let it overcome him.

Recovering from timidity on the second day, he welcomed the dinner conversation on the American war. He plunged in by inveighing against the popular notion that America was under French influence. He described America's acceptance of English manners, its rejoicing at British victories over Napoleon, its attention to English travelers, its preference for English even over American books. On the other hand he declared the French were despised in America just as they were in England. They were the common enemies of mankind. Parents often forbade their children to associate with Frenchmen, their morals being considered dangerous, he said. Surely, though Democratic Republicans were commonly termed Jacobins, Morse was not a Jacobin. After the prolonged exile of Napoleon to St. Helena and the resurrection of France as the idol of the liberals, however, Morse was to plead as vehemently for the French as he now denounced them.

Tirades against the French pleased Thornton but did not convince him of America's fairness to England. To him England's quarrel with Napoleon was the struggle for liberty. The justness of the cause, he told Morse, should secure the indulgence of America for such incidental burdens as the orders in council.

Morse replied flatly. The moment America decided that England's cause against France was just, he said, her neutrality would cease. How could Thornton insist, he demanded, that the English cause was pure when he admitted the purpose of the orders in council to be the universal monopoly of commerce? He had the illustrious parliamentarian quite boxed, or so he wrote his parents, when presently his host whisked him back to the city by carriage.

Morse returned to Clapham to dine at least twice with the indefatigable Macaulay. Morse may have seen his son, the future historian, home from school in the holidays. Young Macaulay was so much a Claphamite that his given name was that of one of the sect, Thomas Babington, and at the age of eight he had already written a treatise intended to convert the natives of Malabar to Christianity. Nevertheless at the Macaulays' Morse found the same abuse of America. A young chap there, when Morse was introduced to him as an American, promptly asked: "Pray how many ships have you in your navy?" On hearing the answer he sneered: "Is that all?" and turned on his heel, laughing.[23]

Closer than either Macaulay or Thornton to the heart of the Morses, father and son, was the leader of the sect. The warm correspondence between Wilberforce and Dr. Morse continued through the war. Wilberforce was pleased when Dr. Morse asked him to cultivate his son's acquaintance. His purpose in consenting, he wrote Dr. Morse, was "to afford the means of innocent social pleasures to those who appear desirous of seeking their relaxation and pleasures in domestic life rather than in the haunts of dissipation."[24] Few had known more of London's haunts than Wilberforce. He knew more than Morse ever knew.

Wilberforce shared the Tory view that Jeffersonian Democrats were disreputable radicals, inclined to be disrespectful of religious and civil tradition, and allies of the Jacobins. When he wrote Dr. Morse his view of "Mr. Madison's war," he tactfully omitted mention of Finley's view, though he very well knew it: "I should almost be afraid of confessing to you, the degree of Abhorence & Indignation in which I hold those who commenced the present war against Gt. Britain. . . . Yet I beg you will observe that my resentment . . . is commensurate with my good will for yourselves, at least for your Northern States."[25]

Hearing such recrimination, Morse was at first inclined to find the Claphamites a burden. With growing familiarity, however, he came to admire their humanitarianism. He knew of their great adventure in founding a colony for enlightened Negroes on the Slave Coast; he knew of their victory over the British slave trade in 1807 and their current interest in the universal abolition of that wretched traffic; he knew of their concern for toleration of dissenters. While sometimes resentful of their coldness and more often of their view of the war, he could easily warm to their benevolence. He wrote home: "Mr. Wilberforce is an excellent man; his whole soul is bent on doing good to his fellow men. Not a moment of his time is lost. He is always planning some benevolent scheme or other, and not only planning but executing; he is made up altogether of affectionate feeling. What I saw of him in private gave me the most exalted opinion of him as a Christian. Oh, that such men as Mr. Wilberforce were more common in this world. So much human blood would not then be shed to gratify the malice and revenge of a few wicked, interested men." [26]

Morse delighted in saying that all Americans in England favored "vigorous prosecution of the war" (a phrase that he was to come to hate in the Civil War), and there was some justice in his assertion. West was notorious for his sympathy for Napoleon; Leslie, while never as bitter against the English as Morse, was pleased when it became apparent that America was sufficiently united to carry on effective war; Allston believed the imperious English needed guidance to better ways; and Ezekiel Cushing, an American medical student, joined his friend Morse on the news of American naval victories in "Huzza, Huzza, for our side." [27] The unity of all Americans in England Morse explained by the persistent discourtesy of their English hosts. It was enough to make any American's blood boil, he had thought early in the war, to hear America called "a nation of cheats, sprung from convicts, pusillanimous, cowardly." [28] English pride and reserve chilled him. The longer he stayed in England the more his resentment grew. He longed to be at home, in the navy.

Fearing for Finley's moral stability and professional success, Dr. Morse inquired about him from Henry Bromfield, the London agent through whom he sent funds to Finley, and the brother-in-law of his companion in orthodoxy Dr. Pearson. The reply confirmed Finley's own explanation of his about-face. "I never heard him converse upon the subject," Bromfield wrote, "otherwise than was actually occasioned by the Occurrence of Events connected with America – but indeed how was it possible for an American to witness the bitter animosity that prevailed here last year, & not deeply to feel for the Honor & Interests of his country, vilified & attacked, as they were?" [29]

But the error of other Americans was no fit excuse for a son of Mrs. Morse. She readily retorted that most Americans in Europe, as he knew quite well before he went there, were "dissipated infidels." [30] She excepted West and Allston.

Just at the time when he most wished to be in the navy Finley was inquiring among English Morses, those who had common ancestors with his forebear Anthony Morse, who crossed to New England in 1635, for the Morse coat of arms. No record survives of his emotion when he thought he had discovered that its motto read: *In Deo, non armis, fido.*

Finley may not have known that Robert Fulton, the painter who had once occupied the room in which he was now staying, had abandoned his art in order to aid the American cause. Fulton was stupidly attempting to persuade America to introduce such a devastating weapon – his newly invented submarine, of course – that men would forever refuse to fight.

Finley himself never went beyond heroic expression in his militarism. Richard went a little farther. When Boston feared a British sea attack, he volunteered for labor on the harbor defense at Fort Strong. All his sons went too far for Dr. Morse. Saddened as he contemplated their " military taste," he yet could hope to see within his time "an end to wars & fightings . . & garments rotted with blood." [31]

Not a few packets that crossed the Atlantic both east and west carried pleas for reformation. But the parents never conformed their politics to the pattern of their oldest son, nor he to theirs. In 1836 when he ran for mayor of New York, he proudly proclaimed in his campaign documents that he had been a Democrat for over twenty years.

CHAPTER *iv*

Painter to the Enemy

One day Morse showed West his drawing from a small cast of the Farnese Hercules. After close examination the master returned it with compliments, saying: "Very well, sir, very well; go and finish it."

"It *is* finished," replied Morse. He had worked on it for two weeks.

"Oh, no," said Mr. West; "look here, and here, and here." The student saw the errors.

In another week he confidently presented West with the corrected drawing. The master flattered him, concluding: "Very well indeed, sir; go on and finish it."

"Is it not finished?" asked Morse in despair.

"Not yet. See, you have not marked that muscle, nor the articulations of the finger joints."

Resolved yet to win an absolute decision from his judge, Morse worked over the drawing again for several days. "Very clever indeed," was West's comment on his third Herculean labor; he added: "Well, sir, go on and finish it."

Morse balked. "I cannot finish it," he protested.

At last convinced by the reality of his pupil's misery, West replied: "Well, I have tried you long enough. Now, sir, you have learned more by this drawing than you would have accomplished in double the time by a dozen half-finished beginnings. It is not numerous drawings, but the *character of one,* which makes a thorough draughtsman." [1] West had seen that Finley still bore marks of fickleness.

In his study for his canvas *Dead Men Restored to Life*, Allston was just then following a practice of some old masters in making clay models of his figures. Putting aside his "unfinished" drawing, Morse followed his teacher. For his painting *Dying Hercules* he modeled the agonized hero in the position which he wished to use in the painting. When Allston saw his work, however, he urged him to complete a rounded figure.

As soon as the completed model had been cast in plaster of Paris, Morse carried it to West. The old gentleman put on his spectacles and walked around it several times. The hero was writhing in the pain of death, his right arm extended in a noble gesture. The model displayed remarkable force for its height of twenty inches. With many exclamations West said: "I have always told you any painter can make a sculptor." [2]

Friends told Morse that the Adelphi Society of Arts was offering a gold medal for original work in painting, sculpture, and architecture. They flattered him into entering his model for the competition. A few days later, while Britons were still killing Americans in battle, the American youth received the gold medal award [3] at the hands of the Duke of Norfolk. Beginner's luck! The model was his first piece of sculpture, the medal his first honorary award. The sculpture was the only piece he is known to have produced, but the award was the first in a long series which entitles him to consideration as one of the most bemedaled of Americans.

By the time he had been honored for his model he had already completed the painting for which it was but an accessory. He applied to Somerset House for permission to enter it in the Royal Academy exhibition. "Six hundred were refused admission this year," he argued neatly to his parents, "so you may suppose that a picture (of the size of mine, too) [it was eight feet by six feet six] must possess some merit to be received in preference to six hundred. A small picture may be received even if it is not very good, because it will serve to fill up some little space which would otherwise be empty, but a large one, from its excluding many smaller ones, must possess a great deal in its favor in order to be received." [4] And even among those accepted, his painting attained recognition. Said the critic of the London *Globe:* "the great feature in this exhibition is, that it presents several works of very high merit by artists with whose performances, even with whose names we were hitherto unacquainted. At the head of this class are Messrs. MONRO and MORSE." [5] The critic placed Morse's canvas among the twelve best in the whole exhibition. And in an article which Morse preserved among his papers until his death the *British Press* [6] placed it among the first *nine*.

His mother feared the éclat would go to his head. As soon as he found he could excel, she lamented, he would weary of trying further. And Dr. Morse relayed the cheerful news only guardedly, as if contemplating the awful relapse that might soon follow. "He has obtained the Gold Medal," he wrote President Dwight, "for his clay figure of the dying Hercules, from the Society of polite Arts in London – & a prize from the Royal Academy for his painting from that figure – so we are informed." [7]

His success, Morse insisted, was due to his American teachers. Proudly he listed America's great painters. First in rank was Stuart, without a rival in England; then West, the highest of the Americans in England; Copley; and finally Colonel Trumbull. They were all old; when they passed along he expected Allston to surpass all the artists of ancient or modern times. After him would come Leslie.* When his parents told friends that he and Leslie were studying in England they were to say, he told them, that they were pupils of Allston, not of West. "They will not long ask who Mr. Allston is," he added; "he will very soon astonish the world. He claims me as his pupil, and told me a day or two since, in a jocose manner, that he should have a battle with Mr. West unless he gave up all pretension to me." [8]

Art commentators have often followed Isham in saying that Morse admired Allston in spite of their utter difference in temperament and upbringing. To be sure, Morse's heritage was that of the stern intellectual Puritan and Allston's of the graceful Carolina patrician. But that Morse had a brother who found leisure to read the Bible through twice before he died at the age of three years and ten months, as Isham delights to record,[9] is not only not true but not representative of Morse's background. The Morses were pious, of

* "Messrs. Leslie, Morse, and Allston . . . ," said *Port Folio* (Ser. 3, IV, 88), a Philadelphia literary monthly, in July 1814, "exhibit . . . the fairest promise of becoming, after their great predecessors shall have disappeared, the West, the Copeley, and the Trumbull of the age."

course; but they were large enough in their sympathies to like the South, just that part of the South from which Allston came. They already had found themselves at home in tidewater Carolina, and Morse himself was to find it a congenial region in which to be dined and wined, to boat and hunt, and pursue his art. Not only could Morse make a good Carolinian; Allston could make a good New Englander. He had gone to school at Newport and to college at Cambridge and had married into a Boston family of standing. He was a God-fearing man, even compared with New Englanders; he was soon to become notable for his piety. Perhaps Allston was the more imaginative, freer in his habits, for after all he was twice an artist, being both painter and poet. But in background, and in ready wrath, impulsive generosity, and comradery they were much alike.

Morse openly admired his master. His affection was not this time the effusion of the moment. Twenty years later he could still say: "I go to Allston as a comet goes to the sun." [10]

In the fall of 1813 Morse took his painting equipment to Bristol, a commercial city that he would not have chosen except for the hope of material gain. He stayed near the home of a patron, Harman Visscher, a merchant relative of the New York Van Rensselaers whom he already knew. Another American merchant, the brother of the Miss Russell who lived in the handsomest house in Charlestown, was attentive enough to permit Morse to do his portrait for his sister, and make it possible for him to know his daughter Lucy so well as to come near being at his "old game of falling in love." [11] Bristol proved profitable that fall and promised further satisfaction.

His income was much on his mind. In Bristol he had been able to reduce his monthly debits with Mr. Bromfield from the usual twenty-two pounds to about thirteen pounds ten. With the encouragement of his new patrons he hoped to support himself as long as he remained in England. His parents were allowing him a thousand dollars for each of his three years in England; by the following summer, when his three years were up, he was able to persuade them in spite of depression in New England * to send another thousand for another year. But that summer he knew that if he wished to go on to France he would have to pay his own way. And he found no

* The mother lamented to Richard: "The *war* the *war* What has it not done *Even deprived us of our bottle Cyder* alass alass," June 18, 1813, COLG.

pleasure in discovering little ways of saving pennies. He despised George Parkman,* the son of a prosperous Boston merchant, who boasted that he would live as a medical student in London for six hundred dollars a year. He despised him for never refusing invitations to dine, for walking three or four miles in order to breakfast with him and Leslie, for "stickling" with washerwomen over half-pennies, for shabby dress. Morse returned to Bristol in the summer with the hope of earning enough to enable him to remain yet some time in Europe and in a manner suitable to his dignity. This time Allston was with him.

For six months that summer and fall, however, Bristol neglected them both. The trouble, he explained, was that both he and Allston were Americans. There were, to be sure, no stupid spying on the Americans of Allston's coterie, no threats of loss of property or internment for the duration of the war, no protests at the honors they received. But irritations were inevitable. Colonel Trumbull as well as Morse attributed his failure in England at the time to national hostility. Few wars create so much resentment as civil wars, and such the war was, an Anglo-Saxon civil war.

Misfortune followed them back to London. Just a week after the Allstons took possession of a new house, Mrs. Allston died. Allston was stupefied. The next day Morse thought him almost bereft of reason. Leslie and Morse tended him affectionately; only they and John Howard Payne were with him at the funeral and followed the coffin to the grave. The new home became a chamber of horrors to Allston, and Leslie and Morse persuaded him to take lodgings in their house. They gradually replaced his morbidness with gentle melancholy. The blow had a profound effect on Allston, however; he turned increasingly to pietism, was confirmed in the Church of England, and grew hypersensitive to purity.

The year that Ann Channing Allston died was the year in which her brother, William Ellery Channing, began to lead a great schism within Congregationalism. It may have been Finley who determined the date on which the long-awaited conflict began. He is said to have found in Thomas Belsham's life of Theophilus Lindsey a list of the New England ministers who were of the heretical Unitarian persuasion and communicated the news to his father.[12] At any rate,

* The Parkman of the famous Harvard Medical School murder.

Dr. Morse found the book and made it the basis for a stout blow at the clergymen named; it was just the ammunition he needed. Dr. Channing took up the defense of the Unitarians, and the process of estrangement within Congregationalism was fairly under way before the year 1815 was over.

The coming of peace to a generation that had hardly known what it meant provided grand spectacles for Londoners. In April 1814, hoping to be the first to send his parents the news, Morse had written that the allies had entered Paris and banished Napoleon. Several days later from among the flags, ribbons, and laurel of Piccadilly he looked up to a hotel balcony at the Queen ("if she was not called a queen," he wrote, "she might as well be any ugly old woman" [13]), the Duchess of Oldenburg, sister of Emperor Alexander of Russia, and Prince Alexander. Amid the thunder of artillery and shouts of "*Vivent les Bourbons!*" he watched Louis XVIII, the first King of France since the Revolution, pass by in a carriage. Skillfully Morse forced his way below a balcony on which Louis was scheduled to appear. When at last the King came before the throng, his smile captivated Morse and he could not resist joining in the mounting cry: "*Vive le Roi!*" During that summer of gala visits among the allied dignitaries the American calculated the number of times he had seen royal guests. Emperor Alexander topped the record with a score of fourteen.

Early the following winter peace brought cheer across the Atlantic as well. America and Britain made an inconclusive end to the war, on which historians yet dispute. The war ended as it began, with significant events taking place after the decisions they might have effected had been made. If Morse's telegraph could have sent instant news of peace to General Jackson he would not have draped himself with the glory of victory at New Orleans and hence might never have been President. But Morse was satisfied with the peace even without the New Orleans victory. America had acquired character, he believed, by her conduct of the war. No European nation, England least of all, would now want to embroil itself with America.

At home in the meeting house on Town Hill the news of peace brought the people together to hear Pastor Morse:

The glad tidings of peace, through thy mercy Oh God, have greeted our ears. . . .
Oh how sweet is thy mercy, & reviving as life from the dead.[14]

Thanksgiving for peace soon seemed vain. The war-weary world gaped as Napoleon gathered an enthusiastic army about him once again, and the ghastly " Hundred Days " followed.

On June 26 the news of Waterloo reached Morse in London. A few days later, when rumors were swarming that the allies had re-entered Paris and had retaken Napoleon, Morse was at dinner at Wilberforce's with Macaulay, Grant and his two sons, and Robert Owen of Lanark. All were talking feverishly, waiting the sound of the guns in Hyde Park which would announce the virtual end of the war – once again. Wilberforce distrusted the rumors, exclaiming repeatedly: " It is too good to be true; it cannot be true." He talked of the hope for universal peace. In the drawing-room after dinner Morse sat near a window which looked out toward the distant park. He heard the dull report of a gun. The company did not notice it. He heard a second report; convinced of its meaning, he called Wilberforce. Running to the window, the old gentleman opened it in time to hear distinctly the next firing of the gun. He stood still a moment, tears rolling down his cheeks, silent. Then without a word he turned to embrace his wife and daughters and shake hands with everyone in the room.[15]

With news of peace Morse was anxious to go to France. He had been intending to go for more than a year. Now it seemed possible. Just a day or two away in Paris were the art treasures of the world, and unlike London's lesser display, they were free for his use. Living was cheaper in Paris, he told his parents. They needn't fear his corruption by the wiles of the city; a man of three-and-twenty had fixed habits. Comptroller Bromfield advised him not to go without positive leave from Charlestown. For months he waited for a reply from his parents, thinking that they had received his requests for permission but refused to answer. In early 1815 his father's letter finally came, coupling advice not to go with the notice that beginning with the coming fall he would have to support himself and that he could make his own decision with these facts in mind. The son decided that the favorable moment had gone, irrevocably. He was already planning his return to America. He may not have known that his father had already asked attention for his son in Paris from Joel Barlow, American Minister to France. If Morse had gone to Paris who knows? Perhaps Barlow would have turned him as he had Robert Fulton from art toward invention.

Two years after his success with his *Hercules* Morse undertook to enter another competition, that of the Royal Academy in historical painting. President West encouraged him to believe that if he went home before the end of 1815, when the judging was to take place, his picture would nevertheless be entered in the contest.

The composition he chose was one that has often appeared on Greek vases: Jupiter sentencing Marpessa to choose the love of either immortal Apollo or mortal Idas. The figures were posed in grandiloquent manner, the trees boldly outlined, the colors brilliant; the whole was a scene of barbaric majesty. It was in just the historical manner that Morse relished, the manner that West and Allston championed.

West's most striking contribution to the history of art had been made in historical composition: in his *Death of Wolfe* he upset conventions by painting the general and those who attended him in the clothes that they actually wore. Both West and Allston scorned portraiture for their pupils. Allston feared that when Morse returned to America, "he shall have been able to raise no higher superstructure than the fame of a portrait-painter." He believed Morse could do better, but that it would be difficult.[16] Leslie was already showing interest in the variety of painting in which he was to acquire fame, illustrating scenes from plays and novels. Morse scarcely needed the advice of friends, however. Before he came to England he had wished to be a historical painter and now he was sure of it. "I cannot be happy unless I am pursuing the intellectual branch of the art," he wrote home. "Portraits have none of it; landscape has some of it, but history has it wholly." [17] His parents might warn, with sound judgment, that commissions for portraits were the most he could expect in a raw country: but he hoped that family influence would find him a fat commission for a painting in a church or hall at two or three thousand dollars. If the people could pay that much for a demoralizing entertainment that is gone in a day, why not for intellectual pleasures and the support of painters? "I do not speak of *portrait-painters*," he wrote extravagantly; "had I no higher thoughts than being a first-rate portrait-painter, I would have chosen a far different profession. My ambition is to be among those who shall rival the splendor of the fifteenth century; to rival the genius of a Raphael, a Michael Angelo, or a Titian; my ambition is to be enlisted in the constellation of genius now rising in this country; I wish to shine, not by a light borrowed from them, but to strive to shine the brightest." [18]

By the middle of July his *Judgment of Jupiter* was finished, his funds exhausted, and he prepared to sail for home. He left in disappointment. In spite of West's encouragement, the council of the academy refused to permit him to enter his painting in the competition unless he would remain in the country to be able to receive the award in person. After studying his painting West advised him to remain. And the letter that Allston gave him to take home to his father was equally encouraging. What more could any father ask?

London
4 August, 1815

My dear sir,

I cannot suffer my young friend to leave me without some testimonial which, however unnecessary for his welcome reception by the friends who so well know him, may yet shew my esteem for his character, and the interest I take in his welfare. It is a subject of no slight gratification to me that I can with sincerity congratulate you on, what religious parents must above all others appreciate – the return of a son from one of the most dangerous cities in the world with unsullied morals.

This should indeed be a cause of lasting satisfaction to you, that the foundation you had laid in his mind was too strong to be shaken even by the assaults of those who have been trained to, and grown formidable in vice; for this may be said with truth of multitudes who dwell in this metropolis.

With respect to the progress made by him in his art, I trust that the specimen which he takes with him (Apollo Marpessa & Idas) will justify the expectations of his friends. This picture was intended to be offered next winter at the Royal Academy for the prize. But that he could not be allowed to do unless he should remain here until November, to make a sketch at that particular time, which should entitle him to stand as a candidate: a piece of mere formality which they might & ought to have dispensed with. But they resist all kinds of improvement from . . . a dread of innovation. I regret much his disappointment, as I have every reason to think he would be successful: his picture being much superior to any I have seen offered on such occasions. If he meets with encouragement he will be a great painter.

I cannot conclude this without expressing the deep sense I have felt of his kindness to me in my affliction. From him and my young friend Leslie I have received every attention which distress could receive from kind and compassionate natures. They were kind to me when kindness was indeed needed. Pray present my respects to Mrs. Morse, and believe respectfully.

Y. rs
W. Allston [19]

Morse had some right to the magnificent dreams with which he left London, for the warm testimonial which he carried with him to his father was written by one who was a sound judge.

Morse reached Liverpool four years to a day after first landing there from America. Little remained in him now of the dainty æsthete of college days. His brown curls were still carefully disposed about his temples in his recent self-portrait; it was not these he now emphasized in himself, however, but the full lips, wide jaw, long, straight nose, firm set of neck and shoulders, and direct countenance. His face approached the "hatchet class," he said; yes, its boldness was like that of his tongue and pen. He had grown sure in these years in England; he talked positively, praised wholeheartedly, excoriated thoroughly, gave generously. As he thought of his art he dreamed of supporting himself in Bristol and schemed to make money out of the Emperor of Russia himself, or now, as he faced across the Atlantic, he considered the possibility of accepting commissions at thousands of dollars and rivaling Titian. In extravaganzas he had grown more American than ever during his English sojourn.

It was probably after consulting Morse that the art historian Dunlap wrote many years later that Morse had given his years in England to the study of historical painting, except for "two or three portraits, painted principally with a view to study the head." [20] Certainly Morse's passion went into his *Hercules* and his *Judgment of Jupiter*. He painted not a few portraits, however: Leslie; John Howard Payne; Zerah Colburn, the mathematical genius; James Russell; two for a " gentleman " in Bristol at ten guineas each; two self-portraits, one in oil, the other pen and ink; and his intention of painting two others is recorded, Stephen Van Rensselaer and Elisha Goddard, the former of the New York patroon family, the other a Boston medical student, an associate of Morse's acquaintances Parkman and Cushing. Further " non-intellectual " paintings were his two landscapes at ten guineas each for Mr. Breed of Liverpool, probably Richard Breed, who was a business correspondent of his father; his illustration in Leslie's manner, Dorothea from *Don Quixote;* and an album drawing, *Knight in Armor*. Probably no historical paintings but many portraits and landscapes from this period remain unrecorded.

In England he had gained particularly in drawing and modeling. He had already learned what most of the American resident artists of that time and even Copley never knew: how to avoid harsh, flat tones by gentle modeling, transparent shadows, and blending of colors. His taste for rich tones was already apparent. His compositions, if grandiloquent, were less stiff.

The prestige of European experience was very real for anyone those days and was still imperative for a distinguished career. He had been to the best masters that American painters knew – if not actually the best – and had come away with their blessing. Few of those with whom he was to associate in his profession were starting with his advantages of a father of distinguished name, education in the best schools of New England, and study abroad. Leslie perhaps approached them, but he became an exile in England; Vanderlyn and Rembrandt Peale, possibly; but not Inman, Jarvis, Durand, Cole, Sully, Jocelyn, or Cummings.

The final disappointment over the rejection of his *Jupiter* did not weigh him down. He had soaring hopes for his career at home as he boarded the *Ceres*. Fourteen days the vessel waited in Liverpool harbor, becalmed with upwards of two hundred others. At last wind brought the sails of all the ships full to the breeze at the same time. From the *Ceres* he watched the sails gradually disperse and, as evening fell, scatter far over the horizon. By morning a gale had set in and presently came the usual tedium of seasickness.

Alternate storm and calm plagued the little vessel for one month and twenty-eight days. On the twenty-ninth Morse entered in the journal of his voyage:

> *Wednesday, 18th October.* Last night was a sleepless night to us all. . . . Rainy, thick. . . . A dreadful state of suspense, between feelings of exquisite joy in the hope of soon seeing home, and feelings of gloomy apprehension that a few hours may doom us to destruction.
>
> *Half-past seven.* . . . Heaven be praised! The joyful tidings are just announced of *Land!!* Oh! who can conceive our feelings now? The wretch condemned to the scaffold, who receives, at the moment he expects to die, the joyful reprieve, he can best conceive the state of our minds.
>
> The land is Cape Cod, distant about ten miles. Joyful, joyful is the thought. To-night we shall, in all probability, be in Boston. We are going at the rate of seven knots.
>
> *Half-past* 9. Manomet land in sight.
> *Ten o'clock.* Cape Ann in sight.
> *Eleven o'clock.* Boston Light in sight.
> *One o'clock.* HOME!!! [21]

CHAPTER v

Itinerant

THE WHITE parsonage under the Town Hill elms was much the same. Nancy was still presiding over the kitchen in her abrupt way. Prince was still driving Dr. Morse to and from Andover for conferences on orthodox strategy. Mother Morse at nearly fifty (she was insisting on conspicuous floral designs for her dresses now) poured out affection and advice to her sons as warmly as ever. Brother Richard, unwell and often uncertain of himself, was in and out of the house while studying for the ministry in Andover. The enterprising Sidney was launching a journal in Boston. The owners of most Boston newspapers, like most wealthy Bostonians, were partisans of the easy way of Unitarianism. Sidney with the support of Nathaniel Willis and Jeremiah Evarts, with whom Dr. Morse had edited the religious monthly the *Panoplist*, was now editing the weekly *Recorder* to redress the balance in favor of orthodoxy.

Having temporarily driven the Unitarians in his own parish to cover, Dr. Morse could more freely give time to his sons. Just as he pushed Sidney's paper and Richard's search for a pulpit he encouraged his eldest son's efforts to establish himself as an artist. Boston he envisaged as a great seat of the fine arts. Allston and Finley together might establish a gallery that would make it so.

Morse felt the united force of family behind him. At home in America, finding the Federalists much weakened by their unsavory course in the war, he suddenly dropped his political controversy with his parents. His career demanded all his energies.

When the *Dying Hercules* had arrived from England, Dr. Morse had it framed and exhibited in a hired room in Boston; he hoped to send it to Philadelphia and possibly on to Charleston, but before the artist himself arrived the exhibition had failed.

Two months later the canvas was again on display, this time in the painter's own rooms. Near Mallory's bookstore, where he had worked in misery five years before, he now achieved a studio, rented by his father. In his brother's new *Recorder* he invited his public:

MORSE'S

EXHIBITION OF PICTURES.

Joy's Buildings, Cornhill-Square.[1]

Polite attention was showered upon the artist rather than upon his paintings. Senator James Lloyd, a Federalist acquaintance of Dr. Morse, took the lead in introducing him into the polished circles where patrons might be found. The excitement of social recognition was at first satisfying, but something more was necessary. At the end of the winter not one Bostonian had bought a painting or given him a commission, while the receipts of the exhibit did not half cover expenses.

Dr. Morse watched his son feel the chilling touch of neglect and saw him shrink. The father was frightened. He sent Senator Lloyd an appeal: "We consider his present situation extremely critical. . . . Should he fail in his object of obtaining the means of completing his education in Europe, I much fear either that he w.d leave his native states with such feelings as w.d lead him to resolve to spend the remainder of his days as an adventurer in Europe, or in Phil.a or N. Y., or that after the expectations he has excited by his past efforts, & the expense to whh he has subjected his parents, his spirits w.d break, & his ambition sink, & as he is fitted to pursue no other profession, his ultimate sink w.d follow. Perhaps the apprehensions are too strong; but having known and marked his disposition from a child we think that they are not. He is a son of our hopes. He is amiable, affectionate, obedient, grateful, kind & generous in his feelings – no spendthrift, addicted to no one vice – & an enthusiastic lover of his country, of its improvements in science, & especially in the elegant Arts. . . . All that he requires to inspire him with life & energy in his professional pursuits, & to draw forth his best efforts, & to preserve all his talents . . . is simply *patronage*."[2]

To occupy himself, the young artist painted his brothers, his Grandmother Breese, and his Grandfather Morse. In the hope of stirring attention he even gave away a painting to the Boston editor Nathan Hale. As he smoked his "solitary segar" of an evening, it seemed to him that his hope of returning to Allston and Leslie in London was fading. In the spring he sent his *Hercules* to Philadelphia for exhibition. In July he abandoned one of his two rooms, and in August the other.

He might easily have crawled into himself during this period of neglect; he might have become bitter against the crassness of American taste; he might have gone into his "ultimate sink," as his father feared. But his father did not know his resiliency or versatility. In this crucial year, his twenty-fifth, he proved that he was not the usual youth of fortunate birth and education. It was during this year of frustration that he chose his wife, undertook the serious practice of a branch of his art – portraiture – which he had disdained but which was to carry him to the top of his profession in America, and promoted an invention which was to give him a reservoir of experience for the crowning labor of his life, the telegraph. And he was even more versatile than his public ever knew. Many have forgotten that in this year, reveling in his discovery of new powers, he turned with confidence to the idea of becoming an architect or even a theologian.

With midsummer heat the roads were dry in Boston's hinterland and he started north. If patrons would not come to his studio, he would seek them out. There were views aplenty in New Hampshire, but his real object, loath as he might be to admit it, was cash; in America that meant portraits. His father had prepared the way with useful introductions.

In early August he appeared in Concord. On "The Street," as the only roadway of the village was called, he found Pastor McFarland's square, white, wooden house, of restful proportions, with a hip roof and an ell tacked on behind for a kitchen. To Finley as a pastor's son the house was familiar in both its outward aspect and its inward disposition. It was almost as much of a public hostel as Stickney Tavern across the way. On winter Sabbaths during the interval between forenoon and afternoon service meeting-goers from distant parts of the town crowded into the warmth of the parsonage to eat their box lunches. All clerics who visited the New Hampshire capital stayed at the parsonage, and apparently Morse did as well. Dr. McFarland knew the family through the *Panoplist,* which he thought a soundly Calvinistic journal, while his wife, a Boston Kneeland, had often heard Dr. Morse preach in the Old South pulpit. The McFarlands readily consented to introduce the young artist into Concord society. They played their part well.

When he had been in Concord less than two weeks, he dined at Samuel Sparhawk's, the house in which the Upper Bank (of which Sparhawk was cashier) had its office. It had a romantic tradition. When it had been built, about thirty years before, the owner, Daniel Livermore, had it placed slightly out of line with the street. He was courting one of Judge Walker's daughters and he wanted it skewed nine inches from the line at one end so that from a window he could look north up the street to the judge's house. In this house now began the courting of a daughter of the next generation. Here at dinner Morse met for the first time the judge's granddaughter, Lucretia Pickering Walker. Decades later Morse returned to Concord to look once more on this house.

That Lucretia was the town belle did not discourage him. The first Walker in Concord had been its first minister and the builder of its first two-story house. His son, Judge Timothy Walker, still lived in that house at the North End. Now a venerable gentleman, he was president of the Upper Bank. Across from him, behind a row of elms, was a house much like the parsonage, the home of Judge Walker's son, the lawyer Charles Walker. There were five children in the household, all of whom Morse soon came to know: Charles, "in his Junior year at Cambridge, an excellent scholar, and a pleasant young man," Susan, "a very fine girl about 15," Augustus, "about 12, at Exeter Academy," Timothy, "about 6, as wild as a bear, and I fear a little too much indulged," and Lucretia.[3]

Concord soon proved agreeable to Morse. In three weeks he had earned a hundred dollars with his painting. But that was not all.

"I have other attractions besides money in this place," he wrote home. "Do you know the Walkers of this place? Charles Walker Esq.r, son of Judge W., has two daughters, the eldest very beautiful, amiable, and of an excellent disposition. This is her character in

Courtesy, Herbert L. Pratt

LUCRETIA PICKERING WALKER

By Morse

Wife of the artist, who said: "Her beauty and simplicity of manners first attracted my attention."

town. I have enquired particularly of Dr. McFarland respecting the family, and his answer is every way satisfactory except that they are not professors of religion. He is a man of family and great wealth; this last you know I never made a principal object, but it is somewhat satisfactory to know that in my profession.

"I may flatter myself, but I think I might be a successful suitor. . . .

"There is still no need of hurry; the young lady is but *16.** . . . Of course all that I say is between you and me, for all it may come to nothing; I have *some experience* that way."[4]

In college there had been two names to quicken his heart, Ann Davenport of Stamford and Jeannette Hart of Saybrook, but he had resolutely decided that love must yield to painting. In Bristol, England, only a year before, enamored of the daughter of his patron James Russell, he had decided that "love and painting are quarrelsome companions, and that the house of my heart is too small for both of them," and had "turned Mrs. Love out-of-doors."[5] Now Mrs. Love was entering the house of his heart by the front door, welcomed.

The Walkers soon knew his intentions. He called repeatedly during his last two weeks in Concord, and the reticent Mr. Walker and his chatty wife encouraged him by asking him again and again to tea and dinner. Everywhere in town he inquired about his Lucrece. Was she a coquette? Was she of amiable disposition? Everywhere he got the same answers, and his own knowledge of her satisfied him. She was slight, dark-haired, of high color, vivacious, the pride of Concord; and yet modest, quiet to the point of diffidence, and frank and open-hearted too. It was nearly his last day in Concord when he ventured to tell her his whole heart. He knew she would not refuse him. Yet he was delighted that instead of replying in words of obscurity that would tantalize him she answered timidly but frankly that her heart was like his. She was willing to wait two or three years.

He left his love behind in Concord, and eight portraits too. Among them may have been that of Lucretia's uncle, Samuel Sparhawk, whom he portrayed as a graceless, peaked Yankee. His likenesses were so candid that Concord was startled; they could be recognized

* She was seventeen. Her birthday was July 15, 1799.

at sight! They were small portraits, on millboard, and thinly painted. They had to be. He was paid only fifteen dollars apiece for seven of them, and for the eighth, because the subject had obtained four sitters for him, only ten dollars. A hundred dollars was not enough. He and Lucretia could not "subsist long upon air," his mother unkindly reminded him. "Remember it takes a great many hundred dollars to *make* and *keep* the pot a-boiling." [6]

From Concord he went west to Walpole and then followed the Connecticut north to Windsor on the Vermont bank. There he painted six portraits for fifteen dollars apiece, a small one for ten, and one for board and room. Even there the fame of Lucretia's beauty had spread!

Long before he went on to Hanover, he heard the noise of the war that was racking that little town. The Dartmouth College trustees had recently ousted President Wheelock. The Federalists took sides with the trustees and their new president, Francis Brown; Democrats took sides with Wheelock. The Democratic state legislature seized the opportunity to attempt to reorganize the private college into a popular state university with Wheelock as president. One of the few officials of the old college to espouse the new university was its treasurer, Judge Woodward, the brother-in-law of Wheelock. His transfer of the college seal and records to the new university was later the basis of the famous plea of Daniel Webster before the Supreme Court in the Dartmouth College case.

As he neared the unhappy town, the scene of two institutions fighting over the same property and students, Morse thought to turn the dispute to advantage. On the huge canvas he had brought home from England he would paint all the figures involved — the officers, trustees, and students; he would finish it in a week and ask five thousand dollars for it. Then he would come home in a coach and six and put Sidney to shame with his paltry nineteen subscribers a day for the *Recorder*. Five thousand a week is two hundred sixty thousand a year. In ten years he would be worth two million six hundred thousand!

In Hanover he was soon modestly painting single portraits. Having learned to be less of a partisan than in England, he succeeded in painting both Judge Woodward, the traitor to the college, and a little later President Brown, Woodward's enemy. He was soon reconciled to the prospect of averaging two or three thousand dollars a year; that would be tolerable, he thought, though far from two million six hundred thousand.

By October he was back in Concord, as glad to see Lucretia as ever. The time had now come to notify her parents of a formal engagement. He did not know how to proceed. What should he say? Could he send the message in writing? He wrote his parents for advice and, after consulting Lucretia, prepared a letter with care:

Monday morn.g. Oct.r 14.th 1816.

Charles Walker Esq.r
Dear Sir,

After various ineffectual attempts to overcome my diffidence sufficiently to communicate with you, or Mrs. Walker, on a subject of much importance to you and family, I have at length ventured to do it by letter; Waiving further preamble, I shall briefly state that on my former visit to Concord, I became acquainted with your *daughter Lucretia;* her beauty and simplicity of manners first attracted my attention, and on acquaintance finding that her *disposition, education,* and *acquirements,* were equal to her personal attractions, I became almost unconsciously strongly attached to her, on farther acquaintance I found that my attentions were not disregarded; and it is by her permission, dear Sir, that I now inform you that our *attachment is mutual,* as you will doubtless learn from her own lips, if you should enquire of her. I felt it my duty in the earliest stages of our attachment to acquaint *my parents* with my partiality, and I have the satisfaction of possessing *their entire approbation.*

My acquaintance in your family being of so late a commencement, I am well aware that my *character, education,* and *acquirements* can be but partially known to you; for a knowledge of these, dear Sir, I must refer you to those who know me, and to whom I appeal with a degree of confidence that their representations will be perfectly satisfactory to you and family. In the meantime, Sir, shall I beg the indulgence of visiting in your family to continue my attentions to your daughter, and also to give you and family, an opportunity of personally knowing me better.

With much anxiety, Sir, I shall await your answer at M.r Thacher's store.

With the highest respect
Y.r Mo. Ob.t hum.e Serv.t
Sam.l F. B. Morse

He sent the letter at noon and waited in suspense.

During the afternoon Mr. Walker asked him to call. By five he had come away rejoicing: "Everything successful! Praise be to the giver of every good gift!"[7] Yes, his blessings were indeed coming fast upon him, even though that spring he had had to give up all hope for a career in historical painting. He had proved that he could earn a reasonable income in portraiture and he had won the constant love of the girl he chose.

When Finley came home he found that Ward Stafford, once Richard's roommate at Yale, had been holding conferences in the parsonage parlor. Jeremiah Evarts, editor of the *Panoplist,* and Samuel Worcester, Salem pastor, at first told Stafford that Sunday-schools were not fit for New England. To hold schools of any kind on the first day of the week would be a profanation of the Sabbath. But Stafford convinced them. In October 1816 the Charlestown Sabbath-school, one of the first in Massachusetts, opened with Finley as superintendent and Sidney among its teachers.[8]

A few weeks later Finley became a member of the church,[9] perhaps as a result of his Sabbath-school experience. In later years he did not write of his conversion, and its circumstances remain unknown. "Finley appears to be alive in religion,"[10] Dr. Morse wrote, delighted with his eldest son. He could not say as much for Richard, though he was studying for the ministry; nor for Sidney, though he was editing a religious paper. The younger brothers were immensely concerned for their souls; they brooded over what it would mean to come forward at communion; they dwelt on their impurity. Finley had simply considered, prayed, and come forward.

Not that his conversion was half-hearted. His experience convinced him that he was not loving Lucretia fully unless he impressed upon her the necessity for a similar change. In January she came to Charlestown to make the acquaintance of the Morse household. There Morse urged her to know her "false peace." A daily routine for self-examination would help; he had tested it himself. Write down your thoughts on paper, he told her, to bring even the most secret ones directly before you. Ask yourself such questions as these:

"What have I done this day?"

"Have I not had such and such thoughts?"

"How did I pray; did I ask sincerely for certain blessings, or was there a secret disinclination to have them?"

"Did I feel weighed down with sin, or did I pray as the self-righteous Pharisee?"

"Have I not received particular blessings this day whh I have not been thankful for?"

Self-examination he considered the only security; but Lucretia, like Richard and Sidney, was tormented by it. After several weeks in Charlestown under Finley's and his father's direction, the seventeen-year-old girl came to know the depravity of her heart. She found that what she had thought innocent now appeared sinful. She was troubled, even agonized.

Finley had known that she would suffer; yet his love demanded that he bring the pain of this knowledge upon her. "I might flatter you, dear, as some would," he wrote from Portsmouth; "I might tell you that your amiable disposition, and your correct conduct would certainly recommend you to God, that you need only go on, live correctly, be charitable, and you have nothing to fear; and whilst I thus deceived you, you might love me most sincerely; but think, my dear, what a part I should act; I could see one whom I loved so tenderly resting in false security, (which if I did my duty, ought to be disturbed), and I could live with her through life, and when death separated us, know for an awful truth, that if I was saved, we were separated *forever*. Could I love you, dear girl, if I could do this?" [11]

Methods of saving souls were the subject of tense conversations at Boston tables these days, for the Unitarian controversy was raging. Church after church was leaving the Congregational Trinitarian for the new Congregational Unitarian fold. In Charlestown, since the liberals could not carry the whole church with them, they resigned to form their own church. Dr. Morse persuaded himself that the purgation would be healthy. But it was not easy to lose old friends. Even the family physician resigned. And Miss Russell, too, the fairy godmother who in years gone by had stuffed Finley's pockets with cakes and fruit. It was gratifying to Dr. Morse at this time of testing that Finley should be of " serious " mind. If Finley inclined to Jeffersonianism, at least he had been dutiful enough not to follow Jefferson into the Unitarian heresy.

During the winter Finley was often painting in Portsmouth. Lucretia had many relatives there, her mother being a Portsmouth Pickering. Unfortunately some of the Pickerings were Unitarians, and hence inclined to cotillion and card parties. And most unfortunately one of them, the husband of Lucretia's aunt, was Nathan Parker, the minister of Unitarian persuasion. Morse tried to keep on good terms with both Parker and the orthodox pastor, Dr. Morse's friend Putnam. But he found that Parker and Putnam did not get along together well enough to respond to his earnest pleading for a town Sabbath-school.

As a painter, if not as a theologian, Morse could still understand both Unitarians and Congregationalists. In Portsmouth he painted both " Uncle " Parker and Professor Pearson, the vigorous promoter of the Andover institutions of orthodoxy. The portrait of Pearson was of remarkable power. A ruddy complexion and a dull red background provided ample color; the massive head, the deep-set eyes, the long, straight nose, the bold mouth tempered faintly with kindly wisdom, were enough to fill the whole canvas with commanding interest. While Pearson was heavily painted, in marked contrast Parker was thinly done; while the one depended for its effect on the strength of the composition, the other, because Parker was youthful and pensive, depended on richness of color and skillful, delicate modeling. Morse understood both the explosive Pearson and the diminutive Parker and could give each the treatment he deserved.

Suddenly Morse came to believe that his concern for the souls of men was more fundamental to his nature than painting their faces. At home he wrote Lucretia: " I long, dear, to see you; I have . . . something to communicate to you of great importance as it respects our future prospects; it is no less than *a change of my profession,* for *Divinity;* at present dear I wish you not to communicate it; it is a subject which requires the greatest deliberation, and earnest seeking of divine direction, all my most judicious friends and among them many of the first divines in the country, Andover professors &c. advise to it; I hope that I shall be directed from above." From this time for thirty years Morse's life was to be a search for a career.

As if it were not surprising enough for Lucretia to hear that she was to become a minister's wife, she read on to discover that she was to become an Episcopal minister's wife: "I shall study probably at Andover *one* year and the rest of the time at the *Episcopal College* just commenced at New York – my reasons, dear, for being an Episcopal Clergyman, (should I determine on divinity) I will tell you when I see you; they are various." [12]

His leap in the direction of Episcopalianism was made easier by his frequent attendance at Anglican services in England, by his association with Allston, who entered the Anglican communion, and by his friendship for Samuel Jarvis, one of the founders of the new Episcopal General Theological Seminary in New York. All his friends encouraged his change in profession, he told Lucretia. In the current confusion of Congregationalism some were looking with envy at the orderliness of a hierarchical church. For one who called himself a Jeffersonian, however, and who was to become vigorously anti-Catholic, the readiness to leap from a church of congregational to one of hierarchical polity was significant.

The trend among the leaders of thought in New England in Morse's generation was rather toward Unitarianism than Episcopalianism. With the discipline of the old Calvinism still in their bones, and the joyous freedom of the new faith opening their eyes, Parker, Emerson, Thoreau, Fuller, and Channing ushered in New England's classic age. If Morse had been influenced by this trend, in later years he might have found himself a part of more progressive political movements than nativism or the defense of slavery. As it was, he could break with his parents more easily on politics and on the form of religion than on doctrines.

Professor Spring met Richard on the Andover Seminary campus one day and, with what Richard called "one of his *ha ha's*," remarked: "Why, I hear that the *painter* thinks of being a minister." The professor untactfully reminded Richard of Finley's reputation for volatility.[13]

Whether Professor Spring had more than a "ha ha" for the painter's attempt in architecture is not recorded. With characteristic boldness Finley determined, in what was probably his first competition in architecture, to compete with Charles Bulfinch himself for the designing of an Andover Seminary building. Bulfinch won. But the painter was not satisfied to be stretching out toward theology and architecture alone. During the same six months he was also the promoter of the Morse pump.

Since March [14] Sidney and Finley had been spending their Charlestown evenings in testing little models of what they humorously dubbed "Morse's Patent Metallic Double-Headed Ocean-Drinker and Deluge-Spouter Valve Pump-Boxes." [15] It was intended as an improvement on the force pump, which would be useful for boats, fire-engines, or blacksmith's bellows. When friends saw it tested with Mrs. Morse's pump in the parsonage yard they thought the idea salable, likely to make hand-operated fire-engines cheaper. Though they had only applied for American patents, in August the brothers began to dream of European profits. They agreed to reserve them for their mother. It was Dr. Morse who wrote Bromfield in London and an acquaintance in Paris to offer the agency for European patents.[16] As with the *Recorder* and the geographies, the pump was a family enterprise.

The invention itself was the joint product of the Hare and the Tortoise. They always spoke of it as "ours." The American patent was in both names.[17] Sidney probably took the lead in both designing and perfecting the machines they built; but it was clearly Finley's special function to make the drawings that were used in applying for patents. And he was the more active in promoting sales. If the fire-engines proved sound, he was promised orders from Andover, Hanover, and Concord.

The brothers succeeded in finding a speculator to lend them between four hundred and five hundred dollars; he was to be repaid and receive one third of the profits from the fire-engines sold. Only one application of the pump ever found many buyers. During the next summer the "small engines for gardens and streets" sold so fast at twenty dollars each that the hired mechanics could hardly keep up with the demand. But the fire-engine speculator was paid only two hundred dollars on his loan; this was the price paid for what was probably the only machine sold, the one sent to Concord.

While there was yet hope for profits from the pump, Finley wrote his Lucretia: "Surely an Inventor earns his money hard. It appears to me I would not go through the vexations, and delays, and disappointments, I have gone through, for double what I expect to obtain from them."[18] Experiments with the pump and with a steamboat design were gently introducing him to the patience requisite to invention – patience which he did not naturally possess.

One day in September, when the seminary year was about to begin, Morse had a long conversation on his future with parents and friends. "They have concluded," he wrote Lucretia, "that, considering my disposition of mind, which was never that of a student's, and considering the time I had spent in acquiring my present profession, which on trial is found to be sufficient not only to give me a support but also to make me a man of fortune, and thus enabling me to do good in that way, and also considering that for 7, or 8 years past, I have formed habits of life in a totally different profession, and which are opposite to those which I must acquire should I study divinity, I say considering these things and many others, they have concluded that it is not my duty to change my profession."

Those blessed with many capacities often find the choice of a career difficult. Finley's task was made doubly difficult because he knew that many of his friends had not yet forgotten his reputation for changeability. "*However, dear,*" he urged Lucrece, "*do not say that I shall not study Divinity, not even to your nearest friends: for I mean still to consider of it;* I wish you to say always on that point, *that I am quite undecided whether to pursue my profession or not,* that I shall not enter the Institution at Andover *this* year, that I shall probably spend the winter in Charleston (S. C.) or somewhere at the Southward; and that it is *your opinion* that I shall probably continue in my present profession. Say this dear, or I shall be thought to be the most *fickle* being in the world, and indeed my conscience accuses me strongly of some-like it; it is indeed true that I am often *too precipitate, too sanguine,* and *too positive* when I think of any new scheme." He well knew his weaknesses. But his knowledge of them could not discourage his faith in his invention. "We are just going to try our New Engine which answers all expectations," he added; "we have it in our barn."[19]

Slack orders for paintings had given him time to consider theology, architecture, and invention; architecture and theology had been dropped, and now slack orders for his pumps gave him time to consider the state of his professional career. How long should he be content with fifteen dollars a portrait? When he first came home from Europe he had hoped to return after a short time to complete his study on the Continent. He had not been successful enough in his painting to make that possible. He had hatched wild schemes of going to the West Indies, to Haiti, for lush profits. He had abandoned them too, but there remained the more reasonable plan of going south among those who accepted the graceful and fine arts as contributions to the art of living.

Perhaps there were more family connections among the stern clergymen and educators of New England, but there were not a few among the gentility of the Carolina seaboard as well. Years earlier Dr. Morse had briefly been pastor in Midway, Georgia. While the boys were in college, for the sake of his health he and Mrs. Morse had spent one winter in Charleston. While there, they were entertained by Major General C. C. Pinckney of Pinckney Island, Dr. Lemuel Kollock of Savannah, and the Legarés of Johns Island, and they strengthened their ties to the Beaufort physician Dr. James E. B. Finley, Mrs. Morse's uncle. Now Dr. Finley lived in Charleston; his family were constant correspondents of the Morses. Even in 1816 Finley had been invited to come to Carolina to try his profession and make his home with the Legarés. Some of the Carolina relations of his teacher Allston had been in Boston and met Morse; and one, John Ashe Alston, led him to believe the South would be generous. In the fall of 1817 Morse wrote Dr. Finley for advice and was encouraged to try Charleston for the winter.

Multifarious duties held him until the moment of departure. As he left he wrote Lucrece: "Portraits and engines, and pumps and bellows, and various models of various things, letters to write, and visits to pay, and preparations for voyages by sea and land, all crowd upon me." [20] On his way south the pump won precedence. In New Haven he showed a model to his former professors Benjamin Silliman and Jeremiah Day, of whom the latter had succeeded Dwight as president of Yale, and also to a new professor, Eli Whitney. Silliman exhibited the model before one of his classes; President Day wrote a letter of recommendation, declaring that it united "simplicity in the construction, with effectual security against friction." And Whitney, already long famous for his cotton gin, wrote a cautious note of approval.[21] In both New Haven and New York he tried to find an agent for his pump. In New Haven he was successful; in New York he did nothing at all. The whole pump affair suddenly sickened him; there was little profit in it and much vexation. He would continue with it, but make it subservient to his painting. As he boarded his packet in New York, he felt that of all the occupations in which he knew he could succeed, it would be in painting that he would find independence.

CHAPTER *vi*

Winters at the South

EXPECTANTLY he settled at Uncle Finley's on King Street near the Battery, surrounded by the town houses of Carolina's leading planters, lawyers, and merchants. The Finleys introduced him pleasantly into some of these homes. The gracious warmth of the Southern winter was agreeable enough; the luxuriant vines and trees idling over the garden walls, the clean steeple of St. Michael's always visible above the city, the rolling walk of the Negroes may have diverted him; but no sitters came. Charlestonians, among the most practiced patrons of the arts in America, expected proof of his skill before they would entrust themselves to his brush. The days drew themselves out wearily. How long could he afford to wait? His confidence in magnificent Southern patronage gone, he may have desperately resolved, as his friend Dunlap records,[1] to paint Dr. Finley as a memorial to his hospitality and leave for home. If so he kept his decision from Lucretia and his parents.

Whether or not the sudden change in his affairs resulted from exhibiting his portrait of Uncle Finley, before the end of his third week in Charleston constant applications for sittings were buoying him to impetuous decisions. He wrote Lucretia that he would bring her to Charleston as his wife the next fall. She consented with a proviso that indicated her affectionate understanding of her lover: Yes, if by that time " you don't have *another plan.*" [2]

Planters, merchants, judges, clergymen, generals applied to the young Yankee for portraits. In less than two months eighty commissions for portraits were on his books, most of them at sixty, seventy, or eighty dollars apiece! A magnificent gain over the paltry fifteen from his New England compatriots. Calculating that he could make a thousand dollars a month at this rate, while the uncertain pump enterprise required "a person altogether of different education from myself," he gave himself with a will to painting the best families of Carolina. They seemed to flock into his studio on King Street over Mr. Aubin's store.[3] John Ashe Alston of Georgetown,* who owned paintings by West and Vanderlyn and well knew what good painting was, offered two hundred dollars for a full-length portrait of his daughter Sarah. General C. C. Pinckney offered three hundred for a portrait of his brother, General Thomas Pinckney. Colonel William Drayton considered his own portrait worth three hundred dollars. A Yankee had become the fashion in the metropolis of the South.

If he finished fifty-three portraits before he was ready to leave in May, as has been asserted,[4] he must indeed have painted swiftly. Even so, his high level of excellence in recording likenesses, his understanding of his sitters, and his direct technique indicated that his painting approached maturity.

With sketches of portraits to complete and a purse of more than three thousand dollars he returned north for the summer. A year before, a full purse would have meant his return to Europe. Now he went home to prepare for marriage.

From Charlestown he pelted Lucretia with questions. Couldn't she prepare as well in Charlestown as in Concord? What would her father be likely to give her as a dowry? (To this question they referred in their correspondence as "a question on a certain affair.") Were his parents to go to Concord for the wedding? Would it be in the morning or afternoon? Where would they drive that day? "How far is Amherst dear, (don't laugh, now) you promised to tell me all about the road and the taverns &c. &c."[5] Her answers were warmly affectionate, and often annoyingly evasive as the appointed 1st day of October approached.

It was from Lucretia that Morse first heard of the ludicrous failure of one of his pumps. In April, through Mr. Sparhawk, Concord had purchased a fire-engine which the town paper described as "a new

* A town of 17,500 population, of which 15,500 were slaves, Finley wrote to his father for the Morse gazetteer.

invention of Mr. Morse . . . procured for about half the usual expense – say one hundred and fifty to two hundred dollars. It requires much less manual labor, and throws the water to as great a distance and in as large quantities."[6] When the engine arrived it was tested in Mr. Sparhawk's yard. It failed to spout water at all. Lucretia heard of the sarcasm of the spectators, and thinking Finley would be "a little diverted" by it, wrote him that one man had said: "Mr. Morse better stick to his brush, *he will do well enough then.*"[7] Several months later an entry appeared in a family notebook: "Engine back from Concord."[8]

On September 2 he was calculating that he would go across the bridge to Boston to meet the Tuesday Concord mail only two or three times more. "I count the days with eagerness," he wrote, "28 days from to-day. Well, love, on the 10th inst. I shall speak to the *town-clerk* to publish the banns of marriage between *Sam.l F. B. Morse* of Charlestown and *Lucretia Pickering Walker* of Concord, N. H. What does the *lady* say; is she willing? are there no misgivings? would not she like a little longer time to make up her mind whether she can love the above named gentleman? As for the *gentleman,* I believe he has made up his mind to take her '*for better for worse*'; and run the risque of her being a termagent, or scold, or vixen, or the like. I should like to know the lady's opinion."[9]

Her answer was slow in coming. When he had not heard from her at all for two weeks, he was in a torment. He couldn't paint. He made excuses for her; perhaps the post office had made an error. Another mail came without a letter. Then he could only conclude that she was ill. For nearly three weeks he had not heard. All his arrangements for the end of the month were thrown into confusion. And then at last came Lucretia's soft touch to his wound: "So then I am to be published next Sunday to Mr. Sam.l F. B. Morse and you wish to know if the lady has made up her mind whether she can love the above named gentleman? Strange question, when you know the lady made up her mind two years ago and has loved him ever since; but how is it that the gentleman can *cooly and deliberately* run the risque of her being a termagent or vixen and thus be teased and tormented and have the consolation of reflecting that this connection was made for *life,* oh dear, if I thought I should ever be such a torment to you, dear Finley, I should shudder at the thought and I should be unwilling to have your happiness entrusted to my keeping." [10] She had replied a little late, and her letter had been delayed in transit.

About two years after he sent his first letter to Miss Walker at Concord he sent his last:

Charlestown Sept.r 16.th, 1818.
Wednesday even.g

Dearest Lucrece,

Your letter of Monday has *just* been handed me, through the delay of the P. Master; I thank you dear, for your promptness, and I in my turn begin *almost* to feel sorry for the letter I wrote last week, since it has caused my dear Lucrece, so much pain. . . .

The plan which you propose of being married in the morn.g dearest, you will perceive, I was *most inclined to* in my last letter, and only mentioned the other, for your consideration, I am glad you decided on the one you have; I shall be with you, dear, probably the latter part of *next week,* only think, dearest, in so short a time; shall you *really* be glad to see me, love, when you see that your Finley can "*blame*" you? You know he loves you dear, and I am afraid too ardently for his comfort; if he did not love his Lucrece, he would not feel so distressed at not hearing from her; So, dearest, you consent to be married the 1.st Oct. you say your father must go to P.[ortsmout]h on that day, as the ceremony will take place early in the morning it will not prevent his going; for we must set out early in order to reach *Amherst* in good season; (*don't tell any one dear the rout we shall take*). . . .

You did not tell me in your letter dear whether your father rec.d my letter sent by the same mail with the last to you requesting him to speak without delay to the Town Clerk of Concord to *publish* us there; was it done? On Monday next I shall obtain the *certificate* here.

Only think, dearest, your next letter will be the last to me, as L.P.W. This W. must be turned the other way thus (*M.*) and *this* too is probably the last to Miss *Walker;* can you realize it? It is a *joyful* and yet *solemn event,* to be married, dear, I cannot help feeling great joy, and we may lawfully feel it, it is intended we should feel joy; Our blessed Savior honored a marriage supper with his presence, thereby giving countenance to all the joys of the occasion.

Let your last letter, dearest, be full, and say all you have to say to me before you see me; and now how shall I close my own last letter but by assuring my dear girl of the undiminished love of her Finley, who will soon give her proof of the same when he takes her to his arms as his own dear companion and partner for life. . . . Remember that your Finley loves you as ardently as ever, if not more so.

Believe me lovely Lucrece,

Y.rs till *death us do part*
as the proverb goes.
Finley ∴ –

P. S. I shall come up to C.–d in a chaise, probably on Saturday week, be married *Wed.* or *Thurs.* go to Amherst the first day, *spend the night,* then journey slowly on to the *Stafford Springs,* stay a little while, then to Concord again *perhaps,* and then *home.*[11]

They both wrote on folio sheets, of the same size, but their handwriting was not alike. His was firm, precise, clipped, the style of one who is accustomed to make his hand do his bidding on canvas or drafting board. Hers was loose, flowing freely.

Concord 21.st September 1818.
Monday morn.g.

My dearest Finley,

I have determined to sit down and answer your last dear letter before I engage in any of the duties of the day before me lest something should occur to prevent, and knowing too what a disappointment it would be to my ever *dear* and *affectionate* Finley if he should not hear from his Lucretia at this *important* and *interesting* crisis. I could not rest until I had discharged my *duty* to you, dear.

I received your last on Friday evening, and wish I could tell you how much pleasure it conveyed to the heart of your Lucrece, I could not help bestowing many kisses upon it for the *dear* writer's sake. In my joy I entirely forgot that my dear Finley had ever "blamed" me so *liberally* as he did in his last, and I could only feel happy that the time was so near at hand when we should meet face to face. . . .

My father received your line and your wishes were promptly attended to, and the following Sabbath your name together with Doctor Chadbourne's and Dr. Long's and I don't know how many others was posted up full length. Mary wishes me to tell you that Dr. McFarland has dropped the word "obey" in the marriage service, oh by the way Charles abuses *us* very much for wishing to be married in the morning. . . .

Dear you certainly must return by the way of Concord from the Springs, can't you? Now dearest I must close, all friends unite in an affectionate remembrance to you and yours, for want of time I have left much unsaid, again I assure you of my ardent affection, whh I trust will not cease to exist after I have lost the name of Walker.

In the glad expectation of soon embracing you I bid you farewell,

Y.rs with increasing affection dear Finley,
Lucretia Pickering Walker.[12]

The date for the wedding was advanced to Tuesday, September 29.[13] At the request of the Walkers, Morse's parents were not present; they could be more conveniently entertained another time. Early in the morning, in the north parlor of the Walker home, Pastor McFarland read the wedding service.

Lucretia was the second Walker girl of Concord to be carried away by someone who was to become known as an inventor. The first became the wife of Benjamin Thompson, later famous as Count Rumford.

By nine o'clock they were in a gig on their way to Amherst, New Hampshire. The roads were bad, but they had completed the thirty miles by night; the next day they bumped over the rocky way, up and down hill, which led along the Souhegan Valley through Wilton to New Ipswich, near the Massachusetts line; they had intended to go on into Massachusetts, but hearing the roads were only cross-roads and that there were no taverns along the route, on the third day they turned back, arriving in Concord on the fourth day. They remained several weeks in Concord and Charlestown, and on November 12 sailed from New York.

The voyage was soon over. The schooner passed between Fort Moultrie and James Island and docked in Charleston. As the crew began to unload the cargo of crusty barrels of rum, ale, cider, beef, flour, and Digby herrings, Morse and his wife stepped onto the dock. They soon found the Finleys, and under their kindly directions settled at Mrs. Munro's boarding-house on Church Street at ten dollars a week. The boarding-house was as much of a home as they were ever to have.

Presently they had as much attention from hospitable Charleston as they could accept. The Legarés asked them to dine, the eccentric Mrs. Yates asked Lucretia out to ride, and Mrs. Keith wrote the Morses that Lucretia was " a charming little woman & all who have become acquainted with her are much pleased with her. I am glad she likes Charleston – & particularly as your son will have to be much more here for some time to come – having such constant employment."[14]

Lucretia dressed well – noticeably well even for Charleston. Though, as Finley said, all her dresses had been made "in Boston under Mama's superintendence," brother Richard, who was now teaching at Savannah, thought her trousseau indicated extravagance and ostentation.[15] Finley was surprised and possibly not a little pleased to hear it. As she sat at tea one evening Morse was suddenly struck by her pose,[16] and drew her in black and white crayon. She wore a fluffy muslin, with loose sleeves caught up with ribbons at shoulder and elbow. In her right hand she dangled a fan. Her features were mild, her expression gentle; with the characteristic slight tilt of her head and the strength of her fingers they suggest a delightful animated repose. She looked content, and Finley thought she was. "She has grown quite fleshy and healthy," he wrote home, "and we are as happy in each other as you can possibly wish us."[17]

When Finley left Lucretia of a morning, he had but to walk from Church Street through a short length of St. Michael's Alley to his painting room. His formal address was Broad Street, but his windows and private entrance were on the alley, in the shadow of St. Michael's steeple.

Sitters came to him in the alley more frequently than before. Soon after his arrival he raised his minimum price from sixty to eighty dollars a portrait, and still the patrons rapped at his door. Late in January he predicted that he would be obliged to come again next winter to fulfill his engagements. By the first of February he declared he would still find ample orders if he spent five or six winters in Charleston. Early that month commissions to the value of $3,000 had been recorded since his arrival; a month later, $4,295. This was the season which justified his later remark that one year in Charleston he had earned beyond his expenses $9,000.

Soon afterward government patronage first came to him. When President Monroe announced that he would pass through the city on the first presidential tour of the country since Washington's, the City Council unanimously voted $750 for Morse to paint his por-

Courtesy, Mrs. Aiken Simons

WASHINGTON SALA DUNKIN

By Morse

Her husband, Benjamin F. Dunkin, was at one time chief justice of South Carolina.

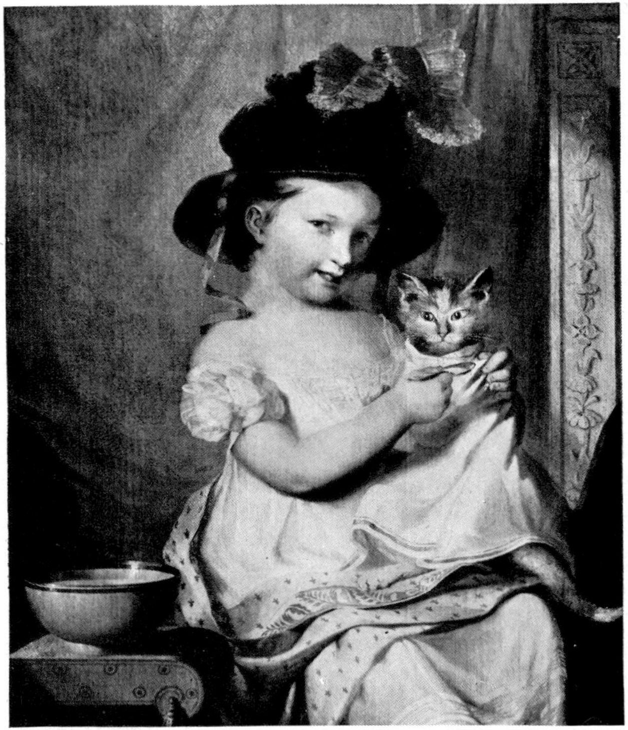

Courtesy, Mrs. Edward Bok

LITTLE MISS HONE

By Morse 1824–5

Probably the niece of Mayor Philip Hone.

trait.[18] In April, when the President was in the city attending dances, theater parties, fireworks, and military reviews, the Council requested him to sit. He protested that it was impossible to discover the time, but Morse had a long interview with him, making plans for sittings in Washington in the fall.

The luxury of work! His itinerant days seemed to be over. In his good fortune he was aware of some less fortunate artists. Three were New Yorkers whom he thought he had drawn to Charleston by his remarkable success.[19] The Boston painter Alvan Fisher he considered talented and well deserving of encouragement; and the lawyer-sculptor-painter John S. Cogdell he invited so often to his room that Cogdell demanded to pay a share of the rent.

By June, with many orders still unfilled, the Morses went north for the summer. Lucretia was with child.

Charlestown was in a black mood that summer. At his installation more than thirty years before, Dr. Morse had been warned that only sustained moderation could smooth away the petulance of his congregation. Dr. Morse was not the man for that task. His gentle voice and manner had commended him as a peacemaker, but controversy was fundamental to his nature. He would not be silenced no matter how unpopular his Federalism and orthodoxy became. When President Dwight had visited Charlestown in 1796, he had observed that "division prevents much of the pleasure of life, which might otherwise be found on so charming a spot." [20] In that year disputants within the church delayed the pastor's salary and he threatened to resign. In 1803 he again threatened to resign. The following year prominent parishioners refused to pay their taxes to the church unless compelled by law. With the movement away from tax support for churches and toward liberal theology dissatisfaction grew, while with the establishment of a Unitarian society in town the church lost its most prominent and wealthy members: Russells, Hurds, Gorhams, and Bartletts. Dr. Morse remembered only too well the prophecy of one of his Yale professors on hearing he was to enter the ministry. At first your people will dote on you, the professor had said; they will say: "Poor pussy, poor pussy." Then they will cool and simply say: "Puss, puss." At last they will mutter: "Scat, you!" [21]

The malcontents who remained in the church set themselves, as Mrs. Morse put it, to "looking up all the Dirt" on their pastor.[22] In the winter of 1819 twenty-five members signed a request for Dr. Morse to resign. They complained, among other things, that he devoted too much time to his geographies. Again a Morse was condemned for his versatility!

The news did not surprise Finley. "It is what might be expected from C[harlestow]n people," he had written his father from the South. ". . . I can't help wishing that nothing may occur to keep you any longer in that nest of vipers and conspirators. . . . Why not come to Charlestown? Here is a fine field for usefulness, a pleasant climate especially for persons advanced in life, and your children here; for I think seriously of settling in Charleston. Lucretia is willing, and I think it will be much for my advantage to remain through the year; Rich.d can find a place here if he will, and Edw.ds can come on and be *Bishop* or *President* or *Professor* in some of the Colleges. . . . A veteran soldier like Papa might be of great service here in the infancy of the *Unitarian hydra.*"[23]

Troubled, uncertain whether or not he was running from his duty to fight wrong, Dr. Morse finally yielded at least to the extent of leaving his pastorate. Finley and Lucretia had been home for several weeks when on August 29, 1819, Dr. Morse announced his resignation from the meeting house pulpit.

When the fullness of the Town Hill elms had once again shrunk into stark patterns, Finley prepared to go south again. This time he knew that when he returned, this home of his twenty-eight years would no longer have the familiar rows of scholarly books in the study upstairs, or his family portraits hanging in the living-room. He already knew that the family had resolved to move to New Haven to escape incessant bickering with mission-despising Unitarians and geography-despising Trinitarians. He left his Lucrece behind in Concord with their little Sue, aged two months. Concern for the family treasury and wrath at the Charlestown "vipers" accompanied him on his lonely way.

To fulfill his engagement with the city of Charleston for painting President Monroe, he paused in Washington. The arrangements for the sittings were neat. He set up his easel in the White House, in the room next the President's "cabinet." But the sittings were too short; the President could spare only ten or twenty minutes at a time. One morning Morse prepared his palette at ten o'clock and waited until the President was able to leave his work at four; in ten minutes, when Morse had just begun to feel that he was capturing the correct expression on the canvas, they were called away to dinner. He enjoyed being with the Monroes none the less; he felt no uneasiness in their society. He dined with the family three times, took tea with them as often, and made his bow at one of Mrs. Monroe's "drawing rooms." Madame President dressed splendidly but tastefully, he thought; and when Dr. Morse, seeking government assistance for study of the needs of Indians, met her in Washington a few weeks later, he described her to his wife as "very Beautiful and about your age & size my dear." [24] Once the painting was under way, five days were all he needed at the White House. The family liked what he had done: the President preferred it to his portrait by Stuart, Morse proudly wrote home, and his daughter wished a replica of the head for herself. Satisfied after a month in Washington, he set out by stage through Fredericksburg, Richmond, Raleigh, and Fayetteville.

It was a miserable journey. In the coach it was so cold at first that when he closed his eyes, his eyelashes were frozen to his cheeks. In Fayetteville he found the best hotel was "a hole of a place." From there on to Charleston the coach was contrived most ingeniously for inconvenience: in rain and fog the seats were wet, the top leaked. That night it was so dark that he could not even see the white horses ahead; at midnight the coach crashed into a tree, breaking its tongue. He passed a sleepless night and was rewarded only with an execrable breakfast at a log hovel, costing seventy-five cents.

In Charleston at last, he had the difficult task of facing the Finleys. He knew that Dr. Finley, after calling the youthful orator Robert Young Hayne * into his sick-room and hearing his promise to

* Mrs. Finley was Hayne's aunt, as well as, by courtesy, Morse's. By her first marriage she was Mary Peronneau Young, probably the Mrs. Robert Young who cared for Hayne as a boy. See S. C. *Hist. and Geneal. Mag.*, V, 170–4 (1904); XXV, 36 (1924); and P. and H. Hayne: *Lives of Robert Young Hayne and Hugh Swinton Legaré* (Charleston, 1878), p. 10. Morse's painting of his cousin by marriage, Hayne, delineates the charm which had already made him, at the same age as Morse, the president of the South Carolina legislature.

be a son to Mrs. Finley, had died several months before. He was uneasy as he called on the widow and children.

"The moment they saw me," he wrote to his wife, "they all burst into tears & were silent; I never felt more depressed than at this time, jaded out by a long, fatiguing sleepless ride, finding Aunt and little cousins in a different house; in black; Aunt so altered I should scarcely have known her, everything reminding me of Uncle's absence; this too combined with the absence of my dear Lucretia; at Mrs. Munro's, the room where we slept, and dined, and supped, the places where we walked, all, all made me, dear wife, feel most miserably, I felt by anticipation, what might take place, were we taken from each other by death."[25]

For two seasons he had prospered in the South. For two more he continued to move in the society of tidewater Carolina, but now with diminishing success and increasing loneliness. He missed the guidance of Uncle Finley. He was depressed among those whom Lucretia had known and who asked for her return. It was fortunate during his third season that Richard was preaching in the Presbyterian church of Johns Island, only some twenty-five miles south, and occasionally would come to town.

In Finley's new exhibition room on Broad Street hung a portrait of John Ashe Alston's daughter Sarah in an elaborate landscape setting. Finley had given the painting unusual care in order to please her father; in doing so he discovered that he had pleased Washington Allston and Gilbert Stuart as well.* Upstairs beyond a door marked private, was a dark room in the far corner of which a window admitted light only through its upper panes. Here, behind a screen of black gauze, stood Finley's easel.[26]

* Allston said the painting would "make a figure even at Somerset House." J. B. Flagg: *Life and Letters of Washington Allston* (New York, 1892), p. 161. Stuart declared himself pleased with both its conception and its execution; his praise is said to have made the portrait so popular that Morse painted several replicas. *Godey's Magazine*, XXXIII, 213 (1846). When the Charleston *Courier* announced on Jan. 22, 1820, that the painting was on exhibition in Morse's rooms, it quoted a fulsome description of it from the *New England Galaxy:* "Mr. Morse had dared to construct . . . a background of poetical and new materials. The whole canvas is filled with the ruins of a venerable architecture — gothick — crumbling — and falling; — encumbered with ivy, and festooned with the luxuriance of nature — with glimpses of a blue sky between: It is indeed a most felicitous idea — and we hope it will lead others to . . . abandon the tame, unmeaning, straight, graceful colonades of Greece."

It did not trouble Finley that his livelihood depended on the brilliant success of a few Carolinians in wringing wealth from their slaves. Though his father was a champion of the Negroes of Boston, he accepted the presence of slaves with indifference. There might be more Negroes than whites in Charleston, but of course there was no question of painting their portraits, and genre-painting was foreign to his habits. He spoke of Negroes casually as lazy servants. They were no problem for him. The time was to come when he would be a publicist for slavery.

Artist though he was, when judgments of the South took shape in his mind they were judgments of personal morality rather than of beauty. Often they were judgments he might as well have made in Concord, Boston, or New York. If cards were brought out at the home of the editor of the *Courier*, Willington, he would take care to ask that one of the ladies entertain him on the piano. When cousin Mary Finley was about to attend her first ball, he feared that she lacked the inner stability that would prevent flatterers from turning her head. All the Finleys – Mary, Ann, Rush, Peronneau – were too frivolous for him.[27] Other judgments referred distinctly to the South. Sabbaths were kept less strictly than in New England, it seemed to him; revivals were less frequent, ministers less respected; dueling evoked his quick reproof.

On the whole he accepted the best standards of the South and felt at home as much, he thought, as a religious person would anywhere. As long as patronage continued, and as long as he could play the piano now and then with his cousins at the Finleys', or take an oyster with Cogdell, or chat about the future of art in the South with the local miniaturist Charles Fraser, he was content with the prospect of bringing Lucretia to Charleston in a year or two to make a permanent home.

During the third season, however, his orders dropped away; during the fourth season they plunged toward zero. Foreseeing squalls ahead, after a struggle between "Mr. Pilot Pride" and "Mr. Pilot Reason," the former was thrown overboard as Reason "put the helm *hard up*": he left his comparatively expensive lodgings with Mrs. Munro and slept in his painting room, now again in St. Michael's Alley. His living became as frugal as when he roomed with Leslie in London. "We rise a little after daylight," he wrote his wife, "say ½ past 6, and Henry [Pratt] * makes a fire and puts on the tea kettle; by the time we are dressed and have our beds out of the way, and the room in order, our tea is ready, (for we have tea for breakfast;) we then have prayers, (by no means the least advantage we enjoy in our new manner of living;) then comes the business of the forenoon until 3.o'clock, when one of the negroes brings up our dinner in a large wooden box sets it down, and makes his exit; our dinner consists of a *beefsteak*, or perhaps a *roast fowl*, a *little rice* and some *Irish Potatoes*, with this we contrive to get along in excellent health and in good trim for study after dinner; then comes the afternoon's study and at night we have our tea, *simple bread and butter and tea*, our milk for tea and breakfast is a pint bro't to us at night, which allows me a tumbler of bread & milk at 10 o'clock just before we go to bed; prayers close the day, and we get out our beds again, and retire. So you now have particularly all the *varieties* in our mode of living; I never enjoyed my health better, I feel that I have enough, and I am consoled under some considerable self-denials with the thought that I am laying up the more for my dear family at home, and can the sooner be able to remain with them altogether." [28] Well knowing what good living was, he could yet do without and thrive.

But why stay in Charleston if work failed – if he had to write repeatedly of "Business dull," or of "*Poverty rocks* and *Embarrassment breakers*"? [29] The cotton and rice markets were so sluggish that bills were hard to collect. Even after he lowered his price for portraits he was obliged to write drearily: "I receive no new commissions; cold and procrastinating answers from those to whom I write, and who had put their names on my list; – give less satisfaction to those whom I have painted; I receive less attention also from some of those who formerly paid me much attention, and none at all from *most*, everything says 'Go.'" [30] He was no longer the fashion.

His last days in Charleston were soured by a wealthy widow, Mrs. Ball. He had painted her portrait, a large one, for six hundred

* Henry Pratt entered the Charlestown parsonage as an errand boy, March 29, 1818. Impressed with his good sense and talent in painting, Finley later hired him as an assistant and promised to give him lessons.

dollars exclusive of the frame. In the summer in the North, Trumbull and Vanderlyn had praised it. In Charleston he exhibited it in his painting room and those who knew her murmured sweet nothings like "the very image of her." Eventually she swept into the painting room to see it herself, with her many children about her. She promptly expressed her pleasure with it and her children down to the smallest called it "mother." But within five minutes she did not like it at all, wished she had not had it done, turned to the portrait of Sarah Alston on the wall and said: "It is beautiful," turned to her own and said: "It is frightful."

Suddenly she knew just what was the matter with it. She had never liked brown, she insisted, looking at the curtain in the background. She preferred purple.

With an effort Morse said he would make it purple to please her. She exploded again. She just could not bear the color in the guitar. And it was not the right shape. Couldn't it be altered?

Remembering that he had painted in the guitar as an exact copy of a real one, Morse muttered: "Yes, ma'am."

"Could you not put a gold chain around the neck?"

"Yes, ma'am," said the painter wearily.

Even when the changes were made she asked postponement of payment. In reply to protests, she came to the conclusion that the painting was not a likeness at all and never paid the whole amount.[31]

Before the close of February, the height of the social season, he announced in the papers that he would leave Charleston permanently in four weeks. The threat brought only a few additional sitters. He took especial pains to please those who did come and felt aware that he was painting better than when he first came south, but to no evident purpose. The founding of a new art academy in which he, Cogdell, and Joel R. Poinsett were leaders [32] brought no change. In April he quit the Carolina tidewater for good, leaving behind him portraits that have been treasured ever since.

CHAPTER *vii*

Congress Hall

GRADUALLY the whole family sought the comfort of New Haven, the town where Unitarianism had not yet penetrated. Lucretia, following the death of her second child, came from Concord with her little Sue. After leaving the unprofitable *Recorder*, Sidney had studied for the ministry at Andover, but now fell back on the New Haven home. Richard came from Johns Island, and finally, as Southern patronage dropped away, Finley came from Charleston. By the spring of 1821 a harried father harbored three sons, aged thirty, twenty-seven, and twenty-six, all without regular income.

Their new house was shabby, Lucretia thought. A cottage, it was built so low that in the cellar during rainstorms vegetables and barrels of cider bobbed about in murky water. As a saving virtue it could boast of its neighborhood, Temple Street near the Green. Hillhouse, the United States Senator and father of a poet friend of Morse, lived next door on one side. On the other lived the old family friend Professor Silliman. Soon Noah Webster moved into the neighborhood.

Shabby though their house might be, the demands upon it for hospitality were frequent. The supply of "15 good cotton sheets 4 good linen do 4 homespun do"[1] often had to be replenished to welcome the occasional Charlestown faithfuls who passed through town. Cider and buckwheat cakes had to appear for breakfast, lobsters for dinner, "hearts round" cakes on the white and gilt china for callers at tea-time.

Wherewithal for rent was hardly available, much less for hospitality. The parish income had vanished. The free parsonage was only an unhappy recollection. Even the sales of the Morse geographies were reduced. The acid of Dr. Morse's disputes had spilled over into the daily journals; one after another the "Harvard Controversy," the "Hannah Adams Controversy," the "Dorchester Controversy," and the "Unitarian Controversy" added to the list of his enemies. However Dr. Morse might relish the excitement of righteous embroilments, they had reduced his income from his writings and prematurely aged him. At fifty-eight, as Mrs. Morse bluntly announced to her sons, he had already "lost his former energy of both body and mind." [2] The Morses could not avoid the humiliation of borrowing.

During their first three years in New Haven they borrowed from Samuel Sparhawk of Concord; from Lucretia's father; from Timothy Dwight, son of the Yale president; from neighbor Eli Whitney; from banks in New Haven, Hartford, and Boston. In a bold venture Dr. Morse bought the house in which he lived for $4,000. Soon he was obliged to mortgage it, and presently to offer it for sale to Whitney, with a request for a lease and an option on repurchase. And though books were the tools of trade for the father and his two younger sons, part of the family library was sold at auction in Washington and Boston, yielding a needed $500 and more.

The womenfolk were often gloomy. Notes seemed to fall due when Dr. Morse was in the West traveling on a federal commission to study Indians, or in Boston or New York pushing the sales of the latest editions of the geography and gazetteer. "I am sorry you & Finley will feel so concerning our affairs . . ." Dr. Morse once wrote to his wife. "But it is of no use to multiply words on a subject on whh so much has been painfully s.d. We *might* be one of the happiest of families – & I trust shall be, as we have been, very soon." [3]

Lucretia quieted her unsatisfied desires in the round of household duties. She directed Nancy in the care of Sue and the third child, sickly little Charles, and ordered Betsey in preparing the dinners, the oysters, clams, or lobsters that Dr. Morse loved only too well, or the rice and sweet potatoes Finley had sent up from the South, or the tea and coffee of which Richard was the connoisseur, or the ale that Finley had ordered. If not busy otherwise, her worktable was waiting for her in the parlor under the portrait of her husband.

When she was ill, as she often was, the financial burdens of the family most oppressed her; it was they, after all, which kept her from having a home of her own.

Not that the men lacked enterprise. All but Finley were busy with their pens. Day after day Dr. Morse bent over his Indian report, Richard over his revision of his father's gazetteer, and Sidney over his revision of his father's geography.

Finley, too, was creating. After pushing the founding of an art academy in Charleston, he swiftly imagined himself in the role of the founder of an academy at New Haven. Before coming home, he had already written out lectures to use in its school. But the academy never opened. He went on with his painting of portraits even while dreaming of painting in West's and Allston's grand manner. For four hundred dollars he had made a portable wooden house, a painting room, he called it, which could be attached to the family house or moved into the garden at will. There he not only painted but worked on his new invention, a marble-carving machine, designed like many similar inventions of the period to make copies of statues by machine rather than chisel.

From the painting room spattered with paint and marble dust Finley would come into the house to find Richard's face often clouded, Sidney limiting his social intercourse to his desk, his mother fretting for the day when she could pronounce an amen to her husband's Indian report. Even at the dinner table he would find the family interrupted by printers' boys with proof to be read. In the living-room, trying to talk with his Lucrece of the days when they might have a home of their own, he would discover again and again that the house was a thoroughfare. The Morse home throbbed with need, creative force, and ambition. It might be a bit grim, even a little unhappy, but he chose to think of it as an uncommon home.

One of his most erratic friends was the poet geologist James Gates Percival. "Is he a smart fellow?" a New York friend once asked Percival about Morse. "In the few words we passed with each other I was pleased with him. At any rate, his face is good, – not handsome, but lighted up and intellectual. Have I hit right?" [4]

Percival was in one of his customary sour moods. "I have not a solitary friend here," he replied from New Haven, "not one whom

Courtesy, Mrs. Howard Field

NOAH WEBSTER

By Morse 1823

Courtesy of the Gallery of Fine Arts, Yale University

BENJAMIN SILLIMAN

By Morse 1825

I associate with. I have lately had some intimacy with Morse, while taking a portrait of my phiz. Your judgment is not far from correct. He is a good artist, and has a mind much above the common level." [5] The poet liked the portrait so well that he persuaded Morse to lend it to a publisher to engrave for a new edition of his poems.

Several of Morse's portraits were of Yale College officers and friends. After a youthful professor of science, Alexander Fisher, was lost in a storm off Ireland, at the request of faculty friends Morse painted him in a melancholy pose against a background of a dark sky, flashing lightning, and raging sea. Morse painted President Jeremiah Day, and his neighbor, Eli Whitney, whom he was often to recollect in years to come. He painted another neighbor, Noah Webster; the portrait was so esteemed that in 1828 it was engraved for the frontispiece of the first Webster dictionary, where it has been republished for over a century since. For De Forest, an American merchant who had once lived in South America and was now attempting to secure recognition for the new Argentine Republic, Morse painted two of his best portraits. Candid studies, searchingly honest, they reveal stodgy vigor in the husband and self-conscious grace in the wife.

But Morse soon found that commissions for painting in New Haven were too few. The academy plan had collapsed; the marble-carving machine was not ready to patent; a scheme to use palmetto logs in cleaning rice had not yet matured. He was often in the company of Professor Silliman at his house and on geology explorations in the Berkshires and Adirondacks,[6] and occasionally studied with him in his laboratory. But experiments with cameras or the latest batteries appeared to lead nowhere. Again he dipped into his reservoir of schemes.

Not a few artists were wondering at America's reception of Granet's painting of the interior of the Capuchin Chapel in the Piazza Barberini in Rome. Shown at an admission fee of twenty-five cents, it was an exhibition success, a remarkable phenomenon in the history of American art. Painters were startled into imitating. As many as three copies of Granet's painting were shown in New York alone, one by the distinguished Philadelphian Thomas Sully. Other Americans, former pupils of West in the historical style, were exhibiting with fair success. At about this time Rembrandt Peale earned nearly $9,000 in thirteen months showing his *Court of Death*, and John Trumbull received $3,000 from a short exhibition in Boston alone. These paintings were elaborate compositions in the storytelling manner to which Morse wished to devote his life.

If a foreign interior like Granet's could excite the American public, Morse asked himself, would not the interior of the congressional halls at Washington excite them more? [7] Would not every spectator take pleasure in recognizing at least one portrait in the painting, that of the congressman from his own district? A painting of Congress might be a means of returning, after six years of portrait work, to his first love, and at the same time obtaining a tidy profit that would at last permit him to establish a home for his wife.

Early in the winter of 1822 he went to Washington, called on President Monroe, congressmen, and his former rival Charles Bulfinch, now the architect for the rotunda which was to join the House and Senate Chambers of the Capitol. Through them Morse secured a room for his use next to the House Chamber. When he was ready to sketch the "members," they could easily drop in for sittings. The House Chamber was to be painted first, with congressmen and Supreme Court justices, then the Senate, and finally executive officials in the White House drawing-room.

Just as he had found that the wrinkles of his mother's face were softened by painting her in candlelight, so he discovered that the House Chamber would seem more enchanting by the light of the thirty lamps in the huge brass chandelier. The grouping of eighty-odd figures of the same size and interest was not easy. Nor were the irregular dome and the curved rows of seats. "I have had a great deal of difficulty with the perspective of my picture," he wrote. "But I have conquered, and have accomplished my purpose.* After having drawn in the greater part three times, I have as many times rubbed it all out again. I have been, several times, from daylight until eleven o'clock at night, solving a single problem." [8]

In a few weeks he began to call congressmen into his room. Through the wall they could hear those who were speaking in the Chamber. When voices rose in feverish debates on the United States

* Morse's "view of the lofty and splendid Hall . . . is mathematically correct," said the Washington *National Intelligencer*, Feb. 16, 1822.

Bank, canals, or recognition of the new South American republics, they could return to the Hall to defend their cause.

Sketching the congressmen soon sucked out the painter's energies. "I am in the vein now," he wrote once, "and must have my way." [9] He did. He would not stop to rest. He would rise at daybreak, finish breakfast and prayers long before the bell called the Capitol workmen to their labors. He would work over his composition or receive the morning congressional sitters – perhaps Van Rensselaer, or Randolph, or Joel Poinsett – two hours to a sitter, until one o'clock. Then he would dine in fifteen minutes. In the late afternoon other sitters – perhaps editors Gales and Seaton of the *National Intelligencer*, or Justices Marshall and Story – would find him with a cup of tea in one hand and a pencil in the other. He was so absorbed in his great endeavor, his friend Prime declares, that one night he mistook moonlight pouring into his room for sunlight and started to be about his work.[9] Fourteen hours was his usual working day, he wrote Lucretia. His continued health he attributed to the discipline of simple fare.

Dr. Morse was also in Washington that winter, at last ready to present his Indian report to Secretary of War Calhoun. Finley barely had time to see him, but his frequent presence in the House gallery in expectation of hearing his report read probably suggested the caprice of putting him onto the canvas. Next to his father in the gallery he painted Professor Silliman, and to represent his father's Indian interests a Pawnee chief then visiting Washington.* Morse thus signed his picture quite as effectively as in placing his name in the lower left-hand corner.

As the number of completed sketches of congressmen grew, so did his pleasure in his creation. He observed that the members liked to come to his room to sit to him, and those who were not asked to do so courted his favor. "Every day gives me greater encouragement," he wrote home, "to believe that it will be more popular than any

* Dr. Morse told a story about this chief in his *A Report to the Secretary of War . . . on Indian Affairs,* finally printed in New Haven in 1822 (pp. 247–8), to illustrate his thesis that Indians had character. When the chief was a youth, his tribe once prepared to burn at the stake a female Indian of another tribe. Just as the awful scene was to begin he snatched her in his arms and rode off with her. After taking her back to her own people, he returned, expecting hostility. But his people did not question him, viewing his act as that of the Great Spirit. Thereafter there were no human sacrifices among the Pawnees.

picture heretofore exhibited." [10] He found additional income in doing small portraits of congressmen for twenty dollars at the same time that he did sketches for his own use. At the end of January Dr. Morse described him as "much encouraged – in good spirits – has 63 heads – has become thin with labor." [11] In two weeks more he was ready to leave for home with sketches of more than eighty members and officers of Congress, and justices of the Supreme Court.

Just as when he had painted President Monroe two years before, his way had been made smooth in Washington. Gratefully he arranged to have the Hillhouses send a dozen of their famous elm seedlings from New Haven to the President's Virginia estate. And to Mr. Bulfinch, the same Bostonian who had designed the spire of the First Church of Charlestown and a building on the Andover campus, he gave a cast of his *Hercules.* Fate took the little statue as a sport. It was sent down from New Haven by boat, carefully wrapped, as Mrs. Morse wrote, with "an old table cloth that passes under him," [12] along with butter and sausages for Dr. Morse. The vessel was stranded in the ice of the Potomac. Part of the cargo was cast overboard. The butter and sausages were ruined, wrote Dr. Morse, but "the *cast* is safely lodged with Mr. Bulfinch, who says he will take good care of it." [13] He took good care of it by allowing it to remain in a dusty cellar of the Capitol. Years later, when Morse was stringing wires in that cellar for a telegraph experiment, he came across the cast on a shelf. It was already the only one of the six casts remaining. Today it is at the Yale Gallery.

Riding night and day, Finley and Henry arrived home on February 16 with bad colds. Exhausted as Finley was, his mother could see he only needed rest "to recruit." At last he could work at his great canvas under the encouragement of his wife and the admonitions of his mother. It was while he was giving nearly all his time to a work on which he could not hope to realize a cent until completed, and while the family finances showed no sign of recovery, that Finley chose to indulge in a glorious gesture. He gave five hundred dollars to Yale for the expansion of the library. But he heard on all sides that he was expected to make fame and fortune out of his picture.[14] From Boston came a prediction that he would take in three or four thousand dollars by exhibiting it there alone.

In the fall he hired exhibition rooms in Boston at ten dollars a week. In the early winter of 1823 the great painting was shown briefly in New Haven.[15] On February 11 Morse and Henry arrived in Boston. The Jocelyns shipped the " key plates and descriptions " from New Haven, and *Congress Hall,* packed to weigh six hundred and forty pounds, came by sleigh. As soon as it was properly placed, Morse asked Allston to leave his work on his great Belshazzar to see it. He told Morse that it was magnificent, and then, as Morse wrote, " suggested some small improvements which I can do in 2 days." Morse accepted the advice of the teacher he idolized as much as ever, and postponed the opening until he could make the changes. He expected the suspense to help the exhibition along, for curiosity was on tiptoe.

It was not until February 22 that the *Columbian Centinel* first carried the advertisement:

MORSE'S PICTURE
of the
Representatives Hall at Washington,
containing
EIGHTY-EIGHT PORTRAITS,
Is now exhibiting at Doggett's Repository,
Market Street
Open every day from 9, A.M. to 5, P.M.
Admittance 25 cents – Key and Description 12½ cts.
Season tickets only 50 cents
H. C. Pratt, *Agent* [16]

As the exhibition opened, it seemed to Morse that everything promised success.

The first day more than one hundred persons came in. If they could spare the twelve and one-half cents for a key and description they read:

The Hall of the House of Representatives of the United States is, without doubt, one of the most splendid Legislative Halls in the world.

The *Dome* is ornamented by painted imitations of sunken pannels, with a flower in the center of each.

The *Eagle* upon the frieze over the Speaker's chair, is ten feet between the wings.

The *Columns,* 28 feet in height, are of breccia, a concrete of various kinds of stones, of all sizes and colours.

Between the columns and behind them are suspended *Curtains* of scarlet moreen, fringed with yellow drops.

The *Time* chosen is at candle lighting while the members are assembling for an evening session. The *Portraits* were taken at Washington about a year ago, each person sat for his likeness, with the exception of the Hon. William Lowndes, whose portrait was sketched from the gallery.

The primary design of the present picture is not so much to give a highly finished likeness of the individuals introduced, as to exhibit to the public a faithful representation of the National Hall, with its furniture and business during the session of Congress. If the individuals are simply recognized by their acquaintance as likenesses, the whole design of the painter will be answered.

New Haven, Feb. 1st, 1823. SAML. F. B. MORSE [17]

Morse watched his visitors study the painting and peep now and then at the key. He was soon encouraged to open the room in the evening, and permit Henry to install oil lamps with tin reflectors which dimmed the room so much that the chandelier in the painting seemed to be the brightest light in the room.

Leaders of Boston opinion came to see the painting. Richard Henry Dana, recent associate of Bryant and Allston in publishing stories and poems, was satisfied. After William Ellery Channing had seen it, Allston was able to persuade the Unitarian champion to write a newspaper article in praise of it. Lieutenant Governor William Phillips and Judge Josiah Quincy, a future Harvard president, cast Federalist eyes on the congressmen. Former Senator Harrison Gray Otis recognized nearly every portrait without the use of his key. Friends of other years came in to express their continued interest: Alvan Fisher, Jeremiah Evarts of the *Panoplist,* and Nathaniel Willis of the *Recorder.*

Many citizens of Charlestown crossed the bridge to see Finley's painting, among them the occupant of the Town Hill parsonage, Pastor Fay, Deacon Tufts, and former Congressman Gorham. But those who did not go to Boston could hardly escape the newspaper puffs for Finley's painting, or the new Morse gazetteer, atlas, and geography that were just coming into Boston bookstores, or Sidney's newspaper defense of his father's title of "Father of American Geography," or extracts from Dr. Morse's Indian report.

Corcoran Gallery of Art, Washington

CONGRESS HALL, OR THE OLD HOUSE OF REPRESENTATIVES

By Morse 1821–3

Extreme left, Gales and Seaton, the reporters of the House; against the back wall and opposite the left aisle, Supreme Court justices, Chief Justice Marshall and Justice Story at right of group; in the gallery at right, Jedidiah Morse, Benjamin Silliman, and a Pawnee chief.

As the weeks went by, *Congress Hall* apparently found effective competition, perhaps in a rival picture exhibited by Henry Sargent, a former pupil of West and Copley, or in the museum of "Living Animals," or in concerts of the Handel and Haydn Society, or in Mr. Wallack as Rolla in *Pizzaro*. The attendance at Morse's rooms was falling away. After he had returned to New Haven, during the last three weeks of March the receipts dropped steadily from less than seventy dollars one week to less than thirty the next, and nearly twenty-five the next. One rainy day only three people came in. A debt to the landlord was growing.

After a run of about seven weeks, on April 12 [18] Henry ceased stoking the wood stove and consigned the congressmen to wrappers. Allston wrote Morse his sympathy.

Boston, 15th April, 1823

Dear Sir:

. . . Your Picture can hardly be said as yet to have had a fair trial. If its exhibition here has not been profitable to your purse, it has yet gained you a full harvest of praise. I believe all amongst the higher classes have been to see it, and, as far as I can learn, there is but one opinion concerning it – that it does you great honour. I have heard many praise it highly, and *not* a *single voice* against it. It is especially admired by the best judges – such as M.r Dutton, M.r Codman, Dana, and others whose opinions go a great way in the circles where they move. Indeed it is so popular amongst these that I cannot account for its lac [*sic*] of profit except in the circumstance that the lower classes must have been wanting in curiosity; and as they make the mass of the town, if it does not attract them, the receipts must of course be small. But I do not think it likely that the same result will happen in the other great towns – New York, Philadelphia, Baltimore, & Charleston. The common people there, if I mistake not, are more accustomed to visit places of public amusement; and those that are in the habit of attending them, I should suppose, would find entertainment in this Picture. Besides, its career is but *just begun.* Be of good heart then. I have no doubt of your success. . . .

Yours sincerely
W. Allston

. . . I wrote to Leslie the other day, and among other things which I said of your picture, I told him it ought to make you an Associate if you were in London. When you carry it to New York, I will write to M.r Verplanck, who is a particular friend of mine, to give it a good word in the newspapers.

While Boston could boast of being the home of Allston, the Puritan capital had not yet risen to the opportunity that Dr. Morse and Finley had seen for it years ago. New York had far outstripped it as the seat of the fine arts. So in New York *Congress Hall* faced a public which could choose among many alluring subjects by competent painters. Rembrandt Peale was exhibiting his celebrated *Court of Death*. Presenting a gloomy cavern, with the imposing figures of enthroned Death and the victims of his empire, War, Desolation, Want, and Dread on one side, and Pleasure, Crimes, and Diseases on the other, all on a canvas larger than Morse's, the painting made a startling impression on the moralistic public. With his copy of Granet's *Capuchin Chapel* Thomas Sully was still basking in its reflected glory. An enterprising Philadelphia marine painter, Thomas Birch, capitalized on a famous shipwreck in his *Loss of the Albion*. Indeed, there was only one publicized painting on exhibit that was not in the historical style. Three years after West's death, four of the current exhibitors, Morse, Sully, Vanderlyn, and Peale, who had been his pupils, were now all exhibiting in the historical style that he loved, while the only picture then showing not in that style was a portrait of West himself by Sir Thomas Lawrence.

Besides following the doubtful career of *Congress Hall* the Morses had other concerns in New York. As in Boston, new editions of the atlas and gazetteer were just coming into bookstores. But more than that, Sidney, assisted by Richard, was launching a newspaper in New York, a religious weekly after the manner of his earlier paper, the Boston *Recorder*. The first number of the New York *Observer* noted that Morse's painting had arrived in town. The first number in which advertisements appeared included Henry's notice that the *House of Representatives* was exhibiting at 144 Fulton Street, near Broadway. It was fitting that news of Morse should appear in the early issues of the *Observer*, for his life was to be reflected in his brothers' famous weekly for nearly half a century to come.

The enterprise of the two younger sons advanced painfully as the subscription list slowly lengthened. But the venture of the eldest son threatened to collapse. The weekly receipts were less than in Boston. An ominous editorial note in a paper of July 4 accompanied the notice of the last few days of the exhibition: "We would only remark that the labour and expense which it has cost the artist have been thus far but ill rewarded in New York."[19] After exhibiting about seven weeks in New York, Finley announced the closing date as July 16.[20] Two days later Percival wrote a New York friend: "I will tell you one thing *sub rosa.* Morse's picture of Congress Hall, (have you seen it? if not it is too late now,) that picture has cost him one hundred and ten dollars to exhibit it in New York. Tell it not in Gath! He labored at it eighteen months, and spent many hundred dollars in its execution; and now he has to pay the public for looking at it, 'largess, largess.' Allston says it is a masterpiece of coloring and perspective. Who would write or paint any good thing for such a *fashionable vulgar* as ours? For my part, I am tired of patting the dogs. I will now turn to kicking them. I believe they will use me better then. If some sign-painter had only painted Nettleton * preaching up an awakening, and sent it about the country, he would have filled his pockets with it, and so would Morse too."[21]

Had Percival touched on the truth? Had Morse's ingenious scheme collapsed because his painting, while a faithful representation of the subject, lacked the imaginative dash which the public wished? Or was it that Morse had no message, no evident moral to teach? Few painters even in that age of precept could have had more passionate views on religious or social conduct than Morse. For some reason he avoided painting scenes from religious history or even scenes which told a moralistic story. Possibly the figures in the painting were too small; Henry thought this the chief objection expressed by visitors. Perhaps his subject was too prosaically American in an age when artistic and literary taste was dependent on Europe.† None of the other paintings then exhibiting in New York was of American subject matter.

* Morse had painted this popular evangelist when as a student of theology at Yale he had served as college butler.

† Ironically enough, when Leslie was exhibiting the painting in England several years later, he thought it would be more popular in America. "I am delighted with its color & effect," he wrote Morse, "& still more with the management of the figures, the strong individual character you have given them small as they are, & the perfectly natural manner in which you have grouped them. The character of the picture altogether is that of the soundest art & its perfect freedom from trick or affectation of any kind is a very rare excellence & in my opinion a very great one. I only regret for your sake that so much talent has been wasted on such a subject, one which you must be aware cannot excite near so much interest in this country as in America." Sept. 13, 1828, LC.

Further exhibition was dropped, and so was the plan to paint the Senate Chamber and White House drawing-room. Morse still had other schemes for turning his *magnum opus* to advantage, but at home in New Haven he gave increasing attention to his marble-carving machine. If his historical painting would not make it possible for him to establish a home of his own for his wife and children, there was still a lingering hope that his machine might. If not, he would have to go on with his portrait-painting. It was after all what he could do best; he completely understood the sort of people he was likely to paint, the shrewd, graceless, comfortable, moralistic gentility of the day. But New Haven was becoming sterile for an artist. He thought of New Orleans, not knowing that Audubon was there, longing to paint birds and finding only a miserable income even in portraiture. He thought of New York as well.

It was not wanderlust that drove him from his parents' home again. While he was seeking a few portrait commissions in Albany he wrote Lucrece on August 16: "Roaming becomes more and more irksome. Imperious necessity alone drives me to this course. Don't think, by this, I am fainthearted; I shall persevere in this course, painful as is the separation from my dear wife and family, until Providence clearly points out my duty to return."

His few weeks in Albany were miserable. There were many promises for commissions but he painted only three portraits, and one of these, that of patroon Stephen Van Rensselaer, was a gift. For days there was nothing to occupy him. There were no pictures or statuary from which to draw. Several families were polite enough, but that was all. Doing nothing was torture.

Albany was a good point of vantage, however, from which to judge the effect of the completion of the Erie Canal. Already Morse could see the mounting stores of fruit, grain, and lumber that had come into Albany from as far as the canal was already in use, waiting for transshipment to New York. He had the advantage of knowing several of the most eminent promoters of the canal. He carried a letter of introduction from his father to Elkanah Watson, whom he soon painted. Chancellor Kent, whom he also painted, once said to a representative who favored spending for defense instead of a canal: "If we must have war, or have a canal, I am in favor of a canal." The chief promoter of them all, DeWitt Clinton, had long been a non-political acquaintance of Dr. Morse; * and in Albany Finley was invited to call frequently at his house. Whether or not Morse knew that he had cut himself from intellectual New England, he did know from his Albany experience that New England's economic predominance was gone, and that New York's star was rising. "N. York does not yet feel the influx of wealth from the Western canal," he wrote his wife on August 27, "but in a year or two she will feel it, and it will be advantageous to me to be previously identified among her citizens as a painter. It requires some little time to become known in such a city as N. York. Colonel T[rumbull] is growing old, too, and there is no artist of education sufficiently prominent to take his place as Pres.t of Acad. of Arts. By becoming more known to the N. York public, and exerting my talents to discover the best methods of promoting the Arts, and writing about them, I may possibly be promoted to his place, where I could have a better opportunity of doing *something for the Arts in our country,* the object at which I aim."

He hurried home for a few days in New Haven. Continued poverty was again forcing him away from his wife. Coyly Lucrece had confessed herself "*so interested*" that she could not advise him between New York or New Orleans, and now of course she was pleased with the decision. At least he would be near enough to get home during the "sickly seasons" and for short visits. We must all make sacrifices, she told him, "and the sacrifices we are called upon to make of each other's society now, I hope will be made up by your being able to remain permanently in the bosom of your dear family – how delighted I shall be to welcome you there! My health is not very good, *spirits ditto!*" [22]

Once more he turned away from Lucrece, children, and parents. He took ship for New York, intending to become the most prominent artist in the city.

* When Dr. Morse was on his way west to study Indians, he sailed from Utica on "Clinton's big ditch" with Clinton. While the Governor was entertained at landing-places, Dr. Morse found opportunity to gather geographical data. "You are like an exhausted receiver," the Governor called out to one of Dr. Morse's informants as he was leaving the barge. "The Doctor has pumped you dry." RCM to Mrs. JM, June 19, 1820, COLG.

CHAPTER *viii*

Fulfillment Comes Late

HE HAD emptied himself of his energy and enthusiasm in his drive to conquer New York. He had "advertised, and visited, and hinted, and pleaded" [1] with his acquaintances, all to little purpose. His friend Van Shaik had been generous enough to request two illustrations for scenes in Irving's *Sketch Book,* but rent and board had soon devoured the returns. Charles Walker had requested a likeness of the lawyer with whom he was studying, the Irish orator Thomas Addis Emmet. Charles hoped it would lead the painter into a series of portraits of professional New Yorkers, but orders had not followed. He had talked with fellow artists. They agreed that New Yorkers were driving too hard at making money to be willing to spend it. Other possible sources of income for him failed. Someone else had patented the principle of his marble-carving machine. His *Congress Hall* had been exhibited by another agent in Albany, Hartford, and Middletown, again at a loss. To economize he had been sleeping on the floor of his Broadway studio, against Lucretia's wish. At last a crisis came when his hat was stolen. In buying a new one he had broken his last five-dollar bill and his confidence at the same time.

Suddenly his *Congress Hall* had appeared to him in a new light: it might prove more of a curiosity to Mexicans than to Americans. And just as Rubens had painted some of his best portraits when he was Spanish Ambassador to London, he might paint his best portraits as attaché to the American Legation in Mexico.

Briefly in New Haven, while Sue and Charles frolicked about him, he said good-by to his mother. Lucretia accompanied him by boat back to New York, for two final days before they separated for two or three years, perhaps more; they could not know. Then Finley took boat to the Jersey shore, stage, boat across the Delaware, and stage through Philadephia and Baltimore.

In Washington he haunted the lobbies of the Capitol, waiting to snatch a few words with those who had won him his position as attaché to the first American minister ever appointed to Mexico: with the aged patroon Van Rensselaer, Robert Y. Hayne, the relative of Aunt Finley whose compelling charm he had caught so well on canvas in Charleston, and Joel R. Poinsett, who was himself a likely choice as first minister.

It was now the spring of 1824, a presidential year. The Federalist Party was dead, and within the conglomerate Democratic Republican Party were opening the divisions which were to transform the "era of good feeling" into a boisterous upsurge of the common people. The appointment of the Mexican minister played its part in the jockeying of the candidates. Already President Monroe had offered the post to General Jackson in order to get him out of the way, but Jackson understood the ruse and refused the appointment. Then one day, when Finley was in the House Chamber, Congressman Edwards of Illinois, who had finally been appointed minister, charged one of the prominent candidates for the presidency, Secretary of the Treasury Crawford, with fraud. Crawford men demanded congressional discipline for Edwards, his preparations for departure for Mexico were halted, and the whole Mexican expedition was thrown into uncertainty. Morse sought his advisers. Poinsett recommended that he go on to Mexico without the Minister; others urged him to go home and wait; still others, to give up going altogether. The President told him the departure of the Minister would be delayed at least five or six weeks.

He returned to wife, children, and parents, still dreaming of the gold mines of Mexico. For several months he still hoped; then word came that Edwards had been maneuvered into resigning his post and all the legation appointments were void.

The collapse of the Mexican venture was the collapse of just one more of his extravaganzas. Dreams whirled in and out of his feverish brain: a studio on Cornhill, a wealth-spouting pump, munificent patronage in the Carolinas, a New Haven art school, a machine to carve copies of great statues, conquest of the American Academy from President Trumbull himself. Each dream had claimed his vitality and for the time being departed, leaving him older, somewhat less pigheaded, but still dreaming vastly.

His days of itineracy returned. He followed the whimsical tune of the call for portraits: to New Brunswick, to New York and New Haven, north to the relatives in Concord and Portsmouth; down East to Portland; and back to Hartford and home.

No flag-waving cheered Lafayette as he left France for his fourth and last visit to America. Police of the Bourbon King would not permit it. But across the sea other treatment was in preparation.

Eight steamboats, flecked with banners, escorted his ship as it arrived in New York Bay. Throngs on the Battery cheered, bells clanged, cannon roared. The general disembarked at Castle Garden on a specially constructed stair, decorated with flags and laurel. At the City Hall Mayor Paulding welcomed him as one of America's honored parents.

The next day, while the new song, *Lafayette's Welcome*, was being sold in the streets, it was proposed that the Common Council request Lafayette to sit for a portrait to hang with the full-length portraits of Washington, Clinton, Jay, and Hamilton in the City Hall. In the enthusiasm of the moment the Council agreed.

While Lafayette toured the country, adding to the amazing number of plates-from-which-he-ate and beds-in-which-he-slept, artists scrambled for the honor of painting him for the city. Vanderlyn, J. W. Jarvis, and James Herring made formal requests to the Council for the privilege. Others soon entered the contest: Sully, Waldo, Inman, Ingham, and Morse.[2]

Morse had come to try his luck in the city again. His painting room was again in lower Broadway, near where his mother was born on Wall Street.

In the scramble for the Lafayette commission his advantage was his facile sociability. While only in one period of his life is his record essentially a story of friendship — the period when he was to be with Cooper in Paris — nevertheless he was eminently sociable.

He cultivated his brothers' and parents' friends. He knew the artists of the city better than most of those who had been there for years knew each other. Anyone who could prove himself a companion to the sparkling Allston, the moody Coleridge, the scholarly Silliman, and the erratic Percival could make himself agreeable in the drawing-rooms of New York's merchants, the leaders of city society. Their standards of public and private morality were like his own. Their social tastes were aristocratic and their political tastes, often enough, conservatively Democratic, as were his. Their homes provided the background for the intellectual and artistic life of the city, for the poets Hillhouse, Halleck, and Bryant, for the novelist Cooper and the young author Dana, for the critics Dunlap and Verplanck.

Hillhouse had introduced him to Isaac Lawrence, a wealthy merchant, when *Congress Hall* was being exhibited in New York. Through Hillhouse, Morse had painted Lawrence and his father-in-law, Dr. Beach, and had come to know his son, William Beach Lawrence, the future expert on international law. It was through Isaac Lawrence, as Dunlap records it, that Morse found favor in the eyes of the Common Council. Through Lawrence Morse came to know Philip Hone, the retired auctioneer, who already owned Morse's portrait of Chancellor Kent. Philip Hone was a member of the Common Council committee for receiving Lafayette. Just the last month before the decision on the commission was made, Morse was painting the daughter of Philip's brother Isaac. "I am engaged in painting the full-length portrait of Mr. Hone's little daughter," Morse wrote home, "a pretty little girl just as old as Susan. . . . I shall paint her with a cat set up in her lap like a baby, with a towel under its chin and a cap on its head, and she employed in feeding it with a spoon." [3] And so he did, in a delightful painting that Horatio Greenough compared to Sir Thomas Lawrence's work. At the same time he was painting the wife of Elisha King, also a member of the Common Council and a member of the Lafayette committee.

Presently Morse heard that he had been chosen to do the Marquis's portrait. He was to be paid at least $700 and perhaps $1,000, and was to go to Washington for the first sittings. Without knowing the truth of his words, he wrote home: "The only thing I fear is, that it is going to deprive me of my dear Lucretia." [4]

In January 1825 it seemed at last possible for him to think of a home for his wife and children. "When I consider how wonderfully things are working for the promotion of the great and *long-desired* event – that of being constantly with my dear family – all unpleasant feelings are absorbed in this joyful anticipation, and I look forward to the spring of the year with delightful prospects of seeing my dear family permanently settled with me in our own hired house here."[5] It was bad enough to be away from Lucretia at all; but in addition the family complained of her being in New Haven. "The whole arrangement of your two families at one in New Haven," brother Richard declared, "is a bad one, & the evils inevitable."[6] A way out was at last in sight.

At the end of the month he was at home a few days with Lucretia and her new-born baby, "Fin." He read aloud to his wife from a biography of Lafayette. Mother and child were doing well.

Morse reached Washington on February 7 and took a room in the same hotel with Lafayette – Gadsby's. That day Dr. Morse wrote him: "Your dear wife is convalescent. We shan't hurry her from her chamber at this season – the children all continue as hearty & playful as when you left them. . . . We suppose you begin the Marquis to-day."[7]

That afternoon Lucretia rose as usual to have her bed freshly made. She spoke cheerfully of soon being with her husband in their own house in New York; and getting into bed again, she shuddered a moment and lay back on her pillow. In five minutes, just as Dr. Morse came into the room to pay his usual visit, she was quietly gone.[8]

The next day, Tuesday, Morse called to see Lafayette. Finley remembered he had heard that his features were poor: a slanting forehead, bulging eyes, a bulbous nose. No! They were noble! Features and character accorded perfectly. They both showed, he thought, just the firmness and consistency for which he was distinguished.

"This is the man now before me, the very man," he thought, as he wrote his dead wife, "who suffered in the dungeon of Olmütz; the very man who took the oaths of the new constitution for so many millions, while the eyes of thousands were fixed upon him (and which is so admirably described in the life which I read to you just before I left home); the very man who spent his youth, his fortune, and his time, to bring about (under Providence) our happy Revolution; the friend and companion of Washington, the terror of tyrants, the firm and consistent supporter of liberty, the man whose beloved name has rung from one end of this continent to the other, whom all flock to see, whom all delight to honor; this is the man, the very identical man!"

He almost melted with emotion as the General shook his hand and said: "Sir, I am exceedingly happy in your acquaintance, and especially on such an occasion."[9] They agreed to meet the next day for breakfast and the first sitting.

The second day after his wife's death, still unaware of it, he passed a gay evening at the President's levee. The votes in the election had been so split among Jackson, Crawford, Clay, and John Quincy Adams that none had a majority, and the choice had been thrown into the House. And the House vote had been close – so close, in fact, that, as Van Buren's story goes, the election of Adams was uncertain without the aid of the aged Congressman Van Rensselaer. As the balloting began he had not yet made up his mind. He prayed, opened his eyes, saw a discarded Adams ballot at his feet, and, considering it a sign of God, voted for Adams. At the White House levee Morse congratulated Adams; he could easily see that the President-elect was in high spirits. He noticed that General Jackson went up to him and cordially shook him by the hand. Jackson, he thought, bore his defeat like a man. Vice-President-elect Calhoun was there, too, and of course the Marquis.

Morse's stay in Washington was nearly over when he received news of his wife's death. Lafayette told him that no one could sympathize more than he; he too had lost a young and beautiful wife.

The next day Morse left for home. In New Haven he found that the funeral had taken place several days earlier, and that his wife's body rested beside those of two of her five children.

Again and again her husband had told her the Lord had given her to him, and the Lord would take her from him in His own good time. He had pleaded that each might be willing to close the lids of the other calmly, even cheerfully, believing that eternity opened before them together. Still her sudden going was not easy for him. The family trembled as it watched him struggle to recover his poise.

When he found among her papers and in her diary fresh evidence that she had faith and was "prepared" to die, he was somewhat consoled. But even then his brothers feared that he was abandoning himself too freely to grief.

Leaving his motherless children to Nancy and their grandmother, he returned to New York. The balm of work served him well. Orders flooded upon him – perhaps because men realized that his need for work was more urgent now than his financial need had ever been. He continued his sittings with Lafayette when the Marquis was in New York being fêted by the new mayor, Philip Hone. In this year he finished the painting of the mayor's niece, received a commission from the city to paint John Stanford, chaplain of the almshouse, and possibly also to paint William Paulding, the former mayor. It was in this year that he painted the strong, sweet portrait of William Cullen Bryant, his friend; the buoyant portrait of Governor Clinton, the triumphant parson at the wedding of the waters of Lake Erie and the Atlantic; and a sensitive presentment of his neighbor Benjamin Silliman.

Naturally enough for one so successful in obtaining commissions, it was a victorious year in social life. Morse was among Cooper's devotees who met of an evening in a small back room of Wiley's restaurant that Cooper dubbed "The Den," on the corner of Wall and New Streets. They all doted on Cooper's wit: Percival, Hillhouse, and Halleck, not inconsiderable poets; Colonel Stone, the editor of the New York *Commercial Advertiser;* the young writer Richard Henry Dana; and of course the ever observant Dunlap. Toward the end of the year Morse was invited to join The Lunch, a club founded by Cooper. Among those soon to be its members were Halleck, Brevoort, Dunlap, Sands, Vanderlyn, Jarvis, and Durand. Morse was flattered by his election. "A literary Society," he wrote home, "admission to which must be by unanimous vote, and into which many respectable literary characters of the city have been denied admittance, have chosen me a member, together with M.r Hillhouse and M.r Bryant, poets. These indicate good feelings towards me to say the least and in the end will be of advantage I have no doubt. Deo Gloria!" [10]

For a time that year he lived with a friend, Dr. Mathews, the future chancellor of the University of the City of New York, who was about to marry into the Hone family. By spring the painter had progressed so well in his vocation that he decided he could hire his own house. He chose one next door to Isaac Lawrence, uptown on Canal Street. At last, just a few months after the death of Lucretia, he could have given her what she had wanted most, a home of her own.

CHAPTER *ix*

Founding the National Academy

During the strawberry season of 1825 Morse invited artist friends to his new house for berries and cream, by simple entertainment hoping to entice them from their stand-offish ways.

His Canal Street house was narrow. The kitchen and probably the dining-room were in the basement, his chamber on the third floor. On the first floor were his parlor and exhibition room. On the second were his painting room, and the room both for his statues, no doubt the products of his marble-carving machine, and for his great "lay figure," the model he used in portraiture.[1] The house proved commodious enough for Morse to entertain at breakfast Governor Clinton and local aldermen just after the gala opening of the Erie Canal.

As gatherings succeeded one another at Morse's house, the artists responded to their unaffected host. They came to recognize their common interest in overthrowing the leadership of the American Academy of Fine Arts, and a significant movement in the history of American art was under way.

Fortunately Morse's ambition to replace President Trumbull as the recognized head of the New York artists now coincided with the dissatisfaction of the art students within Trumbull's academy. Trumbull was unquestionably a good painter. Morse had often been flattered when the president spoke well of his works. But Trumbull had begun his active career while a soldier in painting scenes of the American Revolution and he was still painting them; he was embittered and set in his ways. The organization of his academy encouraged him to remain so. Since its foundation twenty years before, it had been under the control of art patrons rather than artists. Most of the stockholders and even directors were not artists. It was an institution for artists, but of merchants and by merchants.

The students were particularly irked by the management of their study hours. When they came to the academy building on City Hall Park at the opening hour of six in the morning or even at seven, they were frequently debarred, and sometimes insulted if they presumed to knock at the door. Eventually the inevitable incident occurred that drew the students and older artists together.

At nearly eight one morning, as the one-eyed Dunlap came as usual to the academy building, two students, Cummings and Agate, found the doors still locked. Dunlap advised them to complain to the academy. Wearily they replied that it was useless, and moved away.

Then President Trumbull himself appeared, heard Dunlap's remark, and tumbled into a crabbed speech, not against the doorkeeper but against the students. "They must remember that beggars are not to be choosers," he said.

The incident went the rounds of the artists. Cummings drafted a petition to the academy, and Morse invited a few artists to his house to consider means of supporting it. Smoldering resentment burst into flaming revolt. Morse recommended that New York artists form an association of their own.

Up to now they had no body of their own, no common meeting-place; in spite of his hospitality many of the least conspicuous of them did not yet know each other. Soon afterward, on the night of November 8, they held the first general meeting of artists in the city. With Durand in the chair and Morse as secretary, the New York Drawing Association came into being. Morse was elected president. The members included Inman, Durand, Cummings, Agate, Dunlap, Wright, Danforth, Town, Morton, Ingham, Cole, and Maverick.

The sober progress of an evening session of the association was rudely broken one night. Some forty students were at work – the number of members had doubled and then trebled in the space of a few weeks – each with his own small oil lamp and drawing materials on his table. Trumbull stalked into the room, went directly to the president's seat, and, looking authoritatively around him, beckoned to Cummings, who was that evening in charge. He asked him to see that all the students signed in the roll book of the American Academy as its students. Cummings declined, bowed, and moved away to talk with his friends. The students determined to ignore the president's order and continued to draw. The complacent gentleman waited, and then, remarking that he was leaving the roll book for the signatures, walked out in the same haughty manner in which he had entered.

The artists jumped to life, talked earnestly in groups for a few minutes, and were called to order as the Drawing Association.

"Have we any relation to the American Academy of Arts?" they asked themselves.

"None whatever," they replied.[2]

They resolved to inform the academy that they wished to become affiliated if it would grant a larger share in its direction to artists.

While both societies appointed committees on union, their joint conclusion has never been certain. It was clearly agreed that to mollify the students six artists would be elected to the board of directors of the academy at the next election. The association, however, afterward insisted that the academy committee had agreed to use its influence to elect the particular artists that the association should nominate; the academy denied any such agreement, and some evidence supports the denial.[3] Be that as it may, the association was sufficiently confident of the election of its nominees to pay one hundred dollars to the academy to qualify four of them for office as stockholders. The other two association nominees, Morse and Dunlap, were already stockholders.

On the evening before the election, Cummings and the one-eyed veteran Dunlap were strolling in the City Park when an old woman, apparently a beggar, walked up to them, put a letter into their hands, and vanished. The letter was anonymous. It said that through the intrigues of some of the directors only two of the artists proposed by the association would be elected.

Warned by they knew not whom, the artists rashly replied with a threat in the papers the next morning that all their nominees must be elected or none would serve. According to Cummings, Dunlap was responsible for this;[4] but it has been attributed to Morse.[5] It is patent that the newspaper notice had his approval and that of all those who were on the association slate, for it presumed to speak for what they would do, and events proved that it did.

It is little wonder that four of the association slate were defeated. The vote might have been even more disastrous if the stockholders had known that the newspaper notice was written as a result of a single anonymous letter. The two association nominees who were elected were Durand and Morse. They promptly resigned.

If the academy committee, as the association itself maintained, had pledged its influence to elect the entire association slate, the artists' newspaper notice displayed little faith in that committee. On such sand no useful union could be built. Could the artists have viewed the situation as hopeless and have taken this means to rid themselves of their obligations to the academy? Probably not; money meant so much to them that they would not sacrifice a hundred dollars to the academy treasury to qualify their candidates for nothing. The newspaper notice was in all probability just bad taste and bad politics. Morse, however, always insisted that it was "*brief, temperate, respectful.*"[6]

As Morse saw the situation, the only logical move for the artists now was to form an academy of their own. At the next meeting of the New York Drawing Association he proposed that its members elect fifteen professional academicians who would thereafter be self-perpetuating directors of what Morse wished to name the National Academy of the Arts of Design. His recommendations being adopted, on January 16, 1826, the association chose the following original academicians: Morse, Inman, Durand, Ingham, Dunlap, Cummings, Wright, Danforth, Town, John Frazee, William Wall, Edward Potter, Hugh Reinagle, and Gerlando Marsiglia. Morse was elected president and Morton secretary.

President Morse introduced the new academy to the public with the stout statement: "The National Academy of the Arts of Design is founded on the common-sense principle, that *every profession in society knows best what measures are necessary for its own improvement.*"[7] This was a bold knock at the art patrons who not only controlled the American Academy but also held the whip hand over the livelihood of all New York artists.

Trumbull felt "gloomy anticipations of ruin," as he afterward confessed.[8] His academy did its best to woo back the young artists of the city. For the first time it warmed its study rooms, enlarged its library, and furnished instructions. Its very statues sympathized in the blow that Morse had delivered. As one commentator put it, Laocoön's agony was doubled, and Apollo, scowling, seemed to exclaim: "Mr. Morse! Mr. Morse! I'll make you sweat for this!"[9] But Trumbull and his statues writhed in vain.

In May the first annual exhibition of the National Academy opened with the flourish of a private reception. The academicians, with white rosettes in their buttonholes, greeted guests on the second floor of a house at Broadway and Reade Street, and ushered them into a room of not more than twenty-five by fifty feet, lighted, as they proudly pointed out, by the new method of gas burners. The exhibition was highly praised, but it left a deficit of $163.

The next year the exhibition policy was revised to contrast with that of the American Academy. Whenever anyone asked whether one had seen the American Academy exhibition, it was a standing joke to reply: "No, I saw it last year."[10] The National Academy found favor by insisting that all works exhibited should be by living artists only and should never before have been exhibited in the city. The second annual show yielded more than $500, the third more than $800, and the fourth more than $1,000. The artists had proved themselves against the tradition and wealth of the older academy.

During the National Academy's years of slow growth, Morse, who continued to be elected president, championed the artists against the recurring gibes of the old academy. As one newspaper correspondent put it, he and his friends were "trumpeting forth their own fame" by directing "deadly shafts at their parent Institution."[11] Trumbull himself was drawn into the press argument and inadvertently paid a mighty tribute to the leadership of Morse. The separation was all his doing, Trumbull said; Morse was "the author and finisher of the entire plan."[12]

In addresses, pamphlets, and letters to the newspapers Morse easily picked his way through this first public controversy. He had well learned the art from his father – perhaps too well. The effect of his defense, however, and of his two series of historical lectures before the New York Athenæum, was to enhance his credit with artists and public alike. He had proved for the first time that he was an able organizer.

Undissembled pride flowed into his talk with his brothers and into his letters home. Self and academy were inextricably mingled. He would begin to tell of his own leadership and conclude by exclaiming at the brilliance of a National Academy exhibition. Or he would begin with an account of the growing income of the academy and conclude with his own hope that he would soon have funds to return to Europe to complete the study he had left unfinished more than ten years before. His disingenuousness was patent when he said that his academy had "*the best Exhibition of the kind that has been seen in the city*";[13] while the American Academy was showing only "*execrable trash.*"[14] Cummings suggested a not improbable reason for Morse's pride: with the possible exception of Washington Allston, there was no artist at the time in America with more advantages of birth, education, and travel than Morse.

CHAPTER *x*

Discovering Versatility

DAY after day he was at his work from seven in the morning till twelve or one at night, with only an hour's intermission for food; sometimes at the end of the week he would be so nervous that his limbs and whole body would shake. He was so occupied that more than a year after his portrait of Lafayette had been interrupted by the death of his wife it still remained unfinished, and the family began to prod him. Just before sailing for France, Lafayette gave him a final sitting. But then academy affairs absorbed him and the portrait long remained incomplete. "I have many times resolved to let everything else suffer and finish it," he wrote home, May 10, 1826, " but some unforeseen event has from the very commencement constantly broken in, and obliged me to delay it. . . . I am now called away by 50 people."

A few weeks later Finley dropped his palette again to hurry to his father's bedside in New Haven. Dr. Morse soon died, and there passed from Finley's life the quiet little man who had been the author of the first American geography, a founder of the American Board of Commissioners for Foreign Missions, and projector of Andover Seminary, but who was to be best known as the father of Finley.

Returning to New York, Finley labored so hard that in a few weeks the portrait of Lafayette was hung in the City Hall, where ever since it has been a record of New York's gratitude to France, and in its grand melancholy, some say, a record also of the griefs pulling on Morse as he painted it.

The applause he received for his *Lafayette* and his presidency of the academy encouraged him to believe that he was now assured of a steady income. But if so, of what use would it be? He was lonely. After Lucretia's death he had brought little Susan to live with him, only to find that he could not look after her. Now after his father's death he asked his mother to come to New York and bring all three children with her, but she preferred the quiet of New Haven, and he had to acknowledge that New York was no place for children.

It has been said that Morse was not now interested in women, because Cooper once described him playfully as a celibate.[1] Actually, within three years of Lucretia's death a love affair was interfering with his work. That spring he made a proposal of marriage. " You will be anxious to know the result of the affair . . ." he wrote to his mother, in a letter from which some good soul has scratched out crucial words; " it is *unsuccessful;* God's will be done." [2] Other letters sketch the story of his attachment and blasted hopes. A few days later brother Richard wrote brother Sidney: " Finley's affair is up at A.," [3] probably referring to Albany. Still later Finley wrote his Albany confessor, De Witt Bloodgood: " Is there more than *one* in the opposition? This is a point on which I really want information; I should wish to know if his *dissent* is sanctioned by any other of the friends or relatives, I am not aware that it is; but if in your intercourse you can directly or indirectly gather any information on this point you will much oblige me, and also whether any are *favorably* disposed. Will you also ascertain the *age* precisely of a certain lady, a point which I never knew." [4] Several years later he again wrote Bloodgood: " My profession is that of a *beggar,* it exists on *charity*. . . . Twice *you know* I have suffered disappointment in a matter where the heart feels strongest, once at least on account of my profession and whatever may be the ostensible cause of failure in the other instance were the truth known, I believe that the cause would be found remotely if not immediately the same. Nor is the objection on that score irrational. A profession so precarious as mine is made to appear and really is from the *motives* of encouragement, is looked at by fathers, brothers, &c. with suspicion, and objections are of course made to any family connection with it." [5]

In their judgment of his income " fathers, brothers, &c." were right. The reputation that he thought amply justified him in hiring a large house and in seeking a wife did not provide him with the income he anticipated. He might rank first among New York artists, but there were times after his *Lafayette* was completed when he was willing and had no work.

Impatiently he sought commissions upstate, wrote for the *Observer,* tried to sell his old "painting room," talked of selling his *Congress Hall* and many of his books at auction, and threatened never to produce a historical painting again. Longing for a home, uncertain of his career, he grew increasingly irritable. When a request for money came to his brothers from home in New Haven, Richard hardly dared to tell him of it.

His mother and brothers began to worry more than ever about him. With his father gone and the *Observer* subscription list growing but slowly, it was disturbing to have Finley continue to borrow from them. He left his large house on Canal Street only to take rooms – a bedroom and two drawing-rooms on Murray Street near Broadway – that were even more expensive than his house.* A month later he was still in debt to his brothers. He seemed to them incapable of the careful planning and persistence necessary to ensure a regular income. "I despair of ever seeing him rich or even at ease in his pecuniary circumstances from efforts of his own," Sidney had written.[6] They pounded it into him now that he was financially incompetent. There was just enough truth in their dinning to make him half believe it all his life. Reputation and capacity for steady work they granted that he had; but when the debts of their father amounted to more than eleven thousand dollars, and he himself was borrowing, he wished to go to Europe!

These complaints brought the shadow of a family division before the mother's eyes. In her now trembling hand she pleaded for harmony unless her sons wished her to go in sorrow to the grave. Finley tried to regain the good graces of his brothers; he sent home his promissory note, endorsed by Charles Walker, for more than seven hundred dollars.

Family peace was restored none too soon. Shortly after exacting from Finley a pledge never to sign another promissory note, his

* His restlessness is suggested by the fact that in the 1820's during the five years in which he was listed in a New York directory he had as many different addresses.

mother died. She had been her warm self, busy with mince pies, marlboro puddings, and the care of Finley's children, to the end. The summer before, she had refused an invitation to visit friends with the explanation: "At the age of 61 years I have three little motherless children to take care of beside three young men all without wives who have never yet been from under my care at home or abroad." [7] Her charm was her extravagance in both sternness and affection.

The first exhibition of French dancing in America was Madame Hutin's appearance, nearly naked, in the new Bowery Theater in New York in February 1827. That night every lady in the first tier of boxes indignantly left the house. While the daily papers would only say: "She never lets *concealment* prey on her charms," or "she put many gentlemen in the pit to the most extraordinary extatics," [8] the religious press of New York and the secular press of much of the rest of the country protested loudly. The *Observer* led them in a thundering moral judgment.

His days of frustration in his wooing and painting coinciding with Madame Hutin's arrival, Morse threw himself passionately into the *Observer's* crusade, becoming its chief writer.[9] He had long been skeptical of the influence of the theater, and now that French dancing was invading the comparatively clean American stage, he concluded that the stage could not be reformed. In an appeal to American women he cried: "Let an institution that has dared to insult you, be forever proscribed." [10]

In the metropolis of the British Empire Parliament would license only two theaters. New Haven prohibited theaters altogether. But New York already had five or six, with no control over the performances at all. The city papers, Morse believed, encouraged the acceptance of the immoral dance by puffing about "respectable" audiences witnessing the new "poetry of motion." Did New York editors have no sense of social responsibility?

With mounting enthusiasm Morse talked of establishing a journal that would force the offending papers to raise their standards. Arthur Tappan, once an apprentice of Morse's Uncle Josiah Salisbury in Boston, now a silk merchant, and later to be famous as an arch-abolitionist, threw his wealth behind the proposal. He asked

Morse to draw up a prospectus.[11] From the *Observer* office Richard wrote home: "Two thousand of the 1.st article [by Finley] 'Mad. Hutin – Bowery Theatre' reprinted together with the pieces in last paper . . . are ordered by M. A.[rthur] T.[appan] & will be distributed with the Prospectus of the new paper. Finley is writing the prospectus – show'd me some of the tho'ts it is to contain – the name 'Journal of Commerce.'"[12]

Morse found his new role a release. The next day he wrote Sidney:

New York, March 20th, 1827

Dear Brother,

I am well in health, but at times feel desponding in consequence of having no commissions for pictures, I am absolutely entirely without anything to paint for anyone, I have told my friends, but all to no purpose, and I am at a loss almost what course to pursue; at present, however, the part I am called on to act in the Observer seems to be duty; to have roused the attention of the public to the licentiousness of the theatre, and to find such success attending the effort, is no small reward and consolation, under my disappointment as to business, and I feel satisfied that whilst engaged for God he will not suffer me to want. . . . In the mean time bear with me at home, knowing as you may for certain that every effort shall be made by me to send the first monies I can get to you.

As to the New Paper there is every prospect of complete success, the prospectus will be out tomorrow, and from the energy displayed by Mr. T. and the reports he brings from all quarters, everything is ripe for such a paper.

Mr. T. is exceedingly anxious to have a first rate man for its Editor, and is very desirous that you should think of it. . . .

With respect to my being the author of those pieces . . . it is important on every account at present that I should be unknown. . . .

Yr. Affec. Brother
Finley[13]

His injunction to secrecy served its purpose only too well. His role in helping launch a paper that has had a distinguished career of more than one hundred years has been forgotten until the present study. He wrote the article on the theater which gave rise to the proposal for a new paper. He wrote the prospectus for it. Strong indication that he chose the name *Journal of Commerce* appears in Richard's letter already noted; and Morse himself made the direct claim many years later: "I accordingly wrote and printed its *prospectus* and gave it the name of the Journal of Commerce." [14]

The prospectus [15] promised that the new paper would exclude not only theater but also lottery advertisements, and that in order to avoid the violation of the Sabbath by setting up type on that day, the paper would come out late on Monday morning. It pledged that in timely and authentic news the *Journal of Commerce* would suffer by comparison with no other commercial paper in the city.

Upon Sidney's declining the editorship, Finley conducted the correspondence leading to the appointment of William Maxwell, a Virginia lawyer.[16] The first issue appeared on September 1, 1827. After short periods under Maxwell and Horace Bushnell, the paper passed under the control of David Hale and Gerard Hallock. Both Hale and Hallock came from pious New England homes; both, like Sidney, had written for the Boston *Recorder;* through them the Morse brothers continued in sympathy with the new paper for many years. It was in the *Journal of Commerce* that Finley issued his reply to the *North American Review* in defense of the National Academy; when he went abroad he was asked to become its special correspondent; later he found in it occasional support for his political ambitions. He became proud of Hale's and Hallock's resourcefulness in gathering news, proud of their boat, which raced out of the harbor to meet news-bearing packets from Europe, proud that their relays of horses to Washington beat the other city relays.

Somewhere in a round of parties in Albany an aristocratic painter met an aristocratic Englishwoman. The delicate sensibilities of Mrs. Basil Hall were outraged by America's overflowing inns, impassable roads, impertinent curiosity, spitting, and women who could not pass the test of evening dresses. Meanwhile she was pining for the niceties she had known in London and Madrid. "I have lately met here," she wrote home in the autumn of 1827, "with an American painter, a Mr. Morse, who feels this want in his countrymen and women to the full and was delighted to get hold of someone to whom he might express it. He spent several years in England and feels the contrast of this plodding, money-making society to that which he there enjoyed very severely, and sighs for the companionship of thought which in his native country he cannot expect to find." [17]* If Mrs. Hall understood that Morse had no doubts about the virtue of European society she was mistaken.

While he was in Albany that autumn there came to him an experience of the delicacy of spirit that could flower even in the American wilderness. At his lodgings Moss Kent, brother of Chancellor Kent, thrust upon him several volumes of manuscripts, explaining that they were the work of a precocious, fragile maiden who had died at the age of seventeen. As the bachelor judge told of the melancholy loveliness of the author, Morse prepared to allow generously for his sentimental affection. As he read the manuscripts, however, his inclination to patronize vanished, and he protested over one poem: " Can this be the work of a girl of fourteen? " Captivated by the exquisite sensibility of the poems, he declared they should be published. That was the signal for which Kent was waiting. He promptly requested Morse to be her editor, and in the heat of the moment he agreed. After all, was not her name Lucretia? Was not her dark beauty, her purity, her early death like those of his own Lucrece?

Lucretia Davidson was the darling of parents of literary tastes and middling means. When Kent first fell under her spell he won permission to become her guardian and take her from her Plattsburg home to Emma Willard's school in Troy. Diffident, the " little Sappho " composed alone, and if someone blundered upon her unfinished lines, she might tumble in a trice from ecstasy to despair, and either burn them or leave them forever unfinished.

Within two years of her death Morse had made his selections and prepared a biographical sketch. Under a secret profits agreement with Kent and Morse,[18] the Carvills of New York issued the volume as *Amir Khan*. Morse sent copies to Sir Walter Scott, Felicia Hemans, and Robert Southey. It has been supposed that he knew

* Not only were her letters published but also those of her uninhibited husband, Captain Hall. They raised what Mrs. Trollope called a " war hoop " from every village in America. Like his wife, the captain gave a singularly kind judgment of Morse. In a series of letters edited by Morse's friend Bloodgood, he wrote: " In Painting, the Americans are doing wonders. . . . Need I name a Newton, Alston, Leslie, Sargeant, Vanderlyn, and Morse, who have all been abroad? . . . There is a new establishment in New York, called the National Academy . . . which . . . has met with great encouragement, and is in the hands of able men." *An Englishman's Sketch Book* (New York, 1828), pp. 189–90.

Southey, but the draft of the note to him gives no evidence of acquaintance.

May 1, 1829

To Robert Southey, L.L.D.

I have ventured to ask your acceptance of the volume whh accom. this.

I cannot but flatter myself that one who has taken so deep an interest in the youthful genius of White, will find something to gratify him in the remains of genius which sprang up and bloomed in the wilderness, assumed the female form, and wore the features of exquisite beauty, and perished like White in the bloom.

Southey replied in an eleven-page article in the London *Quarterly Review.* Following the hint in Morse's letter, he compared Miss Davidson to Kirke White and also to Thomas Chatterton; he paraphrased and quoted liberally from Morse's biographical sketch and criticism, concluding in words that Edgar Allan Poe afterward said were twice as strong as necessary to establish her fame in England-fearing America. "In these poems," declared Southey, "there is enough of originality, enough of aspiration, enough of conscious energy, enough of growing power, to warrant any expectations, however sanguine, which the patron, and the friends, and parents of the deceased could have formed." [19]

The vogue for Lucretia Davidson grew. Chancellor Kent wrote his brother Moss: "The notice that the London Quarterly takes of Miss Davidson's works must be very gratifying to you & her friends. It has quite confounded everybody here, & they grow ashamed of not knowing more of the work." [20] Jared Sparks added to her praise, and the popular critic Catharine Sedgwick used her letters in a fuller account of her life.[21] After several new editions of her poems, Poe was able to write: "The name of Lucretia Davidson is familiar to all readers of poetry. Dying at the early age of seventeen, she has been rendered famous not less, and certainly not more, by her own precocious genius than by three memorable biographies – one by President Morse, of the American Society of Arts, another by Miss Sedgwick, and a third by Robert Southey." It was also Poe who pronounced the sound judgment that her poems have "poetic sentiment," but not "poetic power. . . . And in so saying we startle none but the brainless." [22]

Early in 1827 Morse went north to his Uncle Arthur Breese's home in Utica, seeking rest and perhaps a few painting commissions. As Uncle Arthur's sixteen-year-old daughter, Sarah Ann, was sleeping one night, someone sang below her window. She did not waken. In the morning she was grieving over her lost pleasure when Morse playfully spoke to her of his versatility.

"Cousin," he said, "I am a sculptor, as well as painter, something of a musician, and can write poetry!"

She well knew that he could paint, for he was then painting her and her parents; but could he write poetry?

"Give me a subject," he insisted, "and tomorrow I will bring you the lines."

"Take the serenade," was her decree.

The next morning he produced the lines that she preserved all her days. They were in the manner of Miss Davidson.

Come, ye that know the lovely maid,
    And help prepare the serenade. . . .
Choose ye the softly-breathing flute,
    The mellow horn, the loving lute;
The viol ye must not forget,
    And take the sprightly flageolet,
And grave bassoon; choose, too, the fife,
    Whose warblings in the tuneful strife,
Mingling in mystery with the words,
    May seem like notes of blithest birds! . . .
Softly! now breathe the symphony—
    So gently breathe, the tones may vie
In softness with the magic notes
    In visions heard; music that floats
So buoyant that it well may seem
    With strains ethereal in her dream,
One song of such mysterious birth
    She doubts it comes from Heaven or Earth!
Play on! my loved one slumbers still;
    Play on! she wakes not with the thrill
Of joy produced by strains so mild,
    But fancy moulds them gay and wild;

Now as the music low declines,
 'Tis sighing of the forest pines;
Or 'tis the fitful varied roar
 Of distant falls, or troubled shore.
Now as the tone grows full or sharp,
 'Tis whispering of the Aeolian harp:
The viol swells, now low, now loud,
 'Tis spirits chanting on a cloud
That passes by. It dies away;
 So gently dies she scarce can say
'Tis gone; listens! 'tis lost, she fears;
 Listens! and thinks again she hears,
As dew-drops mingling in a stream;
 To her 'tis all one blissful dream –
A song of angels throned in light.
 Softly! away! Fair one, good night!

In New York not long afterward the embryonic poet met his friends Gulian C. Verplanck and Robert C. Sands, who were gathering materials for the second number of the gift annual which they and Bryant were publishing. They asked Morse if he would make a contribution.

"If this suits," he replied, drawing from his pocket a copy of his poem, "you are welcome."[23]

Unabashed, a few weeks later they requested the poet to prepare an illustration for his poem. And presently in *The Talisman for 1828* appeared "The Serenade" accompanied by an engraving of a vine-covered turret before which serenaders played in the moonlight. But his first published poem was probably also his last; wisely he directed his facile pen into forms which lent themselves admirably to his vigor and logic – into politics, denunciations of social wrong, and the defense of his academy and eventually his telegraph.

Morse had reputation to lose now. He could no longer afford to make such painting excursions as that in which he rode all the way from Portsmouth to Portland only to find that two prospective sitters were away and a third had "no more taste than a cow."[24] He was learning to depend on upstate friends and such relatives as Uncle Arthur in Utica and Uncle Samuel in near-by Sconandoa. Under their guidance these summers he painted in Utica, Sconandoa, Cazenovia, Whitesboro, Trenton Falls, Cherry Valley, and Cooperstown.

In the summer of 1829 he was upstate for a long stay in Cooperstown at the foot of Lake Otsego. Cooper had already christened the lake " glimmerglass " and introduced a whole series of traditions that hallowed the little town. The novelist was not there now; three years before he had been sent off to Europe with an enormous banquet by The Lunch. There were others whom Morse now knew in Cooperstown, notably the future general John A. Dix, who had once courted the dark Concord beauty Lucretia Walker, but held no resentment against his rival now.

After the visit Mrs. Dix wrote that she was a little afraid of Morse, " considering that I had seen him only twice before, besides his having been to Europe, and being a member of the *ton*, as well as literary and philosophical societies. He is a very agreeable man, and the admiration of all the young ladies here, notwithstanding he is a widower with three children, and here and there a gray hair. He takes admirable portraits: the price is twenty-five dollars." [25] Morse was a lion of society even while he condemned some of its standards.

From the lawn of Apple Hill, the Dix house, Morse painted a charming view. Below the hill in the far distance lies the source of the Susquehanna, " glimmerglass," enclosed by distant hills. In the middle distance a carriage is crossing a bridge. From the foreground rises in a gentle curve a thin pine, silhouetted against a brilliant sky. Near the pine on the lawn are two women, posed with Japanese daintiness. Perhaps it was the charm of the composition, or perhaps the comparative absence of the brown sauce characteristically pervading the landscapes of Morse and his friends, that made the painting so desirable. Dix was enthusiastic, but Morse had already found a buyer in his editor friend Bloodgood. It was not until many years later that this painting, one of Morse's best landscapes, found its way again into the Dix family.

As he left Cooperstown he was concluding plans for study on the Continent at last. Only his poverty had kept him from crossing the

Channel from England to France years before; now he was receiving financial encouragement from commissions to paint in Europe.

He had accomplished much without Continental study, but many of his accomplishments were in other fields than painting. The combination of versatility and leisure was producing in him an astonishing breadth, both in directions usually associated with the introvert – toward poetry, toward literary criticism, and toward inventiveness; and in directions usually associated with the extrovert – toward leadership of men, toward politics, toward ready talk, firm, bold, and informative. The artist had revived his interest, apparently as a Clintonian Democrat,[26] in what his mother would have called "poison politics."[27] He had become recording secretary of a library society, the New York Athenæum.[28] Continuing his interest in science, he heard Professor James Freeman Dana give his brilliant lectures before the Athenæum[29] on electromagnetism, which had been discovered in Europe two years before; in the audience together, unknown to each other, were three persons who were to be associated in harnessing the electromagnet to human needs: Morse, Joseph Henry, and Leonard Gale. Electricity was now so much on his mind that a description of the flowing of electricity through wire would occur to him as an illustration in an art lecture.[30] No wonder James B. Longacre, of Philadelphia, one of the best engravers in the country, said that his conversation was "rich and instructive" especially on the arts but also "on almost every subject."[31] Still Morse was not satisfied with his professional training, first artist in New York though he might be. He was convinced that he not only was not improving as a painter but was declining. At thirty-eight, with graying hair, and deepening lines around his mouth, he believed he still could learn.

Financially he was wriggling more freely within his strait-jacket. After giving up his large house he sold his furniture to his brothers and still owed them $950. Surly brother Richard determined to see to it that he never borrowed any more from him, a fact which Finley was kind enough to forget in the days of wealth that lay ahead. At last he sold *Congress Hall* for $1,000 or $1,100 to Sherman Converse, to exhibit in England. Of this sum Finley used $400 to pay a debt to Arthur Tappan of the *Journal of Commerce*, and the rest to pay his brothers. But it was the various patrons who gave him commissions for painting in Europe who enabled him to go abroad. The list of his patrons included many of New York's business men: Philip Hone, Myndert Van Schaik, Stephen Van Rensselaer, G. G. Howland, Moses H. Grinnell. It included Moss Kent, Charles Carvill, and Morse's brother-in-law Charles Walker; the secretary of the National Academy, J. L. Morton; Morse's cousin Stephen Salisbury of Worcester; New York's best-known physician, Dr. Hosack; and the Albany editor Bloodgood. Some patrons left it to the artist to choose the subject, some specified their desires. The prices ranged from $30 to $500. With the total of over $2,800 offered, and the additional hope that, after he had studied historical painting again in Europe, he would be commissioned by Congress to paint one of the panels for the rotunda which Bulfinch had now about completed in the Capitol, he proposed to sail.

His children he withdrew from the care of nurse Nancy. Little Susan found a home for a time with her namesake aunt, Susan Walker Pickering, in Greenland, New Hampshire. The boys, Charles and the backward "Fin," were placed in the home of Morse's brothers (Richard was married now). With financial and family affairs in comparative order, he sailed from New York in November 1829 for his grand tour.

CHAPTER *xi*

Puritan Seeking Beauty

WHAT meant most to him in his two-week visit to Paris was his evening with Lafayette. It was the first time he had seen the General since painting him five years before. Then Clerical and émigré reaction had recently forced him from his seat in Parliament. Now, although only fifteen thousand out of the twenty-five million French could vote, a liberal trend among voters had reseated him, and he was again a leading voice for the discontented. At one of his soirées, Lafayette instantly recognized Morse, took him by both hands, and pressed him to visit his country home, La Grange. It seemed to Morse now that Lafayette had the respect of all the best men in France; but he could not know that when he next visited Paris, Lafayette would be France's symbol of order in a time of chaos.

Restless to be at work, Morse took coach for Dijon. The fatigue of riding for three days and two nights was relieved by the presence of a pretty passenger. She could not speak English nor he French, but they had a delightful time attempting to make themselves understood.

At Dijon he stopped to rest and avoid travel on the Sabbath. Though familiar with the Anglican service since his years in London, Morse may have known little of Catholic ritual until in Dijon he attended a Catholic church and first recorded the impressions which were to become the emotional and factual source of many of his political books and pamphlets in the following decade. Learning from his landlord that there was no Protestant minister in the city, he entered a Catholic edifice, edged past kneeling worshippers toward the altar, and found a funeral service in process. " There was much ceremony, but scarcely anything that was imposing," he wrote; " its heartlessness was so apparent, especially in the conduct of some of the assistants, that it seemed a solemn mockery. One in particular, who seemed to pride himself on the manner in which he vociferated *Amen,* was casting his eyes among the crowd, winking and laughing at various persons, and from the extravagance of his manner, bawling out most irreverently and closing by laughing, I wondered that he was not perceived and rebuked by the priests." [1] That same day at dinner a hand-organ played waltzes for him and other American tourists. He thought the music disgusting on the Sabbath.

It was Sunday again when his coach reached Avignon. In this old residence of the popes of a divided church he again found no Protestant service. At the cathedral he studied the worshippers for signs of devotion. " Far be it from me to say there were not some who were actually devout, hard as it is to conceive of such a thing; but this I will say, that everything around them, instead of aiding devotion, was calculated entirely to destroy it." [2] Even in the mind of a devout artist, one who had once intended to become a clergyman in a ritualistic church, God and beauty were not readily associated. Music, color, great reaches of stone, only led his mind away from contemplation of the eternal to the charms of mere sense. He thought it must be so with all worshippers. The music at morning mass and a chorus of men's voices which passed under his window that night deeply moved him, yet he shrank from giving himself to sensuous beauty. He needed more on the Sabbath. He needed sober, practical religious instruction.

Through varying rain and moonlight his carriage climbed past brawling cascades into the colorful Apennines. On the long slopes drab clay varied with brown and gold. In the background slate blue and gray were mixed with green and purple; the most distant peaks were deep ultramarine. Coming out of the mountains the coach descended to the Vara River. He was amused by the sangfroid with which the " women of the lower orders " [3] held their clothes above their knees to wade.

More than five weeks after leaving Paris, at nine o'clock one morning he saw the dome of St. Peter's in the distance. By two o'clock the carriage had entered Rome, the city Morse as artist came to love, and as religionist and nativist to detest.

Taking lodgings at 17 Via Preffetti,* he was soon at work in the Vatican galleries, in high spirits over the prospect of spending more than a year on his commissioned paintings. That he might be able to please those who had financed his trip did not seem at all impossible.

Later he visited other galleries, seeing many great paintings for the first time. The comments in his notebooks were often swift and sure, those of a painter who had achieved his own style.

At the Colonna Palace he found a painting with a striking color harmony. It was a sixteenth-century portrait of one of the Colonna family by Paul Veronese. Called the *Green Picture*, it was done in one color; and it proved for Morse that a painting in a single tone could be harmonious in itself. As he related years later to his friend Dunlap, he was standing in front of the picture when he formulated his theory for the distribution of color values in painting.[4] He jotted down: "Curtain in the background, *hot* green, middle tint; sleeves of the arms, *cool;* vest, which is in the mass of light, as well as the lights of the curtain, WARM; white collar, which is the highest light, cool!!!"[5] As he studied the painting the principle came to him: for balance in a painting the highest light should be cold, the middle ground cool, the mass of light warm, the reflection hot, and the shadow negative. That values and color in painting stood in a fixed relationship seemed to him according to natural order.

As time offered, Morse tested his theory. He placed a white ball in a box lined with white. The point of highest light on the ball appeared cold in comparison with the rest of the color of the ball. He repeated the experiment with balls of orange in orange boxes, with balls of blue in blue boxes. The result was the same. He continued to test his theory. A picture of Rubens had affected him as having an unsatisfying, "foxy" feeling; on examination he found the source of the disharmony to be the shadows. According to his theory, they ought to be only negative in tone; in this painting they were hot.

Titian and Veronese were his ideal colorists. He only admired

* A tablet commemorating Morse was erected on this site late in the century.

them the more when friends urged him to study Landi, a contemporary Italian, for color. "I had heard Landi, the Chevalier Landi, lauded to the skies by the Italians as the greatest modern colorist . . ." he wrote. "There is not a redeeming point in a single picture that I saw, not one that would place him on a level with the commonest sign-painter in America. . . . If total disregard of arrangement, if the scattering of tawdry reds and blues and yellows over the picture, all quarrelling for the precedence; if leather complexions varied by those of chalk, without truth or depth of tone, constitute good color, then are they finely colored. But, if Landi is a colorist, then are Titian and Veronese never more to be admired." [6]

In sculpture Morse considered the Dane, Bertel Thorwaldsen, the greatest artist of the age, as did many Americans of the time. Meeting him one evening, Morse found him an old man in appearance, with a "profusion of grey hair, wildly hanging over his forehead and ears. His face has a strong Northern character, his eyes are light grey, and his complexion sandy." [7] Pleased by the affable gentleman, Morse wished to do his portrait. Philip Hone had commissioned him to paint any portrait he might choose. What subject better than the sculptor? Thorwaldsen consented.

Those who considered themselves guardians of taste often accused Thorwaldsen of being an imitator of Greek sculpture. But Morse was not among those many Americans who shouted for sculpture unfettered by classical standards. Studying Thorwaldsen's works, he thought the sculptor to have been born "in the best age of Grecian art; imbued with the spirit of that age, and producing from his own resources kindred works." [8] Thorwaldsen took unusual pains, it seemed to the American, to show him little attentions. To his joy, the sculptor sought him out for evening walks. Unfortunately, Morse felt cut off from the Danish sculptor's fine distinctions of thought by the curse that befell the architects of Babel.

Five months after his first sitting Thorwaldsen was telling the painter of his pleasure in the completed portrait. Shipping it to Mr. Hone, Morse did not hesitate to tell the former mayor it was a fine painting. Hone agreed, as did later a King of Denmark.

When Hone in due time examined several of the European productions of Morse and Cole at the National Academy of Design, he concluded that the sunny skies of Italy had not warmed their imagination. There was no poetry about Morse's painting, Hone wrote, "and his prose consists of straight lines, which look as if they had been stretched to their uttermost tension to form clothes-lines." Nevertheless he was "well acquainted with the principles of his art," and "makes good portraits, strong likenesses; my portrait of Chancellor Kent by Morse is very good, and Thorwaldsen is excellent."[9]

The Thorwaldsen portrait hung in the gallery of patrician Hone, first in his house opposite City Hall Park, then after 1837 uptown in his new mansion on Broadway at Great Jones Street. There it rested in one of the city's best private galleries, beside Morse's *Chancellor Kent* and a study for his *Lafayette,* and beside paintings by many of Morse's companions, Cole, Leslie, Ingham, Dunlap, Gilbert Stuart Newton, and Rembrandt Peale. Twenty-five years after painting the portrait Morse made a pilgrimage to the tomb and museum of Thorwaldsen in Copenhagen. The hospitality of King Frederick VII inspired Morse with a desire to present his Thorwaldsen to the King. Years after the death of Hone it had found its way into the hands of John T. Johnston, the first president of the Metropolitan Museum of Art, who had paid four hundred dollars for it, four times the price the artist had received. Hearing of Morse's desire, Johnston begged him to accept it as a gift. At last the artist presented his beloved *Thorwaldsen* to the King of Denmark, who accepted it as the best likeness of the great Danish sculptor.

Morse's days were filled with painting at the Vatican or the Colonna Palace and visits to the inexhaustible art collections of the city. His evenings likewise were often crowded with concerts, operas, plays; with soirées given by artists or art patrons; and with strolls about the hills or ruins of Rome.

At the theater he observed no wanton women like those who occupied parts of the house in England and America. Not that Rome had less vice; no, he wrote, prostitution in America, like a humor on the skin, deforms the surface; here the whole system is rotten to the core. Without the theater, it seemed to him, thousands of Romans would die of ennui for want of thought, or rather want of matter for thought. The subjects which should occupy their minds, theology and politics, the theater displaced. Of course the government supported the theater, for the government did not want people to think. "But what have we to do with theatres in America? Have we not the whole world of topics for discussion or conversation open to us? Is not truth in religion, politics, and science suffered to be assailed by enemies freely, and does it not, therefore, require the time of all intelligent men to study, and understand, and defend, and fortify themselves in truth?"[10] The artist had no idea of drama as an art. The theater was merely a distraction from both effective living and the enjoyment of domestic bliss. In spite of his heritage of distrust for all things histrionic, Morse knew enough about the theater in New York, London, and Rome to be able to talk about it. He was too curious to ignore it.

In Rome's cosmopolitan society he found admirable opportunity to distinguish national attitudes toward strangers. In company, he discovered, an Englishman, unless requested to do so, greets no one; he treats you like a chair or a table. A Frenchman respectfully greets everyone in a room, converses amiably, and forgets you. Unless there is something peculiar about you, an American will know you after once having met you; he may be too unsuspicious, but is more generously sincere than the other two. The American's openness was the artist's affable ideal for himself as he became at home in Rome.

Spending some evenings with Thorwaldsen or James Fenimore Cooper, he would unlimber his badinage over a cup of coffee in the smoke-filled Caffe Greco, where in years past Reynolds, West, Turner, Keats, and Irving had passed the time.[11] Or he would walk about the hills above the city with John Chapman, the young painter from Virginia, or Theodore Woolsey, later president of Yale. One moonlit evening in June he stole out of his lodgings alone. He walked slowly past the ruined Forum and the Arch of Titus and entered the Colosseum; there he was content, exulting in profound repose. At times he would give himself readily to his companions and draw heavily on their resources; at some poignant moments he was alone.

In the cool mornings of the Roman summer the streets and cafés were alive. At noon the bustle died away, the shops and houses were shut; the city was dedicated to slumber. The heat was unlike anything he had known in America, even in Charleston. The sun scorched his skin; its glare pained his eyes. While the clear evenings were a relief, they could not be so refreshing as excursions out of the city.

Most of May passed with artist friends on a gay tour up the Tiber and Anico to Tivoli and Subiaco. They rode donkeys or hiked about the hills, their painting equipment slung on their backs like knapsacks. They often paused to sketch minstrels, or shepherds, or peasant women, for while the common folk in America – black servants or Yankee fishermen – were not worth attention, like most American artists they considered Italian peasants picturesque. Morse's gift of enthusiasm found ready employment at Subiaco. While walking in an ilex grove in the grounds of a convent he decided that he had found just the right place to retire. He looked to the wooded mountains and recalled the similarly fresh and variegated countryside of home. High peaks were gray in the distance; the near-by hill was marked with a winding track down which crawled a drove of sheep, like a moving pathway. Even the sirocco blowing hot from the African deserts failed to disturb his peace. He soon found the right setting for one of his few landscapes. Peasants in colorful clothing in front of a stone chapel on a wild cliff, swishing trees in a gorge in the right foreground, the town of Subiaco on a hill in the background. He had the composition. Completing the painting later in Rome, he intensified the contrast between the dark figures in the foreground and the misty hill behind them, and romanticized the outline of the trees in the gorge. Although the strength of the stark chapel unbalanced the design of his painting, *Chapel of the Virgin at Subiaco*,[12] it proved that the wild beauty of the Apennines had entered his being.

This landscape was among the many shipments that he dispatched to America during his year and a half in Italy. He did not forget the National Academy; to its secretary, Morton, he sent several casts, listing Thorwaldsen among the donors, and an introduction for his friend Count Hawks le Grice, as a literary correspondent of the academy for Italy. For several weeks after leaving New York Morse himself had considered being a correspondent of the New York *Journal of Commerce*, but declined the offer, believing that the time necessary for polishing his letters would be better spent in painting. Nevetheless, he found time to write letters for the *Ob-*

server, and even to send Dr. Hosack cuttings of the Pergolese and Pizzutello grapes.

As a Protestant among faithful Italians, Morse knew that he was considered a lost soul. And he himself was comfortable among those Protestants who thought Catholics lost souls. Whether or not he may be described as hopelessly prejudiced against Catholics, he may not be fairly accused of ignorance of their form of worship and hierarchy.

He attended Catholic ceremonies frequently; during the Easter period soon after coming to Rome, even avidly. On March 18 he attended the ceremony of presenting the cardinals' hats; on March 19 at St. Peter's, a procession of cardinals kissing the toe of a statue of St. Peter; on March 21 in the Chiesa Nuova, a sacred opera; on March 24, in the Chiesa di Minerva, the Festa of the Annunciation. On Passion Sunday, March 28, he was kept from church in the morning by a toothache (the dentist who extracted the tooth "had the conscience to ask me three dollars – he took two" [13]); in the afternoon he attended a church service, went on to St. Peter's to see the veiled crosses and pictures, and climbed the one hundred and thirty-five steps past throngs of beggars to the Trinità di Monti to hear his favorite choir of nuns. On April 2 he heard the choir again, and a service of consecration. On Palm Sunday, April 4, after services at the Sistine Chapel, he was in the procession which passed the stately bed on which lay the body of a cardinal awaiting burial. On Wednesday and Thursday of Holy Week he went to St. Peter's. With friends he wasted Good Friday morning trying to find the most colorful services; at one o'clock in the Church of St. Sylvestro in Capite they heard the singing of the exquisite *Miserere*, and after dinner they went to the Trinità di Pellegrini for the ceremony of the washing of pilgrims' feet. Anyone attending such a variety of services and churches anywhere would have learned much. But these services were during the most holy days of the church year; these churches were at the seat of the popes. And Morse was a keen observer. In his journal he noted the colors of the priests' robes, the number of candles, the expressions of the attendants, and the order of movements about the altar.

There is no record that Morse was accompanied by any but such similarly distrusting souls as Cooper. Was there, then, no one from whom he might ask an explanation of the ceremonies? In his diary he seldom used Catholic terms; did he, then, misunderstand the Catholic interpretation of the ceremonies, as one Catholic student believes?[14] But Morse had long been familiar with colorful ritual, for he had been introduced to it in the sympathetic company of his own friends in the Church of England. In Rome he met several ecclesiastical officials. One cardinal vigorously combated his religious views; correspondence and interviews followed.[15] Through his English friend Count le Grice he met Cardinal Weld in a pleasant interview;[16] he became acquainted with the son of Earl Spencer, only recently converted to Catholicism and then attached to the English College in Rome, with whom he talked for long hours about conversion.[17] With his blunt curiosity Morse very probably asked for an explanation of any ceremony he did not understand. That his journals do not record his observations in Catholic language, that at mass he did not see the body and blood of Christ but only the movements of the priests at the altar, shows only that the Catholic interpretation did not move him. It could not, for it was not real to him.

Thus among the treasures of the Sistine Chapel he baldly delineates a ceremony: "Procession commences at half-past ten. A cross, with two candles on each side. Cardinals return during chanting from the choir. Cardinals divested of their finery, and appear as ordinary, in purple and ermine. Putting incense into censers. Prayer-book. Many attendants to assist in the ceremony of opening a book. Cardinal says three or four words in a drawling tone. One, in a drawling, school-boy tone, reads from a book in the middle of the room. Great work made in bringing back the book. Chanting; which, for the most part, is a monotonous brawling."[18]

Like a petulant child he seemed to enjoy disrespect of authority. He spoke of fleshy friars, of a priest's eloquence sounding like water gurgling from a narrow-necked bottle, and of a funeral conducted in high glee. Nuns passing in procession looked arch to him; priests at a watering-place, dissipating their time in gambling, were disfiguring the landscape with their uncouth dress. He gave the Pope faint praise for his good nerves: in June on St. Peter's Day, in the midst of the usual "monotonous chant from the choir, the same numberless bowings, and genuflections, and puffings of incense, and change of garments, and fussing about the altar," all that he could discover new in the ceremony "was the constant bustle about the Pope, kissing of his toe and his hand, helping him to rise and to sit again, bringing and taking away of cushions and robes and tiaras and mitres, and a thousand other little matters that would have enraged any man of weak nerves, if it did not kill him." [19]

Even outside the church he could not escape its baleful influence. In the Vatican galleries one morning he noticed a monk who seemed to be observing the pictures. Soon the monk, bowing, approached the artist to offer him a pinch of snuff. Bowing in return, Morse accepted, upon which the monk instantly asked alms. He received them; but when after six months in Italy Morse observed that he could not ask for a cup of water at a cottage without being asked: "*Qualche cosa, signore,*" he remembered the habited mendicants he had seen and, like other Americans in Italy, blamed the Roman Church for surrounding begging with a halo of respectability.[20] One of the usual chanting processions of monks, priests, and familiars passed him one day as he was painting outdoors in Subiaco. "Many of those in the procession were as dirty, unshaved, ragged-looking objects as can anywhere be found," he wrote, "but some of the Capuchins were very picturesque, their long beards gave them grandeur and dignity. . . . I could not pull off my hat as they passed; if it were mere civility I should not object, but it involves acquiescence in what I see to be idolatry and of course in the street I cannot do it. If I go into the church, then I feel bound to remove my hat as a mark of civility, and if I stay they may rightfully if they choose *force* me to kneel, or to go out of the church, but in the street I have my rights as a foreigner; no man has a right to interfere with my rights of conscience." [21] Shortly afterward a man did interfere. While he was watching another religious procession on the street in Rome, a soldier struck off his hat. There was no redress. He could only reflect that the soldier was not to blame; the religion of force behind the order that all hats should be off was responsible for the outrage to decency.[22] Neither then, however, nor when he considered the attempt of the government to hush discussion of politics and religion, did he analyze the relation of the Roman Church to the state.

As a Protestant churchman he distrusted Catholic ritual and its influence; as an artist he loved much of it. On Holy Thursday the churchman's scorn was crowded out by the artist's love of pageantry. From the highest step of St. Peter's he observed the Pope, dressed in robes of gold, appear on a balcony before a great throng of civilians and soldiers. The Pope made his usual sign of blessing, rose, and extended his arms in benediction while the crowd knelt, cannon in the Castle of St. Angelo roared, and the bells in all the near-by churches rang. It seemed to the artist the most imposing ceremony he had witnessed.

What other institution in Catholic Europe, if not in the world, supported architecture, sculpture, and painting as did the Roman Church? He could not but be grateful for that encouragement. Yet he could not avoid questioning his Puritan tradition: did not art provide a setting conducive to devotion? He pondered the use of pictures in Protestant churches.

As the close of his stay in Italy neared, he visited the Milan Cathedral. Its beauty led him to prepare a considered statement, the result of months of concern, upon the conflict between his love of beauty and his fear of beauty within the church. "How admirably contrived," he wrote, "is every part of this system to take captive the imagination. It is a religion of the imagination; all the arts of the imagination are pressed into its service; architecture, painting, sculpture, music, have lent all their charm to enchant the senses and impose on the understanding by substituting for the solemn truths of God's Word, which are addressed to the understanding, the fictions of poetry and the delusions of feeling. The theatre is a daughter of this prolific mother of abominations, and a child worthy of its dam. The lessons of morality are pretended to be taught by both, and much in the same way, by scenic effect and pantomime, and the fruits are much the same."

"I am sometimes even constrained to doubt the lawfulness of my own art when I perceive its prostitution, were I not fully persuaded that the art itself, when used for its legitimate purposes, is one of the greatest correctors of grossness and promoters of refinement. I have been led, since I have been in Italy, to think much of the propriety of introducing pictures into churches in aid of devotion. I have certainly every inducement to decide in favor of the practice did I consult alone the seeming interest of art. That pictures may and do have the effect upon some rightly to raise the affections, I have no doubt, and, abstractly considered, the practice would not merely be harmless but useful; but, knowing that man is led astray by his imagination more than by any other of his other faculties, I consider it so dangerous to his best interests that I had rather sacrifice the interests of the arts, if there is any collision, than run the risk of endangering those compared with which all others are not for a moment to be considered."[23]

In Italy Morse the artist was not hostile toward the Catholic Church, but Morse the churchman was. In France Morse was to find a broader base for his hostility than that of a churchman.

Early in 1830 he had passed through Paris when it was still quiet. In July the Bourbon King, Charles X, occasioned a united bourgeois and proletarian revolt by stupidly insisting on chaining a free press. It was the bourgeois liberal, Lafayette, who used the prestige of his age and military record to avert a conflict between the two victorious parties. He persuaded the revolutionary workingmen to accept a liberal constitutional monarch, Louis Philippe. With the tricolor again waving over the French, liberals everywhere took heart, and Metternich looked out from his Vienna citadel of autocracy upon a restless Europe. The Belgians revolted successfully from the heavy rule of the Dutch. Liberals frightened the Kings of Saxony and Hanover into giving constitutions to their peoples. Encouraged by long friendship with French liberals, the liberals of Poland joined the revolt by rising against their King, the autocratic Nicholas I of Russia. Looking to Louis Philippe for aid, liberals in the Papal States of central Italy were soon to rebel against their temporal ruler, the Pope. With both the Polish and Italian uprisings of early 1831 Morse had immediate concern.

Early in February Morse was hearing and even agreeing with much of a sermon of the son of Earl Spencer, when the cannon of St. Angelo announced the election of a Pope, Gregory XVII. Morse attended his coronation.

Because the new Pope was a follower of Metternich's policy, his election provoked Italians to join the liberal upsurge. The news of rebellion in the papal territory at Bologna and Ancona and in the

Duchy of Modena reached Morse on February 10. Two days later he saw fear on faces he passed in the street; foreigners were being threatened, he heard. Three days more and he was still uncertain of the purpose of the revolt. "Some say it is to deprive the Pope of his temporal power, – and some Catholics seem to think that their religion would flourish the better for it; others, that it is a plan, long digested, for bringing all Italy under one government, having it divided into so many federative states, like the United States."[24] Soon he heard that the Pope was willing to grant a constitution, but that the cardinals refused. Morse chafed at the lack of accurate information in Rome. At night sentinels at street corners cried at Morse as he passed: "*Chi viva?*" Replying: "*Il Papa,*" he quieted his conscience by thinking of the Pope's respectable personal character.

Bitterly disappointing to the Italian rebels was the paltry aid from France. While Louis Philippe merely sent a garrison to the border papal town, Ancona, as in earlier revolts foreign assistance to the papacy came generously from Metternich's Austria. Still the rebels advanced on Rome, and foreigners began leaving the city. Galleries were closed. Fortunately Morse had completed his program for painting in Rome and by the middle of February was anxious to start for Paris. He planned a leisurely journey north, pausing to paint in the galleries of Florence, Milan, and Venice. But it was March before the American consul advised that traveling was safe. With difficulty he, two other American artists, and some Italians secured a coachman to drive them through the military lines to Florence.

The second day they reached the local headquarters of the papal armies. Politely they were detained no more than an hour because a battle was expected. When they crossed the upper Tiber they left the advance guard of the papists behind. Eagerly looking for the appearance of the army that had thrown Rome into alarm for weeks, they drove through about a mile of neutral territory, past abandoned houses, and then came upon a group of dragoons, the tricolor waving over them.

"*Siamo Americani,*" Morse called out when the coach stopped. It was allowed to pass.

Soon a group of officers halted them again. This time the Italians in the coach were displaying tricolor cockades in their hats and the conversation became easy and agreeable. The officers seemed clean and brave. Morse wished them success with all his heart.

The next town the travelers found full of troops in high spirits. At a restaurant soldiers pledged Morse and his friends in a glass of wine and the Americans returned the pledge.

At about six in the evening the coach entered Terni and drew up at an inn. Hearing that Americans had arrived, General Sercognani himself, the leader of the revolutionary army, came out and was introduced to them. The inn was his headquarters. He shook hands cordially, gratified to meet citizens of a country so distinguished in the annals of liberty. He invited them to pass the evening with him. All was bustle as they went in to take accommodations. Soldiers thronged the doorway. Officers were briskly entering and leaving.

At dinner Sercognani introduced them to a courteous gentleman, Baron Stettin, who had traveled in the United States. Morse discovered that Stettin spoke English fluently, and that he had been Prime Minister to Jerome Bonaparte as King of Westphalia.

"You are perhaps surprised," the Baron said, "to find me here at the headquarters of a Revolutionary General."

Morse admitted that he was mystified.

"Well," said he, "I will frankly tell you why I am here. The sons of the late King of Holland, Louis Bonaparte are here, and their friends, anxious lest they should compromise their position, have sent me to persuade them to return."

Morse and his friends were astonished that the Bonaparte brothers should be fighting for Italian freedom. "We could not but applaud the devotion and daring of the noble young men," Morse wrote afterward, "for a cause that appealed so strongly to all our sympathies for the long oppressed Italians." [25] One of those brothers Morse was later to know and admire as Louis Napoleon, Emperor of France.

In Florence the next evening the Americans found themselves beyond the influence of the revolutionary armies. News that they had talked with the revolutionary general at Terni had preceded them, and the American consul had to make elaborate explanations to local police.

The journey had stirred Morse deeply. As he settled down to stay with his fellow American, the sculptor Horatio Greenough, he summarized his deliberations. "I shall be heartily glad to finish my studies in Italy, and return to France, where at least I shall be more in the way of hearing from home, and still more glad to place my foot once more in a land where genuine freedom is understood and enjoyed. We read at home of despotism, but it cannot be known in all its gall, till we feel and see its influence on all around us. . . . The result of all my observations comes to this one point, *that the soul of freedom is true religion exerting its moral power on an educated population.* The patriot of our country to act in character must promote *religion* and *education.* These two principles acting together are a salutary check upon each other. Religion (for it may exist exclusive of education) is in danger of degenerating into superstition, which is tyranny. . . . And education, without religion, is in danger of substituting the wild theories and speculations of the ingenious, for the simple common sense rules of Christianity, and so endangering those thousand secret moral restraints . . . which religion alone can bestow; which all human legislation with the concentrated wisdom of the ages can never supply. . . . There are two ways of governing mankind, viz., by *physical* and by *moral* power; the first is *despotic,* the last *republican.*" [26]

Leaving Florence, he went on to Bologna, Ferrara, then by boat down the Po. Sleeping in a cabin along with vermin and a box of powerful cheese, he passed to Venice within the domain of the despised Austria. Odors from the canals and almost daily thunderstorms made him ill. On the 4th day of July he was taken with a fit of homesickness. Over a cup of coffee with another American he reflected on the contrast between the pestilence, famine, and wars of Europe and the terrestrial paradise at home, the one bright spot on earth. He was anxious to be on his way.

But he could not hurry through Switzerland. Its scenery held him. From the summit of the Rigi he watched the sun rise one Sunday. His companions returned to sleep, but alone he watched the broadening light of day. Thousands have had their love of beauty stirred here, he mused, without one thought of the Being who created this beauty, of His goodness and power, of their duty to Him. "Shut out as I am by circumstances from the privileges of this day in public worship, I have yet on the top of this mountain a place of private worship such as I have not had for some time past. I am alone on the mountain with such a scene spread before me that I must adore, and weak, indeed, must be that faith, which, on this day, in such a scene, does not lift the heart from nature up to nature's God." [27] His experience with Catholicism had strengthened his faith in the uplift of beauty. At least in nature it could lead to the worship of God.

CHAPTER *xii*

Lafayette Liberal

Not a little blood had flowed under the bridges of the Seine since Morse had last been in Paris. A traitor King had been hurled from his throne, and a constitutional monarch put in his place. The old hero of two worlds, Lafayette, was now second in power only to the King. Morse was soon living near Lafayette; he took rooms with Greenough, who had just come to Paris to do a bust of the General.

From hilltop to hilltop by "telegraphic despatch,"[1] as Morse termed messages sent by the semaphore system, news of the fall of Warsaw had just reached Paris. Ever meddlesome Austria not only had quashed the Italian revolt but was helping to subdue the Poles. Still gallantly fighting for freedom from the Czar, the Poles begged France and Britain for aid. But it was not forthcoming. French ministers excused themselves by saying that Poland was boxed by the autocratic powers, Russia, Prussia, and Austria. French liberals were provoked, and Morse heard a mob hissing the Minister of Foreign Affairs.

Calling on Lafayette, Morse was shown into his bedroom. In dishabille the general ran forward, seized both his hands, warmly spoke his pleasure at seeing him back from Italy. Presently Morse asked if there was hope for Poland.

"Oh yes," Lafayette replied. "Their cause is not yet desperate; their army is safe; but the conduct of France, and more especially of England, has been most pusillanimous and culpable. Had the English government shown the least disposition to coalesce in vigor-

ous measures with France for the assistance of the Poles, they woul
now have achieved their independence."[1]

Already Louis Philippe's government was a disappointment t
Lafayette, who, it was being loudly whispered, had crowned th
new monarch by quieting the mob with his timely epigram: "Her
is the King we needed; this is the best of republics." The Gener
seemed to Morse as fresh in complexion and firm in step as whe
in America. He thought of the aged statesman much as he had c
Wilberforce; they were both political leaders who crowded thei
days with plans of benevolence.

Because the plight of the Poles rather than the Italians en
grossed Lafayette, it engrossed his American protégés as well. Con
tributions for the Polish cause were pouring in to the General fro
America. His political duties rendering it impossible for him to dis
burse them personally, without relinquishing responsibility h
turned them over to a committee of his American friends, amon
whom Cooper was a leader.

Cooper had just come from Rome and taken a house on the ru
Saint-Dominique. He usually rose at eight, read the papers, break
fasted at ten, wrote at his desk in his morning gown till one, wen
to the Louvre to banter with Morse at his painting, was home a
six to dine with his wife and children, and in the evening chatte
with Morse and Greenough. Wednesday evenings not only Mors
and Greenough were there, but also the American Polish Commit
tee; Lafayette himself opened the meetings with anecdotes of hi
glorious American days.

The committee wished to put its funds directly into the hand
of Poles who were trying to escape Russian vengeance by crossin
from Poland into Prussia. Young Samuel Gridley Howe was to b
the agent. Already one of the devotees of Lafayette – he had fol
lowed the General in the revolutionary march on the Hôtel de Vill
shouting: "*Vive Lafayette! Vive la Liberté!*" – and eager for dan
ger in the right cause, he gladly accepted the responsibility an
went to Prussia.

When Howe had given nearly all his funds to Poles in Germany
he was arrested in Berlin. Albert Brisbane, an American youth i
search of the formula for a perfect society (who, as Greenough tol
Morse, had gone to Berlin "to refit after the battering his meta

New York Public Library

LAFAYETTE

By Morse 1825

The study for the full-length portrait commissioned by the corporation of New York.

physics had received at your hands "[2]), learned of the arrest and, since there was no American minister in Berlin, notified Minister Rives in Paris. With Cooper, Morse called on Rives to appeal for prompt action. It was not until twenty days after a courier had been sent from Paris with documents attempting to prove that Howe's mission was not political that Morse heard that Howe was freed. Without a trial or the return of his passport he was escorted to the French border.

On the first anniversary of the Polish revolution the Polish refugees in Paris gathered in a hall decorated with the flags of Poland, France, and the United States. Members of the American and French Polish Committees were present, Morse among them. He looked on the melancholy company with emotion. Many were soldiers, " sunburnt victors of 20 battles "; many were nobles, men of science, literature, or art. Nearly all had left relatives behind to the mercy of the Russian oppressor. They were moody; only at brief moments were they caught up by a common enthusiasm. As they were discussing the startling arrest by the French government of M. Chodsko, one of the distinguished revolutionary leaders, " there was a stir towards the door," as Morse explained afterward, " and Gen. Lafayette in the dress of the Polish National Guard made his appearance leading in M. Chodsko also in full Polish uniform. The surprise was great and the greetings which succeeded were in the highest degree animating. Some time elapsed before the gratulations, and explanations were ended. Gen. Lafayette took the chair amidst acclamation; on his right hand sat M. Niemoiowski and on his left D.r Howe. M. Niemoiowski was the last President of the Polish Government at Warsaw, the chief of the nation in its late expiring effort, and here now he sat presiding over the little remnant of his countrymen."[3]

The friendships of the American Polish Committee remained long after the committee had disbanded. Morse was not drawn toward the ideas of Brisbane or Howe, however. He could not follow Howe into the Unitarian associations of Boston and eventually with his wife, Julia Ward Howe, into the extreme of abolitionism; nor could he follow Brisbane among those fiery protagonists of the model " phalanx " communities that were to introduce utopia to mid-century Americans. Morse's orthodox theology and aristocratic social tastes forbade his turning his abundant enthusiasm toward abolition and Fourierism. His sympathies were rather with Cooper, and with Lafayette himself.

Cooper and Morse were constantly together. Whether the Polish Committee was in session or not, Morse spent " almost every evening at his house in his fine family," and in the afternoons " as regularly as the day comes " [4] Cooper would be at the Louvre watching his friend at work copying. Cooper would perch himself astraddle one of the seats and direct the painter at his work: " Lay it on here Samuel," he would say, " more yellow – the nose is too short – the eye too small – damn it if I had been a painter what a picture I should have painted." [5] Visitors were so used to seeing Cooper hovering about, as he himself said, that his face was as well known as any Van Dyck on the walls. With Cooper assuring him that the idea of exhibiting his painting " must take," [5] Morse forgot the dismal tour of *Congress Hall*. All Americans knew about the Louvre; few could visit it; but would not many be willing to pay to see some fifty of the best works of the Louvre faithfully copied into one large canvas? Meanwhile he was learning fine distinctions in the styles of the masters.

In Cooper's " fine family " the eldest daughter, Susan, was aged nineteen. Perhaps Greenough was thinking of her when he told Morse he expected him to marry again soon. Cooper may have already rejected an offer from Morse when Greenough wrote Morse: " I congratulate you on your sound conscience with regard to the affair that you wot of. As for your remaining free, that's all very well to think during the interregnum, but a man without a true love is a ship without ballast, a one-tined fork, half a pair of scissors, an utter flash in the pan." [6] It is a tribute to both Morse and Cooper that the rejection did not disturb their friendship.[7]

Morse learned to know the Cooper who had a passion for " true Rhenish wine "; who was near ecstasy when he discovered the bewitching castle that he described in his new novel, *Heidenmauer;* who felt he was living most fully when, in quest of sensation after the accepted romantic manner, he took a candle, wandered down the corridors of an old convent on the Rhine, and finally locked himself in a room with " images of saints, crucifixes, a dim light, rattling windows, and solitude." [8] But it was another Cooper that Morse most admired, the Cooper of the Polish Committee, the Cooper who distrusted the Roman Church, the Cooper who disliked the hauteur of the English, the republican Cooper who sneered at titles of nobility and "other gewgaws that please the great babies of Europe," [4] the Cooper who supplied Lafayette with information to refute the charge that America was the most heavily taxed nation on earth, and who received thanks for it by being recognized in the Chamber of Deputies as a "well known writer of romance." [9] Cooper was Morse's political godfather.

One evening Morse found Mrs. Cooper and Susan at home weeping over an article about Cooper in a New York paper. It caused Morse no little pain that the very man who was scorned in Europe for his American faith should have cause to believe himself, as Morse put it, "traduced and misrepresented at home." [10] He could easily understand the course of Cooper's relation with his American public; he and Cooper both suffered from American preference for European artistry; they both, in spite of their dislike of stratified society, were accused of being aristocratic to their fingertips.

If Cooper was Morse's political godfather, Lafayette was his political father. In the atmosphere of French anticlericalism Morse became the nativist politician. Many influences were involved: the long line of his Protestant ancestors, the pope-fearing associations of his New England childhood, his father's lashing sermons on the Catholic Bavarian Illuminati, his increasing self-consciousness as an American and Protestant in Italy, and an American and liberal in France, and his loyalty to Lafayette. But Lafayette's influence was outstanding.

Soon after his return from Italy, Morse conversed at a party at Lafayette's with Odilon Barrot, who had conducted Charles X into exile; Salverte, the littérateur and deputy who was famed for his attacks on clericalism and the Jesuits; and the exiles from defeated Italy, the passionate patriot Princess Belgiojoso and General Sercognani, the revolutionary leader who had been so polite to him on his way from Rome. In his account of the party Morse added that he had written a "paper on the state of Italy before and since its repressed revolution." He may have derived information from the

Princess and Sercognani, or perhaps from the cardinals he had met in Rome, as well as from his own experience. "I obtained my information from the very best authority," he explained, "and can therefore vouch for the truth of its statements; I have loaned it to Gen. Lafayette who has already alluded to it in the Chamber of Deputies." [11]

Twelve days before Morse wrote this account of the party, Lafayette made a speech in the Chamber on conditions in Italy. Defending what previous French occupation had done for Italy, he said: "Behold the monuments we have left behind us, the roads we opened; the success with which we subdued the system of *brigandage,* which has since been resumed with more audacity than ever; and must, indeed, ever exist in a country governed by priests and by an aristocracy adverse to every liberal idea." [12] Perhaps Morse was referring to these words when he said Lafayette had alluded to his paper on Italy. Morse often quoted them. He translated the crucial passage more literally: "Robbery, in fact, will always subsist in a country governed by priests and aristocrats, enemies of every liberal sentiment." [13] *

It is probable that Morse's paper contained some such conclusion as that which he had written from Florence for the *Observer*. All his observation on the revolution in Italy, he had said, "comes to this one point, that *the soul of freedom is true religion exerting its moral power on an educated population.*" Being without moral education, religion in Italy was degenerating into "superstition, which is tyranny." [14]

What Lafayette thought when Morse presented his paper on Italy, and in his outspoken fashion talked about the dangers of religious "superstition," does not appear in the few letters that Morse wrote from Paris. Four years later, however, Morse wrote that Lafayette had warned him to the effect that "American liberty can be destroyed only by the Popish clergy." The warning was placed by the author of a book on its title page, and Morse, who was the editor of the book, commented: "It may not be amiss to state, that the declaration of Lafayette in the motto in question was repeated by him to more than one American. The very last interview which

* The Paris *Constitutionel,* Sept. 21, 1831, gave the words as "*Le brigandage, en effet, subsistera toujours dans un pays gouverné par des prêtres et des aristocrates, ennemis de toute idée généreuse.*"

had with Lafayette on the morning of my departure from Paris, full of his usual concern for America, he made use of the same warning; in a letter which I received from him a few days after at Havre, he alluded to the whole subject, with the hope expressed that I would make known the real state of things in Europe to my countrymen."[15] *

Lafayette was not a faithful Catholic. He was in fact hostile to Catholicism both as a state church and as a political force. He was one of the few liberals of 1830 who could remember the days when a corrupt and arrogant church had been a prop of the old regime and all children of Protestants were bastards because non-Catholic marriages were illegal. To be sure, he had opposed the clamor for a cult of reason to replace Christianity; he had only reluctantly condoned the attempt to establish a national church; yet, while his wife was a pious Catholic and he himself had been educated as a Catholic, it is doubtful if he ever received first communion and probable that he did not receive last rites.[16] His faith was a romantic liberalism in which a demand for religious liberty was a corollary of resistance to monopolies, tyrants, or privilege of any kind. He favored separation of church and state on the American model, and accordingly fought the political influence of the Roman Church. He used the phrase: "the intrigues of the apostolic and aristocratic party."[17] While Morse was still in Paris, however, Lafayette also said in the Chamber that if the English Trappists in France were properly understood, they would "not be more dangerous for you, than are the Jesuits of Georgetown to the United States."[18] Morse attempted to explain away the implications of this quotation with sophistry; he did not succeed. Moreover, the statement: "American liberty can be destroyed only by the Popish clergy" excluded the possibility that other known enemies of Lafayette's creed – monopoly, tyranny, or aristocracy – might be the first to destroy American liberty; this statement goes beyond anything that can now be said with certainty about Lafayette's convictions.

Morse's use of the Lafayette quotation produced no denials for many years. Lafayette himself had been dead two years when

* The letter, printed in full in Prime, pp. 234–5, is too general to throw light on the question at issue.

Morse first vouched for its authenticity; Cooper did not deny it; and none of the American friends of Lafayette challenged it, as far as Morse's correspondence shows. It was not until 1855, when anti-Catholicism as part of a nativist movement had captured a large share of the votes of the country, that a Catholic first declared the quotation a forgery by Morse, basing his claim on a quotation from a French book that Morse could not find had ever been published.[19] Discussion in the newspapers brought voluntary letters to Morse from Americans who stated that they had heard Lafayette utter similar warnings on his last visit to America. Some of these statements Morse presented to the public; yet, produced as they were from memory in a heated state of public opinion, they could not validate the quotation.

Whatever Lafayette said, it is certain that Morse's association with him and his circle strengthened the painter's conviction that the Roman Church as an organization was opposed to what he understood to be liberalism, both where the church and state were one, as in Italy, and where they had been forcibly separated, as in France.

"Now talking seriously and now letting ding anyhow,"[20] in Greenough's phrase, he and Morse, and sometimes Cooper too, passed gay hours in their rooms. They once mixed the serious and "ding anyhow" in a whimsical pledge that Greenough wrote on the title page of a pocket French-English dictionary: "In the year 1833 S.F.B. Morse and H. Greenough will be in the city of N. Y. decidedly the merriest and best fellows in the place – given Rue de Surrenne – No. 25 – 1831 – sitting in the dumps without any fire in November."[21]

His bust of Lafayette completed, Greenough returned to Florence and wrote Morse letters on his debts, his loves, and his delight in poetry. For all his verve, Greenough admired Morse's persistence and equanimity. To be seated in Morse's "snug little chamber" he was willing to risk even the cholera, the horror that was sweeping France for the first time in history, snatching five hundred lives a day in Paris alone. "Pardon, I pray you, any thing of levity which you may have been offended at in me," he pleaded when he heard

Morse was to return to America. " Believe me, it arose from my so rarely finding one to whom I could be natural, and give loose, without fear of good faith or good-nature ever failing." [22]

With Greenough gone, Morse was soon talking about his past to his new roommate, a young Georgian art student, Richard W. Habersham. He told him of his days in a London garret with Leslie, of his interest in the Roman Church in Italy, of his color theory. If the youth's memory many years later was correct, he told him as well of plans for the future.

Mondays, when the Louvre was closed, the roommates often went on excursions in the country. One Monday Morse went alone. Two or three times that week he was not at his accustomed place in the gallery. Habersham did not ask why, but on Saturday evening, as they sat by their reading lamps, Morse suddenly broke his silence. " The mails in our country are too slow," he said; " this French telegraph is better, and would do even better in our clear atmosphere than here, where half the time fogs obscure the skies." Habersham laughed at the revelation of Morse's new interest. Morse told him that at the invitation of a French official he had examined the French semaphore system and his imagination had been fired. The semaphore was better than the mail system, he told his young friend. " But this will not be fast enough. *The lightning would serve us better.*" [23] One wonders if Morse would have continued to mull over telegraphy if he had known that Claude Chappe, who introduced the semaphore telegraph into France, had been so beset by rivals that he had committed suicide some twenty years before.

In the presence of Cooper, Mrs. Cooper, Susan, and Habersham, in the comfortable home in the rue Saint-Dominique, Morse continued to indulge his fancy that an electric spark could be used for a telegraph. They all remembered it. Cooper thought it a high flight for a sober-minded artist to talk of sending messages on the wings of lightning and told his family so. But Morse went on talking about what Franklin and Roger Bacon had done in electricity; he chatted on to Habersham about the conveyance of sound under water, or over wires and keys, as in a piano, or by a series of cannon shots, as when the news of the opening of the Erie Canal was relayed along the canal. He went on musing as long as he was in

France, they remembered,[24] but Morse himself could never recall that he did more than study the French semaphore system.[25]

At last his eclectic painting was so nearly completed that he could finish it at home. As he put final daubs on his rendition of *Mona Lisa* he perhaps marveled at the elasticity that made Leonardo da Vinci both painter and inventor. He was nearly ill with intense application those last weeks, yet he could hardly bear the thought of the long voyage home without a chance to work on his painting again; he had no premonition that the trip was to lead him toward becoming the American Leonardo.

The incident that changed the direction of his life occurred because he met the right people on board ship. His friends had conspired to keep him from meeting those people. Cooper urged him to wait till spring and return to America with his family. Thomas Cole asked him to sail from Florence with him. Lafayette, hearing that he was to sail on the *Sully* on October 1, informed him that if he would wait till the 10th he would have the amiable company of Commodore Biddle and a party of young Philadelphians. But a young man whom Morse knew as Dr. Jackson, " son of Dr. Jackson of Boston " who had been " indefatigable day and night in studying cholera " [26] in Paris, had also arranged to sail on the *Sully*. Whether Morse's decision had anything to do with Jackson or not, he stood firm by his appointment to sail from Havre on October 1.

Just before leaving Paris he called on Lafayette to receive his parting injunction. How different the France of 1832 seen through Lafayette's eyes was from the France he had strained to see through the fog from the Dover cliffs nearly twenty years before! Then he had thought the French the enemies of all mankind! The " beast " Napoleon had at last given way to the heroic Lafayette. If the latest French revolution had been something of a riotous comedy, and if the worldly bourgeois had already forced Lafayette and his circle into the anti-administration party again, still the tricolor waved over France, and the General at seventy-three was almost as heroic a figure as when at twenty-five he had returned from his first American adventure. Lafayette's young friend was still an Anglophobe, but also now a mild Francophile, and most of all, through his European experience again, a thoroughly convinced Protestant and American. With confidence Lafayette charged his protégé to give

America a correct view of what had been happening in Europe, and bade him good-by.

Quitting Paris, he dashed to London, staying long enough to sit to Leslie for his painting of *Sterne Recovering His Manuscripts from the Curls of His Hostess*, and recrossed the Channel to sail from Havre on a momentous voyage.

CHAPTER *xiii*

Sully *Voyage*

OCTOBER 1 was the day appointed for sailing. The next day the *Sully* was still in the harbor, windbound, and the passengers were impatiently seeking congenial companions.

Advice about one of the company had just reached Morse from Cooper. "I am told you are likely to have Mr. Rives for a shipmate," the novelist had written. "Touch him up a little." [1]

As American Minister to France, Rives had aided in securing the release of Dr. Howe at the request of Morse and Cooper. Good disciple of Jefferson though Rives might be, he was not of the Cooper and Lafayette set. He had opposed Cooper's effort to prove by statistics that America's republican government cost its people less than Europe's monarchies.

"Yes," Morse found time to write Cooper from the *Sully*. "Mr. Rives and family, Mr. Fisher, Mr. Rogers, Mr. Palmer & family, and a full cabin beside accompany me. What shall I do with such an anti-statistical set?" [2]

In five days more the southwester blew itself out and the vessel moved from harbor.

The first days at sea passed like the days of many other voyages of the *Sully*. The foam crawled up her bow and tumbled back along her crusty sides; the wind whined in her rigging hour after hour; the passengers not leveled by seasickness paced the deck, dined, paced the deck again, and slept at night as serenely as when, a few months before, Emma Willard had written her famous poem on the *Sully*:

And calm and peaceful shall I sleep,
Rocked in the cradle of the deep.

The little packet trembled as usual to the task of plowing the sucking and spouting seas to an ever receding horizon.

Toward mid-ocean, however, when one passenger audaciously undertook to annihilate the horizon itself, this voyage was no longer like other voyages. The *Sully* became a historic ship.

By this time Morse was on good terms with the "anti-statistical set," perhaps only because he was not talking politics. At the close of one luncheon [3] the table talk fell upon the experiments of Ampère with the newly discovered electromagnet. One of the company – Morse remembered it was Mr. Fisher, a Philadelphia lawyer – asked if the flow of electricity was not retarded by the length of the wire.

No, answered Dr. Charles T. Jackson, the dark, round-faced young man of animated tongue, who had found laboratory studies more engrossing than his medical practice in Boston and was now returning from continuing these studies under the best teachers of Paris. No, said Jackson; electricity passes instantly over any known length of wire. Franklin had passed current through many miles, he recalled, but had observed no difference of time between the touch at one end and the spark at the other.*

"If this be so," said Morse, as he later remembered, "and the presence of electricity can be made visible in any desired part of the circuit, I see no reason why intelligence might not be instantaneously transmitted by electricity to any distance." [4] He spoke as if the idea had just occurred to him.[5]

No one noticed his remark. Jackson only observed that he might be correct and went on to describe how magnets could be used to produce sparks.

It was fortunate that no one then or at any time during the voyage told Morse his remark was not new. Probably no one present – not even Dr. Jackson – could have told him that the possibility of instantaneous communication by electricity had already been suggested by several European savants and more than one American. He was allowed to play with his plan in happy confidence that it was all his own. His belief that he had conceived an original idea

* Morse later doubted that Franklin ever performed such an experiment.

thrilled him. It held him sleepless through many nights, tossing in his bunk.

Morse was not ignorant of the basic principles of electricity nor of the comparatively new subject of electromagnetism. The lectures of Professors Day and Silliman at Yale had stimulated his curiosity about voltaic batteries. During his years as a neighbor of Professor Silliman he occasionally assisted him in his laboratory and may have learned of the recent discovery by Oersted and Schweigger of the magnetic effects of electric current on needles. In New York he had been an intimate of Dana, an enthusiast in electromagnetism. He had heard Dana give the first lectures in the United States on Sturgeon's discovery of the horseshoe-shaped electromagnet. For a scientist Morse had little knowledge of electricity; for a painter he had unusual knowledge of this strange " fluid " that was known only by a few in the laboratories and still performed no service for the common man.

He now had in mind the few facts requisite to working out a means of effecting the transmission of intelligence by electricity on paper. He knew that electricity could be passed through wires of considerable length without apparent diminution of the current, that a soft iron bar could be magnetized instantly by passing current through wires wound around it, and that sufficient mechanical force could be effected in the electromagnet to lift considerable weight. More essential to the progress of his idea than knowledge of science were the creative powers within him which could see relationships and possibilities, his manipulative skill, his persistence, and his organizing ability, all of which had been developed by his years of experiments with his pump, his marble-carving machine, his presidency of the academy, and his painting.

He began to consult his fellow passengers. He reported some of his plans to Dr. Jackson.[6] He told Rives of his progress, and when the Minister proposed obstacles he answered them with confidence. He was " most constant in pursuing " the subject of electrical communication, Mr. Fisher remembered, and " *alone* the one who seemed disposed to reduce it to a practical test." [7] " Difficulty after difficulty was suggested as obstacles," it seemed to the captain, William Pell, until " passing from its first crude state through different

MORSE SAYING GOOD–BY
TO THE CAPTAIN OF THE *SULLY*

When asked for a picture of the Sully, *of which none seem to exist, Morse referred to this imaginative engraving from Louis Figuier's* Les Merveilles de la Science (*Paris, 1867–9*).

grades of perfectionment," the idea was seemingly "matured to an available instrument."[5]

Following the precise habit he had developed in his European travels, Morse was entering a record of his thought in his notebook.[8] He knew that it would be desirable to record permanently the intelligence to be sent by electricity. It occurred to him that digits could be used for a code more easily than letters because there were fewer of them. In various combinations they could stand directly for words. He noted down a possible code in dots and dashes:

1 2 3 4 5 6 7 8 9 0

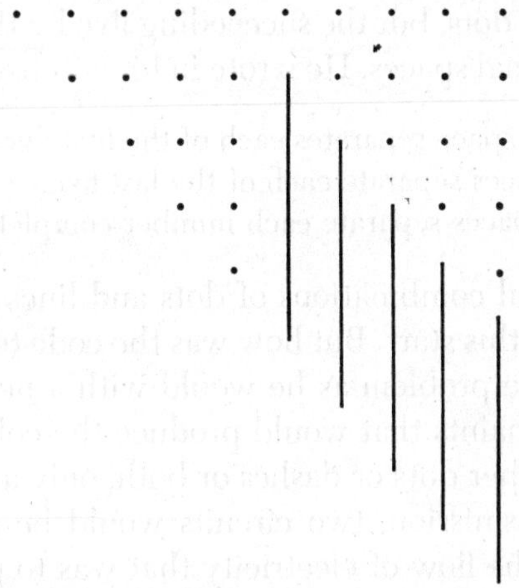

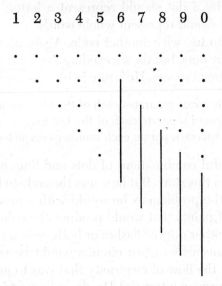

In his mind he formed a dictionary of words represented by various combinations of the digits. Then he tried his code in a message beginning:

He followed the message with its translation:

215	56	15
War	Holland	Belgium

One word that he had written out in the message was not in the code in dots and dashes at all. It was obviously irregular; it was a proper name, Cuvier. In the written message he had put the digits under instead of over it like the others, and had placed dots after each digit thus:

Cuvier
1.6.8.5.4.3.

No code of useful proportions could provide for all proper names; letters must somehow be sent as well as whole words. How he solved the problem at this time is not clear; perhaps he intended that each digit followed by a dot should represent a letter, while numbers without the dot would represent whole words.

He went on to toy with another code. Again he represented the first five digits by dots, but the succeeding five by the corresponding dots with additional spaces. He wrote in his notebook:

> A single space separates each of the first five figures.
> Two spaces separate each of the last five.
> Three spaces separate each number completed.

The most useful combinations of dots and lines or dots could be worked out from this start. But how was the code to be transmitted? He dealt with the problem as he would with a new sitter, seeking combinations of paints that would produce the color and value desired. To send either dots or dashes or both, only a single circuit or, for two-way transmission, two circuits would be necessary. What was to regulate the flow of electricity that was to produce the dots and dashes at proper intervals? He drew in a series of saw-tooth type, thus:

The teeth were to raise a lever which would close the circuit. Obviously he contemplated the use of only a single circuit.

The conducting wires were to go beneath the ground, for he drew in his notebook pictures of clay tubes of two different kinds, with wire running through them.

One method of marking the dots and dashes he talked over at length with Dr. Jackson. The electric spark thrown off when a circuit is broken could be used to form a mark on a chemically prepared moving paper. Evidently this drawing indicates his plan:

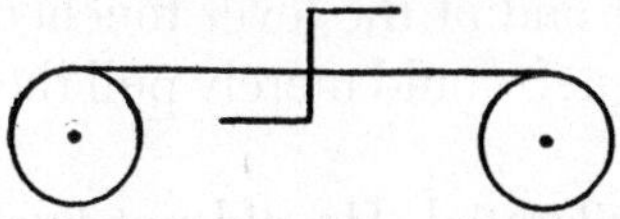

He asked the young doctor, as a chemist, what preparations on the paper would be affected by a spark in such a way as to leave a mark. Jackson suggested some preparations that would do and agreed to experiment with Morse on the subject when they had opportunity at home.[6]

Another mode of marking, however, found its way into his notebook. This one employed the new electromagnet to mark paper by a pencil or pen without any chemical preparations. While most of the rest of his notebook plans he eventually discarded, the drawing for this mode of recording can be recognized everywhere over the world today as the essential telegraph recording instrument. It was a drawing which he may have made with advice from those on board, but without the use of any reference books, without benefit of a magnet or levers or wires to experiment; he made the drawing believing that he was not only the first to attempt to use electromagnetism in transmitting intelligence, but also the first to use any kind of electricity at all. The essential idea sprang Minerva-like from his brain:

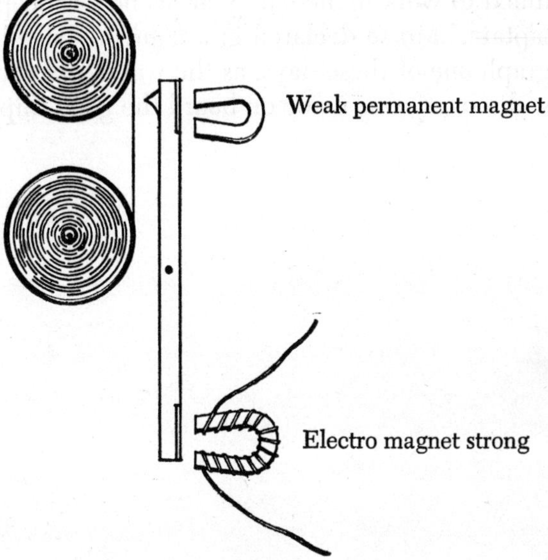

The strong magnet, when electrified, moved the lever, and a pencil attached to the other end of the lever touched a moving ribbon of paper. The weak magnet would merely pull the lever back into position.

The artist was exhilarated. He did not know enough about the abstract principles of electricity to realize the immense obstacles which lay between this simple mechanism and the effectual transmission of messages over long distances. If Dr. Jackson or any of the other passengers knew they did not tell him. He thought he had taken the word "telegraph" – then used to refer particularly to semaphore telegraphs – and placed it beside the word "electric" for the first time in history. Electric telegraph! He would startle the world with his invention.

He forgot how impatient he had been to work at his *Gallery of the Louvre;* he forgot the weighty charges Lafayette had laid upon him; he forgot the errors of the "anti-statistical set." And perhaps, too, he forgot his disappointment with his pump and his marble-carving machine; forgot that he had once written Lucretia: "Surely an inventor earns his money hard. It appears to me I wouldn't go through the vexations and delays, and disappointments I have gone through, for double what I expect to obtain from them." When the *Sully* reefed her sails in New York harbor on November 16, 1832, he was determined to work immediately at his new conception.

"Well, captain," Morse declared in a flourish, "should you hear of the telegraph one of these days, as the wonder of the world, remember the discovery was made on board the good ship *Sully*." [5]

CHAPTER *xiv*

Born Too Soon

THE WANDERER had hardly greeted his brothers on the Rector Street dock when he told them of his vision of wires strung around the world. As they walked over the familiar red brick sidewalks to Richard's and Sidney's house on East Broadway he drew his notebook from his pocket. With these little drawings, he exclaimed, he would astonish the world!

In a few days he was spilling drops of liquid metal on the drugget of sister-in-law Louisa's front parlor. No wonder she long remembered that he had cast the saw-tooth type for his telegraph at her fireplace.

Sidney, once partner in the pump enterprise, freely offered his advice on the undertaking, which this time he believed really would win a fortune for the Morses. Reminding Finley that wire was cheap, he urged twenty-four circuits, one for each letter of the alphabet. More complex though the mechanism for the single circuit might have to be, Finley fortunately recognized its paramount virtue as simplicity, and held to his original decision on the *Sully*.

Delight in astonishing his brothers wore off with the impact of the hard city, its dust, its pigs wallowing in the gutters, its unholy clamor for money and bigness, its prattle about taste when it did not care enough about art to have a single public gallery! His affairs prevented giving his telegraph scheme much time. His children were without a home, scattered. The academy was disgracefully heaping honors upon its own members. His unfinished painting of the Louvre demanded attention. After a few days, for three years the records are silent about his tinkering with type, winding magnets, or stringing wires about his brothers' house.

If Morse had been steadily occupied in painting, the conception of a telegraph might have flickered in his mind and vanished. Necessity was responsible just now for the arrested development of the invention. Nevertheless, "During this time," he wrote many years later, "I never lost faith in the practicability of the invention, nor abandoned the intention of testing it as soon as I could command the means."[1]

Poverty clamped down on his dreams once again. Even the resource of faith in his telegraph may have been denied him. If he had spoken to Cooper about instantaneous communication in Paris, and if he now had faith in his conception, it is strange that he did not write to him about it. If he still believed he would astonish the world, it is strange that he did not write of it to such intimate correspondents as Greenough and Bloodgood. It is strange that Dunlap did not enter a hint of it in his diary along with the multiplicity of Morsiana on the academy, painting, literature, and anti-popery.

When the story of his invention had become part of the great American legend, Morse once read in a New York paper an account of his years just after he stepped from the *Sully:* "His friends were grieved that so short a time had so changed a genial friend into a morose and unfeeling man. He was big with a great discovery that was to agitate and bless the world. He had no thought, no feeling, no faculty for anybody or anything, till the telegraph was a reality and beyond dispute put by the side of the great inventions of the age." Sardonically Morse wrote in the margin: "Rather exaggerated. Ha, ha."[2]

Actually during the five years before his telegraph came to demand his time he devoted himself to painting, guiding the academy, and righting the political decadence of New York. These years deserve more than being blurred into his telegraph career. They played their role in American history.

Morse knew very well that American artists who went abroad could not expect a happy homecoming in a still raw America; and he was no exception. He was by no means that "merriest fellow in the place" that he had hoped to be. "I believe you sometimes have a fit of the blues," he wrote Cooper; "it is singular if you do not with your temperament. I confess to many fits of this disagreeable disorder. . . . You will certainly have the blues when you first arrive, but the longer you stay abroad the more severe will be the disease." [3]

He had little income the first year after his return, perhaps no earned income. His funds were exhausted. The leisurely trip from Italy through Switzerland, the Rhine country, and Paris had been made possible only by payments from his brothers for his letters in the *Observer*. The offer of a room in his brothers' house was a relief.

To be sure, he had been honored with an appointment as professor of sculpture and painting in the new University of the City of New York. Its chancellor was his willful friend, Dr. Matthews. The university, just opened that fall, had no building; it and the National Academy were sharing Clinton Hall, the popular seat of learning built since Morse had gone to Europe by the Mercantile Library Association (of which he was, of course, a member) near City Hall Park. He took pride in his new title. He took care that it was given after his name in formal documents. The next year he declined to present a series of lectures for want of time to bring them up to the university standard. He refused to apply for the professorship in drawing at West Point, though assured he could have it for the asking and though it was remunerative enough to bring Leslie from London. But Morse's judgment was wiser than his old roommate's; Leslie and his English bride found West Point utterly uncongenial, and within a year, after a "collation" in his honor by the National Academy, they sailed back to more appreciative England. And Morse, though he may have had no university pupils his first year, in time became intimately associated with university life, to his great advantage. He did not yet know that his professorship would go down in history as the first professorship of fine arts in an American college, nor that some day he would be known in the university records as its "most famous professor." [4] In the meantime he was not expected to hold regular university classes at Clinton Hall or to receive payment except in fees from his students.

For months after his arrival in New York he worked over his *Gallery of the Louvre*, and then, when he at last placed it on exhibition in rooms over the Carvills' bookstore on Broadway at Pine, it was a failure. It was a good painting, yes. Cooper had expected much of it, and his New York friends liked it. "I can wish nothing better," Leslie told him, "than that you may be as successful in the exhibition of it as you have been in its execution." [5] Dunlap viewed the exhibit several times and wrote a flattering newspaper critique.[6] The painting continued some weeks in New York, bringing in a gross sum of fifteen dollars one week; then it was briefly shown in New Haven, after which it was withdrawn as a total failure, repeating the history of *Congress Hall.*

Morse had despaired of America when he first returned from Europe, a youth of twenty-four, and he was despairing now, a professor of forty-one. As before, he was not alone in his bitterness. After an absence from America of twenty-two years, Leslie had hoped in vain that he would find it more congenial to artists. Friends learned that Dunlap, enthusiastically venerated though he might be, was almost destitute; and they arranged a theater benefit for him, which Morse's scruples forbade his attending. Allston had returned to Boston long before, hailed everywhere as a great master, to find that necessity bore heavily upon him. For twenty years he labored on his great *Belshazzar's Feast,* protesting as he fumbled along: "I can paint under affliction, but to paint under debt!" [7]

Even in the comparatively cultured East Morse felt himself a pioneer. Cooper told him that they both had been born thirty years too soon. That was putting it too mildly for Morse. "I have been told several times since my return," he wrote Cooper, "that I was born one hundred years too soon for the arts in our country. I have replied that, if that be the case, I will try and make it but fifty. I am more and more persuaded that I have quite as much to do with the pen for the arts as the pencil, and if I can in my day so enlighten the public as to make the way easier for those that come after me, I don't know that I shall not have served the cause of fine arts as effectively as by painting pictures which might be appreciated one hundred years after I am gone." [3] If Morse could have foreseen that one hundred years after he returned to New York, one of the greatest museums of the world would hold a "one man show" of his paintings, he might never have gone on to sweat over wires and batteries.

"There is nothing new in New York," he wrote again to Cooper, ". . . except that they are not the same people that are driving after money, nor the same houses burnt, nor the same pigs at large in the street. . . . Come prepared to find many, very many things in taste and manners different from your own good taste and manners. Good taste and good manners would not be conspicuous if all around possessed the same manners."[8] Morse and Cooper were both Jacksonian Democrats. Like many other people of many ages they fought for common men, but did not care to be of them.

The first public use to which he now put his pen was another item in the struggle between the National Academy of Design and the American Academy. The National Academy had loyally re-elected him president during his three years' absence. Partly as a result of his absence, however, the academy had fallen upon dull days. Secretary Morton and Thomas Cole had written Morse that his presence was needed to restrain the academicians from electing an alarming number of themselves as officers. Morse himself had unwittingly contributed to the disorganization by accepting for the academy gifts which were sent to New York with enormous freight charges. Even so the National Academy was in better health than the American. Trumbull's kingdom would have crumbled when his old place on City Park was taken away from him if Dr. Hosack had not built him a new building. But Hosack now whispered to Morse that Trumbull would not insist on being president of a united academy, and again the movement for union was under way. Each academy appointed committees to devise terms. Although Trumbull forbade a meeting of the American directors, one was called.

Late on the night of the American directors' meeting representatives of both academies were to meet on the neutral ground of Dr. Hosack's home – the doctor was a patron of nearly every artist in the city – to hear the decision. Morse, Durand, Cummings, and Dunlap reported that the National Academy had accepted the terms. Then from the meeting of the American directors Hosack himself came in to report that Trumbull, forewarned of the terms, had denounced them at the opening of the meeting, and the directors had then ordered the speech to be printed and stopped further negotiations.

The National Academy council asked Morse to answer Trumbull's address. Nearly a month later Dunlap noted in his diary: "Morse's examination of Trumbulls address I read today. It exposes it fully – but who will read?" [9]

The American Academy was then moribund; and when its patron Dr. Hosack died, it died too. The National Academy bought its property at auction.

"Adversity and the necessity of common defence have united us," Morse reminded his academy in a presidential address. "We have now PROSPERITY to try us, which, all experience shows, requires more moral courage to bear than adversity." [10] There was still work to be done for the academy at Clinton Hall, and the members chose Morse to do it for many years to come.

Writing in behalf of his academy, or reviewing Cooper's *Bravo,*[11] or pleading Cooper's cause in the French finance controversy,[3] or protesting the appointment as Paris chargé d'affaires of an American whom he remembered as being unfriendly to Lafayette [12] – all this kind of writing yielded little or no income; much as it might aid the future of the arts and American institutions, it could not solve Morse's personal problem of poverty. After the discouragement of his *Gallery of the Louvre* exhibitions and perhaps just after another disappointing courtship, he wrote large-hearted DeWitt Bloodgood, in despair: "Hope may revive me in some shape at a future time. But *now* I have more mental suffering . . . than I have ever before suffered; I am in perfect health of body, and yet I would fain think that something in the physical system is wrong to produce such a settled conviction of hopelessness. No, Bloodgood, the causes are tangible, palpable; my profession is that of a *beggar,* it exists on *charity*. Have I not proof of it every day? . . . Well, you say, what do you mean to do? To live if I can; to last through life, to stifle all aspiring thought after an excellence in art which I see and feel I might attain, but which for 20 years has been within sight but never within my grasp. My life of poetry and romance is gone." [13]

Soon afterward a young art student who was about to sail for study in Europe met him for the first time. "So you want to be an artist?" Morse said to him. "You won't make your salt, you won't make your salt!" [14]

Morse had hoped to sell his *Gallery of the Louvre* to Cooper for some such sum as $2,500. The novelist returned to New York against

Morse's advice – he said New York was too commercial for comfortable living and recommended Philadelphia or Boston – and Morse found a house for him on Bleecker Street. There Morse and Dunlap often called and soon discovered that Cooper would not buy after all. When Morse received an offer from George Clark of Cooperstown, he wrote him: "I have lately changed my plans in relation to this picture and to my art generally, and consequently I am able to dispose of it at much less price. I have need of funds to prosecute my new plans." [15] Morse was too sensitive to tell Dunlap that he sold the painting to Clark for $1,200.

A month later Greenough sent Morse a letter from Italy which may explain his change in plans. "Your letter introducing Mr. Bryant was delivered to me here by that gentleman . . ." he wrote. "I am grieved to hear that you have decided on confining yourself to portrait." Morse had again decided to abandon painting in the manner of *Congress Hall* and *Gallery of the Louvre,* the historical style that he considered the highest branch of art. "As for your growing old," Greenough continued, "I must think that a little nervousness of yours for I am sure you can more safely count on 20 active years than most young men." [16]

During this year of despair, his forty-third year, Morse painted gratuitously, for engraving by Durand, a canvas which Bloodgood called "the *best thing you ever did,*" [17] and which according to the subject himself, William B. Sprague, the vigorous Albany cleric, received universal approbation. During this same year Dunlap published his indispensable history of American art, in which he said that Morse had improved while abroad "in every branch of painting, to a degree which has surprised me as much as it has given me pleasure." [18] And at this same time Allston wrote Dunlap: "I rejoice to hear your report of Morse's advance in his art. I know what *is in him,* perhaps, better than any one else. If he will only bring out all that is *there,* he will show powers that many now do not dream of." [19]

He did so, but not in painting, nor immediately in telegraphy.

CHAPTER *xv*

Native American

A NEW nativist flurry was sweeping the country. It first blew strong in 1834 with the burning of a convent in Charlestown, the early home of Morse. It died away a decade later with the Philadelphia riots in which the Morse telegraph was used by police for the first time. Its center was in New York, where Morse was one of its leaders.

The strength of nativism was in the cities of the North and East. One hundred thousand unmannerly foreigners landed there in the 1820's, and in the following decade five times as many. European officials were dumping paupers and criminals on America as a cheap way of getting rid of them; already most of the paupers supported by Eastern cities were aliens. Irish newcomers huddled in the cities where the packets disgorged them. Willing to work for any wages, under any conditions, many of them threatened the positions of established workers. In unionized shops "No Irish Need Apply" was a familiar sign. The older citizens refused to share with the recently naturalized the proud name American.

Moreover, many of these unkempt newcomers were members of a sect whose forms, secret orders, and political affiliations in autocratic Europe the ancestors of most Americans had learned to fear. Hooded figures walking in and out of convents disturbed the peace of mind of descendants of Englishmen, Scots, Scotch-Irish, Dutch, and Huguenots. As the number of immigrants grew the confidence of the Roman Church increased. When it began to object to public-school reading of versions of the Bible on which it had not placed its stamp of approval, Protestants muttered the names of Luther, Calvin, and Knox. A dispute between the trustees of a Philadelphia Catholic church and the local bishop dramatized the difference in organization between the Catholic and the evangelical Protestant sects. The trustees claimed as a democratic right the right to select their pastor and hold their church property in their own names. After a heated controversy extending over many years the local bishop reasserted his authority. To most Americans it seemed that a foreign hierarchy, stemming from Rome, had denied natural rights to Americans. Religious newspapers led the movement to arouse free America against the threat of Catholic domination. While Morse was imbibing the Continental skepticism of Lafayette, there came into being the first anti-popery society in America, the New York Protestant Association.

As the evangelical pulpit began to trumpet reform through the North, the immigrants held aloof. Reformers soon accused them of opposing temperance, women's rights, abolition, and all the other causes dear to the New England conscience. With rising bitterness the native-born called the newcomers paupers, job-stealers, anti-progressives, and papists.

Finally the older voters added the charge of misuse of political privilege. The naturalized immigrants – especially the Irish – were selling their ballots to the city bosses of both parties. There had always been wire-pulling among New York's respectable political leaders – the Clintons, Hones, Pauldings, Lawrences, and Clarks – but it had been done over dinner tables, politely. Now political life seemed to be about to leave the dining-room for the sewer, and nativists were provoked into entering politics in self-defense. They made their first attempt to save the city from mob rule with Morse as a candidate for mayor.

Man of faith, composer in paints and lightning, organizer of artists, Morse had now also become sensitive to what he conceived as the external needs of his city and nation. His political outlook was limited, but considering the range of his interests it is remarkable that he should be politically aware at all. The American Leonardo was approaching the full development of another of his many abilities.

Ever since leaving the stimulus of Lafayette and Cooper in Paris, he had been politically conscious. He had anxiously watched the South Carolina nullification movement led by Robert Y. Hayne and Calhoun. Its sudden end pleased him. Europeans judging us, he wrote Lafayette, "make no account of the great mass of the people, well instructed in their own and their neighbors' rights, that great mass taught by a religion of *persuasion* not of *force*."[1] He wrote freely to Lafayette because he had talked with him on his favorite theme of the need for a religion of persuasion at the base of free government. He believed the general understood him.

The year after his return from Europe, 1833, he sponsored the Italian patriot Piero Maroncelli, who had long been imprisoned in the Austrian fortress of Spielburg, in writing about the papal government as the worst in the world.

In the spring of 1834 he was inquiring into the political power of John England, Catholic Bishop of Charlestown, whom he had once painted.

And before the year was over, Dunlap suddenly discovered that the chief business of the president of the National Academy was repelling popery.

His first nativist work, *Foreign Conspiracy against the Liberties of the United States,* is said to have been a cause of the Charlestown fire.[2] Its hot protest against Catholic intrigue may have stirred the wrath of Lyman Beecher, and the doctor's Boston sermon, "The Devil and the Pope of Rome," in turn may have incited the hoodlums of the city to set fire to the convent. Thus Morse's denunciations of the secret designs of the Catholic hierarchy may have been one cause in burning a convent in the very town where his father had denounced the Bavarian Catholic Illuminati. Morse himself believed that the violence was provoked from within the convent. The lady superior had threatened that ten thousand Irishmen would tear down the houses of Charlestown if the convent property was injured. Her arrogance set the mob in motion, he thought. From a paper he clipped a letter pleading for meetings to honor the nuns of the desecrated convent and the "female innocence" for which they stood. Summarily dismissing the plea, he wrote in the margin: "Another Jesuit affair."[3]

Morse may have been an indirect force not only behind the

Charlestown tragedy but also behind the public career of that colorful flame of the nativist movement, Maria Monk. Morse believed in Maria. He did not know of her mother's testimony that at the age of seven she had rammed a slate pencil into her head and had thenceforth been given to telling "whoppers." Her exposé of the horrors of convent life in Montreal first appeared in "Parson" Brownlee's *American Protestant Vindicator,* the journal which had just printed serially Morse's *Foreign Conspiracy.* The wild tale had been prepared for publication by *Vindicator* associates, including Theodore Dwight, nephew of President Dwight of Yale and friend of Morse.[4] Entitled *The Awful Disclosures of Maria Monk,* it appeared in book form in January 1836. Five months later Morse sent a second edition to Cooper, saying that the new evidence included, especially the plan of the rooms of the convent, proved that Maria was not an impostor.[5] Even two months later his friend Cooper believed he still trusted Maria. He wrote Greenough his fear that "Morse is about to marry a certain Miss Monk, and when you see him I beg you will speak to him on the subject. I am afraid the issue of such a celibate as himself and a regular Monk, who, by the way, has also been a *nun,* might prove to be a progeny fit only for the choir of the Sistine Chapel."[6]

Anti-Catholics twice asked Morse to be among the proposed arbiters of the public dispute on whether Miss Monk had really come from the Montreal convent or, as many already suspected, from an asylum for prostitutes.[7] Investigators did visit the convent in Montreal. One of them, as described by a satirical poet, found in its supposedly horrible caverns not human bones but slimy snails and potatoes, and on leaving the convent assured the nuns:

> Ladies! . . . the trial's o'er!
> Virgins ye are, as pure as ever bore.[8]

It was only through court suits over the proceeds of her books, however, that the teller of "whoppers" was eventually declared a fraud before the law. After being arrested as a pickpocket some years later, she died in a home for prostitutes.

In his early faith in Miss Monk, Morse had such distinguished company as most of the Protestant editors of New York, and the Harper brothers, who surreptitiously issued the first edition of her book.[9] As late as his 1836 election campaign, when many New York and Montreal Protestants had already denounced her, he was still credulous of her tale.

Like most popular movements, nativism was accompanied by violence and fraud. Morse never knowingly abetted them. While lacking in judgment, he made a contribution – notably by his honesty – to the better aspect of nativism, the attempt to introduce order into violent and corrupt city politics.

As he stood for mayor in the heat of the Maria Monk controversy he had two effective campaign documents of his own. One was his pamphlet *Imminent Dangers,* an examination of the city's festering immigrant problem. It was first issued as a series of letters in his own pet paper, the *Journal of Commerce.* The other, *Foreign Conspiracy,* first appeared serially in 1834 in his brother's more or less Presbyterian weekly, the New York *Observer,* and soon after was reprinted in Congregational, Methodist, and Baptist journals, in the two leading nativist papers, the *Vindicator* and the *Downfall of Babylon,* and elsewhere.[10] It appeared in book form first in 1835; then when he was running for mayor, in its fourth edition, issued by Van Nostrand and Dwight, at that time sponsors of Maria Monk; sixteen years later in its seventh edition; and many years after his death in its last edition. His first major work, it was also his most widely read. It was a powerful document for nativism because it came from a respected name, and from a forceful if bombastic pen, well schooled in the overtones of the anti-papist vocabulary. Its warning was thundered from the nativist press, echoed from Protestant pulpits, and re-echoed from the daily press until it created a sensation.

The author was correctly introduced to his early readers as an eminent artist recently returned from Rome,[11] and "an American, who has resided for a long time in Italy and Austria,"[12] because it was during his grand tour that he had developed the emotional source for his nativist writing. He was able now to strengthen his factual sources by general reading, by the use of documents, and by observations of the role of immigrants in New York life.

Morse could easily oppose Catholicism on religious grounds

alone. He had firm faith in his own Calvinism. He practiced his devotions daily. He thought of his own triumphs and failures in religious terms. He constantly urged others to the faith. He had long-tried convictions on theology and ritual. Differing from the anti-Catholics of the *Vindicator* school, however, he prided himself on not meddling with the religious tenets of Catholics. He did not, like most nativists, either ridicule or reason against the confessional, transubstantiation, the celibacy of priests, and Mariolatry.

He argued rather against Roman Catholicism as a political system. Its head is an autocratic temporal ruler, he said. By nature it is opposed to religious and civil liberty. Despotic in its organization, it is anti-democratic and anti-republican, and cannot therefore coexist with American republicanism.[13] If an American Catholic believes in democracy, Morse argued, he does so in spite of his church. He did not use the often effective argument that wherever Catholicism is powerful enough it becomes a state church, an un-American institution, and that everywhere it has an undemocratic, simply because hierarchical, polity. Perhaps he did not do so because he recollected that his father's church in Charlestown had been tax-supported until not long before, that his father had favored introducing presbyteries over the self-governing congregations of New England, and that he himself was now attending Presbyterian services and had once even intended to become an Episcopal clergyman. He was only vaguely aware of the significance of church polity.[14] He viewed Catholicism as undemocratic primarily because its roots were in monarchical Europe.

At Vienna, the central city of Metternich's Holy Alliance, Friedrich von Schlegel, scholar and agent of the Austrian government, declared in a series of lectures in 1828 that monarchy and Catholicism were interdependent and both opposed to the republicanism of the United States. In this same Vienna only a year later, Morse noted, and under the patronage of the royal family, at the request of an American bishop the Leopold Foundation was organized to Catholicize America. The real purpose of the society, Morse believed, was not religious. He knew too well how Austria had aided the Pope in repressing the liberal Italian revolt, and how Austria had aided Russia in repressing free Poland. Was it not natural that

Austria should also be attempting to degrade the republic which was a constant inspiration to oppressed peoples in Europe? And what was more natural, since the United States was inaccessible to Austrian armies, than that Austria should attempt to harness America through its own state church? This was the purpose behind the organization of the Leopold Foundation, Morse charged, behind the enormous increase in the immigration of Catholics, and behind the corresponding increase in the arrogance of Catholics in America. This was the " foreign conspiracy " that he saw.

He deplored the growing clannishness of Catholics; he deplored the waves of rioting between foreign- and native-born in the great cities; he deplored the existence of the O'Connel Guards, a military order of Irish in New York, as a threat to civil order. Observing that priests were interfering with elections, he accused both major parties of propitiating them to obtain the votes of their flocks.

Jesuits are not fools, he insisted. They say they support democracy, as Judas Iscariot supported Christ. Their methods are like those of European despots who press democratic measures to the extreme on the principle that extremes meet. " Anarchy ensues; and then the mass of people, who are always lovers of order and quiet, unite at once in support of the strong arm of force for protection; and despotism, perhaps, in another, but *preconcerted* shape, resumes its iron reign. Italy and Germany are furnishing examples every day."[15]

Ignorant and clannish, Catholics remain under the control of their priests, he declared. The priests may deny it, but they cannot understand our institutions and the church does not want them to. Catholics clergymen must make their records public just as Protestants do. Immigration must be restricted. Naturalization must be made more difficult. Citizens! Do not vote for Catholics!

Morse's accusations, widely read, helped to crystallize the vague anti-Catholic and anti-immigration sentiment and thus widen the nativist appeal. In New York they gave impulse to concrete action against the " foreign " influence in local politics.

A controversy between Irishmen and members of the New York Protestant Association occasioned the first political organization of nativists and in the city. The purpose of the association and its journal, the *Vindicator,* was to attack popery in religious terms. Catholics were invited to attend an association meeting to discuss the compatibility of popery and civil liberty. According to the *Vindicator* [16] and two secular papers, the brash penny *Sun* and the staid sixpenny *Journal of Commerce,*[17] Irish visitors proved their negative view of the subject by breaking up the meeting with violence. Two weeks later, nativists organized several wards of the city for the spring elections of 1835. Democrats were frightened. Naturalized citizens were usually Democrats, but the party needed the support of natives as well. Would the nativist issue draw the few natives out of the party? Democrats accused the Whigs of having fostered nativism to split Democracy. In the voting, however, the "Americans" did not figure in the major battle between Whigs and Democrats. The Democratic mayor, Cornelius Lawrence, under a new charter the first mayor ever elected by popular vote in New York, was chosen for a second term.

The Democrats were right. Nativism was a natural ally of the Whigs, the descendants of the Federalists. The following summer a city-wide Native American Association was organized. While complaining especially against the Irish as a clan, it opposed the election to office of any foreign-born, or of any Catholic on the ground that he took an oath of allegiance to the Pope. Although the association included those who professed to remain in both the old political faiths, it was supported by a Whig paper, James Watson Webb's sixpenny *Morning Courier and Enquirer,* the very paper which, with Philip Hone's encouragement, had given the Whigs their name only the year before. And in the November elections for Congress Whigs supported the American candidate, winning together forty per cent of the city vote. The Democratic Party preserved its position only by reducing the number of "foreigners" in its list of nominations.

In the spring of 1836 nativists asked former Mayor Hone to be their candidate with the expectation that he would receive the official support of his own Whig Party as well. He declined, pleading not disagreement with their views but lack of time.[18] Turning from a Whig to a Democrat, the Americans asked Morse to run for mayor. He at first refused. But to a request to reconsider he replied publicly:

April 6, 1836

To Anson Willis, Esq., Chairman of the Committee of the Native American Democratic Association, and the Gentlemen of the Committee.

Gentlemen:

In compliance with your pressing solicitation urging me to reconsider the decision to which I came of declining my nomination . . . I have given the subject another consideration, and if my understanding of the general principles which govern the Native American Democratic Association be, in the opinion of the Association, correct, I shall in such case deem it a duty to make the sacrifice to which I am called, and place myself at its disposal.

I have conceived, that the Native American Democratic Association is composed, as its name imports, of real Democrats, of American Democrats in the genuine meaning of the term, consequently, that its members cordially recognize the great fundamental principle of the government that the People are, and ought to be supreme; that power emanates *legitimately* only from them. . . .

That therefore, and in accordance with the *established usage of democracy* to take the sense of the people on distinct questions of national policy, the question is now placed, not merely before the citizens of New York, but before the whole American people, *whether it is or is not expedient that the naturalization laws be so altered as to put a stop to evils under which our democratic institutions are suffering,* and to guard against *dangers* with which they are threatened from the influx of a vicious, ignorant foreign population; dangers enhanced by the combinations of these foreigners throughout the country; dangers still further enhanced by the present political movements of the civilized world, and the open as well as secret operations in the United States of Foreign Associations in Europe, and affiliated associations of foreigners throughout the country. That the Association has no intention of interfering with any right of naturalized citizens, but is determined to assert its own right in common with all Native Americans, of choosing whom they please, and consequently of choosing *native citizens only* to office in the various departments of government, and this they determine not merely from its necessity to the safety of the native citizen, but also to the safety and happiness of all naturalized citizens who are *truly* attached to American Democracy. That the members of the Association by thus associating together for the purposes stated, do not yield their opinion of men or measures, as now held by the two great political parties which divide the country, but belonging some to one, and some to the other of these parties, they agree to waive, for the present, their differences to accomplish a common object, and meet on common ground to resist an evil which threatens a common destruction.

If these views, gentlemen, which I entertain, are in accordance with those of the Association, I repeat that I am at its disposal for any situation in which they think I may promote the general good. . . .

Saml. F. B. Morse [19]

A mass meeting of Native Americans, convened to approve his nomination for the mayoralty, resolved that the selection of Morse was " a bright omen of success, the hand which hath stripped the vizor from the Jesuits, will be strong to punish the enemies of our country." [20] The Americans had nominated a college professor, president of a nationally known academy of art, familiar with the intellectual and literary society of the city. Their ideas, if not the political organization they represented, were accepted by the established citizens of New York.

As in November, the Whigs expected to support the major Native American candidates. Two days after the American nominations, however, the Whig *Morning Courier and Enquirer* leveled its leading editorial at Morse. While the Whigs, including Editor Webb, had intended to support Morse, " it was discovered that he is the friend and supporter of Martin Van Buren, and [was] cunningly imposed upon the honest members of the Party who nominated him, by a few designing *Van Buren men* who have acquired an influence in their Councils! " [19] When the Americans turned from Hone to the Democrat Morse they lost much of the support that they might have expected from their numerous Whig friends. Their choice of a devoted Democrat was scarcely politic.

Startled by their discovery, the Whigs made their own nomination for mayor only the day before the three-day balloting began. They chose Seth Geer, the contractor who had just finished the University Building on Washington Square, where Morse had already complained that his " room was a perfect shower bath " and his chimney would not draw.[21]

Morse was obdurate. He was too honest to renounce his Democratic faith for Whig votes. On the last day of the balloting he published a courageous letter:

New York, April 7, 1836

To William Frost, Esq.

Sir, I cheerfully comply with your request to state my views more explicitly on points connected with the next Presidential Election. You have been correctly informed in regard to my preference for Mr. Van Buren for the Presidency. I have always avowed this preference, but it is subordination to *principles* which are superior to any man, or set of men. To these principles I am committed, but not to Mr. Van Buren or any other man. I cannot consistently support any man for office who will not openly and fearlessly espouse the object, of the Native American Democratic Association. . . .

Saml. F. B. Morse.[22]

The American candidate received no publicity for other than his nativist views; and the Democratic papers, supporting the regular nominee, Lawrence, paid no attention to his candidacy. The vote for mayor, tabulated days later, stood:

Lawrence	regular Democrat	16,101
Geer	Whig	5,989
Alexander Ming	anti-monopoly Democrat	2,712
Morse	Native American	1,496[23]

Cooper found somewhat better figures for Morse than were published in the New York press. "What do you think of Morse for a Mayor?" he asked Greenough. "The fellow actually got 1,800 votes for that grave and masticating office, a short time since, and would have been elected had he got 18,000 more."[6]

Morse's nomination had at least been an inconvenience to the Whigs: Webb's *Courier and Enquirer* mourned that Geer could have been elected had he not been nominated so late. In the contest for control of the City Council, however, the Whigs and Americans effected a fusion and won. The Whigs could make no effective move without the Americans' support. The Americans had proved their political stamina by running an independent candidate for mayor for the first time. But they had not yet made the immigrant problem the major issue in local politics. And they could not push more stringent immigration laws through Congress, in spite of much support.

The brusque rejection by the voters of his city did not discourage Morse. During the following summer and fall he championed two victims of foreign and religious autocracy. One was a German liberal and Protestant haunted by fear of the Jesuits; the other was a youthful French priest.

Morse's interest in Clausing, the German liberal, received publicity in the press in July with stories of the youth's suicide in Battery Park. During the previous fall Clausing had heard of Morse as the author of *Foreign Conspiracy*. He appealed to the defender of liberty for aid in publishing his manuscript record of persecution by Metternich's agents. Morse was immediately on guard against imposture. He knew that the youth had only just come from study in Heidelberg and from exile in France. He knew that he was without recommendations. He knew that he used both the names of Lewis Clausing and Heninger. Nevertheless, Morse recommended him to a publisher.

Clausing found employment in the city as a printer for the *Allgemeine Zeitung*. But on November 23 he wrote Morse that he was uncomfortable because his paper had come under the influence of Dr. Julius, a Prussian agent who was persecuting him. " Dr. Julius, travelling through the U. S. A. under the pretext of visiting the different prisons, &c., has been and is still very busy in preparing mischief not only to these persons, whom the despotic of Europe fear to see, at some later period, again on the political theatre in that struggling part of the globe, but also against the institutions of this country, so far as his extensive connections permit him to effect it. A specimen of his machinations can be perceived in three numbers of the Allgemeine Zeitung, where it speaks of the German emigrants, and especially of the '*Native American Association Against Foreign Influence.*' I shall myself have to suffer by those restrictions, which may be found necessary to be laid upon the rights of immigrants, but I see, that some things must be done, to preserve the last asylum of liberty in this much oppressed world." Clausing asked Morse if he could procure him a position in the office of the *Observer* or some paper whose editors were " Protestants and *true* patriots."

Clausing was only imagining the designs of Jesuits against him, Morse thought. He urged him to remain in his position, and to divert his sensitive mind he gave him tickets to lectures at the university and to the current exhibition at the National Academy. Morse wished to "dissipate the idea that he could be essentially injured by any secret machinations against him." [24]

In June, wasted and melancholy, Clausing called on Morse in his rooms at the university. Morse tried to reason him out of his fears. It was no use. Clausing now handed the cautious professor several of his papers: his passports, diplomas, a few letters, and the manuscript description of his persecution by Jesuits and government agents that he had hoped to publish. Morse studied and preserved them.[25] They included a list from a German magazine of 136 political refugees proscribed by the authority of Metternich. No. 16 was Clausing. Morse could no longer doubt that in New York Jesuits and others, agents of the Holy Alliance, and "most perfect adepts in espionage," [26] were persecuting the German youth in his office, at his rooming-house, and at his boarding-house, as he claimed.

Five days later, at the very moment Morse was consulting Cooper on the case,[27] the harassed youth shot himself. To Morse it seemed that real persecution had created the lack of balance through which he saw plots in trivialities and finally release only in death. The papers of July 4 announced the suicide. With the help of Morse the *Journal of Commerce* published an elaborate story on this "genius in the bloom of life" who had died a victim of religious and political persecution. The article was noticed in the *Observer* and the leading nativist papers, the *Vindicator* and the *Downfall of Babylon;* [28] a Georgia paper reviewed it by twitting the "famous . . . 'Native-American' candidate for mayor of New-York" for being a "gull" not to see that Clausing was mad, and advised him to return to his art.[29] Morse wrote to several persons who knew Clausing, seeking advice on the publication of his manuscript. On the one hand a Harvard professor, the German liberal refugee Charles Beck, denied details of Clausing's record of his republican activity in Germany, and on the other hand Beck's refugee colleague at Harvard, the grammarian Charles Follen, supported Clausing's claims.[30]

Morse edited Clausing's manuscript as *The Proscribed German Student*. His introduction did not claim that the details of the script were true but that the main argument was valid. He was wise not to vouch for it all. When he soon entered vigorously into newspaper controversy on the authenticity of Clausing's tales, he was obliged to admit minor errors.[31]

Similar mystery surrounds the French Catholic priest who also put his manuscript in the hands of the sympathetic professor. Morse knew him personally but refused to give his name or describe his life in America since it would injure his Catholic relatives in southern France. In editing his autobiographical work, *Confessions of a French Catholic Priest,* Morse frankly attested that the author was what he professed to be. There was no other proof than his word.

Both the French priest and Clausing, while using colorful terms, wrote as if to please cautious nativists. But the *Confessions of a French Catholic Priest* described the dangers of celibacy, imprisonment of girls in nunneries, perversion of the confessional, and the good living of priests. With the publication of this intimate tale Morse could no longer stand before the public as a political anti-Catholic alone. He was attacking Catholic practices which had very little political implication.

Although Morse was coming closer to the evangelical Protestantism of his truculent father, he was still primarily concerned with Catholicism as he learned to see it through the eyes of French liberals. The leading exponent of the Protestant mission to convert Catholics, the *Vindicator,* never did accept him as an evangelical leader. Its offices and those of its sponsor, the New York Protestant Association, were at 142 Nassau Street, immediately above those of the *Observer.* Morse must have known its editors since he was often in the building; yet it was only with respect to the civil relations of Catholicism that Morse was mirrored in the *Vindicator* as a nativist leader. Long after the *Vindicator* had published his *Foreign Conspiracy,* it listed the bound edition as a valuable study of the civil effects of the papacy for those who were not interested in its religious effects. It noticed his interest in Clausing; it placed his name among the proposed arbiters of Maria Monk's veracity. But it held aloof from politics, noticing neither of his campaigns for the mayoralty.

The year following their first effort to elect Morse, New York nativists nominated Aaron Clark, long a Whig alderman, for mayor. The Whigs endorsed him. The fusion carried the city easily. It succeeded in instituting measures to restrict the landing of undesirable immigrants, which were sufficiently effective to call forth a bitter attack from Morse's idol, President Van Buren. But the victorious Whigs, soon forgetting the fusion, swallowed the nativists. It was not until 1841 that nativists again struck out for independent political action.

Morse had been occupied with telegraph improvement and a trip to Europe while riotous elections followed one another in New York, and still more immigrants were packed into the city slums. Suddenly Governor Seward awoke the New York nativists and with them Morse. In a brief paragraph of his annual message of 1840 Seward argued for schools in which children would be taught by those of their own language and faith. With this proposal as a starting-point, Catholics put forward their demand for public money for their own private schools. New York common schools were being largely run by state funds administered by a private, non-sectarian society, which under the influence of the Protestant majority allowed the reading of the King James Bible. Many Catholics felt obliged to keep their children from these schools. The inevitable " school question " was a major issue in the city election of the next year. Local Whigs followed Governor Seward in the chase for the " foreign " vote; they would no longer associate with the nativists. Having lost most of the Whig vote already, the Americans this time could afford to nominate a Democrat.

The nomination of Morse was adroitly contested. Six days before the election a meeting purporting to represent the city American Party was held at the North American Hotel. The meeting resolved that the party was controlled by a small group of sinister men. Instead of following constitutional procedure " nine men only [had] . . . resolved themselves into . . . [a] Nominating Committee and placed the name of Samuel F. B. Morse, before the people as the candidate." The assembled " deeply regret that so respectable a man as Samuel F. B. Morse should have suffered himself to be deluded by three or four men of little or no influence. . . . And while we disavow his nomination . . . we tender him our best exertions for a nomination to our legislature, or to Congress, in the fall, when his services can be much more advantageously made use of for the advancement of Native American principles." The announcement of this factional repudiation of Morse was published only the morning before the voting.[32]

Supporters of Morse had foreknowledge of the repudiation. They countered on the same day with identical notices in the Democratic *Evening Post* and the Whig *American:*

> AMERICANS BEWARE!
> NO WITHDRAWAL OF THE AMERICAN CANDIDATE!
> SAMUEL F. B. MORSE.
>
> A trick and falsehood of the opposition will appear stating that our candidate has withdrawn. This is *false* – a party trick. . . .[33]

The former three days' balloting had now been cut to one day. That day, April 13, was a bitter one for Morse. In the morning *Express* and in the evening *Commercial Advertiser* appeared a forged letter:

> *New York, April 12, 1841.*
>
> Dear Sir: Seeing the discord among the friends of the Native American Party, and that no good can result from their running a separate candidate at this election, I have come to this conclusion to withdraw as their candidate.
>
> *S. F. B. Morse*

In the confusion only about one hundred voters marked the name of Morse on their ballots. The one Democratic councilman who had supported the Catholic school demand was defeated. Otherwise the Democrats won.

The press denounced or commiserated with the unfortunate candidate according to party lines. William Cullen Bryant's Democratic *Evening Post* accused five or six Whigs within the American Party of having renounced the candidacy of Morse, " a most worthy and amiable man." When the Americans did not succumb to this trick, the *Post* went on, " the Whigs then resorted to a still baser fraud." Their forged letter " did the business effectively." [34] The Whig papers saw Morse with other eyes. To Horace Greeley's three-day-old New York *Tribune* Morse was trying to make capital for the Democrats by a " disreputable stratagem." [35] To the former nativist *Courier and Enquirer* Morse was " one of the most devoted and unscrupulous *Loco Focos* [i.e., Democrats] in the city." This man, it added, " who once wrote a book against the extension of the

Catholic Religion in the United States! is now operating with a party who to their disgrace be it said, strive to introduce religious strife into our political contests! "[36] One of the Whig papers that had published the forgery, Stone's *Commercial Advertiser*, apologized by admitting Morse to be every inch a gentleman: "He is more – being a man of genius and of talent – both of which have been highly cultivated. As a professor of the divine art of painting, his fame is well known – while the polished words of his writings proclaim his scholarship. He is withal a gentleman of great integrity and purity of character. But with all these high qualities of mind and education, his politics have in some way got *awry*, and we can't support him for the office of mayor. . . . But why should such a man desire to embark upon the tempestuous sea of politics at all? If he only knew how anxious we are to get *out*."[37]

Morse declined to drop out of politics to suit the Whigs. His leadership was again acknowledged by nativists the next month with his election as president of the new American Protestant Union. No decisive action had yet been taken on the school question in Albany. The new nativist group hoped to unite all who were opposed to the perversion of the common school fund to sectarian purposes.[38] The union prepared to watch the fall elections for the Assembly, where the issue would soon come to a vote again.

As the election approached, not one regular daily paper supported the Catholic request. Nativist sentiment boomed within both the old parties. Even the Democrats were forced to cut the number of their foreign-born and Catholic candidates. An Irish mass meeting denounced them for doing so. A few days later exasperated Catholics, under the leadership of the bumptious Bishop Hughes, held a momentous meeting in Carroll Hall, where they voted confidence in such of the Democratic candidates as promised support to their school program, and for the other officers drew up a Catholic slate.[39] This move, unprecedented for American Catholics, was immediately met by the Protestant Union. Since Catholics were frankly acting as a political unit, the Protestant Union determined to have a ticket of its own as well.

The sectarian tickets scarcely figured in the election. Catholic candidates received 2,200 votes; Protestant, 470; Whig and Democrat, about 15,000. Whig candidates, except those who contested with Democrats who had received Catholic support, were elected by about 290 votes.[40] Elsewhere in the state, where the school question was not the issue, Democrats won, gaining control of the state legislature.

A compromise school bill, bringing the New York City schools under secular state control, was soon passed by the legislature because the Democrats were anxious to recapture the Catholic vote. Nativists soon regained control of the situation, however. City Whigs repudiated Governor Seward for signing the bill. The nativist sympathizer Stone, editor of the *Commercial Advertiser,* was elected state superintendent of schools; a Protestant majority was elected to the newly formed city school board; and the King James Bible continued to be read in the schools. Soon the Democrats were punished by being split into native and foreign-born factions.

At last in 1844 nativists succeeded in carrying their own candidates to victory. They elected a mayor, James Harper, over both Democratic and Whig opposition. Elsewhere they had similar successes. And that fall they were influential in the nomination of Theodore Frelinghuysen, chancellor of New York University, as the candidate for the vice-presidency on the Whig ticket with Henry Clay.

The fire of nativism temporarily burned out with the Philadelphia riots of 1844. At about that time, when Morse was in Washington guiding the construction of his first telegraph line, he was mentioned again as a possible candidate and was appealed to as an arbiter in a dispute in the American Party Executive Committee.[41] But then he no longer figured as a political leader.

Like most nativists of the period, Morse was now giving what time he could spare to the missionary answer to the Catholic threat. In 1840 he assisted prominently in the formation of the Society for the Diffusion of Useful Knowledge in Italy, which later became the Christian Alliance. In an address in the Union Seminary Chapel on University Place, he stated that it was the purpose of the society to spread " intellectual and religious light " in a country which for centuries had been " the seat of more than Egyptian darkness and . . . pestilential vapours which pervade even our own borders." [42] Through correspondence in English and Italian Morse followed the progress of the society in Italy in opening schools and distributing copies of tracts, the Bible, and D'Aubigné's supernatural explanation of the Reformation. Similarly, as American troops poured into Mexico (he was an ardent expansionist), he encouraged the American Tract Society in proselytizing in their wake.[43] His interest in missions brought requests for contributions. A secretary of the American Protestant Society, an heir to the New York Protestant Association, wrote: "We are aware of your liberality toward the Tract Society, the Christian Alliance, &c. We would not unreasonably press this subject. . . . If you have not money at your convenience, a few shares of telegraph . . ."[44] Shortly after this appeal had come to him, the Christian Alliance operating in Italy, another society operating in France, and the American Protestant Society operating at home federated into the American and Foreign Christian Union, dedicated to fighting popery with missions. Morse supported the union, and eventually became one of its directors. By 1854 it employed one hundred and twenty missionaries and colporteurs.

Even before he died, the fickle public forgot Morse the nativist for Morse the telegrapher. He kept on insisting he was a nativist through new editions of his works and letters to newspapers, but the secular press had now come to the conclusion that to remind Americans that the Catholic Church was undemocratic was intolerant, and to curb immigration was obviously bad business for an expanding America.

CHAPTER *xvi*

Painting Bows to Telegraphy

IN THE FALL of 1835 Robert G. Rankin, a lawyer, was walking along the eastern side of Washington Square when he heard his name called. Turning round, he saw over a picket fence an outstretched arm. Immediately he recognized gray-haired Professor Morse standing in front of the Gothic building just being completed for New York University. Morse took Rankin by the arm.

"I wish you to go up into my sanctum and examine a piece of mechanism," the professor said, as Rankin remembered it, "which, if you may not believe in, *you*, at least, will not laugh at."

They climbed to the third story. Morse had just been given a new title, professor of the literature of the arts of design; he was giving regular lectures now, and was entitled to the free use of a large room. In addition, however, he was paying $325 a year for five more. One was the highest room in the northwest tower overlooking Washington Square; the others were directly below it.[1] Here Morse was painting, teaching, writing, sleeping, and eating. To conceal his poverty he was bringing groceries to his rooms after dark; he prepared his own food. A newspaper critique of his paintings soon referred to the "brilliant" productions of the "school of artists, which is congregated under the roof of New York University."[2] Among them were several of his own pupils, including the promising Daniel Huntington.* Their influence drew many well-

* Morse's pupils living in the University Building at this time, besides Huntington, a pupil from 1833 to 1835 or from 1835 to 1836, according to varying statements attributed to Huntington, included John William Wilgus, a pupil from 1833 to about 1836, and one Loomis; Cornelius Ver Brych, a pupil in 1835, lived on Sullivan Street just off the square. Previous pupils of Morse included Henry C. Pratt, from

known artists to the towered building, including Abbey, Homer, Johnson, and Inness, and eventually helped to bring the section about the square into notice as Greenwich Village, the home of Bohemian artists.

From the third-floor corridor three doors led into Morse's rooms. One was marked on a brass plate: " S. F. B. Morse." [3] Morse ushered Rankin inside. Here the visitor first noticed what looked like a melodeon. Then around the room he saw a clutter of tools, coils of wire, bottles of chemicals, and parts of galvanic batteries.

" Well, professor, what are you at now? " he exclaimed; " magnetism, electricity, music? "

" You see these coils? " the professor replied. " . . . Well, they contain a continuous uninterrupted line of wire. . . . You see that battery there? This the positive pole, that the negative pole, all connected with that keyboard." He launched into a description of his instruments.

As soon as he had moved into his new rooms Morse had begun experimenting with his telegraph again. He had probably been encouraged to do so by their convenience, and his hope of increased income from nativist writing.

Each key in the sending instrument, as Morse had now developed it, was a lever. The remote end of each lever, a conductor, stroked against a disk on which were raised metal conductors, differently spaced and elongated. The contact produced electrical impulses on a wire leading out from the disk, a long impulse for each contact with a long raised metal conductor, a short one for each short raised metal conductor, and none for each space between the raised parts. This pattern of electric impulses was recorded by an electromagnetic receiver at a distant point on the wire as a wavy line which could be read as dots, dashes, and spaces. The sending device was different from the metal type scheme he had proposed on the *Sully*. For recording, however, he used the same device and the same plan of a code of dots and dashes and a single circuit proposed on the *Sully*.

After Morse had made many explanations, his friend fell silent.

1818 through 1823, Frederick S. Agate in 1824, William Page in 1826, Robert Pratt in 1828, and one Field in 1824. Pupils about 1838 to 1840 were Richard William Hubbard, W. J. Bolton, and Robert Bogle. Pupils at unknown times were David Hunter Strother, C. U. C. Burton, and George Harvey.

"Well, professor," he at last expostulated, "you have a pretty play! theoretically true, but practically useful only as a mantel ornament." [4]

Other friends were invited to the laboratory that fall. Professor Henry B. Tappan relished hearing the words that he had given in at one end of the room read from a strip of paper in the instrument at the other end of the room. Daniel Huntington, Cooper, Commodore Shubrick, and Paul Cooper all saw Morse's instruments in operation.[5] It may have been then that Cooper told Morse that he made it a rule never to discourage a new invention no matter how absurd it seemed. He had known the painter-inventor Robert Fulton, he said, when few believed the steamboat would ever succeed, and had learned his lesson.[6]

In January 1836 Leonard D. Gale, professor of science, visited Morse's rooms and saw the telegraph in operation for the first time. From his detailed description,[7] from that of a university student a few months later,[3] and from Morse's recollection,[8] it is certain that Morse had now discarded the "melodeon" sender as too clumsy and returned to the portrule device which he had originally conceived on the *Sully*. The saw-tooth type he had made just after leaving the *Sully* he first put to use, as he said, "before the first of the year 1836." [9]

His printing instrument was still crude. He had nailed an old canvas-stretcher against the side of a common table. On a bar across the middle of the frame he had attached an electromagnet; it was connected by wire to the portrule. From the top of the frame he suspended a lever which at its center hung near the electromagnet and at its base held a pencil. As the magnet was electrified it pulled the lever toward it, moving the pencil. As the paper moved slowly, drawn by an old clock-work, the pencil marked on it a wavy line like a series of V's. Each lower point of the V could be read as a dot, the long intervals between these points as spaces; and when the electromagnet was electrified a little longer than for dots, the pencil marked a V with a wide base, thus:  which could be read as a dash.

He used canvas-stretchers and old clocks as construction materials, for he was poor. Toward the end of the year, when his rent rose to eighty dollars a room, he was obliged to exchange four of his rooms for a large one, which he partitioned and probably sublet to his pupils.[10] He could not afford good equipment or skilled labor. Even had he possessed funds, the New York shops did not carry electromagnets, batteries, or insulated wire. His instruments were necessarily still so crude that he did not wish to exhibit them, much as he believed in the ultimate practicability of the telegraph.[11]

He continued experimenting. In that same year he succeeded in recording by direct application of the electric current on chemically prepared paper, an experiment which he had discussed with Dr. Jackson on the *Sully*. But he was soon satisfied that his magnetic recording device was more efficient.[9]

Rumors of the mysteries practiced in the University Building were spreading. When at Clinton Hall the president walked among his National Academy students, pointing out defects in their drawing, they would lament behind his back that one so gifted should be spending his time in futile experiments. Even his friends whispered that a "miserable delusion" had seized him. Uptown on Washington Square the university students shook their heads ominously; one of the best artists in the country, they said, was sacrificing his genius to a chimera.[12]

They little understood that one of his purposes in telegraphy – perhaps his essential purpose – was to win an income that would permit him to paint as he chose. Though he spent long hours with wire and batteries, and though he ran for mayor that spring, his conception of his future was still bound up with his painting.

The first hint that Congress might deliver a frontal blow to his career as an artist came that summer. John Quincy Adams, thrown out of the presidency by the advent of the people's Jackson, was still a contentious member of the House. Congress had at last appointed a joint committee, of which Adams was one,[13] to secure four painters to complete the decoration of the interior of the rotunda, the great dome that stood in the center of the Capitol between the House and Senate Chambers. The committee chose seven artists to make trial sketches, and Morse was not even among the seven.

He tumbled into despair. As president of the National Academy

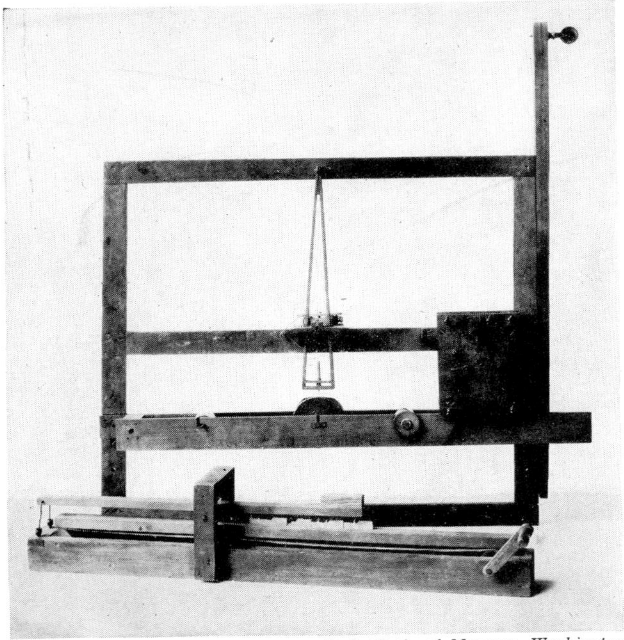

U. S. National Museum, Washington

MORSE'S 1837 TELEGRAPH INSTRUMENT

Above, *the original rectangular recorder used by Morse, with a canvas stretcher for frame and clockwork to move its ribbon.* Below, *the transmitter or portrule is a reproduction.*

Smithsonian Institution, Washington

FRANCIS O. J. SMITH

Drawing by Morse of his telegraph partner.

and as one who had particularly trained himself for historical painting, he had hoped for years that he would be chosen. The support his application had received had given him reason to hope. Allston, the great master, declining a commission himself, had recommended Vanderlyn, Sully, and Morse. The influential literary and art weekly, the New York *Mirror,* named him with Weir, Sully, Inman, and Neagle as the most worthy artists after Allston. And Messrs. Jarvis and Preston, the chairmen of the joint committee, were favorable toward him.[14]

With the news that the plan of sketches had been abandoned, however, agile hope rebounded. All summer and fall he was waiting, waiting for word from Washington. In February the blow fell when it was too late to go south as he had planned, to escape its full force. The committee passed over the president of the National Academy to choose three members, Inman, Chapman, and Weir; and to choose Vanderlyn,[15] the only one of the four who, like Morse, was trained as a historical painter.

As if the wound itself were not enough, Adams applied salt to it. Inman wrote a letter to President Van Buren resigning from his commission in favor of Morse; [16] editors who had originally expressed surprise that Morse had not been appointed now urged that he be asked to fill Inman's place.[17] Humiliating as it was to be considered as a substitute for Inman, again Morse's hope rose. But Van Buren did not accept Inman's resignation, and at the special plea of Adams, Inman took the commission after all.

Adams, Morse believed, was responsible for this humiliation. "He killed me as a painter, and he intended to do it," Morse wrote afterward; "but there was one more powerful than he who chose a path for me, which all the foresight of father's enemies, and my own if I had any, could not have foreseen. May God forgive him as I do." [18] Dr. Morse had had an agreeable acquaintance with President John Adams, but John Quincy Adams had turned from the ways of his father and become a Unitarian and anti-Federalist. Perhaps the younger Adams had never forgiven Finley for being a son of the champion of orthodoxy and Federalism.

According to a doubtful story, Adams had a particular cause of irritation. He had introduced a resolution in the House that foreign artists should be allowed to compete for the commissions, alleging that no American artist was competent. Naturally American artists were provoked, and a caustic reply appeared in the New York *Evening Post*. Adams believed that Morse, accustomed to defending the arts in the press, had written it. Actually Morse had not heard of it until James Fenimore Cooper read it to him — for Cooper had written it himself. So it may have been that Cooper was the incidental cause of Adams's enmity for Morse and his loss of the commission.[19] *

Morse brooded. Disappointments had come frequently in his painting in the last few years: his exhibition of the *Gallery of the Louvre* had failed; desperate attempts to find commissions had left him thinking bitterly that artists lived on charity; at more than forty years of age the parents of the woman he loved had rejected him because he did not have a steady income; and now a hope that had sustained him for more than ten years had collapsed. He threatened to resign his presidency and abandon art altogether.

Friends were alarmed at his loss of nerve. "To you our Academy owes its existence and present prosperity," wrote Thomas Cole, "and if, in after times, it should become a great institution, your name will always be coupled with its greatness. But, if you leave us, I very much fear that the fabric will crumble to pieces. You are the keystone of the arch." [20]

Allston assured his former pupil that he had worked conscientiously to secure him the commission. "But let not this disappointment cast you down, my friend," he wrote. "You have it still in your power to let the world know what you can do. Dismiss it, then, from your mind, and determine to paint all the better for it. God bless you! " [21]

But recovery seemed impossible. He fell ill. Even Cole and Allston could not rouse him from his gloom:

New York, March 20th 1837

Dear Cole,

Your letter found me of course in trouble on account of the decision at Washington. . . .

* Adams seems to have forgotten his grudge in time. Former President though he was, he said to the Reverend R. R. Gurley: "Fulton and Morse have done more by their discoveries, for their country and the human race, than any two hundred Presidents in succession could be expected to accomplish." Gurley to Morse, June 30, 1845, in *Journal of the Telegraph*, June 16, 1871.

I shall do nothing hastily, but I do not now see any way of avoiding exile from New York. My present thoughts are of course turned towards New Haven, and to the interests first of my children, then of myself.

I must leave a city, at least temporarily, in which during seven years of my life I have been compelled by circumstances to look for means, to live, not in the city but in the country. I make no charges against it collectively or individually, I have met with many kind friends here, and I have many connections which will be broken, not without pain especially among the artists, and with the Academy, which is my sorest trouble; but let it pass. I will hope the best for it, and that the experience of the advantages of union of feeling and a spirit of compromise, will prevent any of the evils which you seem to forebode from my resignation of the Presidency. It may indeed be all the better for the institution; I can see some advantages at least. It will have friends added to it from many who perhaps stand aloof from it on my account. . . .

Y.r friend as ever
Sam.l F. B. Morse [22]

A few days later Cummings and Morton came into his sick-chamber at the university with news. They and other artists and art patrons would form an association to raise by subscription, they said, $3,000 for him to paint any historical theme that he chose.

At this he roused from depression. I have never " read or known of such an act of professional generosity," he exclaimed.[23] Among those of his profession contributing were those who brought the message, Cummings and Morton, the three members of the academy who had been chosen by the congressional committee, Inman, Weir, and Chapman, two of his students, William Page and George Harvey, and such other veterans as Cole, Durand, Ingham, Sully, and Dunlap.[24]

His mind went promptly to the theme which he had planned to paint for the Capitol rotunda. He would paint the signing of the compact on the *Mayflower* after all! – though he was to be paid $3,000 instead of $10,000. He would make it just the same size, he told them, as if it were to be used in the rotunda.

Presently he had recovered from his illness, decided to continue as president of the academy, and set about planning a research excursion to Plymouth. He could still rise quickly from despair to exultation.

If the increasing demands of his telegraph venture had not now choked his ambition to paint the *Mayflower*, he would have done it well and his wound would have healed. Even if he had merely gone on painting portraits he might have recovered his poise, for he had the continued confidence of his associates in the academy and generous sympathy in letters which came, as he said, from " the most distinguished artists and amateurs of my own country and also in Europe." [25] But because the telegraph now demanded his devotion, his interest in painting faded and he remembered the rejection of his application for the painting at the Capitol as the end of his art career. Many years later he wrote of his once beloved mistress, painting: " I did not abandon her, she abandoned me." [26] Even a year after his rejection by Congress, however, he had written differently. Then he had said: " I wish as soon as practicable to relieve myself of the cares of the Telegraph, that I may have time to devote more strenuously than ever to the execution of my Picture, and the benefit of the Academy & the Arts." [27] Even then the painter was much alive. It was not Adams with his single blow but the telegraph with its sustained demands on his time and devotion that finally killed him as a painter.

CHAPTER *xvii*

Partners Gale, Vail, and "Fog" Smith

AT THE SAME time that the papers were reporting the commissions for the rotunda panels they were also making a startling announcement of a new French telegraph, the invention of Gonon and Servell. The news led Morse and his companions to believe that his invention had somehow been pirated.

To a prediction in the *Observer* that the new telegraph would send one hundred words from New York to New Orleans in half an hour, Morse's brother Sidney added a vague comment which was the first public notice of Morse's telegraph. "A Gentleman of our acquaintance," it read, suggested an electric telegraph several years ago. Obviously, it went on, intelligence could be transmitted over wires by using twenty-four wires to represent the letters of the alphabet.[1]

Sidney gave away none of his brother's secrets; indeed, his reference to twenty-four wires, though not so intended, seems to have set one rival on the wrong scent.

With the belief that another electric telegraph was winning attention, Morse was now anxious to bring his invention to completed form. Up to this time there is no record that he was receiving financial, mechanical, or scientific assistance in his experiments; but now he hastily secured assistance from Professor Gale, who before the summer was over was part owner in his telegraph rights.[2]

Leonard Gale was of a Massachusetts family, but unlike most of his telegraph associates he was so mild as to be unrecognizable as a New Englander. After winning a degree from the College of Physicians and Surgeons in New York in 1830, he taught there a year, and on the founding of the university, became a colleague of Morse's as professor of geology and mineralogy. Considering his important role in telegraph history, he achieved surprisingly little fame; this may be in part because he is the only one of the four partners who did not leave a mass of papers for the benefit of prying historians. Following him through the series of crises that compose the early history of the telegraph in America, one concludes, however, that he might have played a dramatic role had he not been too mild to do so.

From now on, it is difficult to distinguish between the contributions of Morse and his partners. According to their agreement, any telegraph inventions or improvements by any of them became their joint property. They always called their instruments the Morse telegraph; all legal proceedings were in Morse's name; because the original idea had been Morse's, Gale and the others who became partners permitted their contributions to be known as his. Even if Gale had considered himself wholly responsible for some device he would have hesitated to insist that it was his, for his claim might have had an adverse effect on the interests of the Morse telegraph in the public mind.

Like all inventions, Morse's telegraph was a social product. The ideas behind it had been developed through thousands of years of human history. The discoveries on which it directly depended had been made by others in the preceding century and in the preceding decade. The conversation of his companions on the *Sully* had brought the subject to Morse's mind. Still, the conception itself and its early mechanical form were his. The only other telegraph he knew was that of Gonon and Servell, which in fact was merely semaphoric. Morse had achieved much alone. He would today be remembered in the annals of invention if he had gone no further. But he achieved much more with the help of his partners.

It was early in their acquaintance, as Gale said, probably early in 1836, that they first discussed the principles of the relay.

Gale remembered that he told Morse of his belief that the telegraph would not operate even at a distance of twenty miles. But if a magnet at a slight distance will move a lever, Morse replied, then that lever could close and break a second circuit, and this one could close and break a third circuit, " and so on around the globe." [3]

It was in the spring of 1837 that Morse first showed him this plan of the relay in detail, Gale said, and it thereafter became part of his telegraph system.[4] There is some evidence to the contrary.[5] But the fact seems to be that Morse conceived of the relay independently, as Gale said, though because he had not tried his telegraph instruments with long enough wire to make relays useful, he did not yet know their value. By the time the first Morse line between cities was in operation, it had been learned that the relay principle was necessary only for office or local circuits.

Gale's chief service to Morse was to call his attention to the studies of Professor Joseph Henry of Princeton. More familiar than Morse with current scientific knowledge, Gale was moreover a friend of Henry's. But it is astonishing that Morse, interested in the telegraph over a period of several years, did not know that an article by Henry had appeared in Silliman's *Journal,* in January 1831, relating to the possibility of an electric telegraph. It is all the more remarkable because Morse had talked on telegraphy with Silliman since his *Sully* voyage.[6]

Before Morse had sailed on the *Sully,* Henry in Albany had rung a bell at a distance by electricity and realized the value of his experiment in sending intelligence. Whether Henry's simple device — an armature so placed as to strike a bell whenever it was attracted by an electromagnet (the principle of the common doorbell) — was a telegraph is debatable; Morse himself would not admit that Henry had devised a telegraph. But if sound telegraphs are to be considered as telegraphs — and they were the common forms at Morse's death — Henry's device *was* a telegraph: it conveyed intelligence to a distance by signals. Henry's device may therefore be called the first electromagnetic telegraph. But Henry was not interested in telegraphy as such; his concern was only with its theoretical possibility.

In his article in Silliman's *Journal* Henry pointed out that his proposals for increasing the intensity of electricity and the strength of electromagnets would be useful for such an electric telegraph as Peter Barlow, an Englishman, had proposed in 1824. When Morse finally read Henry's article, he was amazed that anyone had thought of an electric telegraph before him. And as a matter of fact, Henry was mistaken in inferring that it was Barlow who had first proposed a telegraph operated by galvanic electricity; Ampère had first proposed it. And as early as 1774 a frictional electric telegraph had been put in use in Geneva by Lesage. It may have been fortunate that Morse was ignorant that men of science had dabbled with telegraphy before him. If on the *Sully* he had known that Barlow had declared telegraphy impossible because of the diminution of the current over long distances, he might have abandoned telegraphy at once. His ignorance protected his faith, and it also led him to cling to claims of originality which accumulating evidence proved he could not defend.

Gale knew from Henry's article what Morse needed. He knew that the battery of one large cell which Morse was using generated a large quantity of electricity (current) rather than a great intensity of electricity (voltage). Intensity rather than quantity was needed for transmitting electricity to a distance, and it could be increased by using a battery of many cells rather than a single cell, and by increasing the turns of wire around an electromagnet.

Having made the changes Gale advised, Morse found that he could send a message through a hundred feet of wire, then through a thousand, and by November 1837 through ten miles of wire arranged on reels in Gale's university lecture room. Even he was astonished that his telegraph had succeeded so well!

Henry's information was indispensable. His suggestions were new. Whether from the bigness of his heart or otherwise, however, he made no attempt to use them for his profit. While Morse, as a man of his age, was concerned with the relation of knowledge to the needs of man, Henry was other-worldly; he allowed his Calvinism to keep him morbidly sensitive to criticism, fearful of wealth, and content with success in abstract science. Henry's great contribution to telegraphy was not his invention of the first electromagnetic telegraph – a fact which he did not even mention in public through years of court controversy on the invention of telegraphy; it was his discoveries in pure science, which through Gale and Morse became part of the Morse system.

News of still other telegraphs proposed in Europe spurred on the experiments in the University Building.

Partners Gale, Vail, and "Fog" Smith

During the summer of 1837 Morse visited Cape Cod, Plymouth, Boston, and the Antiquarian Society in Worcester, gathering historical data for his painting of the signing of the *Mayflower* compact. After his return on August 27, he wrote his first letter mentioning his telegraph that has been preserved. It was addressed to Catherine Pattison, a girl whom he admired with a protective affection and whom he occasionally visited at Troy. "My Telegraph, in all its essential parts," he stated, "is tested to my own satisfaction and that of the scientific gentlemen who have seen it; but the *machinery* (all which, from its peculiar character, I have been compelled to make myself,) is imperfect, and before it can be perfected I have reason to fear that other nations will take the hint and rob me of both the credit and the profit. There are indications of this in the foreign journals lately received."

From England, France, and Germany, he wrote the next day, he heard of systems which might compete with his own.[7] News of the telegraph of Charles Wheatstone and William Fothergill Cooke had reached America from England as early as May, through an article in the *Journal of the Franklin Institute*, though Morse may not have seen it. His growing fame forced him to read of what the rest of the world was doing in telegraphy. He probably knew also of Edward Davy, for in the same month of May Davy had protested against the granting of an English patent to Wheatstone on the ground that Wheatstone's telegraph was like his own at many points. He may also have known of the telegraph of Gauss and Weber, later developed by Steinheil, which was stirring Germany. Whatever he knew, it is improbable that he yet understood that Wheatstone's, Davy's, and Steinheil's alike were magnetic-needle teleghaphs, and not like his, electromagnetic. It is improbable because he wrote that there was nothing he heard from abroad that he had not already conceived in 1832.[8]

Hounded by the fear that all his work would come to nothing, and released from much of his painting by a financial panic, he moved quickly. On August 28 he wrote his Yale classmate Henry Ellsworth, commissioner of patents, for information on applications. On September 2 he met the person through whom he was to receive financial help. That day he operated a register with 1,700 feet of wire at the university in the presence of several professors.

By accident a young friend, Alfred Vail, wandered into the room. He watched a pencil in a wooden frame scratch a wavy line and was impressed.[9]

Alfred Vail had been a student at the university until the year before and knew Morse as one of its professors. For a time they happened to board at the same house. They seem to have attended the same church, the Mercer Street Presbyterian Church. They both belonged in the peculiar category of Democrats who were also nativists. Vail fell into the habit of dropping into Morse's room.

Uncertain of himself, Vail allowed his interests to pull him now one way and now another. From time to time he worked in his father's ironworks in Morristown, New Jersey; by 1835 he had developed his mechanical skills sufficiently to become a member of the Mechanics' Institute, of which Gale was then secretary. He was president of the Eucleian Society, one of the two literary cliques which set the tone for the university; and in that capacity he paid Morse sixty dollars for one of his paintings, probably the ludicrous *Allegorical Landscape Showing New York University*. By the time he graduated in 1836, however, Vail had decided to study for the ministry. Presently he was ill and discouraged (by habit he was sometimes morose); by the following spring he was asking for work in the Philadelphia mint, and by summer, at the age of twenty-nine, he was still looking for something to do.

After seeing Morse's telegraph in operation, Vail returned to his boarding-house, locked his door, threw himself on his bed, and gave himself to speculating on the mighty results that would follow from the introduction of the telegraph. Seizing an atlas, he traced the important lines that would cover the country.

In a few days he returned to the university and talked with Morse about the problem of distance. Gale remembered that it was Morse's explanation of the relay that decided Vail to interest himself in the invention, while Vail remembered that he realized that if one magnet would work at a distance of eight or ten miles, there was no problem. Vail had no funds of his own, but through his father and his brother George he offered to furnish Morse with money, materials, and labor. On September 23, 1837 he agreed to construct at his own expense a model of the telegraph to exhibit before Washington officials, and other models to aid in obtaining patents abroad.

Photograph from U. S. National Museum

ALFRED VAIL

Morse's telegraph partner for whom has been claimed the honor of devising the Morse Code.

In return he was to receive one fourth of all rights in the telegraph. Inventions of either party relating to the telegraph were to become the property of the whole enterprise.[10] Now Gale, Vail, and Morse were associated together. The partner who was to be equally energetic in promoting the telegraph and maligning Morse was as yet undiscovered.

Soon afterward Morse sent to Washington a preliminary request for a patent. It was in the form of a caveat – that is, a specification of what he intended to patent when it should be in completed form. Vail paid the thirty-dollar fee. On October 6 Commissioner of Patents Ellsworth acknowledged the receipt of the caveat in due order.

Increasing information about his telegraph was appearing in his brother's *Observer* and in the paper he had helped into being, the *Journal of Commerce,* but the caveat is his earliest detailed description of his telegraph. It specified six items of apparatus which he employed to transmit and record intelligence by electromagnetism. First, a system of signs by which words are represented by numbers, and numbers in turn by marks which may be dots, lines, or punctures, 1 by one mark, 2 by two similar marks, and so on to 9 by nine similar marks. Second, a set of saw-tooth type like those he had cast when he landed from the *Sully.* Third, a portrule to hold the type. Fourth, the pendulum recorder or register, marking on sheets of paper that could be bound into volumes for permanent record. Fifth, a word-number dictionary, alphabetically arranged. Sixth, a mode of laying insulated wires through the air on " pillars," or above the ground in tubes, or in the ground in tubes.[11]

No evidence survives that Morse hesitated to apply for letters patent. He had applied for them in the case of his other inventions. His agreements to share his rights with Gale and Vail would hardly have been of value without the assumption that a patent would be obtained. But later, probably when the Morse patent was the basis for a grasping monopoly over which he had no control, Morse felt the pressure of those who asked why he had patented his invention at all. " Personally at that time I was indifferent respecting the securing of letters patent," he recalled. " I was more solicitous that the invention would be a success and that I should be acknowledged as its inventor. It was urged upon me by my friends, to apply for letters patent and the argument that prevailed with me to apply for them, was that only by offering a pecuniary interest, could the funds necessary for bringing the invention into public use be obtained and this was true. Had I given it to the public, as some have since supposed to be the most magnanimous course, others would have claimed the invention, by some plausible modification; and reaped both the honor & the profit."[12] How much "honor & profit" were due the owner of a patent which depended on discoveries of countless men, living and dead, does not appear in Morse's statement; he passively accepted the basic conceptions of patent rights in his time. But he deserved some reward for employing the discoveries of others in a useful combination; and, like Fulton, he deserved it even more for his grilling in the campaign of promotion which followed.

In that same September of 1837 Morse also made his first effort to bring his invention to the attention of the government. In the preceding February the House of Representatives had asked Levi Woodbury, the Secretary of the Treasury in Van Buren's Cabinet, to report on the propriety of establishing a system of telegraphs for the United States. Woodbury issued a circular requesting information on possible telegraph methods.

On September 27 Morse replied, stressing as the advantages of his system the convenient size of its sending and receiving equipment, the ease of recording the intelligence transmitted, its secrecy, its independence of time of day or weather, and its low cost in comparison with semaphores. From the first he believed that his system should be owned by the government, preferably through the Post Office Department.[13]

Five specific proposals for telegraphs were submitted to Secretary Woodbury, four semaphoric and one electric, Morse's. It was not until the end of the year that Woodbury reported them to the House.

That same September Morse was stabbed in the back. One of the persons whom he had consulted on the *Sully* put himself forward as a part inventor of his telegraph.

Several times since their voyage together Morse had visited Jackson in Boston. He had given the doctor none of the details of his telegraph experiments.

Jackson's dagger came in the form of a letter. He had seen notices of "our" telegraph in the papers, he wrote, "but observe that my name is not connected with the discovery." He was sure it would succeed, Jackson went on, as there were many ways of sending intelligence to a distance, such as using twenty-four wires and twenty-four magnets. He intended soon to experiment with such methods, and in the meantime expected that Morse would correct the accounts of "our" telegraph to give him due credit.[14]

It was perhaps not wholly coincidence that the only feature of the telegraph which Jackson mentioned was also the only feature noted in the issue of the New York *Observer* that first told of Morse's telegraph. Unfortunately for Jackson and the *Observer,* Morse never contemplated the use of twenty-four wires. If Jackson had significantly aided Morse, it is inconceivable that he would not have known that Morse had always preferred a single circuit, and that his whole system of using numbers in a code depended upon it.

Morse replied temperately. "I . . . have always said, in giving any account of my telegraph, that it was on board the ship, during a scientific conversation with you, that I first conceived the thought of an Electric Telegraph. Is there really any more that you will claim, or that I could in truth and justice give? I have acknowledgments of similar kinds to make to Professor Silliman and Professor Gale, to the former of whom I am under the same obligations, in kind and degree, as to yourself, and to the latter, I am most of all indebted for substantial and effective aid in many of my experiments. If any one has a claim to be mutual inventors, on the score of aid by hints, it is Professor Gale, but he prefers no claim of the kind."

Dr. Jackson had suggested the train of thought which led Morse to make his initial remark on the *Sully* that intelligence might be sent by electricity. But the remark itself, as Morse now knew, was not original; and it produced no telegraph. While at Jackson's suggestion Morse agreed to try an experiment with him, not original, of marking with a spark on paper prepared with salts, each time Morse called on Jackson in Boston he found him "necessarily engaged" on other matters. Jackson's suggestion had never been tried; it had no connection with the telegraph as Morse had developed it.[15]

Dr. Jackson afterward expanded his claims. Whereas at first he called the telegraph " ours," by November he claimed to be the principal inventor, and soon afterward *the* inventor.[16] Expanding claims in themselves hint loudly of unsoundness. Moreover, Dr. Jackson claimed that the *Sully* passengers would testify on his behalf and they never did. In fact, they testified against him. Morse requested statements from Minister Rives, now Senator from Virginia, Captain Pell, Charles C. Palmer, and J. Francis Fisher. Palmer did not answer, but eventually his brother Frederick testified for Morse. The others, Rives, Pell, and Fisher, in reply credited the idea of the telegraph to Morse and stated that Morse seemed to them the only one on board with sufficient interest to be likely to develop the idea afterward.[17]

But even if the *Sully* passengers had not testified, Jackson's word could not stand against Morse's. Morse was by nature assertive, but also conscientious; Jackson on the other hand become known for dubious claims on his own behalf. Both after the discovery of the uses of ether in surgical anesthesia by Morton and after the discovery of guncotton by Schönbein, Jackson claimed the credit for himself. His claims were contested. His later years were spent in violent controversy, his mind eventually gave way, and he died seven years later in an insane hospital. He was brilliant, versatile, and ambitious, but unsound in his conception of himself.

Meanwhile everyone who had a grudge against Morse could twist Jackson's dagger in Morse's back.

During the fall of 1837 the three partners, Gale, Vail, and Morse, were occupied in preparing the telegraph to exhibit " its *powers* before the *powers that be.*"[18] They were confident of success in Washington if their instruments worked well.

At the university Gale and Morse were applying Henry's principles, using more and more turns on the magnets, and more and more cells in the batteries. The results were satisfactory – surprisingly so. And at the same time Morse was tediously compiling a number-word dictionary.

At the Speedwell Iron Works in Morristown, some twenty-five miles from New York, Vail was supervising the making of new instruments and new lengths of copper wire. Morse often stayed in Morristown himself, visiting the Vails. When he was not busy in the factory he painted portraits of the family and taught one of the women how to paint. When he fell ill with the bilious complaint that he had inherited from his father, Alfred's mother nursed him tenderly.

At the end of December, when he had hoped the instruments would be ready for Washington, they were still unfinished. On January 6, so a story goes, they were at last ready. Morse and Vail tested them and then called Judge Vail, Alfred's father. Hopefully he hastened from his house to the factory.

Alfred was ready at the portrule, Morse at the register. Alfred asked his father to select a message. The judge wrote on a slip of paper: "A patient waiter is no loser."

"If you can send this," he said, handing it to Alfred, "and Mr. Morse can read it at the other end, I shall be convinced."

Slowly the message was ticked off at the register; Morse translated it into numbers and finally into words. On reading his own words again, the judge went wild with enthusiasm. At once he wished to go to Washington to urge the telegraph upon Congress.[19] The Vails, too, were Van Buren men and had hope that Congress would listen.

A few days later, according to the Morristown *Jerseyman,* hundreds of Morristown citizens saw the telegraph operate for the first time:

PROFESSOR MORSE'S
ELECTROMAGNETIC TELEGRAPH

It is with some degree of pride, we confess, that it falls to our lot first to announce the complete success of this wonderful piece of mechanism, and that hundreds of our citizens were the first to witness its surprising results. . . . Others may have suggested the possibility of conveying intelligence by electricity, but this is the first instance of its actual transmission and permanent accord [record]. The fame of Professor Morse . . . must therefore rest on the same basis as that of Fulton. . . .

The communication which we saw made through a distance of two miles was the following sentence: "*Railroad cars just arrived, 345 passengers.*"

These words were put into numbers from the Dictionary; the numbers were set up in the Telegraph type in about the same time ordinarily occupied in setting up the same in a printing office. They were then all passed complete by the Portrule in about half a minute,* each stroke of the lever of the Portrule at one extremity marking on the Register at the other, a distance of two miles, instantaneously. We watched the spark at one end and the mark of the pencil at the other, and they were as simultaneous as if the lever itself had struck the mark. The marks or numbers were easily legible, and by means of the Dictionary were resolved again into words.[20]

A few days later the partners were preparing for their first invitation exhibition. When they had set up their instruments in Gale's geology room at the university the first trial failed. Alfred Vail wrote his brother George that the trials were not successful for several days, during " all which time Prof. M. was rather *unwell;* he is altogether inclined to operate in his own name, so much so that he has printed 500 blank invitations in his own name, at your expense." [21]

What was troubling Morse beyond the task of sending out five hundred invitations and the petty derangements of machinery appears in a letter that he wrote the same day to Catherine Pattison, his Troy correspondent. " The condition of an inventor is, indeed, not enviable," he wrote. " I know of but one condition that renders it in any degree tolerable, and that is the reflection that his fellowmen may be benefited by his discoveries. In the outset, if he has really made a *discovery,* which very word implies that it was before unknown to the world, he encounters the incredulity, the opposition, and even the sneers of many, who look upon him with a kind of pity, as a little beside himself if not quite mad. And, while maturing his invention, he has the comfort of reflection, in all the various discouragements he meets with from petty failures, that, should he by any means fail in the grand result, he subjects himself rather to the ridicule than the sympathy of his acquaintances, who will not be slow in attributing his failure to a want of that common sense in which, by implication, they so much abound, and which preserves them from the consequences of any such delusions.

" But you will, perhaps, think that there is an offset in the honors and emoluments that await the successful inventor, one who has

* *Jerseyman's* note: " The first stroke rang an alarm upon a bell, and put in motion the machinery to receive the intelligence."

National Academy of Design, New York

WILLIAM CULLEN BRYANT

By Morse 1825

Macbeth Gallery, New York

CHARLES T. JACKSON

By Morse

really demonstrated that he has made an important discovery. This is not so. Trials of another kind are ready for him after the appropriate difficulties of his task are over. Many stand ready to snatch the prize, or at least to claim a share, so soon as the success of an invention seems certain, and honor and profit alone remain to be obtained."[22]

As legend has it, Cummings, the treasurer of the National Academy, was in the fashionable throng which attended the exhibition at the university two days later, January 24. Because Cummings had just been given a military appointment, one of his friends proposed as a telegraph message a command on a scale grand enough to suit the occasion:

ATTENTION, THE UNIVERSE,
BY KINGDOMS, RIGHT WHEEL.

According to the story, it was sent in what soon became known as Morse code. A slip of paper with this message was presented many years later by the Cummings family to the National Museum, Washington. It has often been said to be the first message in Morse code that has been preserved.

Unfortunately, several facts prove that the message could not have been sent on January 24, 1838. It was in a form of the code not in use until later;[23] it was marked in quadruplicate, a practice which Morse wrote the following spring had just been worked out by Vail;[24] it could hardly have been sent in honor of a recent military appointment for Cummings, as the records of the New York state militia at Albany show that Cummings received no military appointments from the summer of 1836 to the spring of 1839.[25] In Cummings's own account of this message he makes no claim that it was sent on January 24, 1838, but merely that it was sent on his having just received military promotion.

What is certain about the exhibition in the university building is that the telegraph was now recording symbols which stood directly for letters. "Prof. Morse has recently improved on his mode of marking," the *Journal of Commerce* said, reporting on the exhibition, "by which he can dispense altogether with the Telegraphic Dictionary, using *letters* instead of *numbers,* and he can transmit 10 words per minute."[26] The Morse code had come into being.

	Early Morse (1838)	American Morse (1844)	International Morse
A	...	.—	.—
B	.. ..	—...	—...
C	. ..	.. .	—.—.
D	... .	—..	—..
E	.	.	.
F	. ...	.—.	..—.
G	.. .	——.	——.
H	....	....	....
I	.—	..	..
J	.. .	—.—.	.———
K	—.—	—.—	—.—
L	—	—	.—..
M	—..	——	——
N	—.	—.	—.
O	..	..	———
P	.....	.....	.——.
Q	..—.	..—.	——.—
R	..	. ..	.—.
S	.—.	...	...
T	——.	—	—
U	.——	..—	..—
V	—	...—	...—
W	..—	.——	.——
X	——	.—..	—..—
Y	.—	.. ..	—.——
Z	.—.	... .	——..

Though Morse scarcely realized it, little was new about his code. Two-element codes for sending intelligence may be traced back at least as far as the ancient Greek use of lighted torches, alternately obscured and exposed; two-element codes to represent alphabets, as far back as the 1605 alphabet of Francis Bacon; codes for use by electric telegraphs, as far back as the 1787 code of Lomond, a Frenchman. What is probably the first telegraph alphabet that has been preserved is that of Baron Schilling, a Russian, devised in 1832 (the year in which Morse conceived a number-word code, which he believed to be the first telegraph code); for use by a needle telegraph, Schilling's alphabet was composed of two elements, right or left turns of the needle. The first telegraph code composed of dots and dashes seems to have been Morse's 1832 number-word code, but the first telegraph alphabet composed of dots and dashes seems to have been conceived in 1836 by Steinheil in Germany. The Morse code (or, more accurately, the Morse alphabet) of 1838 was new only in its own combination of dots and dashes.

After careful study of the incidence of letters in ordinary usage and of errors in transmission, Morse and his associates varied the combination in 1844, and in that form, as "American Morse," the code has become standard for telegraphy in the United States and Canada. In altered form as " Continental " or " International Morse " it has become standard for national telegraphy outside of America and for international telegraphy everywhere.

Vail had been Morse's partner since September. Several changes – notably the introduction of the Morse code – had occurred in the telegraph system since then. What share of the system was Vail's?

In his *Sully* notebook Morse left a record that he intended to use dots, dashes, and spaces in a telegraph code. The symbols would stand for numbers and they in turn for words. His special notations on the proper name " Cuvier " may indicate that he thought of the necessity of having some numbers stand for letters rather than words: but even so there is no indication that this line of thought led him to use dots and dashes directly for letters. Furthermore, there is no evidence that in 1832 Morse interspersed the dashes among the dots; in his notebook he used them only after dots to indicate that the number intended was five digits higher; that is, he used a dash after one dot to indicate that the number was 6 instead of 1, a dash after two dots to indicate that the number was 7 instead of 2, and so on. It is clear that up to January 13, 1838, in Morristown, Morse and Vail generally used dots, dashes, and spaces for numbers and that by January 24 in New York they used them for letters; it is clear that up to January 13 they were not usually interspersing dashes among dots, but that by January 24 they were.

These facts would seem to indicate that either Morse or Vail or both might have conceived of the code some time during the eleven days' interval. It would not be likely, however, that one code would be thrown out and another conceived and introduced in a mere eleven days. And there are indications that Morse considered using an alphabet of letters rather than numbers before 1838. In his history of the telegraph published in 1845 Vail intimates that Morse had devised saw-tooth type for letters in 1832. Morse denied it, saying that it was not until 1835 that he first devised type for letters instead of numbers. "The date of the code complete," he wrote, "must therefore be put at 1835, and not 1832, although at the date of 1832 the principle of the code was *evolved*."[27] If so, he may have devised the alphabet long before he met Vail, and before Steinheil had developed his. Other later statements by Morse and two letters, one in January 1838 and the other soon afterward, indicate that Morse may have worked on the alphabet long before it actually came into use. Undated notes in Morse's hand show that at some period he occupied himself in calculating which letters were most frequently used and therefore should be represented by symbols that took the least time to transmit; and a note written in 1870 describes forms through which the alphabet passed before it was used in January 1838.[28] A letter that Vail wrote home from Washington in 1838 gives a strong indication that Morse at least shared largely in perfecting the alphabet. "The machine did not exhibit its working so successfully as at New York," Vail wrote on February 7, "for this reason – Prof. Morse had invented a new plan of an alphabet and has thrown aside the Dictionary."[29]

On the other hand, in his history of the telegraph Vail did not claim that the code was his – in fact, he attributed it to Morse[30] – even though he made other specific claims for himself in the book. Furthermore, his letters and diaries, examined by those who have attempted to establish a case for him, have yielded no claim for the code. To be sure, long after telegraphy had become a great industry, he was warned that if he claimed parts of the telegraph as his own, he would injure the interests of the patentees, including himself. But he did not accept such admonitions as valid. To one he replied that he considered that his contract with Morse did not forbid him to receive public recognition for what contributions he had made. "This agreement with Morse and others," he wrote, "does not refuse me the honor of being the inventor of anything I did invent. Else, why was it not so specified in the agreement? It supposed I might invent or make improvements in the Telegraph, but does not refuse me the honor, but denies me the exclusive right to ownership in such improvement; yet the agreement is such that it makes the invention a unity and the property of the patentees under Prof. Morse, so it was intended and such is its power."[31] Vail affirmed his right to speak. He did stake out several minor claims in his history of the telegraph; but his friends are unable to produce any written evidence that he himself proffered claims to the Morse code.

When Vail died his descendants proffered the claim for him. The only direct evidence they could produce was the statement of a man who was at the time a boy of fifteen.[32] Nevertheless, in 1911 a grandson inscribed on Vail's tombstone in a Morristown churchyard the words: "Inventor of the telegraphic dot and dash alphabet." Morse supporters demanded that the church remove the inscription in the interest of truth. Church officials refused, explaining that the tombstone was the property of the Vail family.[33] Perhaps it is just as well, for if all tombstone inscriptions were corrected in the interests of truth, how many would remain as they are?

Vail probably does deserve credit for several mechanical improvements which made the telegraph a success. When in 1844 a blunt stylus was substituted for the pencil or pen which Morse had used in his first recording devices, it was probably Vail who was responsible. In a memorandum attached to an original model Vail wrote: "I have not asserted publicly my right as first and sole inventor because I have wished to preserve the peaceful unity of the invention, and because I could not, according to my contract with Prof. Morse, have got a patent for it."[34] He claimed to have substituted for the portrule and metal type the key[35] by which millions of messages have been and are still being pounded out by Morse operators the world over.

Vail's contribution to the telegraph was real. He was undoubtedly a better mechanic than Morse. He was honest, if grudgingly so; he was loyal to his obligations. Morse paid him a mighty tribute when he said: "If Fulton had a Livingston to aid him in his early extremities, I had Vail's [*sic*] to aid me in mine." [36] Yet Vail seems to have thought that his greatest contribution of a direct kind was his substitution of the stylus for the pen or pen marker. "Even some little portions of the telegraph which I invented," he wrote, "have never been publicly awarded to me, viz.: the mode of recording by the indentation of paper." [36] Vail unquestionably deserves a place of honor in the history of the telegraph, but since he did not even meet Morse until the telegraph had already functioned, if imperfectly, his niche must be lower than Morse's.

Vail sometimes chafed against Morse's assertiveness and his inclination to be sick whenever there was work to do. As they were about to set out for Washington together, Vail wrote his brother George, "Prof. M. feels better and will perhaps be willing to have us share with him in the honors, etc." [37] Two days later George pleaded with Morse to "bear with A[lfred]. . . . He is easily vexed." But Vail never broke with Morse. During the very period when he was making his greatest contributions to the telegraph, on March 19, 1838, he wrote his partner effusively: "I feel, Professor Morse, that if I am ever worth anything it will be wholly attributable to your kindness."

On their way to Washington in February the two telegraphers stopped in Philadelphia to exhibit their instruments before a committee of the Franklin Institute. It was the first examination of the Morse telegraph by a scientific body. The report of the examiners was adopted by the institute's committee on science and art, and later submitted to Secretary of the Treasury Woodbury. It was a favorable report.

It might be difficult to settle among the different telegraphers the question of originality, it read. "The celebrated Gauss has a telegraph . . . in actual operation, for communicating signals between the University of Göttingen and his magnetic observatory in its vicinity. Mr. Wheatstone, of London, has been for some time also engaged in experiments on an electrical telegraph. But the plan of Professor Morse is, so far as the committee are informed, entirely different from any of those devised by other individuals, all of which act by giving different *directions* to a magnetic needle." [38]

Partners Gale, Vail, and "Fog" Smith

With the hearty encouragement of the institute Morse and Vail went on to Washington. Since September 2 they had exhibited what Durand called their "thunder and lightning 'jim crack'"[39] to increasingly important audiences: first to occasional visitors in the university; then to large gatherings of the people of Morristown, Newark, and New York; then to the Franklin Institute savants; and now to a committee of the House of Representatives. How different from the days when Morse had carried his food to his room at night and felt the raucous gibes of his students! Now he thought he was on his way to a congressional appropriation for a hundred-mile telegraph line.

The House Committee on Commerce invited Morse to exhibit his telegraph in its own rooms in the Capitol. This committee, of which the shrewd Representative Smith of Maine was chairman, was the body to which the Treasury report on proposed government telegraphs, Morse's letter included, had been referred. No action had yet been taken.

Everyone seemed to be coming to see the telegraph in the Committee on Commerce rooms – congressmen, foreign ministers, men of science.

"The world is coming to an end," Vail heard some say.

"Where will improvement and discoveries stop?" others asked, bewildered by the new railroads, and now by lightning to carry words.

"Time and space are now annihilated," was the far-seeing conclusion of one visitor.[40] His comment was to be on the lips of millions.

When Senator Calhoun had seen the wonder he sent in a dozen other senators to see it too. Commissioner of Patents Ellsworth thought Congress would pass an appropriation for it; it seemed to him that nothing in Washington had ever produced such a noise. Vail heard so much wonder expressed that he knew his folks at home would not believe him when he told them about it.

Morse was pleased but cautious. Perhaps he had observed such congressmen as Millard Fillmore come in to see the telegraph and leave unimpressed. And certainly he remembered that he had been to Washington before, seeking cash, and had come away empty-handed. He had spent many days painting in the Capitol, but his *Congress Hall* had been a failure. His attempt to win an appointment for Mexico had been abortive. Would the inventor fail as had the painter and office-seeker?

To Chairman Smith of the Committee on Commerce Morse proposed a plan for government control over the telegraph which indicates his sense of social responsibility as well as his desire for profit and honor. Unfortunately, he did not realize what he was doing when he proposed the plan to Smith, a cool young man of thirty-two, son of a tavern-proprietor. It was clear to Morse now that the telegraph would become an instrument either for good or for evil, depending on its control. To prevent it from falling into the hands of speculators he proposed that the government obtain title to it, under proper restrictions let out franchises for private lines, and build lines for its own use as a check on the private lines.[41]

But what Morse feared came true. The telegraph fell into the hands of speculators, among them the very man to whom he expressed his fears, Congressman Smith. Many persons and situations might be blamed: the preoccupations of a money- and land-mad people, inexperienced in the social control of invention; congressional blindness to the meaning of the first use of electricity for commercial purposes; Morse's poverty and hence his inability to hold out until Congress could understand the value of his patent. As much responsibility for both the subsequent swift unreeling of telegraph wires across the continent and their tarnished condition rests with Smith as with any man.

Soon after writing Smith, Morse was invited to exhibit his telegraph before the President and Cabinet. On February 21 the Native American who had lost votes because he admitted that he was also a "Van Buren man" exhibited his "thunder and lightning 'jim crack'" before Mr. Van Buren, Secretary of the Treasury Levi Woodbury, Secretary of War Joel R. Poinsett, Postmaster General Amos Kendall (who was later to become an intimate of Morse), and other Cabinet members.

Within a few days Morse had discovered that Chairman Smith of the Committee on Commerce believed that his telegraph had vast possibilities and wished to become a partner in the enterprise.

Francis Ormand Jonathan Smith (whose initials his associates later pointedly changed from F. O. J. to "Fog") had crossed Morse's path before. Like Morse he was a New Englander, born in Brentwood, New Hampshire, in 1806. Just as Morse had attended Phillips Andover, Smith had attended Phillips Exeter. By 1822 he was studying law in Portsmouth under Ichabod Bartlett. Morse knew Mr. Bartlett; he had painted him either in 1817 or 1824 or both; he knew his brother Levi Bartlett, a Boston merchant who had married a sister of Mr. Walker, Lucretia's father. Both Morse and Smith knew Levi Woodbury as a Portsmouth lawyer; as Secretary of the Treasury, he had the warm opposition of Smith.

In 1823 Smith's father, Jonathan, moved to Woodfords, near Portland, Maine, to run a tavern. Then or soon afterward Smith followed his father, arriving in Maine, as a political associate later said, without five dollars or five grains of integrity, and continued his law study. At the age of nineteen Smith was admitted to the bar. Soon afterward he wrote a pamphlet against lotteries, praising New York State for having recently adopted rigid laws.[42] In the light of future events Smith's scruples on lotteries seem to have been blatant hypocrisy.

By 1828 Smith had acquired his first real estate in Portland and published his intention to marry Junia Bartlett, of Kingston, New Hampshire, by marriage a second cousin of Lucretia Walker, Morse's wife. In 1831, at twenty-four, Smith won a seat in the Maine legislature; within two years he was president of the Maine Senate and a congressman-elect. When Smith first went to Washington, a former senator from Maine warned Vice President Van Buren: " Smith is certainly a young man of considerable talent, tact, cunning, management and industry, great perseverance, and . . . vindictive." [43] His early intimates in Washington were Franklin Pierce, the future President, and Benjamin B. French, a poet with a lust for life, clerk of the House, and uncle of Daniel Chester French. When French's brother considered going into business with Smith, French confessed to knowing little of Smith's affairs. But he assured his brother that Smith himself " is without exception, the most driving, persevering, energetic man I ever knew. . . . You will always find Mr. Smith a warm hearted friend. When he *takes,* he makes no half way business of it, & *vice versa* – he is, what Dr. Johnson would call ' a good hater.' " [44]

If when the cousins by marriage first met in Washington Morse had been reading the papers, he would have known that Smith was under investigation by a committee of the Massachusetts legislature for shady banking practices.[45] If Morse had taken the trouble to inquire in Maine, he would have found that Smith was building a grotesque mansion in Westbrook, on the outskirts of Portland, with a dome, an ostentatious library, separate servants' quarters, and fountains in the garden; he would have heard that Smith was driving with his Junia to and from Portland in an imported stanhope, with a black coachman (who, Smith told his constituents, had been a servant of John Quincy Adams at the Court of St. James's) seated on a hammercloth fringed with silver and gold.[46]

Morse needed an assistant in promoting the telegraph. He needed a man of wealth. He needed one who could pilot him through Washington's intrigues. But he was a good judge neither of business affairs nor of men. He did not know or he did not care that Smith was a mushroom aristocrat, suspect as a banker and politician. Smith's chatter about common friends and relatives in New Hampshire, his polish and ready talk, and his enthusiasm for the telegraph somehow convinced Morse that here was the needed assistant; Vail and Gale, too, were convinced.

From the first, Smith's relation to the telegraph was unsavory. Morse and Smith knew very well that it would be offensive to public morality for him as a partner of the telegraph to sponsor the telegraph bill. Morse himself testified in a telegraph suit long afterward that Smith became so convinced of the utility of the telegraph that he "abandoned his seat in Congress, and took an interest in it."[47] A later telegraph associate of Morse expanded Morse's statement into the story that Morse insisted that Smith resign.[48] The agreement between Smith and Morse contains no such stipulation. It was signed in March, and on April 6 Smith reported to the House, with understandable enthusiasm, a bill to appropriate thirty thousand dollars to build fifty miles of telegraph.[49] Only on April 14 did Congress vote leave to Smith to absent himself from the House from the first of May to the end of the session.[50] But Smith did not resign; in fact he merely vacated his public trust, leaving the citizens of his district virtually unrepresented for several months. Late in the year he returned to Washington to finish out his term, again using his position as a public officer to further the telegraph of which he was part owner.

Smith's report of April 6 to Congress contained two deceptions. It stated that Morse had already obtained a telegraph patent, a false statement possessing the advantage of giving the invention the aura of governmental approval. It also quoted a letter of Morse's, dated February 15, 1838, in which Morse stated that the rights were owned jointly by himself, Gale, and the Vails. No one else was mentioned. That the report should name some of the owners without adding that its author was himself a part owner was rank deception.

Smith understood his false position. Euphemistically he called his interest in the telegraph " contingent." As late as January 1839 he was still insisting that his ownership should not yet be recorded at the Patent Office.[51]

Whether or not Morse willingly acquiesced in Smith's betrayal of public trust, he allowed Smith to make the report, to return to Congress to finish out his term, and to conceal his connection with the telegraph. Morse's concurrence in Smith's enormities can only be described as a moral lapse. It is the more unfortunate as it occurred just at the time when awareness of Smith's pollution might have kept Morse from introducing into telegraph history one of its most sinister figures.

The four partners fixed their shares in ownership by formal agreement. In the United States this was in the proportion of Morse 9, Smith 4, Vail 2 (George Vail was a silent partner through his brother), Gale 1. Outside the United States it was Morse 8, Smith 5, Vail 2, and Gale 1. Vail and Gale had been willing to reduce their shares in the hope that Smith would swiftly win a cash income for the enterprise. Smith was to present his services as a lawyer; Vail and Gale were to present their services as technicians. Smith agreed to pay the cost of obtaining patents abroad, including his and Morse's expenses for a three-months trip to Europe to begin in April (it was for this purpose that Smith obtained leave of absence from Congress); these expenses were to be repaid to Smith if and when any profits were realized from the sale of patents abroad. All expense incidental to perfecting the mechanism or obtaining patents in the United States were to be borne alone by Morse and Vail.

Whatever mechanical improvements were invented by any of the partners were to become the joint property of all. No contract relative to the telegraph was to be entered into without the consent of all.[52]

On April 2 Morse obtained a passport for travel in Europe. On April 7 he filed a revised specification of his invention at the Patent Office,[53] and immediately requested that the issuing of his patent should be postponed in order that he might have the technical advantage in Europe of not having already secured a patent elsewhere.[54] The House did not act on the telegraph bill before he sailed; the bill failed to reach even a second reading. Congressmen might wonder at the new invention, but they were not ready to risk their reputations in voting appropriations for what might only be a hoax – especially not in hard times.

Morse did not know when he would be free again to pursue his painting career. When he had made his plans to visit Europe for the third time, he wrote a revealing letter to his friend Cummings, the treasurer of the benevolent association which had promised to raise three thousand dollars for him to paint a grand historical work. If Cummings had included in the printed copy of this letter, which he sent to those who had subscribed for the fund, all the words that Morse had written in his draft, Morse might have been spared a public berating. The words which did not appear in the text are here placed in brackets:

T. S. Cummings
Treasurer of the Association, &c.

Circumstances relating to the Telegraph invented by me in the year 1832 will require my attention for an indefinite time, and I am about to visit Europe, principally in reference to matters connected with this Invention. At the same time, indeed, I have in view some studies connected with the Picture which the Association have commissioned me to paint for them. Yet I ought not to conceal from the gentlemen who have so generously formed the Association, that circumstances may rise in relation to the Telegraph, which may make it a paramount duty to me and to my country to suspend for a season, [& maybe eventually to forego] the commission with which they have honored me. In this state of suspense, I have to request that no further collections of the quarterly instalments be made until my return from Europe in the autumn at which time I shall doubtless have it in my power to acquaint you with the course which it may be thought advisable to pursue. If possible I wish as soon as practicable to relieve myself of the cares of the Telegraph, that I may have my time to devote more strenuously than ever to the execution of my Picture, and the benefit of the Academy & of the Arts.

[I need not say that should any event occur to prevent my fulfilling the commission of the Association I hold myself bound of course to refund what has already been advanced.] With sincere esteem truly y.r friend and serv.t

S. F. B. Morse

N. Y. city University
March 15, 1838 [55]

As usual his abilities led in so many directions that a straight course was difficult to follow. Just now he believed that he could abandon painting for the world of lobbying, patent law, and contracts, and yet return to painting at will.

CHAPTER *xviii*

Bureaucracy Abroad

THIS time he was not going to Europe as a student of the old masters. This time, at forty-seven years of age, with a face that had grown sharp and drawn, with a complexion darker than ever under his gray hair, he looked like a master himself. Recognition in America, to be sure, had been slow in coming. The press – with a slavish dependence on Europe which as a nativist he despised – still derived its basic literary, artistic, and scientific judgments from abroad. Even to convince America that he had invented the Morse telegraph he knew he must fight his rivals on their own ground. He was confident. He was carrying his "thunder and lightning 'jim crack'" to London and Paris, where the scientific judgments of the world were made. He would demonstrate that the American art student of 1812 and 1830 had become in 1838 the master of the telegraph.

Sailing with Smith in May, he arrived in London in mid-June along with the "ambassadors and princes . . . pickpockets and beggars"[1] who were gathering to celebrate the inauguration of the Victorian era. In Westminster Abbey with Leslie he watched while a girl of nineteen was crowned Queen of an Empire. Whatever his conception then of the English role in history, by the time he left England Morse thought Englishmen as obstinate as ever.

The round of calls requisite to securing a patent began. He paid the fees at the proper offices, filed a caveat at the Attorney General's, and discovered that two parties, Wheatstone and Cooke, and Edward Davy, were contesting his application. He looked up Wheatstone's specifications at the Patent Office and remained convinced that his own telegraph was different and better. He heard that Davy's telegraph was on exhibition at Exeter House in the Strand and paid his shilling to see it.

Other than his own, Davy's was the first telegraph he had ever seen. It was in a miserable room, small, dark, and dusty, which Davy had hired several months before to bring his invention before the public. Like Morse, he hoped that the government would purchase his telegraph and incorporate it in the Post Office system. Also like Morse, he had found that the government was ponderous to move and he had opened promising conversations with railway and business leaders. He was now exhibiting his telegraph so that prospective investors might see that it really worked, but not too much about how it worked. Davy's telegraph was something like Wheatstone's, Morse thought. They both employed several circuits. They were both needle telegraphs, and hence visual rather than recording. In Davy's receiver, however, as the needles were deflected by the magnetic current they moved little paper screens, disclosing illuminated letters one by one. Davy's sending instrument was a keyboard of twelve keys, similar to the " melodeon " that Morse had once used. The American visitor concluded that Davy's telegraph was even more complicated than Wheatstone's. In a fair fight he was certain that he would win both an English patent and the English market.

His competitors, however, were in a strong position. Wheatstone was not a professor of painting but a professor of experimental philosophy; he had already become known for his research in acoustics and optics, and particularly for his determination, by the use of a revolving mirror, of the speed at which electricity travels through conductors. With the help of William Fothergill Cooke he had already secured his patent a year before, on July 27, 1837. Davy was a chemist, with less scientific reputation than Wheatstone, but the son of a father of fortunate business connections. When Wheatstone first applied for a patent, Davy had protested, alleging that their inventions were similar. The Attorney General had decided that the inventions were essentially different and granted Wheatstone a patent. But when Davy applied for his patent, the Attorney General found that they were much the same after all. Finally the case was referred to Michael Faraday, professor at the Royal Institution, who decided that the telegraphs were sufficiently different to deserve separate patents. On the very day that Davy's patent was sealed, Davy wrote his father: "I have had notice of another application for a patent by a person named *Morse*. Messrs. Cooke and Wheatstone have entered an opposition to this application, and I shall have to do the same, so that one, or other, of us may be able to stop it. We are now both equally interested in keeping a third rival out of the field, and it may save much after trouble and competition."[2]

Morse boldly took a model of his telegraph to a hearing at the office of the Attorney General, Sir John Campbell. Sir John ignored it. His only concern was that the London *Mechanics Magazine* for February 10, 1838, had "published" the Morse telegraph,[3] and thus had invalidated it for a patent. Morse protested that the article merely described the results of his telegraph, not its process of operation. But Sir John reiterated that it had been "published" and denied his application.

While the hearings were in progress, in the anteroom of the Attorney General's office Morse met his most formidable rival, Wheatstone. They introduced themselves. Wheatstone at once invited Morse to come to King's College to inspect his telegraph.

Morse went, and liked the shy young professor. He found him "most liberal minded . . . a man of uncommon genius."[4] In appearance and manner he was surprisingly like Professor Gale.

His telegraph, too, was impressive, but not overwhelming. What Morse had fixed upon long ago as his points of superiority over Wheatstone's he still believed superior. Wheatstone's, operating by five magnetic needles that pointed to the letters of the alphabet, was visual; his own was permanently recording. Wheatstone's employed twelve wires; his own employed four – that is, two single circuits for two-way transmission. All together his was much the simpler mechanism, Morse believed. He did not explain the operation of his telegraph to his host.

When Wheatstone told him that he dated his first thought of his telegraph back to 1832,[5] Morse must have been disconcerted. In 1832 on the *Sully* he had thought himself the only person who had put the words "electric" and "telegraph" together. Now, however, he not only understood that Barlow had conceived such an idea in

1824 and abandoned it as impracticable, and that Henry had thought Barlow's plan practical by 1831, but that like himself another had conceived it in 1832 and gradually brought it to practicability; since neither Wheatstone nor he himself had published their ideas until recently, if at all, they were both independent inventions. He had come a long way even from the summer before, when he believed that every electric telegraph must have been pirated from his! He still believed, however, that his was the first practical invention.

Morse's judgment of his mild young rival was bold; not with the boldness of youth now, but with the boldness of strong, patient faith. "His Telegraph is truly an ingenious and beautiful piece of mechanism," he wrote his brother, "but it is not so simple as mine, and unless my opponents here have discovered my mode from those who have seen it in America, and who may be able to describe it to them (and of which they are now manifestly ignorant) and thus shall adopt mine into their new patent, I shall instantly supersede them. At any rate I shall have the gratification of knowing that my invention is *the one of all others which will prevail, and be generally adopted;* whether I shall be pecuniarily profited by it here, or whether I shall get the credit of it, is as yet uncertainty."[4]

Believing that the Attorney General had unjustly denied his application, with Smith's help Morse composed a letter asking for another hearing. He stated that the only publication of his invention in England did not describe the operation of it, and he defied his opponents to explain its operation with the help of the article or with any other information they had. He believed they could not do it and that their failure would be proof that his invention had not been "published." He wrote an able, closely reasoned argument.[6] He was granted a second hearing.

Appearing again before the Attorney General (the future author of a book that has been termed one of the most censurable publications in English, *Lives of the Chancellors*), Morse learned to his dismay that he had not had time to examine his letter. As Sir John spoke he took it up, carelessly fingered it, and then asked his visitor if he had not taken measures to secure a patent in America. Morse said yes. America is large, he replied, and you "ought to be satisfied with a patent there."

With all due deference, Morse countered, that was not the question submitted for the Attorney General's decision. The question was only whether there was any legal obstacle in the way of his obtaining letters patent in England.

Sir John returned to his original position, as Morse has recorded it. The invention had been published, he said, and therefore Morse's application was denied.[7]

The Attorney General had made his decision on a quibble. There was no appeal except directly to Parliament. That settled the matter.

One admission, though incorrect, the Attorney General permitted himself. When he mentioned that Steinheil of Munich had invented a single-circuit telegraph, he added: "It is probable he took it from yours."[4]

In Paris Morse found that Wheatstone already had a French patent. But whatever his influence in England, Wheatstone was no deterrent in France. The American promptly obtained a patent too. After his experience with the English "pirate law" he was grateful for French liberality;[8] that is, he was grateful until he understood that to continue his patent for more than two years, his invention must be put into actual operation in France. To do so he would have to bring it to the attention of the public quickly.

François Arago, the illustrious director of the Royal Observatory and perpetual secretary of the Academy of Sciences, saw the Morse telegraph in operation one day and was pleased with it. For no reason other than his generous interest, he promptly saw to it that Morse was invited to exhibit before the September 10 session of the academy. Because Morse could not speak French well, Arago agreed to explain its mechanism. He was eminently qualified to do so; for shortly after Oersted discovered that needles were susceptible to the influence of electric current, both Arago and Ampère in 1821 had discovered that a bar or needle in a coil of wire through which current is passed becomes magnetized. This was one of the discoveries fundamental to telegraphy. It was fitting that Arago should sponsor Morse.

Around the hall of the academy Morse arranged his coils of wire. On a table before the most distinguished scientists of Europe, among them Baron Humboldt and Gay-Lussac, Morse placed the register just as it had been made in the Morristown ironworks.

Explaining the instruments, Arago frankly pointed out to the academicians the problems that remained unsolved. To suspend the wires in the air, he said, would appear nearly impossible because it would expose them to the weather. In the rainy season some point on a line between Paris and Bordeaux would be in the area of a lightning storm every day. On the other hand, to bury the lines in the ground, he said, would present major inconvenience in repairing. Morse put the instruments in action.

"*Extraordinaire! Très admirable!*" he heard on all sides. Arago's cautious proviso did not distract the academicians from the imaginative possibilities of the American's machine. As the exhibition concluded, Baron Humboldt rose, took Morse by the hand, and warmly congratulated him. Academicians crowded around the table. The American telegraph pushed all other subjects from the session.[9]

Morse could hardly desire greater recognition. It would be sure to impress American opinion. It would attract the attention of capitalists and the French government.

While Morse was enjoying the acclaim that followed the exhibition, the director of government telegraphs, Alphonse Foy, called to see the American device mark off its dots and dashes. As Morse said was the fact with every Frenchman who saw it, Foy was delighted. He told the inventor that he was investigating telegraphs because the government was about to build one; he urged him to secure a letter of introduction to the Minister of the Interior, in whose department his telegraph bureau was.

Morse carried a flattering letter from the American Minister, Lewis Cass, to the office of the Minister of the Interior. He saw only a secretary. In a few days he again called on Foy, who had now made a report to the Minister.

"I have examined carefully," said the director of telegraphs, "the systems of Steinheil, of Wheatstone, and many others French and German, and I have reported that after patient investigation, yours is the best." Morse saw at last the possibility of an immediate test of his telegraph.

The obstacle to his telegraph would be the expense, Foy added. "It will cost ten times as much as the common mode."

"It would be twenty times better," Morse replied.[10]

He had hoped that the United States would be the first government to erect any electric telegraph line. But before either Congress or the French government acted on his or any other telegraph Bavaria took the honors; its government had agreed to build a line of Steinheil's single-circuit needle telegraph. Still the Minister of the Interior would not see Morse.

Meanwhile private enterprise was also building needle telegraphs. The papers were reporting that Wheatstone was constructing a line in Belgium, and his partner Cooke in England as well. Morse was eager to have his lines constructed under any auspices now, public or private; to validate his French patent some line would have to be opened soon. He began conversations with the directors of the seven-mile railroad recently built by Rothschild interests between Paris and Saint-Germain.

As he waited for action he was developing an application of his telegraph to indicate by sound the presence of a railroad train at any chosen point of the track, on the principle of the later police and fire-alarm telegraphs. He secured a French patent for his scheme.[11] When he showed his plan to the Saint-Germain directors they seemed to hesitate because of the cost of preparing and placing the wires. Morse favored laying them in the ground. When one of the directors told him that he had an estimate for preparing and laying the wires at thirty-six sous per meter, he proposed a method which would reduce the cost below fourteen sous. Wind the wire with cotton, Morse advised; draw it through fluid asphalt; bind the four necessary wires into a rope; draw the rope through fluid asphalt and then into a lead tube; bury the tube in a trench. If he had known how much trouble a similar method was to cause him later in America, he would have been glad that the directors did not readily adopt his proposal.

While the government and the Saint-Germain directors dallied with him, he heard the flattering gossip that the telegraph had been burlesqued at a local theater and that the two most talked-of inventions were the daguerreotype and the telegraph. The curious were now following him even into his unpretentious rooms.

For a time Morse had lived with Mellen Chamberlain, a Philadelphian of means with whom he and Smith drew up a contract to exhibit the telegraph in Prussia, Austria, and the Near East. When Chamberlain commenced his telegraphic tour, Morse took rooms with Edward N. Kirk, the minister of the recently founded American church in Paris, soon to become a leading nativist.

In their "delightful little rooms," three flights up at No. 5 rue Neuve-des-Mathurins, Morse arranged his apparatus. In the parlor he placed his register; in the bedroom one of the new constant batteries of Daniel, and also his "correspondent," as he had decided to name his sending device; and in the small entry between, his railroad telegraph model. The Reverend Mr. Kirk had wide acquaintance in Paris, spoke French well, and hence was a useful as well as congenial companion. On Tuesday afternoon they were regularly at home.

Those who climbed the three flights to see the subject of gossip were a galaxy of the titled and influential. Count Remboutot, the prefect of the Seine, was among them; and M. Jounaid, librarian to the King; Colonel Lasalle, aide-de-camp to the King, and lady; General Charenon, Napoleon's Governor of Poland; M. Fremel, the director of lighthouses; directors of the Saint-Étienne railroad, members of the Institute, professors, editors, deputies, peers, dukes and duchesses.

In the French manner the visitors were delighted and effusive. One official of the telegraph office, M. Moran, observed with incredulity while Morse was operating one of his sending devices, a two-pronged fork. Suddenly M. Moran had a vision of the meaning of the new electric telegraph. With an exclamation of astonishment he held up the fork before the company and said in French: "Behold the fork more potent than that of Neptune, destined to greater triumph, although it has one tooth less than his!" Turning to Morse he added in broken English: "Are you not glorious, sair, to be the author of this wonderful discovery?" Morse recorded the incident with satisfaction.[12]

Several English nobles climbed the three flights of stairs: Lord Aylmer, former Governor General of Canada, and his lady; Lord Elgin, whom Morse remembered from his London student days as "the celebrated *preserver*, not *depredator* (as he has been most slanderously called) of the Phidian marbles"; [13] and the young Earl of Lincoln. Morse did not hesitate to make clear to them the contrast between the simplicity of obtaining a patent in France and England. Perhaps the effectiveness of his comparison led the Earl of Lincoln to press upon him an invitation to call when he passed through London on his way home. Lord Aylmer even suggested, as Morse remembered, that Parliament be asked to grant him a patent by special act. With the help of his new friends it seemed a possibility.

Another visitor to the parlor-bedroom exhibitions was Baron Meyendorf, the agent of the Czar for reporting useful inventions. Meyendorf was promptly struck with the American invention. He told Morse that he had been in treaty with M. Amyot, a French inventor, to establish Amyot's telegraph in Russia. He intimated that if Morse and Amyot could agree to unite their labors he would immediately put matters in train to construct a line of Morse telegraph out of St. Petersburg. Meyendorf brought Amyot up the three flights of stairs, and Amyot, too, confessed his delight with the American invention. In turn Morse and Amyot agreed that Amyot should help Morse introduce his telegraph into Russia and they would both be paid to put the line into operation. "How different a conduct from Jackson's," [14] Morse wrote.

The next time Morse saw the Baron he presented him an estimate of £794 sterling for a twenty-mile line, exclusive of costs of freight, ditching, and asphalt. Call it £800, advised the Baron, and with extras call it £1,000, and add the price of passage to and from America. Morse was planning to go home for preparation, and then go to Russia to supervise the work. He and the Baron agreed he was to be paid half the savings to the government which the telegraph could effect in five years.

"This I will immediately submit to my Government," concluded the Baron.[15] His government largely consisted of Nicholas I, the same Czar whom Morse despised for having suppressed free Poland in 1830.

Now Morse was waiting for news of action from Congress at home, the Minister of Interior or the Saint-Germain railroad in France, Mellen Chamberlain in the Near East, Parliament in Britain, and the Czar in Russia. There were possibilities everywhere, certainties nowhere.

When Smith unexpectedly went home alone in October, he took with him Morse's injunction to kiss American soil. For Morse was dull with longing. Prospects of success might be bright, but he remembered other prospects that had failed to secure him what now seemed most to be desired, a home where he could live with his children.

When he heard that his brothers were constructing a new building for the *Observer,* near Clinton Hall, he sent his daughter Susan a pathetic letter. "Tell Uncle Sidney to take good care of you," he wrote, "and to have a snug little room in the upper corner of his new building, where a bed can be placed, a chair, and a table, and let me have it as my own, that there may be one little particular spot which I can call *home.* I will there make three wooden stools, one for you, one for Charles, and one for Finley, and invite you to your father's house."[16] He knew his children were suffering in their formative years for want of a father and mother. The wound that Lucretia's death had caused him seemed to bleed fresh daily. At times it pained him, he wrote his brother, "so as almost to deprive me of reason, though few around me would suspect the state of my mind."[17]

In his loneliness he walked by the house where Cooper had lived when together they were members of Lafayette's circle. How different it was now! Cooper was in Cooperstown, Lafayette was gone, and the Louis Philippe whom the General had put on the throne had driven liberalism underground. Then he himself had been a painter, sure of his profession, and hoping for a fresh beginning in historical painting when he returned to America. Now his art career was uncertain. In London he had been to an exhibition of the Royal Academy; but in Paris he spent nothing on art exhibits nor did he write about them in his letters; he threatened again to resign his presidency and his professorship as well when he returned home. For the present at least his hopes depended on the telegraph, and they seemed precarious indeed.

Desultory conversations with the government and the Saint-Germain railroad continued. He wondered if the delay were not in part his own fault. The constant chiding of his parents and brothers in his days of prodigality had dinned into him the belief that he was not a business man. But most of all he blamed the "promising-appearance-failing" French character for the delay.[12] "I find delay in all things," he explained; "at least, so it appears to me, who have too strong a development of the American organ of 'go-ahead-ativeness' to feel easy under its tantalizing effects. A Frenchman ought to have as many lives as a cat to bring to pass, on his dilatory plan of procedure, the same results that a Yankee would accomplish in his single life."[18]

Days passed, weeks, months. Paris tossed laurels up the three flights of stairs. But he could not subsist on laurel. He needed sustenance. He needed the opportunity to make his telegraph work. In mockery nourishing fruits only touched his lips, were gone, and touched his lips again.

Patient as could be expected of mortal man, he called eight or ten times at the Ministry of the Interior without even being permitted to see the secretary. Eventually he came to understand that when the railroad directors would promise to settle some detail "in a few days" they were using the French expression for a few weeks. When he asked Minister Cass for advice on how to urge the government or the railroad to act, Cass replied that dilatoriness was the universal complaint and patience the only remedy. It was hard to be patient when he had only intended to be in Europe three months. "I have been dealing too much in lightning lately," the Hare wrote, "to feel easy in travelling on a snail back."[12]

The Saint-Germain directors were awaiting word from the Minister of the Interior whether the government monopoly of telegraphs would permit them to erect a telegraph, if indeed they should wish to do so. Finally Morse understood that the government intended to make no decision. It would neither consent to test the new telegraph itself nor say whether any private company might do so. The hope that the Chambers might force the government to act vanished when the Ministry resigned and Parliament was dissolved for two months pending a new election. Without action by government or private company his patent would be invalidated in a few months. The liberality of French patent practice was specious. In effect it was as piratical as the British. There was no use remaining in Paris.

Three hopes were left to him in Europe. Two were faint: success for Chamberlain's tour in the Near East, and the possibility of securing an English patent by act of Parliament. The third, the hope of establishing a Russian line, he regarded as nearly certain. It demanded that he go home to arrange his family affairs and prepare equipment; he was to be in Russia by July 15.

Seven months of generous recognition in Paris convinced him that Europe knew his telegraph was the best. But as he left Paris with only one commitment to build a telegraph line, and that one not yet signed, it was disconcerting to know that Wheatstone and Cooke in England and Belgium, and Steinheil in Bavaria, were already building lines.

In London the Earl of Lincoln invited him to exhibit the telegraph in his house on Park Lane. Lord Elgin, Henry Drummond, members of Parliament, lords of the Admiralty, and members of the Royal Society attended. Elgin, Lincoln, and Drummond urged him to stay in England long enough to help push a special act through Parliament. But the obstacles seemed mountainous: the inertia of Parliament, the opposition of Wheatstone and perhaps others, national prejudice, the weight of the previous decision against him by the Attorney General. The lure of Russia was before his eyes; he was expecting the Czar's favorable decision by May 10. Considering what he knew, his decision was wise. He chose the comparative certainty of the Russian adventure to the comparative improbability of a Parliamentary victory.

Shortly after reaching home in April, he learned that Mr. Chamberlain had been drowned in an accident on the Danube and all record of whatever he had accomplished had gone down with him.[19] On May 10 word of the Czar's consent had not yet arrived. He shifted his plan of sailing for Russia to the following year. Then news came that Czar Nicholas had refused to sign the contract at all, doubtless because the telegraph as a means of conveying intelligence might prove subversive.[20] All hope of erecting a line in Europe collapsed.

His tour had been a brilliant success in honor for himself and his brain child. Seldom did honor seem more empty.

CHAPTER *xix*

Daguerreotypist

In Paris, when his telegraph and Daguerre's " drawings " were being talked about as the most wonderful inventions of the age, Morse thought it would be fitting to know Daguerre. A few days before leaving for America he asked permission to see the mysterious copper plates on which for the first time in history man had successfully fixed the images of nature. Daguerre consented.

No description of Daguerre's process, or even of his pictures, had yet been published in America. He had announced his discovery only in January, and had confided his process only to such distinguished scientists as those whom Morse knew at the academy, Arago and Gay-Lussac. Like Morse he was one of that select group, among them Fulton and the comparatively unknown Audubon, who combined achievement in science and painting. Fulton had been the first to exhibit panoramas in Paris; Daguerre had employed a similar method in popularizing painting. In his show place, " the Diorama," a revolving floor moved spectators before a series of paintings. With transparencies, openings, and trick uses of light before and behind his paintings, he obtained startling illusions of reality. Having become interested in the effects of light through his Diorama, Daguerre had experimented for years in fixing images, thrown by a camera obscura, on copper plates prepared with chemicals sensitive to light. In association with Niepce he had finally succeeded in what scientists had long been trying to do.

Daguerre showed him his " Daguerrotipes," * as Morse first called

* In French, *daguerréotype*. In America the second *e* was at first sometimes accented, but soon was not pronounced at all. That immediately after its introduction

them. They were like aquatint engravings, Morse thought. In chiaroscuro rather than color, they seemed "Rembrandt perfected." Morse recalled that when he had lived next to Professor Silliman he had played with the possibility of fixing images and given it up as hopeless.[1]

Though the largest of Daguerre's plates were but seven by five inches, the detail visible amazed Morse. No painting ever approached it, he was confident. In one plate, a street scene, he could vaguely see that there were letters on a sign. Through a microscope he could read every letter in the sign. Looking at another plate through a lens, Morse saw in the image of a spider's head, no bigger than a pin, a minuteness of organization which he believed had not hitherto been known to exist. The discovery would open a new field of research, he predicted, with results as startling as when the microscope first came into use.

The next day Daguerre returned the call. He labored up the three flights and spent an hour examining the telegraph. Just as he was expressing his delight with the American invention which vied in popularity with his own, his Diorama, house, plates, and notes of years of experiments were being consumed in flames.

Morse's account of his visit to the Diorama and its destruction were published in his brothers' *Observer*, April 20, 1839. "In the same vessel which brought the above letter," Editor Sidney added, "the writer himself arrived. From him we have received some additional information respecting this very interesting discovery, which we cannot at present communicate." Morse may have known Daguerre's process; there is no direct evidence, however, that he did.[2]

His letter of description was the first report on the daguerreotype written by an American. It was reprinted in newspapers throughout the country.[3]

At home President Morse saw that the National Academy took note of Daguerre's contribution to art. When he proposed Daguerre for honorary membership the vote was passed with "wild enthusiasm." The academicians apparently shared their president's view

---

in New York the *Journal of Commerce* advised pronouncing it "dar-ger-row-type" is a reflection of the New England background of its editors and a suggestion of how Morse may have pronounced it as well.

that the daguerreotype would "banish the sketchy, slovenly daubs that pass for spirited and learned; those works which possess mere general effect without detail, because foresooth detail destroys general effect." [4] On May 20 Morse informed Daguerre of his election. Referring to the English attempt to publicize the different discovery of Talbot, Morse assured him that throughout the United States his name "alone will be associated with the brilliant discovery which justly bears your name." Morse well understood how partisanship could seek to rob an inventor of his due. He concluded by offering his services gratuitously for an exhibit of Daguerre's plates in New York.[5]

Soon afterward the French Parliament passed a bill to reward Daguerre. He agreed to publish both his process and any subsequent improvements; in return the government granted a pension of 6,000 francs to him and 4,000 francs to the heirs of Niepce, who until his death had been associated with Daguerre. The inventor was freed from necessity. If the United States had done for Morse what France did for Daguerre, Morse might have exchanged a life plagued by the jealousy of rivals, distrust of his own partners, and recrimination in the press, for a quiet life spent either in continuing experiments with the telegraph or a return to painting. But telegraphy by its nature lent itself to patents better than daguerreotypy; and the American theory of government did not contemplate direct aid to inventors. The American inventor was not lifted above necessity until too late.

Daguerre fulfilled his agreement with Parliament by permitting Arago to describe his process before the Academy of Sciences on August 19. In a few days mechanically-minded Parisians were enthusiastically comparing the number of smudges on their copper plates with the number of houses out of their windows.

One of the first transatlantic steamboats, the *British Queen,* brought a description of the process to America. With its arrival on September 20, 1839, the history of photography in America began.

On September 30 the *Morning Herald* announced that the first daguerreotype ever taken in America had been taken about three days before. A view of Broadway showing the Astor House and St. Paul's Church, it was on exhibit at the shop of Dr. Chilton, chemist, on Broadway. The daguerreotypist was Mr. Seager, an Englishman.

On October 3 Seager announced in the *Herald* that he would lecture at the Stuyvesant Institute on "the Daguerreotype, or art of imprinting, in a few minutes, by the mode of Mr. Daguerre, the beautiful images of Landscapes, Architecture, Interiors, &c." To convince the public of the importance of the subject he added: "The following scientific gentlemen have given permission to be referred to as being familiar with the process and its extraordinary results: President Duer, Columbia College; Professor Morse; James R. Chilton, Esq.; Jno. L. Stephens, Esq."

Since Morse knew Seager, Robert Taft, the historian of American photography, has assumed that if Morse himself claimed the honor of having made the first daguerreotype in America, he would have protested the claim made for Seager. Lacking any record of Morse's protest, Taft properly assigned the honor to Seager. A contemporaneous letter by Morse himself supports this attribution. On September 28 the *Journal of Commerce* announced: "Prof. Morse showed us yesterday the first fruits of Daguerre's invention, as put in practice in this country. It was a perfect and beautiful view, on a small scale, of the new Unitarian church, and the buildings in its vicinity. The colors are not so strong as they might be, but we understand this defect may be easily remedied." Morse read the article. On September 30 the *Journal of Commerce* published his prompt reply, here republished for the first time:

Gentlemen,

In your mention this morning of the specimen of Photographic drawing by the Daguerrotype which I showed you, you use the phrase, "first fruits of Daguerre's invention in this country" [*sic*], this may convey the meaning that I am the first to produce these results from the process just revealed by Mr. Daguerre to the Institute of France. If there is any merit in first producing these results in this country, that merit I believe belongs to Mr. D. W. Seager of this city, who has for several days had some results at Mr. Chilton's in Broadway. The specimen I showed you was my first result.

Your ob't serv't

Sept. 28th *Samuel F. B. Morse* [6]

Morse's candid letter establishes Seager's priority.

Sixteen years later Morse remembered the trying circumstances under which he took his first daguerreotype. "As soon as the apparatus was made," he began, "I commenced experimenting with it." On another occasion Morse claimed that he had made for himself the first daguerreotype camera constructed in the United States.* [7] "The greatest *obstacle* I had to encounter was in the *quality of the plates*," he continued. "I obtained the common plated copper in coils at the hardware shops, which of course was very thinly coated with silver, and that impure. Still I was enabled to verify the truth of Daguerre's revelations. The first experiment crowned with any success was a view of the Unitarian Church from the window on the staircase, from the third story of the New York City University. This, of course, was before the building of the N. Y. Hotel. It was in September, 1839. The time, if I recollect, in which the plate was exposed to the action of light in the camera, was about fifteen minutes. The instruments, chemicals, &c., were strictly in accordance with the directions in Daguerre's first book. . . . An English gentleman, whose name at present escapes me, but who is, I believe, now living in Mexico, obtained a copy of Daguerre's book about the same time with myself. He commenced experimenting also." [8]

That fall and winter was a low point in the undulating prospects of Morse's life. His years of effort with his telegraph were yielding him nothing but pleasant reputation among the few who understood and disdain among those who did not. The university was split by a row between faculty members and willful Chancellor Matthews which left the professor of the literature of the arts of design with fewer pupils, and led nearly all the regular professors, including Gale, to resign. Vail was busy in Morristown and at the Baldwin, Vail, and Hufty works (later to become the Baldwin locomotive works) in Philadelphia. Smith had been badly defeated in his campaign for the governorship of Maine the year before and the panic had wiped out his investments in Western lands; the construction of his magnificent mansion in the woods near Portland faltered. Gale could not often come to New York from his new position at Jefferson College in Mississippi. He, Vail, and Smith were not contributing anything to the cost of constructing the telegraph instru-

* This camera is said to be the one now on exhibit in the National Museum, Washington. It is an enormous wooden box, with a lens (made in Paris) peeping from the center of one side. Also said to be the first camera made in America and also at the museum is a smaller camera described as built for Draper.

Courtesy of the New York Historical Society, New York City

ALLEGORICAL LANDSCAPE SHOWING NEW YORK UNIVERSITY

By Morse 1836

While the setting is not Washington Square, at the left is the University building, in the left tower of which Morse lived.

ments that Morse wished to exhibit before Congress. Their apparent unconcern led him to wonder whether an effort to interest Congress would be worth the expense this year. The depression beginning in 1837, the most terrible America had known, had worked its way into nearly all public and private enterprises and Congress was a firmer dam to the Treasury than ever. All together, he had little taste for pushing his telegraph now; or for recovering his painting patronage; or, though the opportunity was offered, for writing in the *Observer.* He clung rather to experimenting with telegraph improvements, nativist activity, his few painting pupils at the university, and his academy responsibilities; he directed his ready enthusiasm into the new profession, daguerreotypy.

His purpose in doing so he expressed variously. In the spring of 1840 in an address on the daguerreotype before the National Academy he declared his interest was to discover the effect of the new art on the fine arts.[9] In 1841 in reply to a request to paint a picture he said: " My ultimate aim is the application of the Daguerreotype to accumulate for my studio models for my canvas."[10] In 1855 in one letter he said that he had become a professional in order to reimburse himself for the expense of his first experiments.[8] A few days earlier, in a letter written for a telegraph history, he had said: from daguerreotypy " I derived a small revenue to release me from debt, and to expend in the construction of new & improved telegraphic instruments in the leisure furnished by cloudy days."[11]

Doubtless each of his declared purposes was true for him at one time or another. He became a professional to pay the costs of his early experimenting; then, when these costs were paid, he attempted to accumulate funds for what he still regarded as his ultimate aim, the return to painting; circumstances brought it about that he used his funds for telegraph promotion instead. Just as his desire to paint enticed him into telegraphy and eventually into becoming the chief figure in the history of the telegraph in America, so it also enticed him into daguerreotypy and eventually into becoming, as Mathew Brady said, " the first successful introducer of this rare art in America."[12]

Morse is among those for whom has been claimed the honor of having made the first daguerreotype portrait in America. Other claimants are John W. Draper, who took Gale's position at the University of the City of New York, and Alexander Wolcott of New York.

Daguerre had told Morse that portraits could not be taken because subjects could not keep themselves still. All Daguerre's plates were then still lifes or landscapes, exposed for fifteen or twenty minutes, as were all the early American productions. Of course every enthusiast was wondering if Daguerre were not too cautious; Arago himself had predicted that only a slight advance would make portraits possible. As a portrait-painter Morse was naturally interested, perhaps too much so for the immediate good of his profession. He could not remember afterward whether he or Draper made the first portrait.

The earliest date that Taft can positively accept for a portrait by Draper is December 1839. The phraseology of the letter from which the date is derived, however, does not preclude an earlier date also: "The first portrait I obtained last December," Draper wrote in June 1840, "was with a common spectacle glass." [13] For Wolcott, an instrument-maker, Taft presents an earlier date. In a letter of March 1840 Wolcott wrote that he had made his first portrait in October. Several years later Wolcott's partner said it was made on October 7.

The claim for Morse rests largely on his 1855 letter of recollection: "I have now the results of these experiments taken in September, or beginning of October, 1839. They were full-length portraits of my daughter, single and also in group with some of her young friends. They were taken out-of-doors, on the roof of a building, in the full sunlight, and with the eyes closed. The time was from ten to twenty minutes. About the same time Professor Draper was successful in taking portraits, though whether he or myself took the first portrait successfully I cannot say." [8]

Taft believes that Morse is practically eliminated as a contender for two reasons. First, because he admitted in the above letter that Draper may have been the first instead of himself; second, because on November 16, 1839 Morse wrote Daguerre that he had experimented with his process "with indifferent success." [14] This letter in part reads: "Ever since I saw your admirable results, the day before your disastrous loss, I have felt an absorbing interest in it, and the first *brochure* which was opened in America at the booksellers', containing your exposé of your process, I possess. I have been experimenting, but with indifferent success, mostly, I believe, for the want of a proper lens. I hoped to be able to send you by this opportunity a result, but I have not one which I dare send you. You shall have the first that is in any degree perfect." Did Morse intend to say that he had not made any daguerreotypes worthy of the name? Or did he merely express himself with French modesty in writing to the inventor of the new art? This letter does not indicate how successful with portraits or any daguerreotypes he had been before November 16. And neither do we know how successful an image Wolcott had secured on October 7. The date of October 7 for Wolcott, however, stands as the first reasonably well-authenticated date for a portrait.

The earliest precise record of Morse's experiments with the daguerreotype is in his own hitherto unpublished notebook of January and February 1840.[15] It appears to be the only known journal of an early daguerreotypist.

The extracts here given are mainly a record of Morse's experiments under the oversight of François Gouraud, who came to New York from Paris, so he averred, " as the friend and pupil of Mr. Daguerre . . . with the charge of introducing to the New World, the perfect knowledge of . . . 'The Daguerreotype.' "[16] On Gouraud's arrival late in November, Morse offered him a rent-free exhibition room. By December 4 Gouraud had arranged his exhibit of daguerreotypes, including two taken by Daguerre himself, and invited such figures of the town as the diarist Hone and the officers of the National Academy to see it. Presently Gouraud was admitting the public for one dollar to his exhibit and for an additional fee to his lecture on the process of taking images. His pictures were better than American productions, and he himself was dark, sly, and charming; he soon became a sensation.

No indication that Morse was suspicious of Gouraud appears in the notebook except in Morse's later interpolations. These, recognized by their dissimilarity in penmanship, are here placed in footnotes.

The scratch book indicates that Morse and Gouraud were following Daguerre's directions.*

The first daguerreotype Morse recorded in his notebook was one of the City Hall, the building in which his portrait of Lafayette was hanging. He apparently took the image from the *Observer* Building, which his brothers had just completed near Clinton Hall, on the corner of Beekman and Nassau Streets.

> Jan.y 14 Tuesday 1840. Made proofs with M. Gouraud. Nothing particular in the polishing, except that the acidizing process is more essential than I had supposed, and requires greater delicacy in the manipulation. A drop of acid solution accidentally touched the surface of M. Gouraud's plate. He predicted a particular result, which occurred, the plate in that part became sooner affected with the iodine and while the rest of the plate was well coated with the golden color, the over acidized part, was purple and blue, and the effect after leaving the camera was that it was blurred with a dense mist in proportion as the color departed from yellow to blue. The iodizing process occupied about 10 minutes. My plate had not been well cleaned after the acidizing process and where the acid had not been well and evenly laid on, the light was bluish, and a bluish mist was in part of the shadow.
>
> At 7½ minutes before 3 o'clock the plate was put into the camera. M. G. said 24 minutes was the time necessary; the sky was cloudy, and the principal object in the field of view was the back of the City Hall (a red sandstone), the impression was tolerable with the exception above alluded to. I asked to have the principle explained by which he determined beforehand the time requisite for making the impression. He said he would give me a table.† It was a complicated calculation and one that I should think would only serve in the first trial as an approximation

* Briefly these consisted of five steps:

1. Polish a silver-coated copper plate with powder; rub off with cotton dipped in olive oil, stroking round and across. Spread on equally diluted nitric acid; powder and rub off again; heat, cool suddenly, polish again; apply acid again three times.
2. Place the plate in a box in which iodine is evaporating; when the surface of the plate is coated with a golden yellow – it must not be pale yellow nor yet so dark that it becomes violet – remove in a dark room.
3. Place plate in camera obscura, focus, and expose.
4. Place plate in a box in which mercury vapor, rising from a heated cup of mercury, is allowed to play upon it. When the heat of the mercury rises to 140° F. withdraw the heat; when its temperature falls to somewhere between 131° and 113° F. – whenever the image appears properly on the plate – withdraw it.
5. To fix the image bathe the plate in salt solution, or, better, in hyposulphate of soda solution.

† Morse's note: "Never given to me."

to a good result but in all probability no one can be certain of the first trial of any view. It will be necessary to sacrifice the first plate having ready always another to take advantage of the experience of the first, to correct the time of the second.*

The lights upon the parts of the landscape or other objects are of course first impressed, if objects are dark or the day cloudy the time will be longer.

His last sentence, even including the "of course," suggests that he was still thinking through the theory of the daguerreotype.

Probably later Morse added under date of January 17: "M.r Seager quarreled with M. Gouraud."

The next day he noted: "M. Gouraud and D.r Chilton came to be present at a lesson of M.r Gouraud." Dr. Chilton, the chemist, as before noted, sold tickets for Mr. Seager's lectures. He became the principal supplier for the early daguerreotypists.

The notes for January 18 continued:

Prepared plate as usual with acid, &c. acid better washed over than in former plate but the edges and a small portion of the plate was not so well acidized; the iodine attacked these parts more strongly, and when completed the result was a mistiness in those parts. Put the plate in the camera, 2 minutes before 3 o'clock sun shining bright, but the objects were in shadows mostly. The prevailing color was grey over all objects

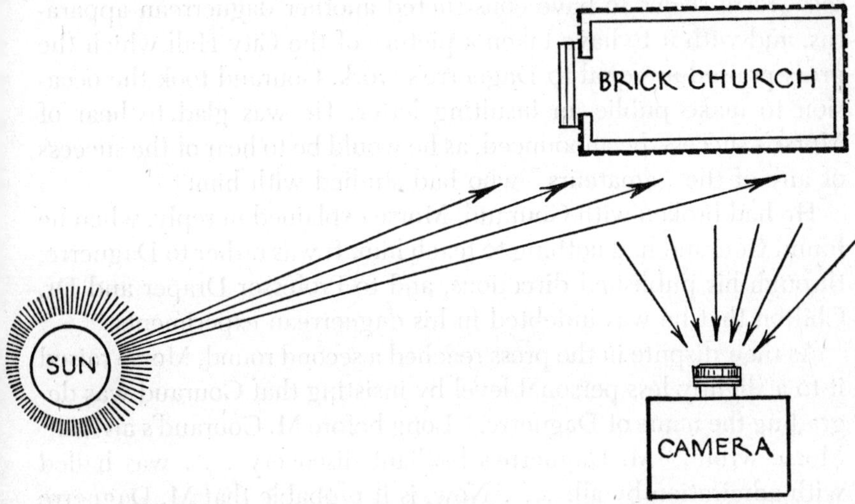

* Morse's note: "as Daguerre suggests."

except the brick church which was red with sunlight upon it striking obliquely thus, the scene towards Barclay Street.

Time required in the camera 16 minutes. Proof a good one for all the objects in shadow, lights a little over-done.

Mr. G. remarked concerning interiors that sometimes a proof was not obtained by a first exposure in the mercury bath, but a second, and third and in one instance Madame Giroux, *four* times, which resulted in a good proof.*

Giroux was the name of the Paris firm which Gouraud represented and which was associated with Daguerre. If the expression "Madame Giroux" refers to a portrait that Gouraud had taken before he came to America, it would be dated at least very early in November. In a publication the next year Gouraud stated that in Paris Mr. Susse made satisfactory portraits, with the sitter's eyes closed, in fifteen- or twenty-five-minute exposures, and that about the same time Abel Rendu had discovered a method of taking portraits with such brief exposures that the sitter's eyes might remain open; Rendu's method, Gouraud said, he had tried before leaving Paris.[17] There is some evidence that Gouraud was correct with reference to Susse, and that his portraits are among the first satisfactory ones in history.[18]

An explosion interrupted the instructions from Gouraud. By himself Morse seems to have constructed another daguerrean apparatus, and with it to have taken a picture of the City Hall which the press praised as equal to Daguerre's work. Gouraud took the occasion to make public an insulting letter. He was glad to hear of Morse's success, he announced, as he would be to hear of the success of any of the "amateurs" who had studied with him.[19]

He had broken with Gouraud, Morse explained in reply, when he found Gouraud had nothing to teach him. It was rather to Daguerre, through his published directions, and to Professor Draper and Dr. Chilton that he was indebted in his daguerrean experiments.[20]

As their dispute in the press reached a second round, Morse raised it to a slightly less personal level by insisting that Gouraud was degrading the name of Daguerre. "Long before M. Gouraud's arrival," Morse wrote, "M. Daguerre's brilliant discovery . . . was hailed with admiration by all. . . . Now, is it probable that M. Daguerre

* Morse's note: "this is all the instruction from Gouraud."

could have sent over a friend of his, a pupil, to give an air of charlatanry to his discovery; to change this flow of admiration for his generosity, and that of his country, for their splendid gift to the world, into disgust by seeing him entering into partnership with such an agent of his apparatus? Has M. Daguerre pretended to give a discovery to the world, and bound himself to reveal it, in all its manifest particulars, and then kept back secrets, to be hawked about this country for a dollar per head?"[21]

Like his father before him, Morse had a way of finding a good fight in whatever he undertook. In art he had found Trumbull, in religion the Unitarians, in public morality the theater and lotteries, in politics the Catholics, in telegraphy Jackson, and now in the field of daguerreotypy he had found a slippery young Frenchman.

The press had extravagantly praised Gouraud when he first arrived in New York. Even the *Observer* was early and loud in its pæans. "A gentleman of taste," it called him.[22] Indeed, it noticed that he had "satisfactory credentials" from Messrs. Alphonse Giroux and Company of Paris, "to whom alone" Daguerre "has given the sanction of his name, in the preparation of all the apparatus of the Daguerreotype." The company had announced that in order to guard against fraud Gouraud would establish a depot for their instruments in New York. "It is gratifying to know," the *Observer* concluded, that "our artists and men of science can be assured of the genuineness of the apparatus by an application at a properly accredited agency."[23]

When Sidney Morse wrote the *Observer's* comment he may have been thinking of his brother as one of the artists and men of science concerned. But it is probable that Morse had no intention of buying his equipment at any prescribed place. Doubtless he resented being told that only one kind of instrument was properly made. Moreover, by agreement with the French government Daguerre had given his rights to the world.

Perhaps, too, Gouraud's sale of toilet articles at his exhibitions seemed to him to degrade the name of Daguerre. And perhaps Morse knew of his plans to publish what has been called the first manual of daguerreotypy in the United States. It was not original: with the exception of additional notes on portraiture, perhaps borrowed in part from Wolcott and Draper,[24] it was without significant deviation from one of the 1839 London translations of Daguerre's brochure, and in fact in whole paragraphs it was identical with it.

If Morse had known what Gouraud's rival later wrote about him it would have been simpler to expose him. Gouraud left New York for Boston on February 26, five days after publishing his *j'accuse* in the press, leaving his trunks behind as security for unpaid rent. In Boston his exhibition materials were attached by court order; he borrowed from a fellow lodger at his hotel and failed to repay; he left Boston with his rent again unpaid. Controversy continued to follow him. After going into the business of taking views of Niagara Falls, he fought his partner in the courts of Upper Canada. Presently he was sued for calling a schoolmaster a blockhead. In 1843 he went through bankruptcy in New York and the following year was accused of copyrighting a work on a trick system of memorizing without giving due credit to the sources from which he derived his system. But in the meantime he had made such an impression with his excellent exhibition plates and his dashing manners that he was able to win not a few editors to his support.

Several months after first leaving New York Gouraud sent to the New York *Commercial Advertiser* what Nathan Hale's Boston *Advertiser* called "a remarkable communication." It was a letter from an officer in the French Ministry of Instruction who, Gouraud said, had developed a new method of taking daguerreotype portraits. It read:

Paris, 25th April, 1840

My dear Gouraud,

. . . As you suggested, I went this morning to see M. Daguerre. I asked him if he had received your two letters; and expressed to him the pain and anxiety which you suffered on account of his silence. . . .

"I have reason to be offended," he said, "with M. Gouraud. I have lately received a letter from one named Mr. Morse, president of the National Academy of New York, in which he tells me that M. Gouraud has represented himself in America as sent by me to *speculate* with the Daguerreotype, and that he has done so in an unworthy manner – a manner dishonoring to my invention. I hesitated at believing this report, but as I received at the same time a *diploma of honorary membership* of the NATIONAL ACADEMY, of New York, signed by Mr. Morse as PRESIDENT, I thought myself bound to *credit* the truly surprising information conveyed to me by him. I have therefore disavowed M. Gouraud as it was my duty to do, in a letter written to Mr. Morse, for that purpose."

Happily, my dear friend, there is nothing really injurious to you in M. Daguerre's disavowal: I give it to you almost in the very words employed by him. He wrote to Mr. Morse that he had sent no person to America to speculate with his discovery in his name; that he had indeed encouraged, and assisted with his advice and experience, all young men of talent who were devoting themselves to the study and the extension of the Daguerreotype; that he had noticed M. Gouraud as one of the most enthusiastic and assiduous; but that he had authorized no one to abuse his name and compromise his reputation.

At these words I begged permission to interrupt M. Daguerre, to express my surprise and indignation . . . for *I saw in a moment* that the *title of honorary member of the* NATIONAL ACADEMY had been given to M. Daguerre by this Mr. Morse, *only to give his slanders more effect, and secure for them a more certain triumph*. . . .

Your devoted friend,
Abel Rendu [25]

Gouraud thought he had delivered Morse a real blow in publishing this letter, and he did convince at least the Boston *Advertiser* and the New York *American*.

Morse seized on the information that Daguerre had disavowed Gouraud, and this according to a letter which Gouraud himself had printed. Replying in the *Evening Signal,* Morse denied that the academy had granted an honor to Daguerre in order to assist a campaign of vilifying Gouraud, and proved it by pointing out that Daguerre had been chosen an honorary member of the academy six months before Gouraud had arrived in America. Moreover, he denied that he had written Daguerre about Gouraud at all.[26]

Before Gouraud could have read Morse's letter in Boston, he announced that the translation of Rendu's letter had included three errors. The editor of the Boston *Advertiser*, Nathan Hale (whose son, Edward Everett Hale, was learning the new art from Gouraud), vouched for the honesty of Gouraud's new translation after having seen Rendu's original letter. Daguerre's statement that he had received " a letter *from* one named Mr. Morse " was retranslated as " a letter *of* one named Mr. Morse." A letter " in which he tells me " was retranslated as a letter " in which it is said." And a letter received " at the same time " as the notification of the honorary membership in the academy was retranslated as " almost at the same time." [27]

While the corrections may have been delayed with the hope that Morse would be forced into extravagant language, in fact they served to validate Morse's reply. And further justification for Morse was soon forthcoming.

The very person on whom Gouraud depended for his defense, Abel Rendu, turned Morse's witness. Rendu was associated with the firm of Messrs. Giroux and Company, which sponsored Gouraud. When Gouraud did not make payments due the Giroux, they sent Rendu to America to disavow Gouraud as their agent. On arrival in New York, Rendu informed Morse that, trusting Gouraud as a friend, he had called on Daguerre and, contrary to the " corrections " that Gouraud had published, he had understood Daguerre to say that he had received a letter from Morse vilifying Gouraud. Knowing nothing of Morse except from his enemies, Rendu confessed, he had sent Gouraud a letter which he had never supposed would be published. He had raised Gouraud from the lowest condition of life, Rendu wrote; he had furnished him with the means to live in both France and America. But now he knew the man was unworthy of his confidence. He begged Morse to accept his apologies.[28]

" Excuse me, Sir," Morse wrote with understandable bitterness to Nathan Hale, " if I feel that my standing in this community for 30 years ought to have protected me in my own native place from the effects of the one-sided slanders of an irresponsible foreign adventurer, who had been already publicly exposed in this city, and more lately disavowed at home." [29]

The controversy did not end with Morse's gloating. Several months later, when what had once seemed of vast consequence no longer interested him, Morse was visiting Niagara Falls. Putting his name on the register of his hotel, he noticed Gouraud. The next morning at breakfast one of the friends with whom he had come to the Falls told him that he had just had a long conversation with Gouraud and found him penitent. Morse announced that he had no animosity against Gouraud, and after breakfast sought out the " charlatan " on the piazza. Presently, while Morse told himself that Gouraud was more to be pitied than blamed, Gouraud was saying: " You are indeed a Christian."

"And now who do you think was my pilot through all the interesting parts of this region?" Morse wrote to his brother. "You never would guess. No less a person than *Francis Gouraud*. . . . He is doing well here; has established himself quite on a large scale, is taking views of the Falls, has made some important improvements in the apparatus, for which he intends to procure a patent, which in his zeal to make amends for what has passed, he has freely confided to me. In short, from all I have seen and heard of him, there has been a great deal of misconception in regard to him. He has doubtless been imprudent, and must blame himself for much of his trouble, but he is not the character which circumstances led us to believe he was. Much allowance must be made for habits of education and temperament, and I would make them for him. Those reports which affected his moral character, I have reason to believe are false; his wife and child are with him here; he assures me that in this he was grossly slandered by Rendu, and I fear that Rendu is not what I had supposed him to be, an honorable, and correct man. How cautious it is necessary to be with these foreigners!" [30]

Sitters fared badly in the glass-roofed studio that Professors Morse and Draper had erected on top of the University Building. Even with the sun streaming through the glass panes the professors were often not satisfied; they concentrated more light on the sitter with mirrors, occasionally attempting to relieve him by interposing a blue glass between him and the mirrors. Sitters were told precisely what to wear and how to dispose their limbs, if Morse and Draper followed Gouraud's advice. They asked men to dress in clear gray coats, pantaloons of a little deeper hue, and for good contrast, vests of a fancy ground and bright color; they asked women to be so modest as to wear black, red, or green. And they placed the sitter's head "on a semi-circle of iron, fitted to the back of the chair" and "arranged" his arms "at pleasure." [19] If Morse and Draper opened their studio as early as March, they then doubtless kept their sitters still under the sun and mirrors for more than five minutes, for in that month Seager published an exposure table which listed five minutes as the shortest time possible in the best weather at the best time of the day.[31] By summer, however, Draper had reduced the time required to sixty-five seconds.

Sarah Anne Breese of Utica, the heroine of Morse's poem, "Serenade," remembered that her deliberate, hazel-eyed cousin made her most uncomfortable under the eye of his camera. "We were in New York," she wrote, "and to gratify our scientific cousin, spent nearly a day on the roof of the University building, which he had specially fitted up for his purposes, as the light was not obstructed by the street or the surrounding buildings. . . . The light was intensified by the aid of mirrors, fastened on the roof, which reflected the sun.

"We remained seated here, exposed to the noonday sun for hours, our complexions becoming actually tanned and the tears often streaming down our cheeks, and we were taken literally 'with a drop in the eye!' It was a fearful ordeal not soon to be forgotten. After repeated failures, Prof. Morse succeeded in producing tolerable pictures." [32]

By the spring of 1841, about the time Morse was running for mayor for the second time, a paper announced that "daguerreotype likenesses are taken at the studio of professor Morse, with the most perfect correctness, in a second of time – as quick, indeed, as the aparture of the lens can be opened and shut again." [33] The daguerreotype had made rapid progress.

By this time Draper, being especially interested in optical theory, had dropped his connection with the studio, and Morse operated under his own name. George Prosch continued to supply him with equipment. Samuel Broadbent of Philadelphia assisted him until about August 1841, and afterward Mr. Young, an acquaintance of Professor Avery of Hamilton College, took his place. Eventually Morse had another "glass" studio arranged for him by replacing a large part of the roof of the *Observer* Building with skylights. He promised to repay his brothers the five hundred dollars that it cost them when he had earned that sum in his studio; when he earned it, however, as he soon did, he had other uses for it.

To Morse's studio, where cameras, batteries, daguerreotype frames, and coils of wire were tumbled together, came students of the new art. His prestige as president of the National Academy, telegrapher, acquaintance of Daguerre, and disputant with Gouraud, brought to him a large number of young men who were willing to pay his fee of twenty-five or fifty dollars in the hope of finding daguerreotypy the way out of the depression. His pupils included some who were to be among the most celebrated of their profession: T. W. Gridland, known as the first professional west of the Alleghenies, Edward Anthony, later founder of a famous photographic supply house, and Mathew Brady, who through Morse's lessons commenced a career that led him to daguerreotype or photograph every president from John Quincy Adams to McKinley excepting only William Henry Harrison.* More pupils came to Morse than to any other daguerreotypist of the time.

When America had its first World's Fair in 1853 in the New York Crystal Palace on Forty-second Street, daguerreotypy had reached its zenith. The exhibition unquestionably proved that America led the world in the new art. In New York alone some one hundred professionals were making daguerreotypes at about $2.50 apiece. Morse's fame as a daguerreotypist was still well known. His pupils were among the leaders of the profession. Although he had devoted himself to the art for probably only two years,[34] he was asked to judge contests among daguerreotypists; he was invited to purchase a partnership in Talbot's United States patents, and to sponsor the new crystallotype; his opinion of the authenticity of Levi Hill's sensational color-photography process, which the first photographic periodical in the world, the *Daguerrean Journal,* declared would rank with Daguerre's original discovery and Morse's telegraph in importance, was asked and his favorable reply unfortunately respected.[35] The exhibits at the Crystal Palace not only included the finest collection of daguerreotypes ever assembled, but also examples of images on paper, capable of being reproduced without limit, talbotypes, collodions, and crystallotypes. By the following year these had become popular and the heyday of the daguerreotype was over.

Already the art of miniature-painting had disappeared, and por-

* Morse's daguerrean pupils during 1840 included D. [?] G. Johnson of New Orleans; Thomas L. Smiley of Philadelphia; a Mr. Dwight, whose fees were paid by Charles Avery of Hamilton College; and probably Albert S. Southworth, later of Philadelphia, and Joseph Pennel of Bowdoin College; in the same year the science professors Avery of Hamilton College and Eben N. Horsford of Albany Female Academy consulted the teacher. During 1841 Charles Taylor wrote from Charleston that he could not pay for his lessons yet because he had failed as a professional, and Professor F. A. P. Barnard of the University of Alabama, soon to be announcing improvements in daguerreotypy, and later to be the president of Columbia College, requested that he might become a pupil.

trait-painting, the only branch of painting which Morse had found profitable, had entered a decline. The age when portrait-painters were a necessity to the vanity of any respectable family had given way to the age when any family could open a plush case to reveal the shiny surface of a daguerreotype; and now in turn it was soon to give way to the age when nearly everyone, rich and poor, could afford pictures of baby's first smile. When the daguerreotype had almost disappeared, Morse was still not forgotten as a daguerreotypist, in part, doubtless, because he had won fame in another field. Up to the time of his death he was known in photographic journals as the father of American photography.

CHAPTER *xx*

Congressional Blessing

THE AUTHOR of "Woodman Spare That Tree" was also the author of a question that piqued Morse. It would have been sufficiently annoying if Morris had whispered it under one of the trees he loved so well in the quiet of Washington Square, but he chose to noise it in the lively pages of his own *New-York Mirror*.

MR. MORSE'S "CABIN OF THE MAYFLOWER"

When the four pictures to be placed in the Rotunda of the Capitol were given to Weir, Inman, Vanderlyn and Chapman, much dissatisfaction was expressed by Mr. Morse's friends that he did not receive one of the commissions. A subscription was entered into to procure a picture from Mr. Morse's pencil, of the same size as those intended for the Rotunda. . . . We ourselves were among the subscribers. Not having heard any thing of this picture for upwards of a year, it has just occurred to us to inquire what has become of it? Is Mr. Morse engaged upon it? and when is the picture to be done? [1]

From the daily papers Morris knew quite well that Morse had been otherwise engaged during the four years since accepting the *Mayflower* commission. He knew that the art professor was heralded as the inventor of a creditable if unused telegraph. He knew that recently the inventor had been a professional daguerreotypist and only this spring had run for mayor, but he put the question just the same.

Morris's weekly was read among artists and writers, and Morse had to answer. How was it that the politician-inventor had crowded out the artist? he asked himself. As he remembered his return from Europe in 1832 on the *Sully,* he had been for the first time in his life conscious of his ability to do a monumental painting. The decision against him had cut him down in his strength.

He began to prepare a reply. But he grew uncomfortable. Were his words ostentatious? Was a public answer seemly?

The *Mayflower* commission, he began in answer to the *Mirror,* had been "a sufficient antidote to any wounded feeling which a rejection by a Com.tee of Congress, implying incompetence on my part, might be supposed to produce." The subscribers, however, had allowed him only about five hundred dollars a year compared with about two thousand for the painters of the rotunda. Moreover, the installments had come in to him with increasing delinquencies, and some who paid were going beyond their means. Then a letter from the Secretary of the Treasury had encouraged him to believe that within a year, by selling his telegraph to the government, he would have ample means to pursue his painting. The government, however, had failed to purchase, and his expectations in Europe had been similiarly defeated. In the meantime he had lost his usual sources of income in New York, and had not been able to work on the painting even when he had given up immediate hope of success in telegraphy. Last May he had abandoned his intention of painting the *Mayflower* at all, and had begun to save to repay the $510 advanced by the association.[2]

Pondering his letter, he concluded that it would be in better taste to return the money without a public reply to Morris. And he soon did. With his first payments he sent each subscriber a printed circular in which he declared defiantly: "A sense of pecuniary obligation is of all things to me most fatal to that independence of mind which is absolutely necessary to a free exercise of its higher powers."[3]

Presently the receipts came trickling in. They came from Chapman and Weir, the rotunda painters; from Fenimore Cooper, Thomas Cole, and the widow of William Dunlap; from one of his former art patrons, R. V. DeWitt, who wrote, "I can tell you one thing, I like your independence in the matter of your Circular & hope you will before long give us a picture such as you can & ought to produce."[4]

Even buying postage stamps noticeably affected the weight of his purse. He had abandoned all painting to find that telegraphy would not win him a bare living.

One of his painting pupils being behind in his quarterly payment of fifty dollars, Morse walked into his room one day saying: "Well, Strother, my boy, how are we off for money?"

"Why, Professor," his pupil replied, "I am sorry to say I have been disappointed; but I expect a remittance next week."

"Next week!" echoed Morse, "I shall be dead by that time."

"Dead, Sir?"

"Yes, dead by starvation."

The youth was astonished. "Would ten dollars be of any service?"

"Ten dollars would save my life; that is all it would do."

Pupil and professor dined together.

"This is my first meal for twenty-four hours," Morse announced as they finished. "Strother, don't be an artist. It means beggary. Your life depends upon people who know nothing of your art and care nothing for you. A housedog lives better, and the very sensitiveness that stimulates an artist to work keeps him alive to suffering." [5]

When an art student was selecting a room in the northwest tower of the University Building, the janitor conducted him into a room in which the student saw statuettes, busts, and models covered with cobwebs, dusty canvases facing the wall, stumps of brushes littering the floor. The only indications of industry were what seemed to him "a few masterly crayon drawings, and little luscious studies of color pinned to the wall."

"You will have an artist for a neighbor," the janitor told him, "though he is not here much of late; he seems to be getting rather shiftless; he is wasting his time over some silly invention, a machine by which he expects to send messages from one place to another. He is a very good painter, and might do well if he would only stick to his business."

When the janitor told him the painter was Morse, the youth was astounded. The presidency of the National Academy seemed to him the most exalted station to which an artist could aspire! [6]

Meanwhile the European rivals of the "shiftless" artist were outdoing him. Steinheil had long ago secured the financial patronage of Bavarian royalty. Wheatstone and Cooke had a private telegraph company organized in their interests, and by the end of 1842 over two hundred miles of lines were in or near operation in England. Moreover, they were commencing a campaign in the United States.

Just a year and a half after they had opposed the granting of a patent to Morse in England, Wheatstone and Cooke had the audacity to suggest to Morse that he secure them a patent in the United States, and grant them half-rights in his American patent, if he had one. In return they offered half their American rights-to-be.[7] Morse hesitated. He asked Smith for advice. That the final decision was a refusal proved profitable, for Wheatstone's system was never generally used outside of Europe. If the interests of the two most promising telegraphs had been united, however, who knows how different world telegraph history would have been?

Unfortunately for Morse's sense of security, Wheatstone and Cooke found other means of seeking an American patent and obtained one before he did. Though he had entered his caveat years before, he had taken no further action because he believed a prior patent anywhere would prove a hindrance in Europe. He finally secured his patent on June 20, 1840, eight days after Wheatstone and Cooke.

In his poverty it was alarming to discover that his English rivals were able to spend a thousand dollars in mere preparation to bring their telegraph into use in America, and it was galling that none of his partners could supply him with funds to meet the English threat. They well knew the danger. Smith expressed the Englishmen's advantage in cynical terms that forecast his relation to Morse. "Money is the only earthly influence to compete with money," he wrote, "and it has the power, in spite of moral considerations, to make itself heard, felt and obeyed wherever directed." [8]

Through dismal days Morse clung to his vision of wires around the world. He was patient with Vail and Smith, knowing that they were suffering financially in the long-continued depression. He quoted the old saw: "Hope deferred makes the heart sick." "It is true," he added, in writing Smith, "and I have known the full meaning of it. Nothing but the consciousness that I have an invention which is to mark an era in human civilization, and is to contribute to the happiness of millions, would have sustained me through so many and such lengthened trials of patience in perfecting it.”[9] That neither the rich nor the powerful were willing to sponsor his telegraph did not dismay him. Years of discouragement in his art and in politics had given him little faith in the judgment of men of position.

His religious faith sustained him. And he was helped also by the encouragement of one of the most respected scientists of the time, Professor Joseph Henry of Princeton. A few days after Morse returned from his tour in unyielding Europe Henry had written his confidence that there were “no difficulties in the way but such as ingenuity and enterprise may obviate.”[10]

Nearly three years later Henry had still not seen Morse's invention in operation. But from descriptions and conversations with Morse he knew the improvements which the inventor had made, and he now gave it more than ever his approval. He sent Morse a letter of endorsement which stands as a record of generous interest by a man of theoretical science in the practical application of a theory which he himself had helped to develop.

Princeton College, February 24, 1842

My dear Sir:

I am pleased to learn that you have again petitioned Congress in reference to your telegraph, and I most sincerely hope you will succeed in convincing our Representatives of the importance of the invention. In this you may, perhaps, find some difficulty, since, in the minds of many, the electro-magnetic telegraph is associated with the various chimerical projects constantly presented to the public, and particularly with the schemes, so popular a year or two ago, for the application of electricity as a moving power in the arts. I have asserted, from the first, that all attempts of this kind are premature, and made without a proper knowledge of scientific principles. The case is, however, entirely different in regard to the electro-magnetic telegraph. *Science is now fully ripe for this application,* and I have not the least doubt, if proper means be afforded, of the perfect success of the invention.

The idea of transmitting intelligence to a distance by means of electrical action has been suggested by various persons, from the time of Franklin to the present; but until the last few years, or since the principal discoveries in electro-magnetism, all attempts to reduce it to practice were necessarily unsuccessful. The mere suggestion, however, of a scheme of this kind is a matter for which little credit can be claimed, since it is one which would naturally arise in the mind of almost any person familiar with the phenomena of electricity; but the bringing it forward at the proper moment, when the developments of science are able to furnish the means of a certain success, and the devising a plan for carrying it into practical operation, are the grounds of a just claim to scientific reputation, as well as to public patronage.

About the same time with yourself Professor Wheatstone, of London, and Dr. Steinheil, of Germany, proposed plans of the electro-magnetic telegraph, but these differ as much from yours as the nature of the common principle would well permit; and unless some essential improvements have lately been made in these European plans, I should prefer the one invented by yourself. With my best wishes. . . .

Yours truly,
Joseph Henry[11]

Thus a man whose basic discoveries helped to make the telegraph possible placed himself on record as believing that Morse was not merely a mechanic, as some were to say, but an inventor deserving scientific as well as popular applause. Henry even told Morse's daguerrean friend Chilton that the telegraph was the most beautiful and ingenious instrument he had ever seen.[12]

Experiments took up much of Morse's time, quieting the tension of waiting, and giving him new faith in his invention. Even in 1840 he wrote a person who had seen the telegraph in Paris that he would hardly recognize it now.[13] Its outward appearance had changed, but the principles were the same which he had sketched in his *Sully* notebook.

On October 18, 1842 he rowed from the Battery across New York harbor toward Governor's Island, paying out wire coated with pitch, tar, and rubber. That evening he communciated successfully from the Battery to the island. He believed that he had sent electric signals through a submarine cable for the first time. As on the *Sully* he was happy in his ignorance. He did not know that Pasley in England and O'Shaughnessy in India had already done so in 1838 and 1839.[14]

The next morning the *Herald* announced that a revolutionary invention would be demonstrated between twelve and one o'clock at Castle Garden on the Battery. Early that morning, however, when Morse had just got the line in working order again, it went lead. Across the water he saw seven vessels lying along the line of the cable. Soon he understood. One of the vessels had raised the cable with its anchor; the sailors, not knowing what kind of seaweed it could be, had cut his cable. The crowd that gathered at noon for the "revolutionary" demonstration turned away with jeers, no doubt believing that once more New Yorkers had proved themselves gullible.[15] Morse philosophized through sleepless nights.

A few weeks later Morse succeeded in crossing a canal by telegraph. And about the same time with the assistance of James C. Fisher, who had received a temporary appointment as professor at the university, he discovered that two or more currents would pass without interference over a wire at the same time. The interest of men of science and his own experiments were distinctly encouraging.

For four years Morse had been appealing to Congress to appropriate funds for a large-scale test of his telegraph. "For nearly two years past," he had just written in September, "I have devoted all my time and scanty means, living on a mere pittance, denying myself all pleasures, and even necessary food, that I might have a sum to put my Telegraph into such a position before Congress as to insure success to the common enterprise."[16] He had looked for private capital and found none. During the last year he had made an agreement with a lobbyist, Isaac N. Coffin, to give five per cent of a congressional telegraph appropriation to him, but Coffin too had failed.

At the moment Washington's mood was friendly. The Whig majority in Congress were likely to favor internal improvements and hence a telegraph test. The partners were not sorry that President Tyler, however, had become a Democrat, for Smith, Morse, and the Vails had all been active as Democrats; in the last election, while Judge Vail had plumped for Harrison and Tyler, his sons had remained true to their family tradition. Tyler had proved himself so friendly to Smith that it had been rumored that Smith might enter the Cabinet as postmaster general. On internal improvements the President gave no sign of having a fixed policy. In spite of the depression and Tyler's attempt to economize, Morse now believed that Congress would pass his bill and the President would sign it if only one of the partners in the telegraph enterprise could be in Washington.

In the fall he once more asked the Vails for funds to permit him to go to Washington. They had none to spare. Against the advice of his sons Judge Vail had invested in local railroad-building, and the sons themselves had their funds tied in the Baldwin locomotive works, which, like all capital-goods industries, was mired in the continuing depression. Morse wished to send Professor Fisher of New York University to Washington for the sake of his influence in Congress. And Morse knew his own value in Congress. He had a host of friends, a confident manner in approaching strangers, and an excellent sense for publicity. Somehow he himself found funds for them both to go to Washington in December.

Morse took care that they lived simply in the capital. The first week they took rooms in the American Hotel at $16.50 for room and breakfast for both. Later Morse found a room for himself at $5 a week, and still later Commissioner of Patents Ellsworth, his classmate at Yale, and the father of a beautiful girl, took him into his house. Presently it was rumored that Morse was engaged to be married.

As twenty years before when he was exhibiting his *Congress Hall*, he found that miscellaneous projects were housed in the Capitol. Just now Edward Anthony, once his pupil, was using the rooms of Senator Benton's Committee on Military Affairs for daguerreotyping every member of Congress. He himself was again given the use of the rooms of the House Committe on Commerce, and this time, the use of the rooms of the Senate Committee on Naval Affairs as well. He began stringing wires to connect the instruments in the two rooms.

Soon two sets of instruments were clicking in each of the two committee rooms, with wires connecting through the vaults of the building. The performances that had proved so dramatic to the uninitiated four years before were repeated. "The mind is scarcely prepared," the *National Intelligencer* commented on the exhibitions, "to pursue even in speculation the mighty results which are soon to follow."[17] Two congressmen and a reporter gave their names to Morse in one of the rooms one day and then walked to the other. As they entered, the telegraph operator in charge, whom they had never seen before, announced their names to a crowded company. Everyone was convinced of the power of the telegraph, the reporter concluded; the only question was the expense of laying the wires.[18] But the reporter mistook excitement for confidence. One skeptical member of the Committee on Commerce, the Whig Caruthers of Tennessee, was convinced only when Morse – doubtless with his tongue in his cheek – correctly sent the message: "Tyler deserves to be hanged." [19] Other visitors were not convinced at all. Senator Smith of Indiana confessed afterward that he studied Morse's face for signs of insanity.[20]

Again Morse had the satisfaction of seeing the House Committee on Commerce report in his favor. In December Representative Ferris of New York, for the committee, reviewed the amazing list of recommendations for Morse's invention, and proposed that $30,000 be appropriated for testing Morse's telegraph by constructing a line under the immediate superintendence of Morse and the general direction of the Postmaster General.[21]

When Greenough and Morse were in Europe they had agreed that Congress did little to keep American artists at home. The unexpected had happened and Congress had given Greenough a commission to model a statute of Washington. He had come all the way from Italy to supervise the installation of the completed statue in the center of the rotunda, only to find that it was so heavy that it threatened to crash through the floor. He was now asking $5,000 to place it on a pedestal in front of the Capitol. But the Tyler administration was priding itself on economy, and his request seemed hopeless. He thought Morse's equally futile. "Poor Morse is here with his beautiful, his magical telegraph," he wrote to his brother. "How he continues to keep alive with the hope that they will vote him $30,000 now, when they propose to cut down West Point and reduce the salaries in the navy, I know not. He goes regularly to the House." [22]

Day after day, as Morse waited in the House gallery, he wondered if his hopes would be defeated as they had been when he had painted his father, Professor Silliman, and an Indian chief sitting in the same gallery. Again and again as he walked through the rotunda and saw the spaces on the wall on which he had hoped to place the great monumental painting of his life, he may have wondered if John Quincy Adams, still a member of the House, would again single him out for his spite. He may have wondered, too, if any opposition to his nativism would flare up in debate; or if, as four years before, the House would merely forget to call his bill to the floor. He hoped for victory, but he had known too many disappointments in his fifty-one years to be confident. "Everything looks favorable," he wrote to his brothers on January 6, "but I do not suffer myself to be sanguine, for I do not know what may be doing secretly against it. I shall believe it passed when the signature of the President is affixed to it, and not before.[23]

He pleaded with Smith to come to Washington to help the cause. But Smith was now busy editing a farm journal,[24] caring for his farm and other real estate, and addressing Maine agricultural societies. When Morse heard that Smith positively would not come he replied in a letter of remarkable temperance:

Washington, D. C., Jan.y 13.th, 1843

Dear Sir,

I have just received yours of the 4th inst. and regret exceedingly that you are not here as I expected you would be; for my bill is just now in a situation in which you could be of very great service to the whole enterprize.

I have had rather an unequal share of the trouble and risks, and expense of urging forward this enterprize. . . . I . . . have been compelled to do all both in invention and in the urging it before the public, at my own expense and risk, while the profits should any accrue must be divided between you all. You will all see how unequally this bears upon me and in the spirit of justness and fairness will no doubt adjust matters right.

My bill is referred to the Com.tee of the Whole *on the State of the Union,* and I am hoping, it will be called up, every day, but you know the business of waiting for the action of Congress. The Vails have not assisted me with any funds, Dr. Gale cannot, and I am here with nearly every cent I own in the world in my pocket; I brought on with me Professor Fisher, who has been of great assistance to me in exhibiting the action of the Telegraph and in visiting many Members with whom he is personally acquainted. I pay his expenses and the delay in acting upon my bill, is operating pretty seriously for me. In a few days I shall have expended everything, and shall not have the means even of paying my passage home.

If the darkest time is just before day, daylight must be close at hand; and I am inclined to think this is the case, for there is a bright side to this dark picture. I find no opposition anywhere, on the contrary every kind feeling towards me, and favorable and even enthusiastic feeling towards the Telegraph. I am told everywhere that my bill will undoubtedly pass. The only hint of possible opposition is that some of the Maine!! Members may oppose it. A few days will decide the matter. The Senate I learn from many Members, will not be long in passing it through when the House shall have passed it. . . .

Yrs truly
Sam.l F. B. Morse [25]

The fickle boy of Andover and Yale had become a memorable example of perseverance. Even Smith knew it. "Since your return from Europe," he admitted in reply, "yours has been the whole expense, yours the whole toil of keeping the principle of life, and hope and utility in the invention." [26]

The tension heightened as Morse watched from the gallery day after day. There were so many congressmen who had to speak for the benefit of their constitutents, or, as Morse put it, "say something to Bunkum," that his bill was not yet called up. He heard debates on the proposal to impeach the chameleon President Tyler, on the fine imposed on Andrew Jackson for his administration of martial law in New Orleans in 1815, on the arrests of American slavers off Africa by British vessels; it seemed to him that the people's time was much wasted. He was reduced to the level, unusual for him, of questioning whether he was doing right. "Am I in the path of duty?" he posed. "When I think that the little money I brought with me is nearly gone, that if nothing should be done by Congress, I shall be in a destitute state, that perhaps I shall have again to be a burden to friends until I know to what to turn my hands, I feel low spirited. I am only relieved by naked trust in God, and it is right that this should be so." [27]

His whole life seemed to turn on the passage of the bill. If it becomes law, he wrote his Charleston friend Cogdell, "I have a work to perform in organizing my Telegraphic system for the country which may employ me for the rest of my life." [28] The issue was life employment and honor versus destitution until he could find new work. Or so it seemed to him now. He forgot that four months before, he had vowed that as soon as the telegraph was established his telegraph partners would woo him from painting in vain.[9] "My history would present a series of conflicts, disappointments, trials and successes," he told Cogdell, "and yet who are without all these in some form or other?"

He studied resignation, but found himself fretful. It was easier to say: "Thy will be done" than to feel it, and he knew he did not wholly feel it. The suspense became increasingly onerous as January closed and he knew that the end of the session, March 3, was not far away.

One day in early February he told the story of his woe to a friend and moved him to tears.

A few days later, February 21, congressmen read in their morning *National Intelligencer* new evidence of distinguished support for Morse's bill. Benjamin Silliman, under whom Morse had once studied about batteries at Yale, had now written his once unpromising pupil: "If I have weight enough to carry only one wavering vote, it may be the very one that will cast the decision in your favor." That same day Morse was in the House gallery when his bill at last came to the floor.

During the morning the House considered Revolutionary War pensions; in the early afternoon John Quincy Adams lectured on state debts; after a brief debate on land claims in Arkansas, Millard Fillmore moved that the House go into Committee of the Whole. Just before coming to Washington Morse had seen Fillmore in New York and changed his distrust of the telegraph into a belief that it might succeed. His motion having carried, Fillmore moved consideration of a navy pension bill. Mr. Adams might now have reminded Fillmore of his pledge that when he had the floor he would relinquish it to Adams, so that he might move to send an American minister to China for the first time. But Adams refrained. His restraint permitted the novelist John P. Kennedy, Smith's successor as chairman of the Committee on Commerce, to ask Fillmore to give him the floor to move the telegraph bill. On the promise that, if debate began, Kennedy would not persist in his motion, Fillmore agreed. Kennedy then moved that the Secretary of the Treasury rather than the Postmaster General oversee the telegraph expenditure. The amendment was carried.

Cave Johnson of Tennessee rose to insist that since Congress was about to encourage science it should encourage the science of mesmerism in Washington. Mr. Johnson did not know that he himself was eventually to administer United States telegraphs.

Houston of Alabama interrupted to propose that along with magnetism and mesmerism Millerism * should be included in the bill.

Stanly of North Carolina said he had no objection to including mesmerism provided the gentleman from Tennessee was the subject of the experiment. ("A laugh," added the *Congressional Globe* at this point.)

Mr. Johnson replied that he had no objection provided Mr. Stanly was the operator. ("Great laughter.")

Morse was leaning tensely against the gallery railing.

Mr. Mason appealed to the chair to rule the amendment out of order as not in good faith and therefore injurious to the character of the House.

The chairman, Winthrop of Massachusetts, replied that it was not for him to judge the motives of members in introducing amendments. Said he: "It would require a scientific analysis to determine how far the magnetism of mesmerism was analogous to that to be employed in telegraphs." ("Laughter.")

A reporter approached Morse.

"I have an awful headache," Morse told him, putting his hand to his forehead.

"You are anxious."

"I have reason to be, and if you knew how important this is to me, you would not wonder. I have spent seven years in perfecting this invention, and all that I had: if it succeeds, I am a made man; if it fails, I am ruined." [29]

Meanwhile twenty-two members of the House voted in favor of amending the bill to include mesmerism and Millerism.

The amendment having been defeated, the House promptly voted without a division to report the telegraph bill from the Committee of the Whole to the House. Immediately thereafter Mr.

* A sect which then anticipated the second coming of Christ in 1844.

Adams asked why Mr. Fillmore had not given him the floor to move his China bill.[30] But Morse's former enemy had already let slip his opportunity to interrupt the progress of Morse's bill, if, indeed, he had any desire to do so. Morse was no longer listening. His friends gathered around him exclaiming that the first crisis was over. Some admitted to him that they had voted for the bill rather in deference to him than from confidence in his machine.

Two days later Durand, the painter, was writing about Morse to a friend who asked Durand when the inventor would be likely to repay a loan. Morse "has been all winter at Washington," Durand wrote, "trying hard to push his 'dunder & blixen' Telegraph thru Congres. . . . I am afraid however that Uncle Sam will be found lightning proof in this case & that his unlucky Godson will return as he went with the exception of having exhausted the $700 salary from the N.A.D. [National Academy of Design], with small benefit to the Fine Arts, and with as little prospect for the benefit of your $50 note."[31]

That very day, however, Mr. Kennedy again moved the bill, this time for its third reading. Someone called for yeas and nays, and not a few congressmen left their seats to avoid responsibility for voting upon a machine they could not understand. Morse was in the rear of the hall. He stood by while the votes on his fate were being counted. He tried to keep tally, but the figures danced before his eyes. The result was announced. Morse hardly knew what happened. Hamilton Fish supported him to a seat.

Mr. Adams did not vote. Among those opposed to the bill were Cave Johnson of Tennessee. Among those in favor were Kennedy, Fillmore, and Winthrop; while Wallace of Indiana, father of the author of *Ben-Hur,* was defeated for re-election soon afterward because he had voted to spend public money for this absurdity.[32]

When Morse recovered he analyzed the vote. Seventy congressmen had not voted at all, an ample number to overcome his slim majority of 89 to 83. He had won a majority of all states north of the Potomac, including Maine, after all, but excepting New Hampshire; he carried four Western states, Ohio, Indiana, Michigan, and Louisiana, and lost one, Arkansas; he carried none of the nine

Southern states voting. His success was in the commercial states, favorable to internal improvements.

His House majority of six might be quite as useful as a thousand — if he carried the Senate. He was a little grim as he wrote Vail of his progress toward victory. "For two years, I have labored all my time and at my own expense, without assistance from the other proprietors (except in obtaining the iron of the magnets for the last instruments obtained of you) to forward our enterprise. My means to defray my expenses, to meet which every cent I owned in the world was collected, are nearly all gone, and if, by any means, the bill should fail in the Senate, I shall return to New York with the *fraction of a dollar* in my pocket." [33]

Eight days only remained before the close of the session. The Senate calendar was jammed. Not only might his bill be defeated if it came to the floor, but it might not even emerge from the calendar. When the last day of the session came, there were still more than one hundred and forty bills before his.

As Morse related long afterward,[34] he was in the Senate all day on March 3. When the lamps were lighted it seemed to him that his bill could not be reached before the closing hour. He consulted senatorial friends. They told him to prepare for any disappointment. He could stand the strain no longer and went to his room convinced that his bill was lost, that he would be returning home without any work ahead of him, and that for a whole year again it would be impossible for him to go forward with his contribution to the world. At his hotel he found that after paying his bill he would have enough for his railroad ticket home and thirty-seven and a half cents more. As he remembered it, he disposed of his fears in his long-tried way of faith and slept like a child.

In the morning, as he walked into his breakfast room, a servant called him. A young lady had come to see him. It was Annie Ellsworth, the smiling daughter of the Commissioner of Patents, to whom even Morse's daughter came to believe he was engaged. He expressed his surprise at the early call.

"I have come to congratulate you," she said.

"Indeed, for what?"

"On the passage of your bill."

"Oh, no, my young friend, you are mistaken; I was in the Senate-chamber till after the lamps were lighted, and my senatorial friends assured me there was no chance for me."

"But," she replied, "it is you that are mistaken. Father was there at the adjournment, at midnight, and saw the President put his name to your bill; and I asked father if I might come and tell you, and he gave me leave. Am I the first to tell you?"

Morse could not speak for a moment.

"Yes, Annie," he said at last, "you are the first to inform me; and now I am going to make you a promise: the first dispatch on the completed line from Washington to Baltimore shall be yours."

Some evidence supports Morse's comely story. Greenough wrote his brother on March 3: "There is no telling what Congress will or will not do. They have passed both Morse's and my bill to-day, and both by a handsome majority." [35] Over a year later Morse wrote that Annie had first told him of "the final passage of the bill." [36] And Annie did eventually send the first formal message over the first telegraph line.

Other evidence, however, negates the point of the story. Careful students have crushed some of this evidence. They have discovered a letter of Morse to Smith saying the bill had just passed. Morse dated the letter March 3. But they take it upon themselves to remark that he must have written it on March 4 and in the excitement misdated it. If so, however, it is odd that in the letter he says that the President has not signed the bill, since Annie is supposed to have told him it was already signed. Moreover, according to the *Congressional Globe*, [37] his bill was not passed after the lamps were lighted on March 3, but in the morning session of that day when he was still supposedly in the Senate Chamber; and according to the House *Journal*,[38] the President announced his signature of the bill not late but early in the evening.

Morse would not spin a story out of nothing. He simply did not remember accurately twenty years after the event. It may be that Annie only brought him the news of President Tyler's signature; or that Annie brought him the news of the Senate vote on the morning of March 3.

Be that as it may, Morse was triumphant. "You will be glad to learn doubtless," he wrote Vail, "that my bill has passed the Senate without a division, and without opposition, so that now the Telegraphic enterprise begins to look bright. I shall want to see you in New York after my return, which will probably be the latter part of next week. I have other letters to write so excuse the shortness of this which if short is sweet at least." [39]

A few days later Morse borrowed fifty dollars from his former daguerrean pupil Edward Anthony and bought a coat and pantaloons.[40] His credit was good.

CHAPTER *xxi*

"*What Hath God Wrought!*"

LIKE many a newly appointed official, the superintendent of the United States telegraphs was confronted with demands from his supporters for rewards. Though his partners had done little to transform the telegraph bill into law, they were on hand for a conference in New York on March 21, pressing for office. Morse was no business man; it was awkward enough to be responsible for dispensing $30,000 in constructing what had never before been constructed in America, but it was still more difficult to appease his partners. He was testing himself as well as his telegraph.

He had already consulted the person who was to administer the telegraph appropriation, Secretary of the Treasury Spencer. Of the two methods of placing the wires which he had mentioned in his 1837 letter to Secretary Woodbury, he now told Secretary Spencer he preferred the plan of laying them in the ground. As he explained later, he favored the underground system because he believed it cheaper, and because he understood that Wheatstone had thirteen miles of underground line operating successfully in England. Whether he knew that Wheatstone also had lines on poles is uncertain.[1]

Already he had proposed to the secretary the appointment of Professors Gale and Fisher, "who have been for a long time associated with me in my experiments,"[2] as assistant superintendents. Somehow by the time of the New York meeting Morse became convinced that Vail also had been long associated in his experiments and deserved an appointment. Fisher offered to supervise the preparation of the wire; since the Mississippi college in which Gale had been teaching was closed, Gale was able to furnish any service Morse might desire; and Vail wished to supervise the manufacture of the instruments at three dollars a day plus travel expenses.[3]

Fortunately Secretary Spencer did not hold it against Morse that he was a nativist. As Secretary of State of New York under Governor Seward, Spencer had proposed a compromise school bill that Morse the nativist had fought. Now Spencer docilely appointed Morse as superintendent at $2,000 a year, Fisher and Gale as assistant superintendents at $1,500, and Vail assistant superintendent at $1,000.

Unhappily no government salary was granted to the most ambitious of the partners, the Yankee from Maine. According to the original terms of partnership Smith was to present his services to the partners gratuitously. But so were Vail and Gale. They argued that to present their services to Morse as superintendent of United States telegraphs would not be the same as presenting them to Morse as their partner; accordingly they felt justified in accepting a government income. Smith, however, was not a trained technician. The United States telegraphs appointed no lawyers. He could only hope — and later developments indicate that Morse encouraged him to hope — that he might derive an income from the congressional appropriation by arranging contracts for Morse.

With organization out of the way, the superintendent prepared an advertisement for Boston, New York, and Baltimore papers calling for bids for No. 15, 16, and 18 copper wire to be delivered in 28 days; bids for covering the wire with cotton twine in 90 days; and bids for about forty miles of lead pipe, half an inch in internal diameter, to be delivered in 28 days.[4] Since returning from Europe, Morse had learned that the ground could be used to complete a circuit; the bids therefore called for only half the amounts which he would otherwise have demanded. He awaited the bids at his office in his brothers' *Observer* Building in New York.

While the advertisements were running in the papers the superintendent concerned himself with the alignment for the telegraph. In consultation with Secretary Spencer he had already decided that the best route would be between the Capitol building, where the congressmen who might buy his patent for the government were within reach, and the populous city of Baltimore, only forty miles distant. After surveying the possible routes, Morse decided that the best right of way would be that of the fifteen-year-old Baltimore and Ohio Railroad. Over slight opposition from members of the board of directors, President McLane granted permission, provided the telegraph did not "interfere" with normal road operations.[5] In consultation with Gale and Vail, Morse agreed to let Smith discover what McLane meant by "interfere" with normal operations and draft an agreement.

In late April the bids were ready for the Secretary of the Treasury's perusal. James E. Serrel, who had invented a lead-pipe-making machine which Morse, Gale, Vail, and Smith had seen and approved, made the lowest of the five bids for pipe. All the bids were well below the estimates Morse had made to the secretary and they were both pleased.

Bids for trenching – that is, the laying of the pipes with wires enclosed in the ground – were not called for with the other bids. Morse gave Smith the opportunity to arrange the trenching contract. Smith proposed as contractor Levi S. Bartlett, his wife's brother, the first of several relatives whom he was to connect with the telegraph. Smith's immediate partisanship for Bartlett and the fact that Bartlett later assigned his rights under the contract to Smith suggest that Smith wished to be the contractor himself, using Bartlett's name as a front. Morse may not at first have realized this. When Smith forwarded his contract from Portland, however, Morse declined to accept it because the expense was to be exactly what he had estimated it to be: "It does not *look* right to have it exactly the sum presented in the estimates." Instead of $6,120 he said he would be satisfied if it were $6,000.[6] Morse may already have suspected that Smith, being denied a lawful income from government telegraphs, was determined to extract an unlawful income.

Perhaps in the hope of appeasing Smith, Morse attempted to have his travel expenses as a lawyer for the United States telegraphs paid by the government. Secretary Spencer ruled against it. "If legal advice was wanted," he wrote Morse, "application should have been made to the Department. Mr. Smith's being a proprietor of the Telegraph as stated by you, can make no difference. The services are not of the description contemplated by the act of Congress."[7]

In June Morse and Bartlett signed the trenching contract as arranged by Smith. The date for completing the work was advanced, approximately as Morse had requested, to December 1. The rate of pay, however, was fixed at $153 per mile, which, at forty miles, was $6,120, the exact sum Morse had originally estimated.

Ezra Cornell liked walking. He liked it because it was cheap and because he could choose his own route. He was walking in Maine when he found the road to the fortune that built Cornell University.

As a mechanic, Cornell had culled no fortune from Ithaca, New York. Disappointed, he had bought the exclusive right to sell the Barnaby & Mooers plow in Georgia and Maine. He found Georgia farmers immovable. But Maine Yankees, while they already had what he admitted were the best plows in the Union, wanted still better ones. One summer he persuaded Editor Smith of the *Eastern Farmer* to try the new plow on his Westbrook farm and testify for it in his farm journal. Later they were together at a fair in Readfield, Smith giving a vacuous oratorical plea for farmers to raise themselves in the social and political scale, and Cornell demonstrating his plow.[8]

The next summer Cornell was again on the road to Maine. He walked from Ithaca to Albany in four days, and from Boston to Portland in two and a half days. In Portland he promptly called on Editor Smith at the office of what was now the *Maine Farmer.*

He found the editor on his knees in the middle of the floor, the mold-board of a plow at his side, and chalk marks on the floor before him. He was explaining a design for a plow to a manufacturer, who Cornell knew by his good-natured grin was dubious of Smith's knowledge.

Smith rose. " Cornell," he said, as Cornell remembered, " you are the very man I wanted to see. I have been trying to explain to neighbor Robertson, a machine that I want made, but I cannot make him understand it." He explained that he wanted a plow that would leave the earth on each side of the trench in convenient form for filling in again by another machine. He told him that it was for laying telegraph wires in the earth.

Cornell looked at specimens of the pipe in which the wires were to be enclosed, and understood at once that Smith needed not two machines but one. He sketched a design and showed it to Smith. The pipe was to uncoil from a reel on the plow and pass into the ground directly behind the coulter; another device on the plow was to scoop the earth back into place over the pipe. The next morning Smith provided the young plow salesman with materials and space in a Portland machine-shop.

When Cornell had built the model, Smith asked Morse to come down East to see it. According to Cornell's unreliable recollection, on August 19 they tested it on Smith's Westbrook farm near Forest Home. The plow was hitched behind eight oxen, driven by an Irishman employed for the purpose. As the three Yankees watched, the Irishman flourished his gad and the oxen pulled ahead in a run. In their alarm Morse and Smith forgot about the plow. When the oxen came to a stop they were bewildered to see that the pipe had disappeared from the reel. Cornell coolly assured them, as he said afterward, that the pipe was where it was intended to be, in the ground. Doubtfully Smith directed the Irishman to dig for the pipe. He found it. The whole length had been successfully laid. At once Smith (doubtless on behalf of Bartlett) hired the ingenious Cornell to lay the pipe for the Washington-Baltimore line with his own machine. Morse is said to have returned to New York confident of the success of underground wires.[9]

For only a little while longer telegraph prospects remained satisfactory. On August 10, 160 miles of wire were ready on reels – the longest wire Morse had ever had available. At Morse's invitation Professors Renwick of Columbia College, Ellet of South Carolina Columbia College, and Draper and Fisher of New York University were present. For the first time Morse used one of the new constant batteries, Grove's, an improvement on Daniel's. The result was immensely gratifying; unexpectedly the battery worked the receiving magnet adequately through 160 miles of wire without relays. With the assistance of the professors Morse made careful experiments on the decomposing power of the current. The results, he believed, confirmed the law discovered in 1826 by Ohm, a lonely Cologne gymnasium teacher, that current equals voltage divided by resistance. "The practical inference from this law," Morse concluded in a report to Secretary Spencer, "is that a telegraphic communication on my plan may with certainty be established across the Atlantic. Startling as this may seem now, the time will come when this project will be realized."[10] These were bold words for one who had not yet tested his telegraph for more than 160 miles and even then not in practical service.

Troubles soon gathered. In September Serrel was already behind schedule in delivering the pipe with wire encased. Cornell did not begin trenching until October 21, when only forty days remained before the whole trenching operation was to be completed. But Serrel was still delivering pipe so slowly that Cornell was delayed. Exasperated, Morse directed Smith to make a new contract for pipe. According to the new contract with the Tatham brothers the charge for the remaining thirty-three miles of pipe was to be $1,176.12 less than what Serrel was to have charged.[11] Smith proposed that the saving be credited half to Morse and half to himself. Morse hesitated, questioning whether Smith's proposal was honest. Finally he credited his half to the government, and let Smith do what he pleased with his.[12]

Cornell's astonishing plow was laying the pipe faster than the plumbers were soldering the ends of each length together; consequently it was not until Cornell had laid nine miles of pipe from Baltimore nearly to the Baltimore and Ohio depot at Relay, Maryland, that Vail and his electricians proved that the Serrel pipe, made by a process which the partners had approved, was defective. Just when the whole enterprise seemed to be well launched, it tilted into a ridiculous pose.

Morse walked along the tracks to where Cornell was still following his plow and team of eight mules.

"Mr. Cornell," he called, and Cornell left his machine. "Can't you contrive some plausible excuse for stopping this work for a few days? I want to make some experiments before any more pipe is laid, and I don't want the papers to know that the work is purposefully stopped."

Cornell knew that the wire had not been properly insulated. He had been expecting some such request, and was ready. "Yes, I can manage that," he said. Stepping back, he called to the mule-drivers: "Hurrah, boys, whip up the mules; we must lay another length of pipe before we quit." The drivers cracked their whips, and the telegraph plow cut the earth, drew the useless pipe from the reel, buried it, and covered it. Cornell watched for his opportunity. While Morse looked on, he canted his plow so that it caught the point of a rock and broke in pieces.[13]

Morse had gained time, he hoped, to salvage what was left of his plans. While the Serrel pipe had been made by drawing soft lead ingots into thin pipe over a mandrel in which were the four wires to be enclosed, the wires were being enclosed in the Tatham pipe while it was still hot. Morse asked Professor Fisher, who had been responsible for testing the Serrel pipe, to state whether he was faithfully testing the Tatham pipe. His duty was to stop up one end of each length of pipe, apply a vacuum at the other, and see if the vacuum was sustained. Fisher replied that he was testing it according to directions. He added, however, that he had expected the Serrel pipe to prove worthless.[14] Either he was skeptical of the test which Morse had prescribed, as Cornell was,[15] or else he had heard reports that it had proved useless. By about the middle of December, when the laying of the pipe was to have been completed, Cornell had reconstructed his plow and laid a mile of Tatham pipe. When tested, it too proved defective, probably because the pipe was so hot when the wires were put into it that the insulation was burned.

Vail and Morse agreed that both processes of manufacture might have been wrong, but that Fisher should have discovered the defects long before. They seem to have ignored the possibility that the test was itself defective. Dismal conferences succeeded one another at the Relay House, in Relay, Maryland, where Morse, Vail, and Smith were staying.

Morse dismissed Fisher, but unfortunately in his desire to be kind did not frankly tell him why. The approach of winter, he said, was halting all trenching. In reply Fisher became insolent. Then Morse was forced to tell him that his unfaithful testing had "well nigh ruined the whole enterprize."[16] Morse took the trouble to recommend him to Gale for a position in the factory of Gale's father-in-law in New York. Gale did find him a place, but presently Gale and Fisher quarreled and Fisher walked out, threatening to reveal the secrets on which the factory depended.

At the same time that he dismissed Fisher, Morse lost another helper. Gale resigned, he explained, because the illness of his father-in-law rendered his superintendence of the New York factory essential. Gale retained Morse's confidence, but just now, in the darkest moment of the enterprise, only Vail and Smith were with him. And Smith soon broke away too.

When the defects in the pipe had become fully understood, Morse shied again from the reality of failure. Without assigning any reason, he wrote Smith that trenching operations should stop until spring, except for completing a short stretch near the Capitol so that Congress might see the telegraph in operation.[17]

Smith, alias Bartlett, refused to comply. He had begun the trenching, he insisted, later than the contract specified, but at Morse's request; after it commenced he had been required to submit to constant delay occasioned by non-delivery of pipe. Now he was being asked by the government to transfer all his means of operation from the part of the line where Morse had ordered him to begin to another part of the line; and after doing an inconsequential part of the trenching, he was being ordered to suspend operations until spring, when, according to the contract, all operations were to have been completed already. He threatened to claim damages.[18]

Morse felt crushed. He had never been so exhausted before, it seemed to him, and never in more need of prayer. He was almost overwhelmed when he could not get away long enough to see his daughter Susan sail from New York for her new home in Porto Rico.

As a solution Smith proposed that Morse secure the Secretary of the Treasury's approval for an advance to Bartlett. Morse would declare that he had vouchers from Bartlett for money paid to him for work done to the amount of nearly $5,000. The $3,000 difference between this sum and what Morse had actually paid him for work done would be an advance to Bartlett in consideration of the inconvenience he had suffered through delay. Bartlett would then finish the work in the spring. Morse, however, stoutly refused to certify to the government that he had paid Bartlett for work done – which was indeed the only basis on which the contract gave him the right to give Bartlett any money – when in actuality he would be paying Bartlett for work not yet done. "I cannot consistently with any consideration of honor," he bluntly informed

Smith, "ask the Secretary of Treasury to approve an agreement which violates truth on the face of it."[19]

Morse did not understand the character of the proposed agreement, Smith countered. The agreement was in the form of articles to be attached to the old contract, thus in effect making it a new contract. It was to be expressly stated in the new contract that Morse was but to advance money to Bartlett in consideration of what he had lost under the old contract, and then Bartlett was to complete the work in the spring under the new terms. If to adjust the old contract Morse had to perform an act that was not provided for in the old contract but was provided for in the new, what was dishonest about that? Smith proposed a meeting at the Treasury Building "to decide finally whether our mutual relations can be preserved or must be broken forever."[20]

Morse's acidity could be justified only if he already suspected that Smith was a swindler. He did. They had already tussled over the original Bartlett contract and the division of the saving from the new contract with the Tathams. Now, hot with dismay over the bad pipe and the uncertain prospect ahead, he had come out in flat accusation. In reality the lifelong struggle between the partners had begun as soon as any money came into their hands to dispute about. Smith "seems perfectly reckless and acts like a madman," Morse wrote to his brother, "and all for what? . . . His profit on the contract. *Hinc illæ lachrymæ.*"[21]

Sharp comments about the telegraph enterprise were finding their way into the papers, and with reason. The Bartlett contract was in dispute; the Tatham brothers' contract had been broken by Morse's order that they stop delivering their defective pipe; Gale had resigned, Fisher was dismissed, Smith was rampant. And what must have stung Morse most of all, Vail chose this time to demand a raise in salary and predict calamity. "Had a conversation with Prof. Morse," Vail wrote in his diary, "and represented to him that my salary was not sufficient to meet my expenses. He has given me the promise that he would represent my case to the secretary and have my salary raised 250 dollars, and that immediately. The mode of conducting the business of the Telegraph I cannot concur in, and doubt if the experiment is ever tried, and I am at a loss to decide whether or not to remain in the employ of the government.

There is much inefficiency in the chief superintendence of it. Much indecision and economy ill devised. . . . I fear if the appropriation is spent without a trial, that utter disgrace will follow all concerned." [22] In after years Morse wisely refrained from referring to Vail's lack of sympathy in the crisis, but it is unlikely that Morse forgot. Several months later he wrote to his brother: "Even Mr. Vail, who has held fast to me from the beginning, felt like giving up just in the deepest blackness of all." [23]

Morse moved in a nightmare of uncertainty. He had lost hope that underground wires would be usable, even if enough of the appropriation remained to pay for repairing the wire and laying it. Fearing the rumors of failure might spread into a wave of popular ridicule that would make it impossible to proceed even if technical problems melted away, he wrote a cautious letter to the *Journal of Commerce*. He felt that he could not afford to be frank. Neither could he distract attention from failure by announcing new plans, for there were none. As yet there were no intrinsic difficulties, he wrote; at present the lateness of the season prevented further operations.[24]

Through the " deepest blackness " Morse retained the confidence of Secretary Spencer. When the inventor asked the appointment of Cornell as assistant at $1,000 a year, the secretary followed his recommendation. If Bartlett wanted a new contract, the secretary informed Morse, he saw no reason why the government was obliged to grant his request, especially since Bartlett had chosen to assign his rights to another person. The government would take the consequences of Bartlett's loss, he said, and reimburse Bartlett in the usual way when the loss was determined.[25]

Morse and Smith made no effort to continue their " mutual relations " on a friendly basis. Instead, Smith entered upon a consistent campaign to vilify his associate. If Morse had been uncertain of the man's character before, there could no longer be any question of it. Smith told Secretary Spencer that Morse had attempted to defraud the government on the Tatham contract, the very contract in which Morse had credited his half of the savings to the government while Smith had pocketed his; and Smith even threatened to bring the contract to the attention of Congress. As one of the proprietors of the telegraph, he informed Morse that he objected to

Vail's receiving any pay for his services to the government because, in the original partnership agreement, he had pledged his services free to the enterprise until the patent was sold. He informed his telegraph partners of his opinion the line would not be completed within the congressional appropriation. Finding Morse still insufficiently distraught, Smith charged the inventor with including improper items in his accounts of the 1838–9 trip to Europe, the expense of which Smith was bound by the partnership agreement to pay. Morse ably defended himself, and countered by demanding compensation for his services in Europe because he stayed there at Smith's request longer than the agreement stipulated. When Smith accused him of ingratitude, he replied bitterly that the charge came with little grace from one who had "during my hours of severest trial, lost sight of no means to discharge, disable and harass me." [26]

Finding that Smith invited vituperation, Morse determined to communicate with him only by letter. Unfortunately communication continued necessary, for there was no way to read Smith out of the partnership as long as the patent existed. "Fog" Smith was like the fog of Portland harbor, cold, relentless, penetrating. Even the ministrations of the friends with whom Morse was staying, the Commissioner of Patents Ellsworth, his wife, and their daughter Annie, could not offset his baleful influence. As often when distressed, Morse fell ill.

When the underground method was abandoned, $23,000 of the $30,000 appropriation had already been spent, and doubtless Smith and Vail were not the only men who increased Morse's irritability by predicting that the line could not be finished without more funds. But Morse had increasing hope that by some new method it could be built within the appropriation. To save money, in February he gave up his telegraph office in the *Observer* Building in New York.

Meanwhile Cornell was attempting to discover whether the defective wire stored in the cellar of the Patent Office could be salvaged; and both Vail and Cornell were reading all they could find on European telegraphy in the Congressional and Patent Office libraries. It was Vail who discovered in an English journal that

Wheatstone and Cooke, having found trouble with underground wires, had put the wires on poles, and it was Vail who persuaded Morse of the importance of his discovery. Morse may already have debated switching to poles. He had rejected the idea because he understood that Wheatstone had proved the underground method sound. Now he assented to the change in plan, Cornell states, before the end of March.[27] As a matter of fact, Morse had advertised for seven hundred posts in the Washington papers of February 7.

Upon the supervision of Cornell and Vail the wire was extracted from the defective pipe, the pipe sold, and the wire recovered with cotton, saturated with gum shellac, and reeled.

By the middle of March, laborers were drilling holes along the railroad tracks north from Washington. Morse cheerfully assumed they were for the first telegraph poles in American history. Again he was happy in his ignorance. In 1826 or 1827 Dyar had erected telegraph poles on Long Isand. His telegraph, however, recorded by chemical decomposition and his attempt proved abortive. By April, Morse's poles were rising for the first electromagnetic telegraph in American history. Placed along railroad tracks, they were providing a stark pole-against-sky pattern which was to become familiar to everyone. The poles sprang up quickly, two hundred feet apart; chestnut poles, twenty-four feet high, unbarked. While behind the scenes Vail reserved his enthusiasm for his mineral collection, and the war between Smith and Morse raged on, beside the railroad tracks towered the symbols of coming victory.

On April 9 the double wires reached six miles north of Washington, and a question telegraphed from the end of the line was answered from Washington in two or three seconds.[28] When a few days later the wires extended twelve miles, Morse told a reporter that he was already so accustomed to telegraphing to his assistants that he sometimes forgot himself and started to speak to them aloud.[29]

Fortunately for the telegraph, both the Whig and the Democratic national conventions were about to meet in Baltimore. With his sense for publicity, Morse knew the dramatic possibilities in a race between his lightning line and the railroad in reporting the presidential nominations to Washington.

On May 1, the opening day of the Whig convention, the wires

reached to Annapolis Junction, about twenty-two miles from Washington. When the news from Baltimore came to Annapolis Junction by train, Vail was to telegraph it immediately to Morse at the Capitol.

At half past three a train arrived at the junction with delegates from the Baltimore convention shouting: "Three Cheers for Henry Clay!" It was not surprising that Clay was the nominee for president; everyone had expected it. But a little-known man, Theodore Frelinghuysen, had been nominated for the vice-presidency. While passengers jeered him for his folly, Vail clicked off the news to Morse.

Morse was almost alone in his Capitol room as the news unwound on a ribbon before him. According to an eyewitness, as the clicking stopped he rose and said: "The Convention has adjourned. The train for Washington from Baltimore has just left Annapolis Junction bearing that information, and my assistant has telegraphed me the ticket nominated." He paused. "The ticket is Clay and Frelinghuysen."

The little group about him objected. "It's easy enough for you to guess that Clay is at the head of the ticket," said one. "But Frelinghuysen – who the devil is Frelinghuysen?"

"I only know," Morse is said to have answered, "that it is telegraphed me so from Annapolis Junction, where my operator had the news a few minutes ago."[30]

It is unlikely that these were Morse's words, for he knew very well who Frelinghuysen was. He was not only a nativist of prominence, but chancellor of New York University, where Morse was still a professor. Fortunately more authentic accounts survive of greater victories for the telegraph soon to follow.

Even with minor success, Morse and Vail were finding it hard to get along with each other. "Professor Morse is so unstable and full of notions," wrote Vail the day after sending the Whig convention news. "He changes oftener than the wind, and seems to be exceedingly childish sometimes. Now he is elated up to the skies, and then he is down in the mud all over under. It requires the utmost patience to get along with him."[31]

When he thought of Smith, the inventor was always despondent. "Prof. Morse is again low spirited," Vail noted in his journal a few days later. "He says that Smith will permit nothing to be done by Congress in reference to a further appropriation. Prof. M's plan is to desist from further progressing with it. Let the patent expire, and then if gov't use it, and remunerate him, he will not see Prof. Gale & myself want. But will not give Smith a cent."[32]

By May 24 the telegraph line had been built within the congressional appropriation and was in working order. The time had come for the fulfillment of Morse's promise to Annie Ellsworth. With the advice of her mother, she had chosen the first formal message to be sent over the first intercity electromagnetic telegraph line in the world.

Annie had selected a sentence from a prophecy of the ancient soothsayer Balaam. The Israelites, having come not long before from Egypt, were encamped in the Jordan valley. On a mountain above them, standing beside a smoking offering, an enemy king was attempting to force Balaam to pronounce a curse on his own people below. Balaam refused. In doing so he spoke his prophecy:

> Surely there is no enchantment against Jacob,
> Neither is there any divination against Israel:
> According to this time it shall be said of
>   Jacob and of Israel,
> "What hath God wrought!"

Morse invited a company to the chamber of the Supreme Court in the Capitol building. His instruments were ready. Miss Annie gave him her chosen words; and in the Morse code he sent the dispatch that indicated to the world that the Morse telegraph was now a reality. That very day he sent his brother a summary of the event:

Washington, May 24, 1844

Dear Sidney:

Could you not put a few facts in relation to the Telegraph into a popular shape for the Journal of Commerce? Such as, for example

THE ELECTRO-MAGNETIC TELEGRAPH TRIUMPHANT

The experiment of the Telegraph on Prof. Morse's system which has excited such deep interest throughout the country, and which has been in the process of establishment under the patronage of the General Government, between Washington & Baltimore, we are pleased to learn has been completely successful. On Friday the 24th inst. the first Sentence was transmitted from Washington to Baltimore, and under the following circumstances: "While engaged during the last session in urging a consideration of his invention before Congress, Prof. Morse learned the news of the final passage of the bill first from the daughter of the distinguished Commissioner of Patents; Prof. Morse in return for the highly grateful news promised that the first Sentence sent by the Telegraph from Wash.n to Baltimore should be indited by her. In fulfilment of his promise, he transmitted the following Sentence letter for letter in one minute, and the same sentence was again received from Baltimore in another minute; 'What hath God wrought?' Nothing could have been more appropriate than this devout exclamation, at such an event, when an invention which creates such wonder, and about which there has been so much scepticism, is taken from the land of visions, and becomes a reality. . . ." [33]

He believed himself wonderfully blessed to have been chosen an instrument of divine revelation. He but believed it the more fully as men rose to snatch away a share of divine patronage for themselves.

It was many years before the story of the first message was in every schoolboy's reader. More than the first message or the news from the Whig convention, however, it was the reporting of the Democratic convention which blasted its way through ignorance and indifference. While the nation's attention was focused once more on Baltimore, the telegraph performed miracles on the floor of the convention itself.

In Baltimore, Cornell and Vail were at instruments in the third story of the warehouse of the railroad depot in Pratt Street. In Washington, Morse was at instruments in a room below the Senate Chamber; he had arranged to post news on a bulletin-board in the rotunda, and to announce it through a window of his room.

As the delegates gathered in Baltimore the day after the sending of the first message, Van Buren was the leading candidate. Someone telegraphed from Baltimore inquiring the capital's momentary favorite. Morse knew that Van Buren was Washington's favorite. The fact did not please him. A few weeks before, when President Tyler had proposed the annexation of Texas, which most people believed would mean war with Mexico, Van Buren had announced that he opposed annexation. Morse was an expansionist; he favored Lewis Cass of Michigan, whom he had known as American Minister to France, and who, like himself, was friendly to expansion and slavery. Morse admitted, however, that the telegraph ought to be impartial. He dutifully sent the message: "Van Buren stock is rising."

On the first day of the convention Vail telegraphed to the Capitol that a motion had been made to adopt a two-thirds majority requirement for nomination. After a hot debate the second day Vail telegraphed that the two-thirds rule had been adopted over the opposition of the Van Buren men. The South, angered by Van Buren's opposition to the spread of slavery into Texas, was deserting his cause.

Then the excitement began. Morse announced through his window that on the first ballot Van Buren had achieved a majority but not the necessary two thirds. Cass was his closest rival. On the second ballot Morse found satisfaction in reporting that Van Buren was slipping, Cass rising. The trend continued until the seventh ballot, when Morse told the astounded congressmen standing by that Van Buren had only 99 votes to Cass's 123. The eighth ballot introduced a new candidate, James K. Polk of Tennessee, a little-known expansionist, with 44 votes.

Senators had been reading Morse's bulletins aloud on the Senate floor. Whigs affected unconcern; Democrats disregarded the chairman's demands for silence. But the ninth ballot put the whole Senate in confusion. Vail kept a journal of the dispatches:

Morse: "Mr. Simons is speaking in the House on pension bill a bare quorum."
Vail: "Yes."
Morse: "Mr. Choate has reported in the Senate. . . .
Vail: "The vote taken will be nearly unanimous for J. K. Polk. Harmony and union are restored."
Morse: "Is it a fact or mere rumor?"
Vail: "Wait till the ballot comes."

When these dispatches were read in the Senate, as Cornell recalled, "the gavel thundered, and the lightning continued its flashes, until the storm burst . . . with such fury that an adjournment was moved and carried."

Congressmen crowded around the window of Morse's room.

The register clicked again: "Polk is unanimously nom. 3 cheers were given in convention for restoring harmony."[34]

The senators and representatives about Morse's window received the news, the *National Intelligencer* said, as the ancients received the responses of an oracle. The Democrats were at first speechless. Suddenly recovering, they gave three cheers for James K. Polk, and calling Morse to the window again, three cheers for Samuel F. B. Morse.

In the Baltimore convention hall a few minutes later a delegate from New York addressed the chair: "Mr. President, the telegraph has announced the nomination of Mr. Polk to our friends in Washington, and I am happy to inform the Convention that his nomination is well received. With the indulgence of the Convention, I will read the dispatch."

There were cries of "Read, read." Polk was the first "dark horse" candidate to be nominated by a national convention, and the knowledge of how he was received at the Capitol was important to the convention.

The speaker held in his hand a ribbon of telegraph paper, several yards long, on which letters had been written in under dots and dashes.

He read: "Three cheers for James K. Polk, and three cheers for the telegraph." Wild applause flooded the convention hall.[35]

As a gesture to Van Buren's followers, the convention nominated Senator Silas Wright of New York for vice president. At the moment Wright was in Washington at the Capitol. Vail sent the news to Morse, and Morse to Wright. In reply Wright asked Morse to telegraph that he refused the nomination. Morse sent the message to Vail and he in turn had it sent to the president of the convention, who read it a few minutes after the nomination. The convention was startled again. By telegraph the convention requested him to reconsider. By telegraph he again refused. And after the still incredulous convention had sent a committee to Washington by train to make sure that the telegraph had reported Wright correctly, it nominated in his stead G. M. Dallas of Pennsylvania.

The telegraph was triumphant. In Baltimore hundreds plagued Vail for permission to enter his office just to be able to say they had seen the telegraph. In Washington Morse felt the keenest pleasure when Congressman Cave Johnson of Tennessee, who had once asked that Morse's appropriation be divided with a mesmerist, walked up to him and said: "Sir, I give in. It is an astonishing invention."[36]

News of the nominations and the part played by the telegraph in effecting them went the rounds of the nation's press. It seemed to Morse that he could hardly take up a paper without coming upon a flattering reference to the telegraph. In a New York nativist paper he read of the editor's pride that he "whose achievements in the world of science, will send his name to posterity, even on the winds of lightning, is an American citizen – a New Yorker – but, more than all, distinguished . . . as identified with the earliest movement and organization of the Native American party."[37] Little else was done in Washington during the convention, he read in the New York *Herald,* but watch "Professor Morse's Bulletin"; his telegraph, the *Herald* declared, "is not only an era in the transmission of intelligence, but it has originated in the mind . . . a new species of consciousness."[38] The telegraph produced an "*electrical* effect" in Washington, noted a Utica paper; the telegraph, it concluded, is "unquestionably the greatest invention of the age."[39] Though Morse had been claiming for twelve years that the telegraph would startle the world, many people were only now convinced that it wasn't a hoax. The Whigs and Democrats who crowded around Morse at the Capitol united at least on one sentiment, said the *National Intelligencer;* they united in "mingled delight and wonder" at the telegraph.[40]

Americans prided themselves on their inventiveness and their willingness to try the new. But for twelve years they had ignored "the greatest invention of the age." Twelve years, and many of them were just waking enough to wonder. Exuberantly Americans were pressing westward, wresting land from those whom they called inferior peoples. But for twelve years an instrument capable of smoothing the westward trek had been in prospect and even now hardly anyone dared to invest in it. Americans now were wondering. Little knowing that the direction of the telegraph's greatest usefulness would be toward breaking down barriers among nations, they were preparing to hail its inventor as an American hero.

In his own way the inventor was also wondering. How remarkable it was that he, an artist, should have been chosen to be one of those to reveal the meaning of electricity to man! How wonderful that he should have been selected to become a teacher in the art of controlling the intriguing "fluid" which had been known from the days when the Greeks magnetized amber, but which had never before been turned to the ends of common man! "What hath God wrought!" As Jehovah had wrought through Israel, God now wrought through him.

"That sentence of Annie Ellsworth's was divinely indited," he wrote to his brother, "for it is in my thoughts day and night. 'What hath God wrought!' It is His work, and He alone could have carried me thus far through all my trials and enabled me to triumph over the obstacles, physical and moral, which opposed me.

"'Not unto us, not unto us, but to Thy name, O Lord, be all the praise.'

"I begin to fear now the effects of public favor, lest it should kindle that pride of heart and self-sufficiency which dwells in my own as well as in others' breasts, and which, alas! is so ready to be inflamed by the slightest spark of praise. I do indeed feel gratified, and it is right I should rejoice, but I rejoice with fear, and I desire that a sense of dependence upon and increased obligation to the Giver of every good and perfect gift may keep me humble and circumspect. . . .

"Mr. S. still embarrasses. . . . I pray God for a right spirit in dealing with him." [41]

CHAPTER *xxii*

In the Fire of Fame

ALREADY responsibility for the test line had sapped Morse's accustomed geniality. Fisher he had dismissed abruptly. With Smith he had begun an injudicious if courageous war. With Vail he was more companionable, but especially after the hot wind of publicity blew over them, even Vail went through miserable days of questioning his friend's motives. Possessing the wisdom of one who had known many conditions of men, the inventor comprehended some of the dangers that loomed before him. He had begun to pray that public favor should not kindle pride in his heart. He probably realized that since the completion of the test line, the devious individual purposes of the four patentees were coming increasingly into play.

Jealousy was surely eating into the Vails. Alfred descended to the pettiness of noting: " Prof. Morse . . . knows full well that it would be difficult to work the telegraph without me." [1] He hinted that Morse did not know how to telegraph even as well as one of the new operators, Henry J. Rogers; and Vail and Rogers joshed their chief for his claims to originality as they telegraphed to each other:

Vail: " Prof. Morse says that my plan of a ladder he planned last winter."
Rogers: " Ah ah." [2]

Again and again Vail complained of Morse's delay in registering at the Patent Office his assignment of Vail's share in the patents. " If he had any objections to do it," Vail wrote in his diary, " he is not frank in assigning a good & valid objection. It looks bad to find him putting off this matter of so much importance to me, and my dependent family." [3] Within a few weeks Morse made the assignment to Vail's satisfaction. But more than a year later George reminded his brother that in spite of repeated requests he had never assigned to George his half of Alfred's telegraph rights. Meanwhile George advised Alfred to restrain himself and befriend Morse as a matter of policy. While a few days later George wrote a prospective telegraph buyer: "I respect no man more than I do Prof. Morse," [4] now he wrote Alfred: "I saw Prof. Morse when in New York. I made up my mind that we could get nothing without his friendship and influence. If he chooses to go against us we are minus. And therefore I would recommend every possible concession to him except in new discoveries which you should now keep secret." [5] A few days later George continued: "I regret extremely that Prof. M. will hesitate for a moment to grant what belongs to us. . . . He longed for fame and has obtained it. His assistants are not without their need of fame either – and may have theirs nearly associated with his yet. Many claim for you all the honor except the original idea but don't you claim it until our slice is in our hands securely. *The important discoveries are to be kept aloof from the publick.* A wider field than an 8 x 10 office may be occupied. First secure your portion in this country. And do that quickly but don't show that you are anxious." [6] The partners were caught in a swirling sea of jealousy and greed.

Sensing that he was being pulled into a vortex, Morse concluded he would be well rid of business connections with the telegraph. He was not concerned for profits that might be found in contracting to build lines. He wished to sell his patent rights and make his gain on the sale, leaving the responsibility for organizing companies and constructing lines to others. If he could hold his rights until private speculators came begging, he knew he would make more money. But he could use cash now. Most of all he wished to sell his whole right to the government at once. It would be simpler than selling piecemeal to private companies. Moreover, he believed in the principle of government ownership of the telegraph. He always had, even as long before as 1837, when he first proposed its use by the government.

Vail and Gale were also anxious to be rid of business responsibilities; but Smith was not. He had visions of a deep-dish pie, and his fingers itched to be in it. He wished to contract with the government to build telegraph lines. Vail, Morse, and Morse as attorney for Gale countered bluntly. Smith might make contracts for constructing lines in some areas, they said, but if so, they would not accept financial or moral responsibility for them. They proposed instead several alternatives:

1.st We propose to sell to the Government the whole Patent, for a definite sum.
2.d We will sell to Gov.t the use of the Telegraph for its own purposes, leaving to us the right to sell rights to others.
3.d We will sell the right to construct at so much per mile.
4.th We will let Government to go on and construct for a certain distance and leave it to Gov.t to say what compensation shall be given us for the use of it.[7]

Negotiations with the government commenced in hearings before a committee of Congress. Cornell and Smith presented estimates of the cost per mile of building telegraph lines. Unfortunately their estimates differed: Smith's was higher [8] and trouble loomed between him and Morse again. Commissioner of Patents Ellsworth occasioned an explosion by taking it upon himself to advise Morse to sell rights to the government for fifty dollars a mile, a lower sum than either Vail or Smith contemplated. Vail consented to accept this figure only after extorting the promise from Morse that, if the government purchased, his salary would be raised and Morse would have only one quarter of the profits of the pamphlet on telegraphy they were to publish. Smith, moreover, was adamant. Although a year before in the *Maine Farmer* he had declared Ellsworth as much responsible for current achievement in agriculture and mechanics as any man in the Union,[9] now he wrote Morse: " If you will induce your friend Ellsworth to mind his own business, we shall not have trouble – otherwise, we shall never get out of trouble." [8] The Bartlett contract dispute was dropping out of sight only to be superseded by another. " Your faith as a Christian," Morse wrote Vail the same day, " will be tried, as well as my own, in the blow up which has taken place. I go before the Com.tee this morning. M.r S. has written me a passionate letter accusing my friend M.r Ellsworth in the most opprobrious terms. Depend upon it, such feeling cannot cover any but the darkest designs upon us all." [10] Day after day Smith gnawed at Morse's faith in men.

Negotiations were fumbled, and Congress adjourned in the spring of 1844 without taking any action. Still hoping that the government might purchase, the proprietors turned perforce toward private enterprise.

Two proposals were made to them. J. Reese Fry and Edward Fry of the Philadelphia *North American* negotiated for building a line from Philadelphia to New York. While discussions with the Frys continued, Morse responded to an inquiry from a Baltimore agent by offering to sell his share of the patent right for $100,000, allowing for an additional $10,000 to the agent as a commission. "I am fully aware," he wrote Smith in explaining his offer, "that this is not a criterion of the value of the whole, nor is it half what I should get; but for the sake of having my mind free for a general superintendence and extension of the system unembarrassed by business details and to perfect it, I will forego the prospects of greater but more distant remuneration." [11] Apparently he wanted now to be free from business, not to return to painting, but to develop his telegraph. Certainly he was willing to make a heavy sacrifice for being free. A few weeks later Vail refused to sell his share of two sixteenths of the patent rights for less than $50,000. At the same rate Morse should have asked for his nine sixteenths twice as much as he did. The Vails agreed to make offers to the prospective Baltimore buyer without telling Morse; Alfred Vail and Morse tried to keep Smith from knowing that Gale was thinking of selling his share to Henry Rogers. But all the proposals fell through, and the proprietors continued in the whirl of suspicion.

At first Washingtonians wondered what it would cost to send parcels to Baltimore by telegraph. Soon they knew better. They came to the Capitol or later up the outside stairs of a dwelling-house on Seventh Street for news of the Philadelphia Catholic riots, in which police used Morse's lines before they used Wheatstone's lines in England; for news of the election that put Polk in the White House; to watch the progress of a telegraphic chess game, with one player in Washington and the other in Baltimore, which, Morse believed, preceded any telegraphic chess game in England by several months. They came to send messages too. A family, hearing that one of its members had been murdered in Baltimore, inquired by telegraph and in ten minutes the rumor was exploded. The Baltimore and Ohio Railroad used the "lightning line" to dispatch trains, business men to certify checks, newspapers for late news.

The evident utility of the telegraph was the principal argument for the congressional bill on which the patentees pinned their reduced hopes. It called for the extension of the telegraph to New York under much the same terms as the first line had been built; Morse would again be the superintendent.

All winter Morse danced attendance on Congress, as he had many times before. In January it seemed to him that the Texas question was driving everything else into a corner. In February a House resolution was offered to ask him to devise a telegraphic method of taking the vote of the House; it was laughed down. Soon afterward, however, he entered into conversation about it with Chairman Pratt of the Committee on Public Buildings. For $1,500 he offered to construct in the center of the floor of the House a light frame, place on it for each member a card bearing a magnetic needle, and attach to each card wires from each desk. To record his yea or nay each member would but turn a handle on his desk this way or that.[12] Doubtless Morse hoped that by his device the House would save time which it could give to his telegraph extension bill.

It was the last day of the session again when Congress finally attended to the government telegraph. Instead of extending the telegraph it merely provided $8,000 to continue the operation of the Washington-Baltimore line and transferred its administration from the Treasury to the Post Office. With the advent of the Polk administration the next day, March 4, 1845, Morse came under the supervision of Postmaster General Cave Johnson, the statesman who had once proposed that mesmerism share with magnetism in the patronage of Congress. Responsibility for extending the telegraph remained in the four partners' inhospitable possession. Their warnings to Congress had come to naught: the telegraph patent remained in private hands and a trend toward a speculative monopoly was inevitable.

It was on March 4, too, that a former Postmaster General offered to lift all business responsibility from Morse's weary shoulders. Amos Kendall proposed to sell Morse's telegraph rights either to the government or to capitalists at a commission of ten per cent. In Kendall, a man of sharp eyes and thin lips, Morse recognized a man he could trust.

Kendall's early life offered a striking parallel to Morse's. Like Morse, he had early read Dr. Morse's geographies, invented a pump, broken with the Federalism of his associates, and married in the fall of 1818 a woman who died a few years later, leaving him a widower with several children. Like Morse, too, Kendall was born into a Massachusetts Congregationalist home, left Congregationalism for another Calvinistic denomination, and remained bitterly anti-Unitarian all his life.

From Massachusetts Kendall went to Kentucky to teach and practice law; instead he became an ardent Jacksonian editor, whom Whigs learned to call "the Robespierre of America." When Jackson became President he appointed Kendall to a minor Treasury office. Through political writing in Washington he became, as Harriet Martineau said, "the moving spring of the administration." Eventually Jackson appointed him Postmaster General, and he remained in office long enough to pull the Post Office out of debt. He had recently purchased a farm northeast of the Capitol (since become the campus of Gallaudet College), and was editing a Washington Democratic magazine, *Kendall's Expository*.

His vision of the future of the telegraph differed sharply from that of the present Postmaster General, Cave Johnson. Kendall expected the telegraph to effect the demise of all newspapers with wide circulations like the *National Intelligencer* and the *Journal of Commerce*. They would be limited to the city in which they were published, he believed, because local newspapers would already have received news by telegraph before the big city newspapers arrived by train.

Congress having failed to extend the telegraph even to New York, Morse determined to commit his telegraph rights to this wise politician, Kendall. He urged Vail and Gale to do likewise. His decision, he wrote Gale, "was advised by our most judicious friends, in consequence more particularly of the movements of Smith who is the same as ever. M.r Kendall will devote nearly his whole time to this matter, and we have made it as you will see for his interest to make sales for us at the rate of $200,000 for the whole patent right. We run no risk, and have perhaps the most competent man in the country to manage such a concern." [13] Vail and Gale joined him in presenting their rights to the agency of Kendall.

Smith retained his own rights, and used them to demand of Postmaster General Johnson one fourth of the $8,000 appropriation for the running expenses of the Washington-Baltimore line because he was one-fourth owner of the patent! Kendall quite understood Smith, but, his assent being necessary to contracts, Kendall determined to work with him, and adroitly succeeded in doing so for a time.

In April the first contract for the private construction of a telegraph was drawn up for a line from Washington to Mobile. Though the terms were announced in the papers in the hope they might stimulate further interest, Kendall had no faith in the contracting party.

In May, Smith's and Kendall's tenuous union led to the formation of the Magnetic Telegraph Company, the first successful telegraph company. Early subscribers to telegraph stock were often expressmen or stage proprietors who had been driven out of business by the railroads. In the first company, however, the telegraphers themselves showed the way. Smith was by far the largest subscriber of the first company with $2,750. And several of his associates were stockholders; his friend, clerk of the House, B. B. French, his brother-in-law, Charles Monroe, and other relatives, J. J. Haley, and Eliphalet Case. Kendall subscribed $500; he became the president. Though his annual salary as superintendent of the new company was to be only twice as much, Cornell made the first investment of his famous career with $500. Charles Page, a friend of Morse who was an examiner in the Patent Office, put himself on the list for $500, but concluded that it was unseemly for Patent Office employees to be interested in companies which depended on patents, and never paid in his subscription. The Washington banker William W. Corcoran, who was later to found an art gallery that would house Morse's *Congress Hall,* subscribed $1,000 for his firm.[14] The total subscription was only $15,000, but double that amount of stock was issued to the subscribers on hope, and $30,000 again to the patentees for the right to use the telegraph.

In the next few weeks one company after another came into being. By August 5 Kendall was able to report to Morse that companies were formed to erect lines from New York through Albany to Buffalo and from New York to Boston. Other negotiations were under way. "An arrangement has been made with Henry O'Rielly Esqr.," Kendall added, "by which he had undertaken to get up a western line through Pennsylvania to Pittsburgh branching to St. Louis and the Lakes. Doubts are entertained whether he will accomplish anything." Kendall was soon to find that O'Rielly did not lack energy. Meanwhile both Kendall and Smith had offered to buy Morse's patent rights, but neither produced the $100,000 that he still asked.[15] And now the lines from Buffalo to New York and on to Washington were giving the patentees half their stock, and the line from Boston to New York more than half. In stock, at least, Morse was a wealthy man.

Just as the formation of telegraph companies seemed to assure freedom from poverty, and Kendall's ability to work with Smith seemed to assure freedom from bickering with his associates, Morse sailed for Europe to enter again into the world of contest. Restless, he desired to make certain that developments abroad did not threaten his success at home. He sailed the day after Kendall's favorable report.

As he was leaving for Europe the papers were shouting that his telegraph might be rivaled by the invention of another New Englander, Royal E. House of Vermont. Shrewdly Kendall advised his client to examine one of the House telegraphs to see how effectively they fulfilled the claim to print Roman letters, and if necessary to effect an agreement with House for the use of his improvements. The day was to come when he would know better, but now Morse had only contempt for House's telegraph. "You need have no fears of it," he wrote Smith. "It is mathematically demonstrable that it is of no use compared with mine."[16]

He showed the same hard certainty in Europe. In England he visited a telegraph office of his chief rival, Wheatstone, and concluded that his system, even with a reduced number of wires, was "clumsy and complicated."[17] Both men had grown calculating since their polite meeting of 1838. Then Morse had respected Wheatstone's system, though believing his own better. Now, with a position to uphold, stock as well as honor depending on the continued pre-eminence of his own invention, he was less gentle in his judgments. Then he had written that Wheatstone dated his invention from the same year as his own, 1832. Now he gave 1837 as the earliest date that Wheatstone could claim. Then he had acknowledged frankly that Wheatstone's was an independent invention; now in a statement prepared for a French telegraph history he declared that he was "perhaps erroneous" in supposing Wheatstone had borrowed his ideas.[18] When he examined one of the Wheatstone lines in the Netherlands, he discovered that Wheatstone had developed a telegraph which used a ratchet wheel to make visible signs. At once Morse claimed the device was his own because it was powered by an electromagnet! He continued to believe that his own system was better because it was simpler and faster, which was true; and because it was recording, which was soon to prove an advantage only because its recording apparatus could easily be adjusted for receiving by sound. Morse understood that Wheatstone, in turn, was saying that the American system was "*impracticable* and *absurd*."[19]

In France Wheatstone's system was not a favorite. "He may crow on his own dunghill," Morse wrote in Paris, "but the French cock crows here."[20] And the American cock did some crowing too. Under the direction of Bréguet the government was operating an experimental line from Paris to Rouen. With his old friend Foy, still the administrator of government telegraphs, Morse inspected the line. Promptly he recognized Bréguet's line as his, too, for though mechanically not like his – it was like Wheatstone's new ratchet-wheel system, and read by sight by arms pointing to letters on a dial – it operated by electromagnetic power. Morse concluded that it would send only about 12 signals a minute, while his own would send 60, and with a few mechanical improvements would send 150. Foy later told him he did not properly understand Bréguet's system; it would send 38 signals a minute. But Morse continued to crow. The French government was again attempting to choose a telegraph system for general adoption. The venerated Arago, the same physicist who had first introduced him to the Academy of Sciences in 1838, was now president of the commission to make the decision. With friends in Paris, with assistance from American diplomats, with the success of the forty-mile line and contracts for thirteen hundred more in America, Morse could present a strong case for his own system. Again he exhibited before the Academy of Sciences, and then before the Chamber of Deputies as well.

His fourth tour of Europe was like his third, barren of all but praise. The General Commercial Telegraph Company of London, which he had hoped would adopt his system, told him it preferred his to all others. Arago agreed. Hamburg received the inventor so joyfully he was sure his telegraph would be introduced there. Meanwhile a friend was showing his instruments in Vienna; Prince Metternich, who doubtless did not know that the inventor's current sixth edition of *Foreign Conspiracy* labeled him as an arch enemy of America, enthusiastically explained the Morse telegraph to the Emperor, and the Emperor expressed his pleasure at seeing in operation the invention of which he had heard so much. But as before, Europe granted the American neither profit nor patents; it could use his instrument without legal obligation to him, and so far it had not even chosen to use it. It was only later that his tour bore fruit. His system was formally adopted by the Austrian government the next year, and by France not until 1856.

Promoting the telegraph in Europe, Morse was no longer either a creative artist, a writer, or an inventor. He still, however, made sensitive judgments of people and country. In a Dutch village he was depressed by the cleanliness so exacting that it crushed the natural liveliness of children; he was cheered when he saw along the banks of a lake a few water reeds left undisturbed. In France he confessed that he liked courtesy even if insincere, for "if one must be cheated I like to have it done in a civil and polite way." [21] As a man his judgments were as nice as ever. As an inventor his mind was hardly ready for new truth; it was closed in defense of legal rights, investments, and reputation.

At home Morse found his lieutenants Vail and Cornell in a huff. When the line from Baltimore to New York reached the Jersey shore, Vail attempted to communicate from Philadelphia to Cornell at the end of the line at Fort Lee. At Philadelphia Vail used one of the Morse electromagnets, as usual locked in a box so that no one could discover its design. Using his own magnet, as Cornell said, he received Vail's signals, but Vail, using Morse's magnet, did not receive Cornell's signals. For three days Vail tramped along the line from Philadelphia, seeking a break in the wire. Every two miles his galvanometer indicated that the wire was sound. Still without discovering a break, he reached Fort Lee, exhausted. Then Cornell told him he was using his own magnet. Vail swore that the new magnet would never enter the Philadelphia office.

Morse joined with Vail in thwarting Cornell. When he heard that Cornell was trying to sell his magnets for use on the Morse line from New York to Buffalo, he wrote the president of the line that Cornell's magnet was cumbersome (as it was), and interfered with his patent rights. "You must restrain your feelings," Morse wrote to Vail. "It is impossible to get along just at present without him, and the violence of your opposition will only create sympathy for him, and he can do us a great deal of injury. I have no more favorable opinion of his proceedings than you have but we must wait a proper opportunity for freeing ourselves from him."[22]

Morse was irritable. Cornell's insubordination was annoying; at the same time he was busy having his patent reissued to include the questionable claim for exclusive right to all telegraphy powered by electromagnetism; and he was also vainly attempting to assist in connecting the line at Fort Lee with the line across the Hudson that ended near Audubon's house in upper Manhattan, using submarine wires or wires suspended on great masts (the *Scientific American* soberly recommended suspending the wires over the river from balloons).[23] Perhaps it was because of his irritability that he did not now become the friend of Audubon while he experimented in the laundry of Audubon's house on methods of crossing the river.[24]

As an antidote to Cornell's magnet Morse introduced a magnet modeled on one used by Bréguet on the Paris-Rouen line. In Washington on Christmas Day Charles Page, who had worked out a modification of Morse's magnet which Morse may have paid him for permission to use as the Morse magnet,[25] was in the telegraph office. The Bréguet magnets were small. Placing one on a Morse magnet, Morse announced: "There is a mouse upon an elephant." Page was delighted. The new magnet was not only conveniently smaller, but also stronger and cheaper than his own modification of Morse's magnet. He declared that it was the most gratifying Christmas present he had ever received. Morse was moved by his ingenuousness.[26] Soon, however, Morse was introducing magnets of the Bréguet model on his lines without making public confession of his indebtedness to Bréguet. Legally he was under no obligation to do so. But even in a letter to Arago, in which he accused Bréguet of having adopted his system and referred to his own recent reduction of his magnet to a very small size, he still failed to admit his debt to Bréguet.[27]

The new Bréguet magnets soon drove the Cornell magnets out of use, and prosecution of Cornell was unnecessary. Cornell and Morse, however, watched each other narrowly ever afterward. Cornell continued to superintend the construction of Morse lines, and to have an increasing investment in the lines that spread through New York and the Great Lakes area. When Kendall and Smith discovered they could no longer work together, Cornell appeared as an ally of Smith against Kendall, Vail, and Morse.

Meanwhile, to prevent another threat from within the growing Morse telegraph family, the patentees ordered that any instruments used on their lines were to be approved by either Morse or Vail. Moreover, they threatened to prosecute anyone who constructed instruments for use on any telegraph line which involved the use of electromagnetism.[28] It is not surprising that a popular cry of "monopoly," fed by the taunts of House and other competitors, rose against the Morse patentees.

It had seemed to Morse a mystery that God should have led him to study painting for so many years and then suddenly stopped him by erecting a wall across his path. Now, still more mysteriously, the wall that he had once pounded in vain appeared suddenly to be giving way.

He had already given up the presidency of the National Academy just before sailing to Europe. He was still listed as an art professor in the catalogue of New York University, and everywhere he was still called "professor," but he had no pupils. On his last visit to Paris he had not even entered the Louvre. Artist friends drifted away from him. When Allston congratulated his pupil on the passage of the congressional bill for the construction of the first line, Morse had replied that he would not give up painting yet, "but pursue her even with lightning, and so overtake her at last." [29] Soon afterward Allston died. Morse went to Cambridgeport to visit the family, and Allston's brother-in-law, Richard Henry Dana, Sr., told him: "You know not . . . with what affection Allston always spoke of you, and, let me add, how highly he thought of your powers as an artist." [30] One-eyed Dunlap was dead too. And Inman. But most of his other New York artist associates – Cole, Cummings, Durand, Morton, and Huntington – were still busy in the academy. Morse seldom wrote them now; he had moved out of the light-hearted circle of artists and "Knickerbocker" authors he had known when he first came to New York.

It was Inman's death that turned him again toward painting. Inman's panel in the ever disturbing series of panels in the Capitol rotunda remained unfinished. "A move is making to get the Rotunda Picture for me," Finley soon wrote his brother Richard; "I have not moved a finger in it, and shall not. After the sore blow I received as a Painter by the former rejection of my claims, I will never of myself put myself in the way to be again rejected. If I should be offered the Picture I will accept." [31] God had interrupted his painting, it seemed to him, in order to direct his attention to telegraphy. But now his part in giving telegraphy to the world was complete. "And at the moment when all has been accomplished which is essential to its success," he wrote to Sidney, "He so orders events as again to turn my thoughts to my almost sacrificed Isaac." [32]

He was still superintendent of the Washington-Baltimore line; he had assisted in detail in the construction of the New York to Philadelphia line and with advice in the construction of many other lines; he still fretted over newspaper puffs for rival telegraphers. It would require a wrench to loose him from these entanglements, but he knew his invention could now stand alone. Investors were behind it; for their own good they would see that his rights were protected. And Kendall would do the rest. Having recently excited his old passion by giving art lectures in Baltimore and Washington,[33] he was ready, as he had said he would be from his first essays in telegraphy, to return to his profession.

Weeks and months passed while once more he waited for Congress to determine his career. In May his Washington friends set in motion a petition in his favor. Friends of his painting years responded, among them Durand, now the president of the academy, Cummings, Chapman, Morton, G. C. Verplanck, Philip Hone, DeWitt Bloodgood, and even the bewildering editor of the *New-York Mirror,* George P. Morris.[34] Under the direction of Vail his portrait of his daughter Susan, completed in 1837, and so far as is known his last major painting, hung in the rotunda of the Capitol as an exhibit of his powers as a painter. While his friends might move to have him return to painting, he would do nothing on his own behalf. He would not be humiliated again.

While waiting, anticipating that he could recover the skill of his brush again at will, he helped unreel the wires of his telegraph into new territory. By the summer of 1846 New York was connected with Boston, Buffalo, and Washington; Philadelphia was connected not only with the main line but now also with Harrisburg, and a line on to Pittsburgh was under construction, as well as feeder lines. Under an agreement with him Livingston and Wells of New York opened the first telegraph line in British North America between Toronto and Hamilton, December 19, 1846.[35] Soon after Yale, whose officials had once concluded he would never prove a useful college resident, had conferred on him the degree of LL.D. (which Morse interpreted as meaning Lightning Line Doctor), a New York paper commented: is not the telegraph "*the* feature of the age? . . . As New Yorkers we are proud of the Doctor, and we are proud too, of that classic pile, in whose silent halls this beautiful philosophical mechanism was arranged and perfected. The University has much to boast of. . . . While England by her government has got with great labor 175 miles of telegraph into operation . . . the United States, with her individual enterprise, has now in successful operation 1269 miles. This is American enterprise."[36] It was immensely gratifying to observe his growing renown and his lines spreading across the continent, but he was ready to leave telegraphy for painting.

More than a year after he had expressed his willingness to accept the commission, the news of congressional action came to him from a Washington friend: "I have just learned today that, with their usual discrimination and justice, Congress have voted $6000 to have the panel filled by young Powell. He enlisted all Ohio, and they all electioneered with all their might, and no one knew that the question would come up. New York, I understand, went for you."[37]

Morse let Congress decide his future. His love of art had lost its power over every other love. At fifty-five he let slip his last chance to become again creative and pathetically drifted back into telegraph controversy.

CHAPTER *xxiii*

A Victorian Takes a Wife

AT FIRST Morse and O'Rielly were respectful even in dispute. O'Rielly had not fulfilled on scheduled time his contract with the Morse patentees for constructing a line from Philadelphia to Harrisburg and Pittsburgh. But more important, he and the patentees differed over the contract. It gave to O'Rielly rights for " a line " from Philadelphia to Pittsburgh, and thence through Cincinnati to St. Louis and the principal Great Lakes towns. It also gave him, however, the same privilege not for " a line," but for " any line beyond Pittsburg, to any point of commercial magnitude." [1] O'Rielly, expansive and ambitious, interpreted the contract to mean that he could set up independent companies in the area west of Pittsburgh to any number he chose. The patentees, on the other hand, insisted that the intention of the phrase " a line " was to keep control in one company in the interests of efficient telegraph service. The dispute went into a court of equity in Philadelphia in February 1847.

Smith asked that the whole contract be set aside because O'Rielly had broken it. Morse, however, desired some kind of compromise. He believed that to abandon it, while legally defensible, would be morally wrong. O'Rielly, he thought, had proved a man of great energy; unfortunate circumstances alone had prevented the completion of the Pennsylvania line on schedule. The patentees asked that their share of stock in any companies O'Rielly might set up be jumped from one fourth to one half if the contract was to be continued. Even this demand Morse was willing to forgo "if they will carry out the *unity* which we intended." [2]

But Morse's inclination to compromise vanished with the decision of the court. The presiding judge threw out the case on a technicality and, going beyond any legal necessity, commented that he believed O'Rielly had interpreted the contract correctly.

A restless Ulsterman, at the age of twenty-one O'Rielly had become the editor of the Rochester *Daily Advertiser,* said to be the first daily paper west of the Hudson. Being a Democrat, and a leader in promoting agriculture and canals, he had been appointed postmaster of Rochester by Kendall. Now he was on his way to head a great telegraph empire and to die penniless in a New York tenement.

Within a few days Morse saw in the papers that O'Rielly was about to build lines under the same contract from Buffalo to Chicago and from St. Louis to New Orleans. "Pray what does it all mean?" he asked Kendall. "Is the effect of the Phil.a decision to give O'Rielly and his Associates the construction of *all the Telegraphs in the Union?* . . . Alas, I confess that my respect for the law as administered is much shaken by the late decision. I feel there is no security. I never was more deceived in regard to a case, and the effect has been to make me doubt everything, and whether in the eye of the law, I have any rights at all." [3]

By September the patentees determined to act as if their contract with O'Rielly were void. They effected a distribution of responsibility so that Kendall handled patent rights in the Middle and Southern states, and Smith in both his home territory of New England and, because he was a good fighter, in the contested West. But O'Rielly continued, as Morse said, "forever puffing, and being puffed in the papers, as so full of zeal and energy in getting up lines." [4]

By November, O'Rielly, who not long before had agreed with Morse that House's letter-printing telegraph was "humbug," bought a share in House's patent. Now the two major rivals of the Morse interests, O'Rielly and House, were allied. They commenced construction of a House line between New York and Philadelphia, and threatened to do so between New York and Buffalo. They continued to build Morse lines in the West. Subscribers who were paying in capital for Cornell's new Morse line from Buffalo across Upper Canada to Detroit delayed payments to await the outcome of the contest.

In New York every journal denounced Morse except the *Herald* and the *Sun*, the despised "penny" papers, precursors of yellow journalism. The sheets with large circulation outside the city, even his pet, the *Journal of Commerce*, opposed him, he believed, because just what Kendall predicted had happened. The telegraph outraced the metropolitan papers in getting news to smaller cities and towns. The metropolitan editors resented their loss of circulation. Knowing nevertheless that the telegraph had come to stay, they cheered O'Rielly and often invested in his companies with the hope that he would break down telegraph patents and cut costs of their telegraph news. In his ready way Morse declared that Hale and Hallock, of the *Journal of Commerce*, were "glad . . . that they are likely . . . to embarrass me, and deprive me of half my property, to get their Telegraph news a little cheaper!"[5]

The same position was taken by most papers the country over. "The press at the West as well as here are prejudiced against me," Finley explained to Sidney, "because they have to pay a certain price (a mere pittance when its value is considered,) for their news. They wish it cheaper; therefore, regardless of all things else, whether I have rights, or whether my opposers have none, they join in the cry of 'monopoly.'"[6] Taking up O'Rielly's charges, they extracted laughs from the garbled messages that came into their offices from Morse lines; cheered the storms that tore Morse wires from their poles; and charged that Morse stole his telegraph system from Steinheil.

Meanwhile O'Rielly gathered strength. Not only did he have the House rights on his side, but he also purchased other telegraph rights, among them those to the telegraph of Barnes and Zook. Hearing of his new moves, Faxton, president of the Buffalo-New York line, of which Morse himself was a director, expressed his uneasiness. Morse replied in a singularly caustic letter. "The Telegraph is a *profitable enterprise*," he wrote, "hence the attempt to pirate. . . . '*Where honey is, the bees will be*,' and not bees only but all sorts of *blue bottles,* and *nasty flies and moths.* . . .

"Now my dear Sir, suppose I were to undertake to answer all the misrepresentations, and abuse, and squibs, that the O'Rielly conspirators, in Albany, Rochester, New York, and out West, perpetrate daily, (and they are many of them Editors of Papers, who want their *dispatches free,* and hence their hostility, hence their desire to break down, what they choose to denounce as a monopoly,) pray, what else should I have to do? . . .

"Put down as much of what I am going to say to partiality for *my own,* as you please, but *remember* what I say. *Nothing has been invented, heretofore, like my Telegraphic system. No improvement has been made in it by any other person since I have had it in operation.*"

Perhaps Mr. Faxton stopped to ask himself if Morse had forgotten that Vail helped him – that Bréguet's magnet had proved useful. Possibly Vail, Bréguet, Page, and Cornell had not made an *essential* improvement in his system, but certainly they had contributed improvements to it.

But when Faxton read the whole statement its import may well have shocked him. "*Nothing has been invented, heretofore, like my Telegraphic system. No improvement has been made in it by any other person since I have had it in operation. No improvement will be made that can at all compete with it.* These declarations I have put in black and white, and you have possession of them. When I am mistaken you may twit me with the boast." [7]

History has long since twitted Morse even if Mr. Faxton neglected to do so. Within eight years Morse himself was consenting to introduce into America a radical improvement, Gintl's process of duplex telegraphy, by which two messages could be sent over the same wire simultaneously in opposite directions.[8] While Morse's system well-nigh conquered all rivals in his day, it has lived with such radical improvements that the sum total of improvements may be said to have supplanted his system. The controversies in which he was engaged had warped his perspective. The controversies were created in part by the circumstance that the United States did not reward him for his invention as France did Daguerre and that the United States did not buy his telegraph outright and run it as a government enterprise as he had at first hoped, and consequently capitalists were scrambling to make the most of the new gold mine. In large part, however, he could have avoided controversies by leaving them to Kendall and the capitalists whose interest it was to defend him. He could not bring himself to do so. By nature he loved controversy and he regarded the defense of the originality of his invention as sacred. Not trained as a scientist, his emotions were so linked to his brain-child that when anyone proposed that it be taught something its parent did not know, the parent felt himself maligned.

When O'Rielly began to build a line from Louisville to New Orleans with the Barnes and Zook instruments, Morse and his colleagues decided the time had come to block him. They believed that the Barnes and Zook instruments were being used in violation of Morse's patent because they used the electromagnet, and according to the claim in Morse's patent reissue, the butt of many jokes in the press, Morse had the rights to any use of electromagnetism in telegraphy. Morse prepared to move against O'Rielly again in the courts, and at the same time to harass him by putting up a Morse line along a similar route to New Orleans.

From Pittsburgh the Morse poles began to sprout toward Nashville. For about fifteen miles the Morse and O'Rielly routes to Nashville happened to be close to each other. Shaffner, the overseer of the Morse laborers, foresaw trouble and armed his men. "This is to be lamented," he wrote to Morse, "but if it comes we shall not back out." [9]

Morse kept his poise. "I emphatically say," he wrote to Shaffner, that "if *the law* cannot protect me and my rights in your region, I shall never sanction the appeal to force to sustain myself, however conscious of being in the right. . . . If the parties meet in putting up posts or wires, let our opponents have their way unmolested." [10]

Nevertheless Shaffner saw to it that the O'Rielly gang was informed that his gang was ready. The moment came when they met on the parallel stretch. The O'Rielly men yelled. The Morse men yelled. For fifteen miles they worked within sight and sound of each other and with the utmost speed. When one man finished digging a hole for a post, he ran to the next location. They shouted back and forth songs like the one written by Reid:

Boys! bear along the lightning thong
Down the O-hi-O.
Four thousand miles already up,
And thousands more to go.[11]

The Morse gang pulled ahead of their rivals, as Shaffner, no doubt disappointed, wrote his chief, "without the loss of a drop of blood."[12]

As the race continued toward New Orleans, Morse found solace in the first ten verses of the thirty-seventh Psalm: "Fret not thyself because of evildoers. . . ."

Before the lines reached New Orleans the Morse patentees brought suit for an injunction against O'Rielly for using the "Columbian," the telegraph system of Barnes and Zook. Morse went down to Kentucky for the court hearings. With him was his second wife.

One summer it suddenly occurred to Sidney that Finley should have a farm. Not only would it be a home for him at last, but it would provide work for Finley's son Charles, whose occupation was the despair of the family; it might even uplift the neighbors. "Brother Finley's taste for landscape gardening would have a fine field for display in the execution of such a project," Sidney wrote home. ". . . The problem sh.d be to produce the greatest possible display of good taste with the least expenditure of money – & especially to furnish models for plain American farmers."[13]

Finley had already searched out a country place when Sidney's letter reached him. After the sale of the government line to a private company he had left Washington and lived for a time in two rooms in the *Observer* Building, taking his meals at a boarding-house. But he no longer needed to hoard his coins. The *Observer* was prospering and his two brothers had families and homes of their own in New York; he, too, had income enough from his telegraph stock to gather his scattered family about him at last. That his brother's letter should come just when he had already selected a "farm" – a large tract just south of Poughkeepsie – seemed a providential intimation that he was acting judiciously.

It was a hundred-acre estate which the inventor purchased, rather than a farm. He agreed to pay for it $17,500, plus an allowance for stock and farm machinery. His neighbors were not ordinary tillers of the soil, but Van Rensselaers and Livingstons. Since before the Revolution this estate had been owned by Livingstons, distant relatives of the man who had assisted Fulton to construct the steamboats that first smoked up and down the river below.

From the house Morse could see over trees, a deep glen, and more distant woods down to the blue and gray Hudson. Across the river toward the north on clear days he could see the Catskill Mountains, and to the south the Fishkills. Near the house was level land cleared for farming, enough for both Sidney and Richard to build houses and have a twenty-acre garden apiece besides. North two miles in Poughkeepsie were good markets, schools, and churches.

By the summer of 1847 Morse had his three children about him in his own house for the first time in twenty years. In the new house he hung his portrait of one of the family who had especially longed for a home, Lucretia. Her oldest child, Susan, could often be with him now for long respites from her lonely plantation life in Porto Rico, and her presence was always satisfying. Poor Fin, a burden for the family ever since he had become mentally deficient from scarlet fever, found the farm a healthful home. The boy whom Lucretia had called "Little Charles," the sickly one, was now an unstable young man for whom the place provided wholesome work. There was even another "Little Charles" now, Lucretia's grandson, Susan's son, to play under the locust trees and pull the tail of the good-natured Newfoundland.

Morse soon felt he belonged in the new home. It pleased him to learn, after he had named it Locust Grove for the many locust trees about it, that Judge Livingston, whose property the estate had once been, had given it the same name. He discovered, too, that Catherine Livingston, the judge's daughter, had been wooed among these same locusts by his Utica uncle, Arthur Breese. And Morse felt more at home than ever when in the spring his son Charles married a granddaughter of those lovers who had once rambled about Locust Grove.

In June of his first season in the new home Morse went to Utica for Charles's wedding. The bride was pretty Mannette Lansing, who was to prove as unreliable as Charles. The wedding party gathered at the house of Mrs. Sarah Ann Walker, where hung the painting Morse had made to illustrate his poem "Serenade," written for Sarah Ann years before. Morse knew Mr. Walker, too; he became a director of the New York-Buffalo telegraph line, later succeeding Faxton as its president.

Many Breeses still lived in or near Utica and doubtless the house was crowded. Uncle Samuel Sidney Breese was not far away in Sconandoa. Uncle Arthur was now dead, but his second wife was still living in Utica, and probably three of his daughters were at the family gathering: Mrs. Walker, the hostess; Mrs. Lansing, the mother of the bride; and Mrs. Griswold, the mother of Sarah Griswold, the bridesmaid.

Morse remembered his cousin Sarah. He had met her before at Cousin Sands' in New York. He had then been, as he now recalled, "struck with her beauty, her artlessness, her amiable deportment, and her misfortune of not hearing, and defective speech."[14] He had found himself in love with her, and her misfortune had only stirred him the more. Reflecting on it, he had felt that he had no right to think of marrying. Both were penniless, and the more he had thought of it, the more certain he had become that he must not even tell her of his love. He had been rejected too many times because of his poverty. He had not wished to be hurt or to hurt her. But then, six or seven years ago, Sarah had been only a girl; now she was a woman of twenty-six. She had been born on Christmas Day in 1822, at about the same time as his son Charles, the present groom.

Morse observed the lovely deaf bridesmaid. She was a dark beauty like his Lucrece. When she saw that his son Fin, because of his backwardness, was being ignored by his sprightly cousins, she took his hand, walked with him among the company, and finally sat beside him, making herself understood well enough to amuse him. Her kindness filled the father's heart; it determined him, now that he was prosperous and she mature, to ask her to marry him. He did so and she accepted.

Uncertainty followed. Sarah's mother, Mrs. Griswold, was not opposed to their marriage, but her sister, the mother of the girl Charles had just married, objected and knew how to make her influence felt. The negotiations lasted for weeks. Mrs. Lansing visited for a time at Locust Grove, where her mother had been courted, and damaged another courtship in so doing. "We had a most violent and (between ourselves) most *selfish* and *imprudent* opposition," Morse wrote his brother, "from Mrs. Lansing, Manette's mother, which communicated itself to Manette and slightly to Charles, till I found, that my home was likely to be imbittered by this most outrageous and impertinent influence of Mrs. Lansing." Perhaps Mrs. Lansing had read the O'Rielly charges that Morse wished to be a millionaire, and perhaps she hoped that his resources would not be dissipated among too many cousins other than Manette and herself. It was only the money problem that Morse mentioned to his brothers as coming between them, though other difficulties may have existed in the disparity of thirty-one years in their ages, in the fact that she was his own first cousin's child, or in her deafness.

Once during these days of family dissension someone told Sarah that it was rumored that she would not have consented to marry Morse if he were not rich. She replied with emotion, in her awkward speech: "Oh, I wish he was poor, and I would then let him know whether I loved him."

"Well, Sarah," someone replied, "suppose his property should be taken from him and it may be in some way not now foreseen, what would you do?" Perhaps someone was contemplating an O'Rielly victory.

"What would I do?" she answered. "Why, support him with my own hands." [14]

Morse did not notify his brother Richard of his marriage until within two weeks of the wedding date, which, as Morse warned, was too late for disapproval. Perhaps to parry censure for having chosen a girl without fortune or social competence, he wrote that he had chosen her in part just because she was dependent. The letter was frank:

Washington, July 29, 1848

My dear Brother,

. . . I wished to inform you myself, before you heard of it from other sources, that I shall shortly be married to that most lovely second Cousin of ours, *Sarah Elizabeth Griswold,* the beautiful daughter of

Cousin Catherine Griswold, who for many years was deaf and dumb, but who has gradually been recovering both hearing and speech, until at present, I, at least, find no difficulty in conversing with her in my ordinary tone of voice. She is 26 years of age and is, therefore, mature. If anything at first blush strikes you with surprize at my choice suspend your judgment till I can explain all in an interview. You are at least aware that in all my movements especially in relation to so serious a subject, I am in the habit of asking counsel from the source of all wisdom, and the paintings of his hand, and his leadings are so manifest that I have not a lingering doubt that he has at length heard my prayer, and granted me a gift worthy of Himself. Of her sincere devoted affection for me, I have no doubt, and I have so many guarantees for it, that it is made *doubly* & *trebly* sure. Sidney, you know, used to say before he was married, that he meant to choose a poor girl of respectable connections who should add to personal affection, the feeling of gratitude for befriending her. These guarantees for strong love, I have in a treble form, in my choice. 1.st We are relatives in a degree which, while it does not forbid (from its nearness,) an alliance, is sufficiently near to produce strong natural affection. 2.d She is portionless, and to some extent both she and her mother have been dependent on M.r Goodrich who married Cornelia her sister. I say, to *some extent*, for she is of noble and independent spirit, and for some years past has furnished herself with clothing by the assiduous labors of her needle, in furnishing some articles of fancy for her brother's store. This trait of character is one that you and Sidney, at least, will appreciate. 3.d Her mother will have a home with me, if she chooses, a portion of the time. These guarantees of affection, aside from mere *personal* love, you perceive are of a nature to warrant a belief in its reality and continuance.

Her mother has given her cordial approbation. . . . I had received her consent by Telegraph yesterday. . . . I have had an opposition of a most unpleasant character from Mrs. Lansing, which threatened to create a breach in the family. I have much to say to you on this point, and I wish to caution you against committing yourself, or any of your family committing themselves, by any word or act, in the present state of affairs, which may be construed into *disapprobation*, until I see you and have had full explanation of matters. . . .

I was called here suddenly to meet my counsel from Louisville previous to commencement of the suit against the pirates in that region. . . .

Love to all. In great haste.

Y.r Affect. Brother
Finley

P.S. My property affairs look *bright,* but keep this fact to *yourself exclusively.*

P.S. 2d. Sarah is not pious, but is very desirous of hearing me explain the subject of religion; I cannot but hope from the way in which she manifests her interest in the subject that God intends to lead this Sweet Child to the Savior, Pray for her and for me. She has been in the habit of attending the Episcopal Church, but is not bigoted. . . .[15]

In an Episcopal church in Utica, on August 10 of the year in which the first women's rights convention in America was held, Morse married the woman he chose because she would be dependent.

Bride and groom left Utica immediately to meet O'Rielly in a Kentucky court. On their way (it was Morse's first trip "over the mountains") Morse found his wife sensitive to the beauty of scenery, never fatigued, always ready at the right time, tastefully dressed for every occasion. "Sarah is . . . amiable, affectionate, devoted," he declared fervently; ". . . I say everything when I say that my dear Lucretia could not be more so." [16] No matter how deranged their room in the Weisiger House in Frankfort might be when she was not there, in her presence it resumed perfect order. She seemed contented, cheerful, continually busy with a needle or book in the corner of the room. Whether because of her poverty or her difficulty of hearing and speech, she quickly became his attentive helper without presuming, so far as abundant correspondence indicates, to be his legal or financial adviser. She showed the dependence he had expected and desired.

Proudly Morse informed his brothers of the attentions bestowed upon his bride. He told them that the lady of Governor-elect Crittenden sent her a "fine packet of peaches from their garden." He copied for them a note from the *Louisville Courier,* "the paper which has been most virulent in its abuse of me": "Prof. Morse the lightning man who is at present in Kentucky engaged in the prosecution of suit against the O'Riellys has recently married a beautiful wife, purchased a beautiful farm, and erected a beautiful house on the banks of the Hudson River where he intends to settle down and live in quiet for the rest of his life." [16]

CHAPTER *xxiv*

On Trial

AT TEN o'clock every morning Professor and Mrs. Morse appeared in the courtroom. At three at the close of the session they returned to the Weisiger House. Between three and six Morse conferred with his counsel, including Kendall and the fight-loving Shaffner, in one room of the hotel, while O'Rielly conferred with his in another. At six the counsel of both sides, Morse and his lady, the bumptious O'Rielly and his sprightly son all dined together, and afterward lounged about the sidewalk and under the trees in front of the hotel. Local lawyers among the counsel told of the raucous days when Frankfort with some six hundred inhabitants was the metropolis of Kentucky. Kendall, quite at home in Frankfort, where he had once edited a newspaper, told stories about Old Hickory, whose biography he had begun. Morse chatted about his wizened teacher, West, and the famous scientists who had heralded his telegraph in Paris, Humboldt and Arago. Jefferson Davis amused the company with accounts of the Mexican War. Governor-elect Crittenden and Senator Metcalfe took the opportunity to make Morse's acquaintance. The little capital knew it was host to a famous trial and made the most of it.

The rest of the country also knew what was going on in Kentucky. "This is one of the most important lawsuits ever contended for in the United States,"[1] said the Philadelphia *American*, fervently hoping that the court would prevent Morse from successfully reaching out his greedy hand to seize all telegraphs that used electromagnetism.

Wearily Morse heard the presentation of evidence on whether he or Steinheil had really invented the Morse telegraph, on the difference between the Columbian and the Morse telegraphs, on the meaning of the claims in the Morse patents. At the end of sixteen days Federal Judge Monroe announced the decision. He declared Morse to be the inventor of the Morse telegraph and granted an injunction against O'Rielly. For the time being, the principle was established that Morse held patent rights to all use of electromagnetism in telegraphy.

The Morse telegraph carried the news of the decision over the country. Said Horace Greeley in the *Tribune:* "Believing the claims put forth in behalf of Prof. Morse to amount to a monopoly of all possible modes and means of communicating ideas by electricity, believing such claims to be absurd, unrighteous and prejudicial to the public interest, and believing that he (or those claiming under him) have made unreasonable and excessive exactions for the use of the patent, we have hoped to see his pretensions somewhat pared down in the Courts. We still hope so." [2]

The Frankfort suit was only the first in a long series. For six years, while bitterness became fixed within Morse, newspapers and investors in other telegraphs urged on the war against him. Their opposition was concentrated at the vulnerable point of his claim of rights over all use of electromagnetism in telegraphy, a claim which first appeared only in his patent as reissued in 1846.

O'Rielly lieutenants sought to evade the injunction by receiving by sound instead of recording on paper. While Morse had once claimed recording as the distinctive feature of his telegraph, in his patent reissue in 1846 he had also claimed rights for receiving by the already popular method of listening to the click, click, of the receiver; the Kentucky court arrested the O'Rielly management for contempt. Again O'Rielly men sought to evade the injunction by moving the telegraph instruments into Indiana outside the jurisdiction of the court. But the posts and wires of course remained in Kentucky, and when they attempted to use these wires for messages received and sent out of state, the court ordered the district marshal to seize them. O'Rielly finally took an appeal from the Kentucky district court to the United States Supreme Court, reaching final decision only in 1854.

Meanwhile in Philadelphia a contest arose with Alexander Bain, a Scotch telegraph inventor, who was advised by the press not to bring his children to America for fear that Kendall would claim them as the inventions of Morse. In Boston a trial issued in the decision that House's telegraph was sufficiently different from Morse's to merit a separate patent. There were suits in Kentucky, Tennessee, Ohio, and New York; there were hearings before the Patent Office at which Morse had to enter "interference" when he believed new patents would infringe on his.

From the suits emerged a mass of evidence, much of it new. Professor Silliman testified that his former pupil knew something about electricity in college days. Cooper offered to furnish a statement about his friend's interest in telegraphy in Paris in 1832 before sailing on the *Sully*, but Morse declined to use it, believing Cooper mistaken. From his brothers he secured depositions attesting to his exultant predictions for the telegraph on disembarking from the *Sully*. He introduced in evidence his own *Sully* notebook and many letters. He secured statements from visitors to his and Gale's rooms at the university that they had seen his telegraph in operation in 1835 and following.

Against him rival inventors and telegraph companies ranged their witnesses. Dr. Jackson gave sensational testimony that the conception of the telegraph on the *Sully* was his. When he inspired a flurry of newspaper animadversions directed against Morse in 1839, a friend called Morse's attention to the lines in *Paradise Lost:*

> The invention all admired, and each, how he
> To be the inventor miss'd; so easy it seem'd
> Once found, which yet unfound most would have thought
> Impossible.[3]

When everyone saw there was money in the telegraph, Morse's enemies begged for Jackson's testimony to strengthen their position in the press and in the courts, and Kendall feared the Boston doctor enough to write a brochure attempting to expose him. But Jackson's evidence was more sensational than effective. It was never given weight in the courts.

More effective was the testimony of Joseph Henry, one of the foremost scientists of the time.

The break between Henry and Morse originated in Henry's weakness of pride. Vail's 1845 history of the telegraph all but omitted mention of Henry as a telegrapher. While Morse owned one quarter of the financial rights to the book, he had not even read the proof of the part which dealt with Henry's contributions, but Henry peevishly blamed Morse. At the request of Morse, Vail wrote Henry an apology, admitting that Henry stood at the head of the science of electromagnetism in America, and promising to correct the omission in the next edition.[4] Henry did not reply.

Unfortunate circumstances prevented Henry from recovering perspective. On the day that Henry was elected secretary of the new Smithsonian Institution at Washington, Morse took the trouble to write a letter of congratulations for the *Observer*, hoping that it would improve their relations. Inadvertently the letter was not published. When the cornerstone of the Smithsonian Building was laid on the Washington Mall, Vail, in an unhappy moment, offered a copy of his book to be placed in it. Henry forbade accepting it, as Vail learned. Still Henry's displeasure reached Vail and Morse only by hearsay. When Vail's book was reprinted from the same plates but with a new date, 1847, on the title page, Henry mistakenly supposed that this was a new edition and looked for the promised corrections in vain.

The next year Morse thought he had at last found an opportunity to regain Henry's confidence. Morse secured the permission of Sears C. Walker of the Coast Survey to attach to a report on telegraphy a summary of Henry's contributions. In preparation, Walker arranged a meeting of Henry, Morse, and Gale. At the gathering, the first time Henry and Morse had conversed for many years, Morse explained that he had not known until recently that Henry had already settled the practicability of a telegraph in his 1831 article in Silliman's *Journal.* Gale interrupted to say that he had told Morse of the article when they first worked together, and Morse had used Henry's suggestions when he first succeeded in telegraphing to a distance. Morse did not answer. As Henry remembered it, the interview was then over, and Henry and Morse never communicated again.[5]

That Henry correctly reported the interview is uncertain; at any rate Morse wrote for the Walker report that he had become familiar with Henry's results, if not his article, in 1837. He went on to give Henry high credit: "While, therefore, I claim to be the first to propose the use of the *electro-magnet* for *telegraphic purposes,* and the *first* to *construct a telegraph on the basis of the electro-magnet,* yet to Professor Henry is unquestionably due the honor of the *discovery of a fact in science* which proves the practicability of exciting magnetism through a long coil or at a distance, either to *deflect a needle* or to *magnetize soft iron.*"[6] While Henry deserves more credit than Morse was willing to grant, at least Morse gave him full credit for his most significant contribution to telegraphy. Again, however, Morse's statement was not published as intended; apparently Walker declined to carry out the agreement. And this time Morse as well as his cause was hurt.

Unfortunately Morse blundered into retracting the credit he had assigned to Henry. Many years later, in 1855, he published what he knew was so strong an indictment of him that if accepted (it was not) it would force him from his Smithsonian office. Morse accused him of lying, and declared: "I am not indebted to him for any discovery in science bearing on the telegraph."[7] Both Henry and Morse had lost perspective.

Henry's testimony, now placed before the courts, did not deny Morse's claim to be the inventor of the Morse telegraph. But being disgruntled, Henry viewed Morse's contributions in as unfavorable a light as possible. "I am not aware," he asserted, for example, "that Mr. Morse ever made a single original discovery in electricity, magnetism, or electromagnetism, applicable to the invention of the Telegraph."[7]

On the other hand Morse was able to produce the letter that Henry had written him in 1842, declaring that Morse was entitled to high scientific praise for having invented his telegraph. Their estrangement continued until their deaths, but Henry's letter prevented his testimony from doing more than personal injury to Morse.

His opponents collected an annoying list of claimants to the invention of electric telegraphs. A list of sixty-two was publicized by William Francis Channing, son of the great Unitarian foe of Jedidiah Morse, and himself an associate in the invention of the fire-alarm telegraph. Sixty-two claimants to what Morse had thought on the *Sully* he alone had conceived! Many of the inventions dated after 1832. The most astonishing of them, however, was earlier. It was the invention of Harrison Gray Dyar, a Massachusetts youth, who had strung telegraph wires on poles on Long Island in 1827 but had been forgotten ever since. He asked the legislature of New Jersey for permission to erect a line from New York to Philadelphia, but it was denied him. Discouraged, and harassed by lawsuits, he left for Europe in 1831. In Paris Dyar won an award of $300,000 for inventions unconnected with the telegraph; he became a wealthy New Yorker with, like Morse, a house near Madison Square and another one near Poughkeepsie. He had no reason to contend with Morse. When Morse's opponents asked him to testify in their favor, as of course they did when they heard his story, he refused. Dyar's telegraph used static electricity, and marked by sparks on moving wet blue litmus paper, producing an acid which left a red dot for each spark. The courts accepted the evidence that he had put up an experimental telegraph line on Long Island, but that fact did not in any way invalidate Morse's patent, for the two telegraphs had little in common.[8] Still, Dyar's case made it clear that Morse was not *the* inventor of *the* telegraph, nor the first American to invent a telegraph, nor the first American to erect a telegraph line, as the public has largely believed.

The many who regarded O'Rielly as the hero of the war against the Morse monopoly endlessly repeated a ditty in his honor:

> The Steed called lightning (says the Fate,)
> Is owned in the United States.
> 'Twas Franklin's hand that caught the horse,
> 'Twas harnessed by Professor Morse.
> With Kendall's rein the steed went shyly,
> Till tamed and broke by H. O'Rielly.[9]

It was O'Rielly, however, who set the stage for the steed's return to the professor's harness. O'Rielly's appeal of the Frankfort case to the United States Supreme Court approached a decision early in 1854. Morse was glad that an end of his suspense was coming. Yet he was uneasy, for he knew that an adverse decision would mean that he would have to study ways of economy that he had long since forgotten.

The majority decision was rendered by Chief Justice Taney.

O'Rielly and his associates had made three charges, as the Chief Justice interpreted their arguments. They charged that Morse was not the "first and original" inventor of the telegraph he had patented; that if he were, the patents were not properly issued to him and did not confer on him the right of exclusive use; and that even so the Columbian telegraph used by O'Rielly was so different from Morse's that it did not interfere with his patents.

In deciding on the originality of Morse's invention Taney reviewed the knowledge of electromagnetism before 1832. Many had suggested the idea of electromagnetic telegraphs, he said, since they first became possible with the discovery of electromagnetism by Oersted in the winter of 1819–20. Henry, he went out of his way to add, had done as much as anyone to develop the knowledge of electromagnetism; but no one had yet produced a practical electromagnetic telegraph in 1832. That being so, "it ought not to be a matter of surprise that four different magnetic telegraphs, purporting to have overcome the difficulty, should be invented and made public so nearly at the same time that each has claimed a priority; and that a close and careful scrutiny of facts in each case is necessary to decide between them." Henry's bell-ringing device was ignored. The four considered were those of Steinheil, Wheatstone, Davy, and Morse. Using legal rules little related to facts, the court dated Morse's invention early in the spring of 1837 as being then in full form and publicly exhibited, and according to rules for judging dates of foreign inventions, it dated Steinheil's and Wheatstone's later in the same year, and Davy's only in 1838.

Even if Morse's telegraph were later than others, Taney declared, his patent would not be invalidated unless one of those other inventors had previously patented a similar telegraph in this country. This they had not done.

To the charge that Morse merely borrowed his ideas and combined them into a telegraph, Taney asserted that the use of ideas of others was natural and proper, "otherwise, no patent, in which a combination of different elements is used, could ever be obtained." The court decided that Morse was the original inventor of the telegraph that bore his name. It did not examine his relation to Vail.

In answer to the charge that Morse had not properly taken out a patent and could not claim exclusive use of his telegraph, the court found that he had taken out his patent in proper order, but that one claim in it, that which appeared in the patent reissued in 1848 as the eighth claim, could not be allowed. This was the claim to the right over the use of electromagnetism in telegraphy. As O'Rielly and the press had often maintained, Taney said, this claim would be comparable to a claim by Fulton of the right to use steam to propel vessels no matter by what machinery, thus preventing any improvements in steam vessels except by himself. Taney wondered, if the eighth claim was expected to hold good, why Morse had bothered to make any other claims, since that one alone would cover all the particular machinery he had developed for telegraphy.

In reply to the final charge that the Columbian and Morse telegraphs were substantially different, Taney found that they were the same and hence the Columbian telegraph did interfere with Morse's patent. O'Rielly was rebuked.

Three justices concurred with Chief Justice Taney. Two others concurred in the minority opinion of Justice Grier, which was even more favorable to Morse.

News of the decision reached Morse in Washington. With doughty Shaffner and his wife, and the son of Kendall, he went to an official reception and was warmed by constant compliments. They were granted to " your *modest* husband," he wrote to his wife on February 17, " whose cheeks so often assumed the rosy hue of his youth some —— years ago, (no matter about filling the blank,) that he began to think the red might, from reiteration, become permanent, and that he might surprize his young wife, on his return." At last the man who had once thought himself like Whitney and Fulton driven by wretched patent laws " to exile, or to poverty, to the insane hospital, or the grave,"[10] felt the law was behind him.

After the Supreme Court decision Morse remained in Washington to ask for an extension of his 1840 patent. Without extension it would soon have run its fourteen-year course and the court decision would have put nothing in his pocket. Morse believed that patents should extend throughout the life of the inventor, but as it was, the Commissioner of Patents could extend them for only seven years. He attempted to prove that he deserved an extension by stating his total telegraph income:

Income from direct sales of patent rights	$36,630.48
Income from telegraph stock dividends	47,090.75
Has in hand stock, which if renewal denied, would be worth only	85,950.00
He has received stock in payment for patent rights, a part of which he has sold for	24,200.00
Total estimate of income from telegraph	$193,871.23

With legal advice he deducted from the total items which he thought properly charged against the telegraph: $3,000 a year for sixteen years, his loss as an artist while developing the telegraph; costs of equipment in his experiments; costs of litigation; the price of his purchase of Gale's share of the patent. The remaining sum was $90,874.[11]

Accepting his low figure, if his income had been divided equally among the sixteen years since his first public exhibition of his telegraph in 1837, he would have had the tidy income of more than $5,500 a year. Since he manifestly had no such income during the years before private investment in the telegraph, his recent income must have been ample.

Morse's figure of $90,874 Commissioner of Patents Mason revised, using the information Morse himself had presented, to $200,000, and then he weighed that sum against what he regarded as the value of the telegraph, some millions of dollars. Yet the inventor could not claim a compensation equal to the entire worth of the invention or he would have given nothing to the world, the commissioner said. Moreover, other persons might well have made the same invention in time. And other persons had prepared the way for him. The reward to the inventor should be liberal, however, he concluded. "The benefactors of their race have rarely received an excess of gratitude, or reward. These should rather exceed than fall short of the proper measure."[12]

After Morse's agents and friends had mistakenly explained that income from the extended patent would go only to Morse and not to the other patentees, and after a magnanimous recommendation by Joseph Henry, the commissioner extended the patent.[13]

By 1845 Morse felt that responsibility for bringing the telegraph into public use could be safely lodged with Kendall, but in practice he found that he could not give it up. The next year he believed he had done his part in giving telegraphy to the world and could return to art, but when Congress did not give him a painting commission he lacked the will power to return to painting after all. Though he knew it was unnecessary, he continued to participate in the world of clashing interests. By doing so he had won wealth and paid for it. He had given up his last chance to return to creating beauty with his brush. He had been hounded by a public cry that he was greedy. He had lost friends by his apparent arrogance.

Somewhere within himself he knew better. He still delighted in the locust trees of home, the laughter of his grandchildren, and the patience of his wife. When he was free of the terrible pressure of lawsuits and the drive for wealth, when his rivals had come to accept him as one of the heroes of telegraph history, at times his magnanimity returned even as he thought of his telegraph. Fame had not warped him so that he did not know at least what he ought to say.

At a great dinner in his honor in London he spoke words of understanding: " When the historian has made his search, and brought together the facts, if any one connected with a great invention or discovery has attracted to himself the more concentrated regard or honour of mankind, or of a particular nation, how significant it is that time, and more research bring out other minds, and other names, to divide and share with him the hitherto exclusive honours. And who shall say that it is not eminently just? Did Columbus first discover America; or does Cabot, or some more ancient adventurous Northman dispute the honour with him? Is Gutenberg, or Faustus, or Caxton, the undisputed discoverer of the art of printing? Does Watt alone connect his name with the invention of the steam-engine, or Fulton with steam navigation? . . . There is a lesson (and a consoling one, too) to be learned from this voice of history. Man is but an instrument of good if he will fulfill his mission; He that uses the instrument ought to have the chief honour, and He thus indicates his purpose to have it. (Cheers.) It is surely sufficient honour for any man that he be a co-labourer in any secondary capacity to which he may be appointed by such a head in a great benefaction to the world." [14]

CHAPTER *xxv*

Atlantic Cable

By the close of the Mexican War Hale and Hallock of the *Journal of Commerce* saw that their old methods of collecting news by horse-express and pilot-boat were outmoded, and they knew that Bennett's *Herald*, odious penny sheet though it might be, had the requisite energy to exploit the still little-tried method of reporting by lightning. One morning after the *Herald* had published another scoop, Hallock, the proud sixpenny editor from Wall Street, walked into Bennett's office, saying: "I have called to talk about news with you," and the alliance that led to the forming of the Associated Press began.

During the war telegraph lines were still few, messages often garbled, and in a single storm 170 breaks in wires occurred between Hartford and New Haven alone. On its face the usual rule of first come to the office first served by the wire was fair; but in fact it was abused by some reporters who retained the wire to prevent rivals from sending news. As more and more editors recognized the value of columns headed "by telegraphic dispatch" (the word "telegram" was unknown until 1852), the advantage of union in gathering news and promoting telegraph lines became evident. The association of Hale and Hallock with Bennett showed the way.

Just after the close of the war, representatives of the major New York papers, the *Sun* and *Herald*, the despised penny papers, and the *Journal of Commerce, Courier and Enquirer, Tribune*, and *Express*, the conservative sheets, gathered in the *Sun* office. The telegraph had effected wonders. The once hostile editors organized themselves into the New York Associated Press, the association since grown to fame throughout the world. The calm, aged Hallock was its first president. Its first known contract was with "Fog" Smith for the use of the line between New York and Boston.

From the beginning the Associated Press was largely occupied with relaying European news from Eastern ports. When poles carried wires into Halifax the Association appointed as agent there a man who had run a pigeon news service but now had the grace to know that lightning could outfly pigeons, D. H. Craig, a Yankee subdued in conversation but savage in action.

True to his reputation, "Fog" Smith was unhappy because the New York press used his lines from New York to Boston and Portland without paying more than ordinary tribute. When the next steamer was due at Halifax, Craig and Smith's news agent, John Smith, met on the wharf, the fastest horses in the province waiting beside them to race for the use of the wire to New York. Half the people of the city were said to have been on hand to watch the contest. As the steamer neared the dock the crowd stirred. When it was within thirty or forty feet the purser of the steamer mounted the paddle-wheel box and to the cheers of the throng tossed a parcel of English newspapers directly into the hands of John Smith. In a few seconds he was riding toward the telegraph office, long before Craig had met the official requirements for boarding the vessel. The purser dined well that night.

In support of his namesake agent, F. O. J. Smith now used his power as controller of the Boston-Portland Morse line, the only one between those cities, to squeeze Craig out altogether. Smith notified the Associated Press that he would telegraph none of its news over his lines unless it appointed a new agent. Refusing to knuckle under to Smith, the Associated Press goaded the public along the whole seaboard route into howls against the Morse monopoly.

Finally Kendall felt obliged to reprove. "What is your position?" he demanded of Smith in a letter made public with Morse's endorsement. "A message comes to your line, after having passed over three legitimate Morse lines, and you assume a right to stop it – to send it no further. For what reason? . . . Simply because the agent of the Associated Press, at Halifax, is, in your opinion, a bad man, not to be trusted by the public."[1]

But what finally brought Smith to terms was neither the rebukes of Kendall and Morse, nor government regulation (for there was none). Instead it was the competition that Morse disliked. Craig arranged for O'Rielly to construct a Bain line from Boston to Portland, providing a non-Morse route from New York to Portland and thus evading Smith's lines.

Like his predecessor Cadmus, the inventor of the Morse alphabet found that his work produced confusion. From his dragon's teeth had sprung an army of companies that fought among themselves, fought the sower, and fought the public whom they were created to serve. Moreover, many of them were shoddy companies, unsound in financial structure. Their equipment was not standardized. They built their lines too cheaply, as Morse and Vail agreed; they used poor wire; their posts were ugly and not set firmly in the ground.

For some telegraphers the confusion pointed toward union in more than news-gathering. Morse had recognized the advantage of union of all the Morse lines from the first. He had hoped for union under government control or ownership; now when a proposal came from a Wall Street capitalist to buy all the Morse companies and rights, Morse favored it, desiring that the union should be "so organized that the public shall have no just cause of complaining of an oppressive monopoly, and may be better served than by independent companies." Kendall favored the plan too. It was a proposal, as Morse wrote him, "originally designed by us, but thwarted by O'Rielly and his abettors." Morse and Kendall were both willing to sell their stock and Morse his patent rights "at a fair price." [2] The proposal came to nothing, but shortly afterward Kendall issued a call for a convention of representatives of all Morse lines from Maine to Missouri. It met in the Washington City Hall in March 1853, and made itself a permanent body for consultation on such matters as means of payment for messages that originated on the lines of other companies, provisions for blacklisting undesirable operators, and the propriety of revising the Morse alphabet.[3] The convention was the germ of future union.

Besides leading toward union, the war for control of the important sources of European news at Halifax encouraged dreams of a cable that would bring news from Europe itself.

Morse left the earliest authenticated prophecy that a cable would reach across the Atlantic. That he did so perhaps as early as 1838,[4] and surely as early as when the Washington-Baltimore line was hardly begun, is a tribute to his powers of prophecy. In 1843, after a successful experiment with the principles of Ohm's law, he wrote the Secretary of the Treasury two sentences that were repeated endlessly after the cable came into being: "The practical inference from this law is that a telegraphic communication on the electro-magnetic plan may, with certainty, be established across the Atlantic. Startling as this may now seem, I am confident that the time will come when this project will be realized." In England in 1845 J. W. Brett registered a company with the express purpose of laying an Atlantic cable, but it remained a paper corporation. Morse afterward cheerfully acknowledged that Brett was the father of European, but not American, submarine telegraphy.[5]

But in the terrible and glorious history of the laying of the Atlantic cable Morse's role was largely that of lieutenant to a lithe young man in his thirties who had just retired from his paper-manufacturing business, Cyrus W. Field.

Morse and Field could talk each other's language. They were alike sons of New England pastors of Old Testament fear in the Lord; they were alike hardheaded. Their shrewdness made it all the more difficult for people to understand how they could propose laying a wire under the ocean.

But the public was not aware of previous experience in cable-laying. Morse had proposed a submarine cable from New York to Charleston as early as 1837.[6] Both Pasley in England and Dr. O'Shaughnessy in India had already communicated under water by 1839. Morse's experience with the Governor's Island cable in 1842 was known to anyone who cared to look up the facts. In the late forties a daring English company laid the first cable under the English Channel, but like Morse's Governor's Island line, it was hooked up by a fisherman who mistook it for a new kind of seaweed. In 1851 a Channel cable was permanently laid, and two years later Charles Bright, an engineer of twenty-one, laid a cable from England to Ireland. By this time speculation on the possibility of an Atlantic cable was abounding.

Early in 1854 F. N. Gisborne, an English engineer who was seeking funds for the company by which he was engaged to lay a cable between Nova Scotia and Newfoundland, called on the Field family. After talking with him one evening, Field was fingering his globe when the idea came to him, as it already had to others, that Newfoundland and Ireland were neighbors and could also be connected by cable. The newspaper scramble for European news at Halifax indicated that an Atlantic cable would meet a need. Inspired with his idea, Field dispatched letters to Morse and Matthew Fontaine Maury. Both were in Washington at the time, Maury in his observatory, and Morse celebrating his recent Supreme Court victory over O'Rielly. Morse went to the observatory to see Maury and obtained from him an account of what he could better describe than anyone else in America, the plateau which lay under the sea between Ireland and Newfoundland. "The plateau is neither too deep nor too shallow," Maury explained. "Yet it is so deep that the wires once being landed will remain forever beyond the reach of vessels, anchors, ice-bergs, and drift of any kind; and so shallow that the wires may be readily lodged upon the bottom." [7] Morse wrote to Field that he had always believed a cable possible, and recommended that Maury be associated in the enterprise in some remunerative way. He remarked that Maury's soundings of the Atlantic had brought forth, in answer to Field's questions, "an echoing yea." [8] Morse soon called on Field in New York and their strange association, varying from admiration to enmity, began.

Field gathered about him a notable group to forward the enterprise, among them Morse; Peter Cooper, the venerable ironmaster and inventor, soon to be loved for his generosity in founding Cooper Union and laughed at for his fear of the conscienceless moneyed aristocracy in America; Cyrus's brother David Dudley Field, a well-known lawyer; and the bankers and merchants Marshall O. Roberts, Moses Taylor, Wilson G. Hunt, and Chandler White. During that spring and summer they often met at Cyrus Field's house on Gramercy Park, calculating in millions of dollars, tracing routes on the globe. From their meetings emerged the organization for building the Nova Scotia-Newfoundland line, ambitiously named the New York, Newfoundland, and London Telegraph Company. Cooper was chosen president, Morse vice president, and Gisborne engineer.

Young Cyrus Field, however, who impressed the group with his cold calculations and warm zeal, remained its guiding genius.

The imaginations of millions on both sides of the ocean had been stirred. The company found itself able to secure exclusive rights to anchor a European cable from Newfoundland, Prince Edward Island, Nova Scotia, and Maine, and subsidies from both the United States and Britain.

For his one-tenth interest in the company Morse paid in ten thousand dollars. Over the protest of Kendall, for one dollar and "certain advantages" Morse also gave his services in the attempt to persuade the Morse lines from Maine to New York to send messages for the new company at half rates; and as a threat if they failed to do so, Morse granted the new company the exclusive right to build parallel lines. He also made the magnificent gesture of giving the company his rights on a line across Britain's Atlantic Ocean and Britain's North American provinces, in neither of which he had rights to dispense. His telegraph was used in the provinces, but he had failed in attempting to secure a patent in the Canadas by act of Parliament.

Next year, while lines of poles crept over Newfoundland, company agreements with the Morse lines were completed as Morse had promised. Morse told everyone that in three years through his telegraph instruments at Locust Grove he would be asking a Yankee's questions of persons in London, Paris, Vienna, Constantinople, and Canton, and would be receiving replies in five minutes. As yet the company had not even laid the short stretch of cable from Nova Scotia to Newfoundland.

One day toward the end of summer the passengers on the *James Adgar* were chatting merrily in the sunshine on the first day out of New York, expecting that a cable-laying expedition would be as carefree as a deep-sea fishing cruise. Some of the passengers idly watched the Long Island shore while others gathered about Morse to see his model telegraph instruments. One of those who heard him explain his toys, Henry M. Field, the young minister brother of Cyrus, was later to remember that he understood telegraphy for the first time that day. Cyrus himself was on board and their lawyer brother, David Dudley. To enjoy the amenities of cable-laying several older men had come along, too: Peter Cooper, the elder Field, a pastor in a small town in the Berkshires who looked and spoke like a Hebrew prophet, and Dr. Spring, a New York pastor, son of the Professor Spring whom Morse had known at Andover. Ladies were also aboard, Mrs. Morse among them.

The call at St. John's was not disillusioning; with the fussy ceremony of the times the passengers were dined in the city and in return entertained on board. But in giving these dinners the passengers prepared for the failure of their enterprise. They placed at the head of their table not the captain of the ship but the venerable Pastor Spring.

From Newfoundland the *James Adgar* and a brig bearing cable from England sailed across Cabot Strait to anchor one end of the cable to Nova Scotia. The Americans had supposed that the English vessel would pay out the cable under its own power, but as it was only a sailing-ship whose course would be too indirect for cable-laying, it was decided that the *James Adgar*, a paddle-wheel steamer, would tow the brig. The first time the captain got the *James Adgar* under way it rammed the brig. The second time the tow-rope caught in the paddle-wheel, and in the confusion that followed the brig nearly drifted on a reef. The third time the captain got the *James Adgar* safely off shore, and the cable engineers ordered him to set his course toward Newfoundland by a white rock on a mountain in the distance. But the captain was stubborn, the more so because he remembered that he had not been given the seat of honor at dinners on his own ship. Peter Cooper saw that he was not following directions. As president of the company he told him so. "I know how to steer my ship, I steer by compass," said the captain, and that was all that Cooper could get him to say. He first went far out of the way in one direction and then in another. As the ship continued its crazy course a storm broke over it and the once gay excursion party was glad to abandon the cable to the deep.

The next summer the Newfoundland-Nova Scotia cable-laying expedition again prepared for its task and this time succeeded. Morse was not on the expedition; at Field's invitation he was on company business in England, for the decision had been made to prepare for laying the Atlantic cable itself.

Before stopping long in England Morse briefly toured the Continent with his wife and his niece Louisa. Crossing France, he passed miles of telegraph poles that seemed to be presenting arms to him. In Paris he listened affectionately to the chattering of his "children," his instruments, in a great government telegraph office. He could hardly be lonely anywhere in Europe now.

In Copenhagen he made pilgrimages in honor of heroes of two periods of his life. Recalling his painting days, he spent several hours in Thorwaldsen's Museum admiring the works of the man whom he still regarded as the greatest sculptor since the classic age. He then visited the room in which Oersted made his discovery of the deflection of needles by galvanic current. For a moment Morse sat in the great scientist's chair and reflected that without his discovery the telegraph would have been impossible.

Soon afterward, for the first time in his life, he was in St. Petersburg, the city from which he had once expected to set up his first telegraph line. No metropolis ever impressed him like the capital of Russia. The wealth and splendor of London or Paris faded into insignificance before it, he felt, as a candle fades before the sun. Presently he was wondering at the magnificence of the Peterhof itself. When Morse and his party disembarked at the quay, imperial carriages met them by appointment, whisked them through town while bystanders uncovered their heads, plunged through extensive gardens, and halted before the palace buildings. Passing lines of liveried servants, Morse reached an apartment in which the master of ceremonies was reviewing the roll of the guests to be presented to the Czar. Suddenly Alexander II himself entered, a bold blue sash across his breast. The master of ceremonies began calling the roll, and the Czar spoke a few words of greeting to each of his guests. When it was Morse's turn, the master of ceremonies announced: "Mr. Moore."

Quite himself even in Peterhof, Morse instantly replied: "No, Morse."

"Ah," said the Czar, "that name is well known here; your system of telegraph is in use in Russia." [9]

A few days later the Morses were in Germany calling on Baron Humboldt in the imperial residence at Potsdam. Although Humboldt had received him effusively when he first exhibited his telegraph before the Academy of Sciences in Paris, still Morse had taken the precaution of asking the Prussian Minister in Washington for a letter of introduction. The moment Morse entered his room, however, the short, stooped man at the table strewn with papers called him by name, saying: "Oh, sir, you need no letters; your name is a sufficient introduction." The naturalist chatted rapidly of the Wilkes exploration in the South Pacific and finally presented his visitor with a photograph of himself, on which he wrote in French: "To Mr. S. F. B. Morse, whose philosophic and useful labors have rendered his name illustrious in two worlds." Morse had the photograph framed and hung in his library.[10]

An unforeseen obstacle to the use of a long cable had occurred to Dr. Whitehouse, the electrician of the Atlantic Telegraph Company which Field had recently organized in England, and to the physicist Michael Faraday. In cables in water or in earth, current might be retarded by reverse currents induced in the surrounding media; in a long cable such a retardation might be formidable. One night after Morse's return to England, when one of the subterranean telegraph lines running into London was not in use, Morse, Whitehouse, and the English Channel telegrapher, Brett, sent messages through a circuit of two thousand miles. As Morse reported the result of the test to Field: "The doubts are resolved . . . and the great feat of the century must shortly be accomplished." [11]

Though the three experimenters were up all night for the test, the next evening they met again at a banquet for Morse. Many honors had come to the inventor on the Continent, many in London, but this seemed to him his greatest. The chairman was William Fothergill Cooke. He and Wheatstone had become estranged in a dispute that was like the quarrel between Jackson and Morse over the credit for inventing the telegraph, and also like the dispute between Smith and Morse over their common ownership of the patent.

"I was consulted only a few minutes ago on the subject of a telegraph," said the promoter of the Wheatstone system in a toast to Morse, "for a country in which no telegraph exists. I recommended the system of Professor Morse." The audience cheered. "I have been thinking during the last few days on what Professor

Morse has done," he continued. "He stands alone in America as the originator and carrier out of a grand conception. . . . But I think we have a right to quarrel with the Professor for not being content with giving the benefit of his conception to his own country – he has extended it to our own colonies of Canada and Newfoundland, and beyond that, he has now got it introduced all over Europe, and the nuisance is that we in England are obliged to communicate abroad by means of his system." There were cries of "Hear! hear!" [12]

Such a banquet in recalcitrant Britain was a magnificent triumph, even if Morse's old friend Leslie did mix his congratulations with questioning: "I had the pleasure of reading the report of your dinner in the 'Times' today. How was it that Wheatstone was not present and that no allusion was made to him?" [13] The *Times* was wrong. Mr. Cooke himself had discreetly alluded to his estranged partner, the quiet King's College professor, praising his efforts in the commercial use of the telegraph. "I for one," explained Brett to Morse, "was the first to name him when the dinner was proposed as had he been present I was to have proposed him (for a toast), but it was hinted to me as he was not present I had better leave him and Mr. Cooke did it so gracefully that I do not regret it." [14] But no matter what Leslie or the editors thought, Mr. Cooke had spoken Morse's praises, Morse had responded generously, the gathering had cheered, and as when years before he had won the medal for his *Hercules,* Morse was happy once more even in England.

Soon afterward at home in New York Morse drew away from Field. The inside story of the division between them has never before been written.

With Field's shift from paper-manufacturing to telegraphy, he had concerned himself increasingly with the problem which had previously concerned Morse, telegraph unity. Shortly before their voyage together to Newfoundland, Field had made known his interest in founding a company that would unify all the telegraph lines in the Eastern states and provinces. Both Morse and Kendall had approved, being willing to lease their stock and patent rights to Field. Aided by the ever wily Craig of the Associated Press,

Field and his associates organized the American Telegraph Company with the intention of effecting the union. When they bought the rights to the Hughes printing telegraph, however, Morse promptly questioned whether Field intended to damage him. "As you say," Kendall wrote him, "Field and Co. are shrewd business men not unfriendly to you or me but more friendly to themselves. It was not friendship to us which induced them to buy the Hughes instrument; but it was in fact, say what you will, to hold in *terroreur* [*sic*] over our heads and the heads of our Companies to induce us to let them have our lines at a reduced rent."[15] Morse began to deal warily with his Atlantic cable associates.

Shortly after purchasing the Hughes rights, as Morse understood it, the Field associates withdrew their offer to Morse. Presently the Morse interests and the Field-Cooper-Craig interests were building rival lines in New York State over the same routes. "Keep your eye on this excellent friend of yours – Mr. Cyrus Field," advised Cousin Walker of Utica.[16] Morse did.

While visiting England to assist in preparations for laying the cable, Morse had been elected an honorary director of Field's Atlantic Telegraph Company, incorporated in England. But he was not satisfied. Not only had he given his services to the company while in England, but the rights for connecting the cable from the Maritime Provinces to New York, which he had given to the Newfoundland company, had been transferred by Field's influence to the new company. He felt he deserved more reward.

Kendall hinted at Morse's hurt to Field. He observed that Morse was an honorary director, and asked, pretending not to know, if he were also a stockholder. Field understood the hint well enough, but in response only offered to sell Morse one or two shares of one-thousand-pound stock at par. Field was himself the largest American stockholder in the company.

"I have lost all faith in the professions of those gentlemen in relation to your interests and my own," Kendall wrote to Morse on learning of the offer. ". . . What respect have they shown . . . for your property or fame? . . . They got from you $10,000 in their Newfoundland scheme in addition to all your rights on any new line from New York to the British Provinces for which they paid you nothing; they have made use of your time, labor, name and reputation in their transatlantic scheme and now that they feel strong in the patronage of governments and capitalists, they will allow you to *purchase . . . at par!*" In short, Kendall wished to be rid of the agency of Morse's affairs altogether, and go back to completing the work of which he had already published one volume, the biography of his old chief, Andrew Jackson.[17]

Morse protested violently to the one of the American Company in whom (though a Unitarian) he had most faith, Peter Cooper, its president. For more than sixteen pages he raged on.

Cooper replied plainly. He admitted that the Hughes patent might hurt Morse's interests. But, said he, we must all submit to the judgment of practical tests. "It should be our ambition as well as our pride not to allow the paltry questions of *meum* and *teum* to dwarf the noble enterprise of working the electric telegraph around the world by the machinery best adapted to accomplish that end."[18]

Time has proved Morse right in believing his invention more useful than Hughes's. However that may have proved itself eventually, and whatever Cooper's and Field's and Craig's intentions in purchasing the Hughes rights, the fact remained that when they held those rights they could expect to be able to buy the Morse lines at a less and perhaps even a ruinous price.

On the other hand it is clear that Morse was not free to deal with his Atlantic cable associates as he would have been if he had not had investments of his own to protect. His property entanglements weakened his perceptions until he was indeed well-nigh bound by the paltry question of *meum.*

He allowed himself to be persuaded by Cooper, however, to continue for the time being to co-operate with his fellow cable promoters. He did so though Kendall dubbed Field another "Fog" Smith. For Morse he could have chosen no stronger epithet.

After being forcefully persuaded, the Secretary of the Navy placed at the disposal of the cable projectors the new steam frigate *Niagara.* In preparation for a peaceful expedition her guns were removed at the Brooklyn Navy Yard, her decks cleared, and her bulkheads knocked out to make room for the stowing of the cable in England. As one of the honorary directors of the Atlantic Telegraph Company Morse applied to the secretary for permission to be a passenger on the vessel. He sailed on the *Niagara* in the spring of 1857.

Anchored in the Thames, the *Niagara* for days was the center of a fleet of bobbing craft. It was the first time in many years an American war vessel had been in English waters, and this one was the biggest in the world. Moreover, Britons thrilled at the thought that this vessel was to lay a little wire under the ocean to link the Old World and the New. One day another historic vessel, the *Agamemnon*, which had come out of the jaws of death in the bombardment of Sebastopol, and now had been detailed by the British government to aid the cable enterprise, came up the Thames to take its place beside the *Niagara*. The *Niagara's* crew cheered lustily.

When the stowing of the cable on board the two vessels finally began, it was apparent that it would take several weeks. Since Morse was anxious to confer with the French Premier on the possibility of the governments of Europe giving him an honorary gratuity for their use of his telegraph, he took the opportunity for a trip to France.

In Paris he pretended disappointment that the fashion for billowing crinoline prevented him from judging the form of French women. "Who could have predicted," he wrote to his wife, that, because an heir to the French throne was expected, "all womankind, old and young, would so far sympathize with the amiable consort of Napoleon III as to be in appearance at least, likely to flood the earth with heirs?"[19] Whether or not he overcame the obstacle of crinoline as he proposed by using a lorgnette to see the ladies and a trumpet to talk with them, he did succeed in impressing ladies and gentlemen of influence. After having published a memorial on his behalf to the governments of Europe,[20] he left Paris in June with the hope of obtaining financial recognition for their use of his invention.

It was more than a month later that the cable fleet, four British and four American vessels, was ready to sail from Liverpool. Morse was on the *Niagara* as the fleet steamed out of the harbor. Throngs on the docks waved handkerchiefs, vessels of war fired salutes, sailors cheered from the rigging.

The *Niagara* looked as strange as her voyage was unique. Between her main and mizzen masts was a towering coil of one hundred and thirty miles of cable. Much more was below. Abaft the mizzen was ponderous machinery for paying out. In a row were five horizontal drums, geared together, each about five feet in diameter. As the cable was drawn out from the hold, it was to pass back and forth among these drums until from over the last one, which hung over the stern, it fell into the sea. The passing and repassing over the drums served to reduce by friction the speed of the paying out. A balance indicated the strain applied to the cable, by the weight of the part dropping into the sea and the speed of the vessel, so that a brakeman could apply the brakes to the drums accordingly.

Experiments proved to the satisfaction of the engineers that the cable would stretch as much as twenty per cent without breaking. That decided, Morse suggested that the cable be stretched in the presence of the officers in charge of paying out in order that they might be impressed with the necessary care.[21] If this test had been made, it is possible that the history of the expedition might have been other than it was.

Across the Irish Sea in sight of the high green hills of Queenstown, the attempt was made to test the entire two thousand five hundred miles of cable, half on the *Niagara* and half on the *Agamemnon*. During the experiment Morse was stepping from one rowboat to another when one of his legs slipped between them, scraping his knee. It pained him, but he successfully sent a message through the entire cable for the first time that day.

A few days later the little fleet sailed out of the Cove of Cork along the southern coast of Ireland. The *Niagara's* deck was now a confused mass of machinery, it seemed to Morse; here and there were " steam-engines, cog-wheels, breaks, boilers, ropes of hemp and ropes of wire, buoys and boys, pulleys and sheaves of wood and iron, cylinders of wood and cylinders of iron, meters of all kinds, – anemometers, thermometers, barometers, electrometers."[22] Picking their way among them were a motley company: the ship's crew, the cable crew, observers for the governments of Russia and France, reporters, company officials like Morse and Field, electricians under the supervision of Dr. Whitehouse, and engineers under the supervision of young Bright.

On August 4 the telegraph fleet entered the Bay of Valentia off a rocky promontory of Ireland that reached out toward America. That night there blazed on shore a bonfire of peat piled as high as a two-story house; rockets chased the gloom from above the ships; there was music and dancing and a banquet in the harbor town. At the banquet the Lord Lieutenant of Ireland used a happy expression: the cable fleet, he said, was to be "beautiful upon the waters, even as are the feet upon mountains of those who preach the Gospel of peace." [23]

The next day the harbor was gay with flag-decked vessels of all sizes as a shallow-bottomed boat towed an end of the cable from the ships toward the shore. A hundred men broke from police restraint to rush forward to haul the cable onto the beach, the Lord Lieutenant among the first. In a few moments the cable was spliced to a wire that in turn was spliced to other wires reaching across Ireland, under the Irish Sea, across England, under the English Channel, over the whole Continent, and to Asia.

As Morse, a little lame, stood listening on the shore, he may well have been moved as a clergyman pronounced the prayer that he had repeated to himself so often since praise first came to him for his telegraph: "Not unto us, O Lord, not unto us, but unto Thy name give glory."

On August 6 the fleet sailed. It soon returned ingloriously. The cable had snapped in an accident. Morse was sure it would not happen again.

The next day the fleet sailed once more, the *Niagara* paying out the cable in its wake. Dr. Whitehouse having worn himself out in the preparations, Morse was now in charge of the electricians aboard, and young Mr. Bright of the engineers.

This time the first few hours passed without alarm. The cable slipping back and forth over the drums and into the water was specially prepared for duty near the shore to withstand rubbing against sharp rocks. It was night when the eight miles of heavy cable neared its end. There was anxiety for the moment when its last length should slip into the water. Could the first section of the lighter cable – the cable that was scarcely an inch in diameter – bear the weight of the end of the heavy cable dropping into the deep?

By a physician's order Morse was lying in his berth to rest his leg. Above his head he heard the rumbling of the drums, and every now and then a tremendous thump when a splice in the cable went over them. He could not sleep. He knew the critical moment was approaching.

Suddenly the rumbling ceased. In the confusion of voices that broke the silence he heard one saying: "The cable is broke." The dreaded had happened. There was nothing he could do but strain to hear the sounds of remedial action. Providentially the engineers had contrived to catch the end of the heavy cable on a buoy. Now he heard them grappling for it in the sea. In half an hour came the joyous shout: "All right." Above him the machinery commenced its low rumbling, like the purring of a great cat, it seemed to him.[24] The first crisis was past.

The next morning was clear and land was still in sight. The coil in the hold was still unwinding itself without kinks, and the cable slipping smoothly into the water. Everyone was in fine spirits. From thirty miles out Morse sent a cable message to Valentia to be forwarded to his wife.

The third day out soundings showed the depth gradually increasing to about four hundred fathoms, and the charts warned it would soon drop suddenly to seventeen hundred and then to two thousand fathoms, nearly as great a depth as they would find anywhere on the voyage. The engineers narrowly watched for increase of strain on the cable.

"Stop her! Stop her!" was the cry from all on deck at six in the evening. Morse was able to rush on deck now, and he did. He found riotous confusion. The cable had somehow slipped off the drums and was running out swiftly. Ropes were applied to the slipping cable, and while it strained, "perspiring at every part great tar drops,"[25] it came to a standstill, holding together long enough to be returned to the drums.

In the gray morning of the fourth day out, there was a heavy swell. The stern rose and fell, young Mr. Bright at the brakes applying and releasing them as usual in accordance with the swell. Then Mr. Bright went below to see how the cable was coming out of the hold. He left as brakeman a mechanic who had been familiar with the brake system since its construction. The stern rose and fell again, rose once more, and the cable parted, the end slipping into the ocean with hardly a swish.

The drums stopped rumbling. All hands came on deck, gathering in little groups, talking as silently as if one of their number had gone overboard. There was no confusion this time. Three hundred and forty miles of cable lay on the bottom. The only way to fetch it up – if any of it could be fetched up – was to return to Ireland. The *Niagara* put about, and soon the rest of the fleet after her. There was nothing else to do.

While the argument raged on board the next day as to what had caused the break, Morse wrote his explanation. "At 3.45 yesterday morning . . . Mr. Bright spoke to the man in charge of the brakes, asking him what strain was upon the cable, to which the answer was returned about 3000 pounds. Mr. Bright directed him to put 100 lbs. more of force upon the brakes to check the speed of the cable. This was demurred to by the man for a moment, who expressed a fear that it would not be prudent. Mr. Bright, however, persevered in his orders. The brakes were applied with the additional force, which suddenly stopped the wheels of the paying-out apparatus, and of course brought the force of the unchecked speed of the ship, as an addition to the strain. At this time, too, there was a moderately heavy sea which caused the ship's stern to rise several feet, and to the same degree to fall; when the stern fell the cable under its immense strain, went down into the water easily and quickly, but when the stern was lifted by the irresistible power of the succeeding wave the force exerted upon the cable under such circumstances, would have parted a cable of 4 times the strength. . . . It did snap, and in an instant the whole course and plan of our future proceedings were of necessity changed. . . . I feel sorry for Mr. Bright."[26]

Morse's explanation – essentially the same as that of Field and the reporter for the *Herald* aboard[27] – was published in American papers. When Mr. Bright heard about it he sent Morse a letter of protest. After reading it, Morse had it published with his apology. Mr. Bright had written that he had given the brakeman no orders to alter the adjustment of the brakes. The fault, Mr. Bright believed, was that the brakeman did not regulate the brakes as usual in rhythm with the swells.[28]

The whisper went round the world that the Atlantic cable was a hoax.

In America Morse soon found that the alliance of Field, Cooper, and the Associated Press was still pursuing " unity," otherwise called " monopoly." Where they could not buy out the lines they wanted, they were building Hughes lines of their own, waging ruinous wars on the Morse lines.

" I intend to withdraw altogether from the Atlantic Telegraph enterprise," Morse wrote to his brother Richard soon after reaching his beloved wife and home on the Hudson, " as those who are prominent on this side of the water in its interests, are using it with all their efforts and influence against my invention, and my interests, and those of my assignees." [29] Meanwhile Kendall advised his client to appear neutral. He would protect the Morse interests, he proposed, while Morse himself should maintain pleasant social relations with both sides.

That winter Morse called at Field's counting-room for a letter from Field in London. Before he had an opportunity to read it one of the clerks drew his attention to a newspaper article excoriating Field for the cable failure. Morse's first impulse was to write an indignant reply. Walking the few blocks to the house he had taken for the winter on Twenty-first Street, however, he read Field's letter and changed his mind.[30] Field had notified him that a new British corporation law forbade the election of an honorary director who was not a stockholder. With apparent solicitude, Field warned him that he should immediately secure stock or else he would not be re-elected. But there was no cable to permit Morse to notify him in time, even if he had cared to purchase stock.

As he replied to " Fog " Field, an impulse to threaten seized him. He forgot that he had intended to withdraw from the company. He would have liked, he wrote, to accompany the cable expedition again the next summer, as Cooper had requested, but his failure to be re-elected made it impossible for him again to ask the navy to permit him to sail on the *Niagara*. " Many of my assignees," he added, ". . . deem the success of the laying the cable to be the basis of operations by . . . the American Telegraph Company for monopolizing and controlling all the Telegraph lines of the United States.

. . . This . . . is sufficient, I think, to show that my continued and ardent wish for the success of the Ocean enterprize has another foundation than any expectation of personal pecuniary advantage to myself.

"I wish you distinctly to understand, however, that . . . I am not responsible for the schemes or plans of self-defence, and self protection of those interested in the established lines, whom the antagonistic course of the American Telegraph Company has arouzed in opposition. I hear of plans, the details of which are not imparted to me . . . which may well occasion you some uneasiness in regard to your anticipated profits." [31]

With new cable and improved equipment the *Agamemnon* and the *Niagara* were on the Atlantic again in June, Mr. Bright still in the service of the company. In mid-ocean the cable on the two ships was spliced together, and they sailed in opposite directions. After some three hundred miles of cable had slipped into the sea, it snapped again. Better prepared for disaster this time, they were ready again in July. From mid-ocean the *Niagara* sailed for America and the *Agamemnon* for the British Isles. On August 4 the vessels safely reached their ports, in Trinity Bay, Newfoundland, and Valentia Bay, Ireland. A few days later, August 16, 1858, the first official cable message was sent from Queen Victoria to President Buchanan.

Somehow a parody of the inaugural exchanges found its way past Bryant's desk into the *Evening Post:*

"Dear Buchanan: I send this by my rope."

"Dear Victoria: I send this to *Eu*rope."

Gladly the papers resurrected Morse's fifteen-year-old prophecy: "A telegraph may with certainty be established across the Atlantic." At the office of the New York *Sun* hung a sign: "S. F. B. Morse and Cyrus Field, Wire-Pullers of the Nineteenth Century." The celebration was one of the lustiest and most enthusiastic in American history. Across the continent bells clanged and bonfires lighted the countryside, preachers talked of the blessing of God, poets of human brotherhood, and immigrants of telegraphing home. In the excitement New York nearly burned down its City Hall.

The news of success found Morse in Paris in a somber mood. He was cautious as he addressed the company of Americans that had gathered to do him honor as their part of the world-wide celebration.

"On the pure management of the Atlantic telegraph," he said, "as a political or commercial engine of vast power, for good or evil, will depend whether the hearty congratulations at its success as a scientific enterprise (which is the ground on which I can and do unite in these congratulations) shall be weighed with regrets that its vast capacity for good in the world is to be perverted to evil, to be contracted by a narrow policy, or used oppressively or offensively." [32]

As Robert Fulton had naïvely supposed that his invention of a better submarine would bring an end to all war, so Morse at first had assumed that his telegraph would be of social use. But as early as when he first proposed government control he had wondered; during his long conflicts with Smith, the Associated Press, and Field, his dreams of 1832 had soured. He must have seemed more sober now to those who remembered him in Paris in 1838 proclaiming the wonderful results his telegraph would bring to mankind. Now he may have glimpsed, as few of his generation did, that material progress might be no progress at all.

Exultation in America, rejoicing in France, and approval in England all died soon afterward. For the cable itself had died. Why, no one has ever surely known. Morse is said to have predicted that it would fail because it had been stored improperly before being laid. Many refused to believe that any signals had been sent over the cable at all. They said that Field had mocked them with a gigantic hoax. They charged him with having stultified the President and the Queen by pretending to send their messages over a tiny wire lying among shells and seaweed at the bottom of the sea.

The next year a union of interests closed the rift between Morse and Field. The Magnetic Telegraph Company, the first Morse company, "saw the light" and became part of Field's American Telegraph Company. The leading stockholders of the Magnetic Company, including Morse and Kendall, accepted an offer of $500,000 of American stock (a sum greater than that for which Morse had offered the whole of his patent rights to the government fifteen years before) in exchange for $369,300 of Magnetic Company stock. Barnum of the Magnetic Company became president of the reorganized American Company, and Kendall, Morse, Field, Hunt, and Abram S. Hewitt were among its new directors. The company now owned all the important lines on the Atlantic seaboard, except Smith's Boston to New York line, and Field, not being anxious to associate with Smith, finally bought him out, too. The company operated seven different lines from Boston to New York alone.

About the same time the Morse patentees sold their remaining patent rights. Most of the rights for trunk routes had already been sold. And the patent had not long to run – only until June 20, 1861 – unless again extended. Even so, Smith sold his patent rights to the American Company for $301,108.50, a tidy sum for a man who had made but a small investment of cash. And Morse and Vail sold theirs jointly to the American Company and its allies in the United States and Canada. With the sales a series of nasty lawsuits between Smith and Morse, which threatened to last indefinitely, came to a sudden conclusion. The American Company with its allies soon controlled the patents and lines of Morse, Hughes, and Bain.[33]

In vain the company attempted to secure another seven-year extension of the Morse patent, promising to pay over to the patentees the sum of $30,000 if it succeeded. Smith opposed extension. He planned to build a new telegraph line and wished to avoid paying patent royalties.[34] He had squeezed his tumbler full of juice from the Morse patent and was ready to throw the rind away.

Smith's war with the Associated Press had forced it into the arms of the American Company. But now the Associated Press feared the American Company as a coming monopoly, and moved to thwart it. Craig, still agent of the Associated Press, maneuvered behind the scenes. He secured enough backing from the press generally and from the "Six Nations," six companies including the young Western Union which were only loosely associated with the American Company, for the Associated Press to threaten to build rival lines of its own. Field and his friends, Peter Cooper, Abram S. Hewitt, and Wilson G. Hunt, immediately declared for conciliating Craig. Kendall declined; he knew too much of Craig's wiles to care to truckle to him. Morse at first was uncertain.

A statement said to be signed by every editor of New York and

Boston was presented to President Barnum of the American Company. It demanded reduction of rates, the election from the stockholders of three directors approved by the New York press, and one each by the Boston and Philadelphia press.[35]

Morse read a copy of the statement and indignantly called at the American Company office in Wall Street. He found the Englishman Russell, the willful secretary of the company, in excitement. Russell said that he was determined to break the Associated Press by getting up an opposition news-gathering association, with its own agents in Europe, and giving it special privileges on the company lines. Morse listened to his threats with complacency, almost with approbation, since the Associated Press seemed to have determined on war.

Soon after returning to Poughkeepsie, Morse received a note from Hewitt inviting him to dine at his Gramercy Park house – which was also his father-in-law's, Peter Cooper's, house – to meet representatives of the Associated Press. After having made the two-hour trip to the city again, Morse found at the Cooper-Hewitt house not only his hosts, the ironmasters, and their next-door neighbor, Field, with all of whom Morse was now in harmony, but Raymond of the *Times*, Beach of the *Sun*, Hallock, Jr., of the *Journal of Commerce*, the son of the Hallock who had been first president of the Associated Press and whom Morse had long known, and Brooks, who had once fought Smith for election to Congress in Maine, now editor of the *Express*.

The hosts, Field, and Morse persuaded the editors to keep open the questions at issue until they had an opportunity to bring company officials to reason. Raymond of the *Times* convinced Morse that the Associated Press was strong enough to build its own lines if it wished. Morse's new interest in peace, as he explained it at length to Kendall, was wholly to save his telegraph interests.[36]

A few days later the city papers published a notice of a demand for a meeting of the stockholders of the company, signed by four of the directors: Hewitt, Field, Hunt, and Morse. The signature of three was enough to force a meeting, and Russell and his friends howled against Hewitt, Field, and Hunt as the henchmen of Craig and the Associated Press. Morse they somehow avoided. He was, after all, a national institution now, the venerable inventor of the telegraph, almost too old to engage actively in business wars, and too respected to be brashly accused of misdemeanors in the brochure warfare that followed.[37]

That he stood a little apart from the name-calling made it possible for him to be more forward in conciliation. It was due to him that two officials of the company who had been appointed by Russell's influence ceased to be convinced of Russell's wisdom. With Morse's encouragement in the soothing Delmonico atmosphere they engineered social gatherings which concluded in a treaty of peace.[38]

At last the Morse, Field, and Associated Press interests were all in harmony. Not only were the attacks on Morse's patent now over, but also his attacks on the lines he had founded. One would think that he would have shrunk from further controversy.

In that year of 1860 thirty-one ships coming in from Europe were met by Associated Press reporters at sea off Cape Race, Newfoundland, and their news telegraphed over the continent. But Field persisted against the inertia and suspicion of the world and the threat of poverty for himself. In 1865, in the fourth attempt, the cables snapped again. When the next year the *Great Eastern,* the largest steamship in the world, left Valencia, the town had grown so weary of seeing cable expeditions depart that enthusiasm could hardly be wrung from it. But this time the cable slipped into the water from the *Great Eastern's* stern without a break all the way across the Atlantic. The scramble for news in Nova Scotia and Newfoundland ceased. At last the Americas and Eurasia were united by cable, never again to be separated.

Morse was now seventy-five years of age, unable to participate in cable expeditions except by wishing them well. If he erred in accusing the brilliant young engineer Bright, if he was often too much bound by his own interests in judging Field, still for a man of always decided views he had shown much grace in relinquishing his untenable positions when the occasion demanded it. The honor of linking the Old and New Worlds belongs principally to Field for his indomitable perseverance and to England for providing most of the capital. The original conception, however, was Morse's and no one was more pleased than he that he had lived to see Europe and America united across the sea on which the idea of the telegraph had first come to him.

From the peace of his home above the Hudson the conjuror saw the lightning flash over more and more of the earth. But the bolts did not go where or when he wished. They flashed nearly as much on the Sabbath as on most other days, lighting the holy day with a brash glare. They lighted the pages of thousands of newspapers now, both the pages of those which told the truth and of those which spoke for the selfish interests that controlled them. The secrets of his magic he entrusted to companies which treated his lightning disrespectfully, asking it to travel on ugly posts, on posts that were not firmly set in the ground. The companies themselves quarreled and some refused to accept transfers of lightning which had been called down from heaven by other conjurors, as if heaven-sent impulses should be subject to man's petty jealousies. His lightning served the ends of greed as well as of generosity, hate as well as goodwill, destruction as well as creativity, war as well as peace. Like many other great men of his century, he had presented a new power to man and, having made his gift, saw little more that he could do than abandon it to man's desires.

CHAPTER *xxvi*

Copperhead

WHEN a New York Negro married a white woman a mob fired the officiating parson's house.

That night Morse asked his Georgian friend Habersham to go with him to hear an abolitionist speak. Coming away, Morse prophesied: "The Northern people will never override Constitution and laws under the lead of fools and fanatics to slay the goose that lays the golden egg." [1] He may have been thinking of the nest egg he had won in his painting days from the gracious slavocracy of Charleston.

From the beginning of the 1830's Morse was an anti-abolitionist. His support of slavery was popular then, but he became a leading apologist for slavery when being so meant that his wisdom, patriotism, and Christianity were questioned by most Americans. His courage, if not his wisdom, may be an inspiration to believers in unpopular principles.

Years before when the Morse brothers came home from college they sometimes found the yard of the Town Hill parsonage crowded with Negroes, for Dr. Morse was conspicuously friendly to the Negroes of the Boston area. He established evening services for them at which he preached Sunday after Sunday himself; he led in founding a school and a church for them; he assisted the half-Negro, half-Indian Quaker Paul Cufee in colonizing Boston Negroes in Sierra Leone.

Visiting in Georgia, Dr. Morse had witnessed the death of a slave in the family in which he was staying. "If a valuable negro die," he commented, "it calls forth the remark that some old worn-out slave could have been better spared. Can this be right? Are not the slaves immortal beings? Should they not have the opportunity of rising in the scale of humanity as the whites have?" [2]

During his four years in Charleston Dr. Morse's son, however, enjoyed the highest income of his painting career without leaving any record of concern for the Negroes on whose labor his income depended.

They disagreed, yet the father was indirectly responsible for his son's attitude. Dr. Morse had awakened in Finley on the one hand a loyalty to an orthodoxy that he came to associate with the social order of the immediate past, and on the other hand an antipathy to Unitarianism that he came to associate with abolitionism itself.

In time Morse came to accept slavery as a positive good. "Slavery *per se* is not sin," he wrote. "It is a social condition ordained from the beginning of the world for the wisest purposes, benevolent & disciplinary, by Divine Wisdom." [3] Like Bishop Hopkins and others, he arrived at this conclusion through a study of the Old Testament. He could do so because he regarded the Bible as the Word of God come to earth untouched by human experience.

Unlike many pro-slavery men, however, he frankly admitted that his belief contradicted the Declaration of Independence. When he read in Rousseau's *Social Compact* the words: "Man is born free," he reacted violently. "I repudiate his fundamental postulate," he wrote in his notes on the book. ". . . There is not a living thing born into this world which is at its birth, and for so long a time subsequently so utterly dependent, bound hand and foot with no will of its own, more completely helpless, more subject, more perfectly enslaved as man." This, he added, "is the source of the error of the Dec.[laration] of Indep.[endence], the equality paragraph, and the inalienable character of liberty." [4]

Jefferson's declaration might not suit him, but he considered himself a member in good standing of Jefferson's party. Even in his excursions into third-party politics he had remained a Democrat on national issues. He believed in the party system. He favored Lewis Cass for president in 1844, but after the Democratic convention had announced its nomination of Polk by the new Baltimore-Washington telegraph line, he supported Polk, believing it in the interests of democratic procedure to accept the convention nominee. He remained a Democrat through the Mexican War. While he was proud of his family motto: "*In Deo, non armis, fido*," and thought "My country right or wrong" a false axiom, in this instance he believed his country right. The Catholic Mexicans are "a worn out race," he declared, and God would regenerate them through American influences; "Our Bible and Tract Societies and Missionaries ought to be in the wake of our Armies."[5] As his telegraph came to assist armies to move, his gifts continued to assist missionaries to preach the Gospel of the Prince of Peace.

A few months after his Supreme Court victory in 1854 he ran for Congress in the Poughkeepsie district. An opposition paper admitted that he might bring outside strength to his party.[6]

More cautious than in his two previous campaigns for office, he committed himself as little as possible. He was nominated by the Soft faction of New York Democracy, but in his campaign manifesto[7] he professed not to know the difference between Softs and Hards.

"Bronson and good rum, Seymour and bad rum, Clark and no rum,"[8] was a popular slogan of the campaign. Governor Seymour, the leader of the Softs, had vetoed as unconstitutional the state "Maine law," so called after the Maine liquor law of three years before. Bronson, the Hard nominee for governor, was an outspoken wet, and Clark, the Whig nominee, an outspoken dry. Morse would only say that he favored the most stringent liquor control the state constitution would allow. On its face his statement might appear to follow the lead of the Governor, but it was susceptible of the interpretation that he was dry, as one opposition paper said.[6]

On slavery, too, he was weak. He would not say how he would vote in Congress on the proposal to open the Nebraska territory to slavery; with many words, after the manner of many candidates for office, he said he would vote as he thought best after debate indicated which vote would defeat sectionalism. He probably suspected that his district favored free soil, the policy advocated by local Whigs, and determined to keep quiet. He was rightly accused of dodging the issue, for he had written his brother that he favored opening Nebraska to slaves.[9]

If equivocal on prohibition and slavery, his position on the third issue of the campaign, nativism, was clear. He could hardly burn his early animadversions on foreign influence. Indeed, in this very year two of his nativist tracts were reprinted. In his campaign statement he only needed to say he had not, "at this late day, for the first time to make an opinion on this subject," and his readers knew what he meant. The nativist Know-Nothing Party nominated its own candidate for governor, but did not nominate a candidate for Congress in Morse's district. Nativists were still the natural allies of the Whigs, however, being generally for prohibition and free soil, and Morse, described as "an original unadulterated Know Nothing,"[9] was ridiculed as a remarkably fit candidate for a party which condemned Know-Nothingism.

As it was, Morse ran slightly ahead of his ticket in his county.[10] If he had won all the Know-Nothing vote he would have carried it. Nativism was at a new crest just now, and in neighboring Massachusetts all but three of the representatives chosen were nativists. But his district was more concerned to preserve Nebraska from slavery and its sons from drink than to preserve older Americans from newer Americans. Everywhere through the state the Whigs were victorious. By the following year the Know-Nothing attempt to save the Union by diverting attention from slavery, a purpose which Morse lauded,[11] had failed both North and South.

Having been defeated three times for office, Morse never tried again. But when next politically active, he was more bold.

When the chasm between North and South finally seemed to Morse impassable, he proposed that each go its way as a separate nation. The old flag could be sliced from corner to corner, he said, the South taking one half, the North the other. Whenever the issues dividing them melted away, as he was certain they would in time, the two flags could be reunited. Until then the fact that when these two flags were placed side by side they appeared to be the old American flag would be a constant reminder of the common ancestry of the two nations, a reminder of the shame that had come between them, and an encouragement for them to work together toward common goals.[12] A common goal on which they could profitably unite, Morse believed, was a war against England; a war for which unanimity could be so easily obtained would drive the issue of slavery into the background and prepare the way for reunion.

The attack on Fort Sumter was for the nation a signal for war, but for Morse a signal for renewed effort toward conciliation. He planned a visit personally both to Washington and to Richmond, seeking a formula for union. Deciding not to go because of his age, he nevertheless paid the expenses of a friend for the same purpose. That the expedition was futile did not discourage him from looking for some circumstance which might provide a basis for negotiations.

In part the war was the fault of the South, he believed. Southerners had encouraged their ambitious politicians, deserted their friends at the North, and cried against union on any terms. But the South was by no means alone to blame. "Many look no farther back than the attack on Fort Sumter," he wrote within two years of the event, "and thus charge upon the South the commencement of hostilities. This is neither just to the South nor to impartial history. The previous years of abolition provocation inflicted systematically, & incessantly, upon the South, will not be ignored in the Historians' summing up of the causes which have generated our national troubles."[13]

Soon after the attack on Fort Sumter Andrew Carnegie was called to Washington to organize a military telegraph system. The next month during the Battle of Bull Run, Lincoln and most of his Cabinet were in the War Department's telegraph office until the news came in Morse code: "Our army is retreating," when they scattered to prepare for the invasion of Washington. The North enrolled some 1,800 boys, mostly under twenty, in the telegraph corps, and the telegraph became, as in Europe during the Crimean War, what Secretary Stanton called the right arm of the army.[14]

Meanwhile the inventor of the telegraph system was serving as president of a pro-slavery society, the American Society for the Promotion of National Unity, which became, as the historian Lossing, a Poughkeepsie neighbor of Morse, described it, "the germ and the powerful coadjutor of the peace faction which played such a conspicuous part during the last three years of the Civil War."[15] In its official program the society thanked God that four million beings, incapable of self-care, were entrusted to Southerners. In answer to the righteous protests of his former pastor at Poughkeepsie, Morse defended his society as having "as warm-hearted, praying . . . Christians as ever assembled to devise means for promoting peace."[16] Among them were Episcopal Bishop Hopkins of Vermont and Leonard Woods, president of Bowdoin, the college in which Calvin Stowe was teaching while his wife was writing *Uncle Tom's Cabin.*

When Lincoln announced his Emancipation Proclamation,* Morse and his remnant of the faithful knew that rabid abolitionism had at last captured the Republican Party. To meet the threat Morse and his friends needed a new organization. This time they found substantial backing.

At a private conclave in Delmonico's luxurious restaurant on Fifth Avenue at Fourteenth Street the new "conspirators" first met. Someone among the number – perhaps Morse – sent an invitation to William Cullen Bryant, editor of the now Republican *Evening Post.* Bryant sent a reporter in his place. Because he held an invitation the reporter was greeted only with upraised eyebrows, while the reporter for Greeley's *Tribune* was ousted without ceremony. The company was admonished to secrecy, but the *Post* reporter, considering himself not bound to be polite to Copperheads, wrote a sensational account of the proceedings. Bryant himself introduced it in the *Post* as the record of an "unscrupulous campaign against the government of the nation, and in behalf of a body of rebels now in arms."[17]

The *Post* published the whole list of those who had signed the call for the meeting, emphasizing the fact that many were millionaires, and many New Englanders. Among them were August Belmont, an agent of the Rothschilds and reputed proprietor of the *World,* E. H. Miller, Wall Street operator, David E. Wheeler, wealthy lawyer from New Hampshire, Henry Young, Troy millionaire, Samuel J. Tilden, corporation lawyer of Wall Street, "S. F. B. Morse, artist and inventor, born at Charlestown, Massachusetts," George Ticknor Curtis, a lawyer at one time retained for Morse, a "fresh importation from Boston," and three editors: Manton Marble of the *World* from Boston, William C. Prime of the

* Lincoln drafted the proclamation in the telegraph office of the War Department. On the day it was made public the President was again in the office, his feet on a desk, recalling the time in March 1857, in Pekin, Illinois, when he first saw the Morse telegraph.

Journal of Commerce from Connecticut, James Brooks of the *Express* from Maine.[18] As Bryant defined the purpose of the new Society for the Diffusion of Political Knowledge, as it called itself, it was to " raise a fund for the circulation of political ignorance, as of treasonable newspapers and speeches. The rich men of New York are to supply the money, and the reactionist editors of the *World,* the *Express,* and the *Journal of Commerce* the brains." [17]

The meeting at Delmonico's was held on Friday night. The revelation was made in the *Evening Post* of Saturday. By that time those who attended the meeting were uneasy, declared the *Post.* " The Sunday papers," another paper explained, " copied the astounding revelations. The Monday morning papers took up the cry, and paraded the names of the traitors and conspirators; the telegraph spread the news to the end of the land." [19] *Professor Morse,* of this region," observed a Poughkeepsie paper, " who is making thousands out of the government through his telegraph, figured among the infamous gang of conspirators." [20]

Tilden, Sidney Morse, and a little later Finley Morse made public letters defending themselves. Tilden, who was later to court Morse's daughter Cornelia, declared that " War Democrats " and even one Republican were present. He insisted he had heard no suggestion at the meeting that was not " moderate, patriotic, and constitutional. No allusion to peace was made." [21]

The *Post* named Sidney Morse of the *Observer* as chairman of the meeting, confusing him with his brother. Because of the error the *Observer,* now being edited by Morse's future biographer, Samuel I. Prime, whose Republican editorials made Morse rub his eyes, lost many subscriptions. Sidney denied that he was present at the Delmonico meeting, or that he favored the purposes of the meeting as explained by the *Post.* Both the rebellion and abolitionism were wicked, he said.[22]

The role of the Morse brothers as conspirators was the subject of a newspaper letter by a writer who styled himself " Bunker Hill," no doubt intending that his appellation should be cutting to the Charlestown-born brothers. " Bunker Hill " forgot that Dr. Morse had approved the Hartford Convention when he wrote that the Morse brothers owed veneration to their father as one loyal to New England and his country in war.[23] One of the Field family, Cyrus's brother, David Dudley Field, also took it upon himself to chide Morse. His fame, Field said, was a national inheritance that should be jealously guarded.[24]

So many sensible people seemed carried away by hysteria that Morse wondered if he would wake up some morning to find all his Protestant friends becoming Catholic, or, worse still, free thinkers on the Theodore Parker model. He was obliged to censure members of his own family, to condemn clergymen for political sermons, and even to repudiate the opinions of the *Observer*. He heard that he was considered a marked man and had been recommended by a Boston paper for incarceration in Fort Lafayette. As a man of means he probably ran less risk in flouting popular judgments than a person dependent on employment, but it took stout conviction to withstand popular pressure at all. Whatever other effect they had, his courage and that of his associates at least helped persuade the administration to maintain a modicum of civil liberty at home.

While the epithets of "Copperhead," "traitor," and "peace man" were flung at his head, Morse allowed himself to be elected president of the new society. During the year and a half between its organization and the Democratic campaign to put McClellan in the White House, Morse's name appeared as president of the society on some twenty pamphlets issued from its office in the *World* Building. He himself read many of the manuscripts. The authors included George Ticknor Curtis, Samuel J. Tilden, James Brooks, Governor Horatio Seymour, Charles Mason of Iowa, Thomas P. Kettell of *Hunt's Merchant's Magazine*, and the Democratic candidates themselves, McClellan and Pendleton. Morse appeared as author of three of them.[25] Bluntly he denied that his purpose was to undermine the American government; it was rather to undermine the administration, he said, which indeed, in a free country, was often the only way to save the government itself. Unanimity of support for an administration is not essential in war-time, he insisted; in fact, when an administration grows arrogant it is dangerous. It was the abolitionists who had urged the administration into unconstitutional measures. It was they, aided by English intrigue, who united the South against any peace negotiations. He declared that the abolitionists were the conspirators themselves; they were "conspirators, freedom-shriekers, Bible-spurners, fierce, implacable, headstrong, denunciatory, Constitution and Union haters, noisy, factious, breathing forth threatenings and slaughter against all who venture a difference of opinion from them, murderous, passionate advocates of imprisonments and hangings, bloodthirsty, and," he asked, "if there is any other epithet of atrocity found in the vocabulary of wickedness, do they not every one fitly designate some phase of radical abolitionism?" [26]

While Morse upheld slavery, his primary aim as the leader of the Diffusionists was to restore the Union, if necessary first by war, then by conciliation. He explained his attitude toward Lincoln in a letter to J. D. Caton, an Illinois telegraph promoter and leading Democrat, after Caton had conferred with him in New York. "The present incumbent is the legally appointed, lawful President of the United States, and must, therefore, be sustained in all his Constitutional acts, whatever opinion we may form, and howsoever severely we may criticize (and we have a right to criticize) his acts and those of his advisers. He must be told, however, with perfect plainness that the People, the Power above him, will hold him to account for any and every infraction of their instructions, embodied in their solemnly enacted will, the Constitution, given by the People for his as well as our guidance. The emancipation proclamation, the illegal arrests, the confiscation acts, the suspension of the Habeas Corpus, under the plea of military necessity, must be repealed and annulled. He has overstepped his powers in these acts." [13]

In their judgment of Lincoln the Diffusionists were by no means alone. In the 1862 congressional campaign, in which the preservation of civil liberties was a major issue, the Republicans lost Lincoln's own state and Pennsylvania, and barely kept control of Congress; even New York re-elected a Democratic Governor, Horatio Seymour. When the conscription act came, Horace Greeley of the *Tribune*, the oracle of abolitionism itself, declared the principle of conscription repugnant to a free people. Just after Gettysburg, draft rioters controlled New York for three days, often overpowering police and militia, and firing the homes of abolitionists and Negroes. The rioting brought Morse down from Poughkeepsie to look to the security of his Twenty-second Street house, and Governor Seymour, who detested conscription, down from Albany to quell the bloodshed with a promise to postpone conscription in his state.

For a man of seventy-two, the patriarch of the telegraph performed a surprising number of promotional duties during 1863. With Governor Seymour's encouragement he obtained Democratic speakers for Poughkeepsie; when the Ohio Democratic leader, Vallandigham, was arrested for a speech in which he said the administration was needlessly prolonging the war, Morse attended a meeting to protest; in June he attended a peace demonstration in Brooklyn and in July the Democratic Independence Day celebration in New York.

With the approach of the presidential campaign he increased his efforts. By January 1864 he reported that his society was supporting General McClellan to a man. Generals were not often of presidential timber, Morse admitted, but if Democracy was to save the union he believed it should nominate someone like a popular general who had a chance to win. In preparation for the campaign Morse conferred with his associates on purchasing a New York magazine for the cause. With Morse's donation of $500 and an equal sum from other sources J. Holmes Agnew bought the old literary monthly, the *Knickerbocker,* which had once sparkled with the wit of Bryant, Cooper, Sands, Irving, and Halleck, and converted it into a servant of Democracy. The new magazine became what Morse told Editor Agnew was the "ablest of all the periodicals of that class with which I am conversant." [27] To campaign funds that year Morse contributed more than $2,000.

By summer, shuttling between Poughkeepsie and New York, he was attending conferences, revising manuscripts for publication, presiding at a peace convention, and attending great mass meetings which sang in the light of torches and rockets to the tune of *Vive l'amour:*

When secessionists tried the Union to sever
Up rose the man we love;
Little Mac drew his sword and boldly said "Never!"
Hurrah for the man we love.

He'll win the race, to the White House he'll go
Whether Beecher or Greeley are willing or no.
Hurrah for the man, hurrah for the man,
Hurrah for the man we love.[28]

In September, at the age of seventy-three, he declined to accept the presidency of the Young Men's Democratic Union Club of New York. As the campaign grew hotter his Diffusionist friend Mason, on behalf of the Central Executive Committee for Campaign Documents, asked him to spend ten days working in the committee rooms; he replied that he would try. On the news from Antietam he was among those who signed a letter to Democratic Mayor Gunther congratulating him for refusing to permit New York to celebrate the victory over "our brothers."

In the last week of the campaign he made the mortifying discovery that what he had thought was his family motto was not its motto at all. When he had first come across it in London long before, its words: "*In Deo, non armis, fido,*" had scarcely been agreeable to him, for he was then the super-patriot. Now, when convinced that God could not be on either side of a war, he discovered that there was more than one branch of English Morses, and that the motto of his branch was only a bad pun: "*Mors vincit omnia.*" I prefer to adopt the old one, he wrote the family genealogist plaintively.[29]

Five days before the election Morse presided at a meeting on behalf of Brooks of the *Express*. He delivered good advice for himself when he said: "The application of opprobrious epithets to an opponent never convinced him."[30]

It was a sad circumstance for the veteran campaigner that his own brother became one of the opposition. Richard told him that if the Democrats did not submit to the election of Lincoln they would do so at their peril. Morse in turn threatened to leave the country if Lincoln won.

On the Saturday night before the election the torchlights of Democracy glittered on Broadway in an unbroken line from far downtown through Union Square, where the great meetings of the campaign had been held, to within a short block of Morse's Twenty-second Street house. When the trembling forest of torches, transparencies, and flags first reached Madison Square, the waiting throng burst into cheers. The disbanding paraders, pressing in front of the white marble Fifth Avenue Hotel, raised a swelling clamor for McClellan himself to appear. Inside the hotel the passages were so packed that Morse, conducting McClellan to the balcony, was nearly crushed; three policemen could scarcely force a way for the hero and his patriarchal escort. As they stepped onto the balcony it seemed to Morse that the mass of heads beneath him reached as far as he could see in every direction. Somehow the shouting died away. In his forceful way he introduced the candidate who would defeat Lincoln, bring a quick peace, and save the Union. As he stopped speaking, there came up from the people such a shout as he could compare in his memory only with the reception given in London to Blücher and Platoff after Waterloo.

Exhausted from the excitement, he slowly made his way from the crowded hotel around the corner to his orderly brownstone house.

The day after the election he informed his recalcitrant brother Richard: " When I can believe that my Bible reads '*cursed*' instead of '*blessed* are the *peacemakers*,' I also shall cease to be a *Peace* man." [31]

CHAPTER *xxvii*

Patriarch

THOSE whose claim to fame is their ability to bend nations to their will may win renown in their own lifetime. But those who present a great gift to mankind – a painting, story, or new way of looking at life – are seldom sung until they are dead. The sage of Locust Grove was a brilliant exception to the rule. He won a measure of honor at home even with his painting, his writing, and his promotion of daguerreotypy. He won a measure of recognition for his telegraph at home and abroad even before the world had accepted it. But when the world knew its value, he attained recognition which is seldom accorded a living hero of the arts of peace.

Before building his first telegraph line he had been honored for his invention by the Academy of Industry in Paris, the American Institute in New York, and the National Institute for the Promotion of Science in Washington. Soon after the opening of the first line the Archæological Society of Belgium and the American Philosophical Society granted him membership, and Yale conferred on him the degree of Doctor of Laws. When the Sultan of Turkey became the first sovereign to decorate him, opponents of the "monopolist" observed that according to the first article of the Constitution no American might accept foreign titles without forfeiting his citizenship, and that therefore he, along with the showman Barnum and the railroad-builder Whistler, ought to be denationalized. Eventually the American who had once complained of decorations as "gewgaws that please the great babies of Europe," received decorations from the sovereigns of France, Spain, Portugal, Denmark, Prussia, Württemberg, Austria, and Italy.[1]

Even greater recognition came to him. In 1858 representatives of ten European nations met in Paris to honor him, an American to whom they had no legal obligation. With the encouragement of Lewis Cass, then Secretary of State in Washington, and of Premier Walewski of France, Morse had published a memorial asking for a personal gratuity in return for the savings effected by his invention in Europe. He had addressed his memorial directly to the governments, for in Europe the telegraph was government-owned – except as yet in England, which was thereby excused for not joining in the award.

At the meeting Premier Walewski presided over representatives of Belgium, the Netherlands, Sweden, Austria, the Papal States, Piedmont, Tuscany, Russia, and Turkey. The principles on which the Morse telegraph rests, he said, were not Morse's, but the telegraph itself, commonly used all over Europe, was. It was one of the most useful inventions of their epoch, and of great economy to their governments. It was only just, he concluded, to offer compensation to the now aged inventor.

As if by prearrangement the representatives accepted the sum of 400,000 francs as the total to be awarded to him. The apportionment presented a difficult problem. But eventually each representative agreed to pay to the French government as administrator 311.55 francs for every telegraph instrument in his country. France was to pay the largest sum, having 462 instruments, and Tuscany the smallest, having 14 instruments.[2] The award of a sufficient sum to support Morse in reasonable comfort the rest of his life was a magnificent gesture from the Old World to the New.

Some of his associates, however, wished to share in his new prosperity. According to the original agreement, his partners were entitled to a portion of any income from the telegraph property acquired by "letters patent or otherwise" in Europe. Morse could not believe that these terms gave them any claim upon a personal gratuity. But both Vail and Smith did ask for a share. As usual Smith would miss no opportunity to put his hand into a promising grab-bag, and prepared to do so through the courts. When he and Morse agreed to refer the matter to three lawyers, to Morse's amazement the lawyers decided that the word "otherwise" in the original agreement gave Smith a share in the gratuity in the same proportion as from any other telegraph income from Europe. The value of the award seems to have been less than $60,000. One third of this sum went to Morse's financial agent in Paris; of the remainder five sixteenths went to Smith, and two sixteenths to Vail's widow, Morse terming it a gift, and Mrs. Vail a right. The residue, about $19,000, was Morse's.[3]

He remembered the award as an honor rather than as a contribution, for his income was sufficient. In 1860, a year in which he applied for the extension of his patents, he had already concluded that he had enough money to "satisfy the desire of any reasonable man."[4] In 1863, a war year, his total income was $31,711.30.[5] By 1867 he and his Sarah owned 7,517 shares of Western Union Telegraph stock alone, and other shares in oil wells in Kentucky, California, and Canada, in the "Morse Association" mines on the California-Arizona border, and in an insurance company. As he worked over columns of figures at his great oak desk, he regretted again and again that he was so stupid with his money affairs. But for all his anxiety, and for all the money that he threw into bottomless pits in the West, his income permitted a handsome program of spending and giving.

Even in the early fifties he felt justified in building a new house at Locust Grove. If he had never provided a house for Lucretia's children, certainly he would do his best for Sarah's.

Mid-century Americans had somehow convinced themselves that Gothic or Italian churches were suitable models for houses. Quite unlike the buildings Morse had known in Charlestown, any new house of pretension sported latticework on the veranda, swirls in the gable verge boards, or carvings on the finials. In the most elaborate of the current modes, the Italian villa manner, a campanile took the center of interest, broken and unbroken surfaces vied with one another, and gables, balconies, bay windows, projecting bracketed roofs, or encrusted verandas, often in a confused jumble, provided the desired romantic detail. A chief protagonist of this Italian style, A. J. Downing, compared anyone who preferred simple houses to a person who preferred simple tunes be-

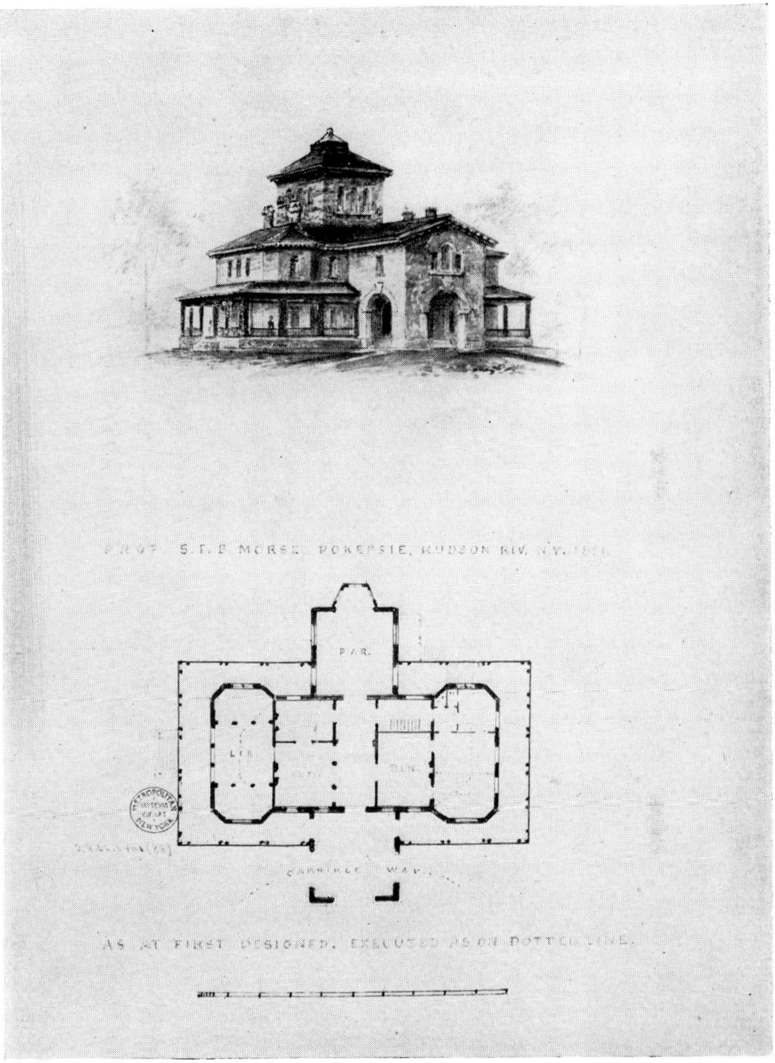

Metropolitan Museum of Art, New York

LOCUST GROVE

1851

Architect's drawings, by Alexander J. Davis, for Morse's house overlooking the Hudson.

cause he had never been educated to appreciate harmony.

After poring over the books of Downing and Loudon, Morse accepted the popular judgment and chose for the design of his house an Italian villa, and for his architect, Alexander J. Davis,[6] who had planned many mansions overlooking the Hudson. Davis designed a central four-story campanile flanked by north and south wings. In the south wing was the most important room to Morse, a half-octagonal study. The outside of the study Davis encumbered with a veranda draped in latticework; the inside Morse encumbered with bookcases, paintings, and relics of his past years of creativity, poverty, and honor. Morse also entrusted the landscaping to Davis. Soon larches grew by the gaping porte-cochère, old locusts bordered a delectably curving driveway to the post road, and Morse was walking from his study veranda toward the garden on paths edged with tulips, hyacinths, or fuchsias, discovering enticing vistas of lawn, field, river, and in the distance blue and green hills.

As age crept on him, he still often rose at half past six in summer, and was at his work at his great oak desk by eight o'clock. There in his firm hand and meticulous grammar he wrote letters defending his telegraphic reputation, inquiring as to the state of his bank account, deploring acceptance of abolitionism, and refusing to endorse inventions, donate funds, or accept office in societies, though he did allow himself to become a vice president of the new Metropolitan Museum of Art, and a founder of the Dutchess County Society for the Prevention of Cruelty to Animals. In the afternoon he walked about his garden, particularly his vineyard, the pride of his heart, or consulted with his farmer on the state of the hay, cows, and hogs, or inspected his stables to the north of the house and the greenhouse to the south, or played with the flying squirrel he had taught to sit on his shoulder, eat out of his hand, and sleep in his pocket.

In the winter friends might find the Morses in a brownstone house on Twenty-second Street, near Madison Square, but through a long summer they were likely to be at Locust Grove. There callers would be shown around the garden by the host, a magnificent figure with a white beard flowing to his breast and soft hair reaching to his shoulders. In the tower living-room, surrounded by his wife, his children, and their Swiss nurse, Clare Subit, he would talk of his former hardships; or with a sparkle in his eye he would bring out his box of medals; or would exhibit the telegraph instrument that he had connected by wire with the line that ran along the riverbank below and through it with the world.

Visitors concluded that he was a grand old man. Benevolence seemed to beam from him, neighbor Lossing thought,[7] and one telegrapher decided he was unassuming, dignified, and considerate.[8] Morse the monopolist had become in the public mind, and perhaps in truth, Morse the kindly patriarch of Poughkeepsie.

He doubtless followed what his telegraph associates were doing with the income they derived from his invention. He may well have been pleased that Cornell, hard and closefisted though he might be, had founded a university in his home town of Ithaca, and that Kendall, too, led in founding Gallaudet College in Washington, for many years the only college for deaf mutes in the world. Only recently Kendall had come to the conclusion that to remain outside the church was to be in standing opposition to Christianity, and with gusto had begun teaching a Sunday-school class. Surely this step pleased Morse, for when Kendall made a large gift to the building fund of his church, the Calvary Baptist Church of Washington, Morse also contributed.

If Cornell's and Kendall's stewardship gratified Morse, certainly Smith's did not. Smith was early interested in women's education – he was the first treasurer of Westbrook Seminary, a girls' school on the outskirts of Portland, and he hoped to be remembered after his death by the establishment of a home for indigent women. But his compassion for women may have been only sublimated remorse for his treatment of them. Before the completion of the Washington-Baltimore line his first wife, Junia Bartlett, had died, and he found a mistress. Some ten years later, when he became engaged to a willful young woman of respectable family, this family discovered the existence of the mistress. On his fluent protestations of good intentions, his fiancée consented to marriage. He brought her to Forest Home and took a house on South Eighth Street in Brooklyn as well. For a time he satisfied her with the elegance of his mansion in the woods and the glitter of life in New York; but when he became involved in a series of lawsuits with Cornell he could not meet her rising demands for a Fifth Avenue home and better dresses, servants, and carriages. She accused him of bringing his mistress to Forest Home when she was away, and turned her children against their father. She called him mercenary and tyrannical. He called her a green-eyed monster and took to drink. Under these circumstances, when he explained that his purpose in founding his home for women was to honor " the goodness and greatness of a mother occupying her true place in the mystical chain of God's Providence," his neighbors would not believe that he was sincere. His brick house with fantastic vaulted ceilings in every room was never used for the purpose he had intended, and has since become a convent school. He died in 1877, still a lover of books – his library was said to be the best in Maine – and still estranged from his sisters, his wife, and some of his children. He left behind him a curiously frank will, explaining how his wife had compelled him to pay over to her certain sums, referring to her " indulgent indiscretions," making gifts to his several natural children by name, and describing one of his legitimate sons as " disobedient and disrespectful towards myself " and " the most destitute of them all of ambition for even a common education." His Forest Home soon crumbled. Because his tomb, too, was shabbily built, its top slab being filled with newspapers instead of concrete, several years after his death rotting newspapers were waving over the remains of Francis Ormond Jonathan Smith, one of the most gifted public figures of his generation in Maine.[9]

Morse also concerned himself with the welfare of women. Considering his age, wealth, and conservative taste, his interest reveals his amazing vitality. As early as 1851 he gave $1,000 to the Cleveland Female Seminary. Then he joined fervently in the movement to set up colleges conducted on the assumption that women could learn what men could learn without losing the feminine graces. Shortly before the Civil War a group of Poughkeepsie neighbors, including Matthew Vassar, Milo P. Jewett, and Morse were quietly planning to act on this revolutionary principle. Jewett informed Vassar, a wealthy brewer (and proud of his beer), that what Fulton and Morse had done for the physical and material in life, he might do for the higher realms. Vassar was determined to found a college.

He and Jewett, both Baptists, wished the college to be evangelical but non-sectarian; and to guard against perversion of his purpose, Jewett recommended that he follow the scheme that Jedidiah Morse and Eliphalet Pearson had adopted in legally fastening upon Andover a creed that would prevent it from becoming infested with Unitarianism. But even law cannot chain the future to the past; and Jedidiah and Finley Morse would today find little theological peace about the hill of Andover-Newton Seminary or the lake of Vassar College. Morse was a charter trustee of the new institution and attended meetings as much as his health would permit.[10] He was proud of his part in establishing the college that opened in 1865 as Vassar Female College. Pleased with its progress, at the age of eighty he assisted in founding another women's institution, Rutgers Female College. He gave it $2,500 for a lectureship; he presided over a course of lectures in its turreted and balconied building on Fifth Avenue at Forty-second Street opposite Croton Reservoir; and he loaned it such a large sum that he embarrassed his household arrangements.

In his poverty he had given $500 to the Yale library. Now in his wealth he was still generous to Yale – in spite of the fact that because his alma mater insisted on honoring Northern soldiers for killing their Southern brothers he refused to attend commencements. He purchased his teacher Allston's great painting of Jeremiah for $7,000 and gave it to the Yale gallery; and soon afterward he gave $10,000 to the Yale theological school.

More than thirty years after his father's death, he paid the greater part of the costs of erecting a monument, a shaft surmounted by a globe, over his tomb in New Haven. In memory of him he also gave to the Union Theological Seminary in New York $10,000 in Western Union stock to found a lectureship on the relationship of the Bible to the sciences;* this with some misgiving, for he knew the Union professors were wrongheaded on slavery. "If I did not believe that a time is coming when they will ignore their present opinion," he wrote, ". . . I should feel that I was misspending the means which God has given me." [11]

* Among the lecturers on the "Morse Foundation" have been Arnold Guyot, geographer of Princeton, William Jewett Tucker, sociologist of Andover, and James Henry Breasted, Egyptologist of Chicago.

But most of all he wished to honor his father through a biography. Richard at first seemed the proper person to write it. He was not now actively engaged on the *Observer;* phlegmatic as always (Finley informed him that his gloom was really the result of overeating), he was the stay-at-home of the family and had the time and taste for scholarship. Consenting, he spent five years in arranging his father's enormous correspondence preserved by the family. In attempting to borrow other letters he found that some persons, like Professor Park of Andover, feared the poisonous smoke of Dr. Morse's controversies would blow down the paths of time, and refused to lend the letters in their possession. His work completed, Richard presented it to his brothers only to find they were dissatisfied.

They finally agreed to select someone, whose expenses Finley would in large part pay, to put Richard's work into a shorter and more acceptable form. They selected William Buell Sprague, the editor of the many volumes of the *Annals of the American Pulpit,* a series of biographical studies of clergymen of all denominations, and hence well qualified to smother Dr. Morse's denominational controversies. When he had completed his drastic revision he came to Locust Grove to read his biography aloud to the three brothers. His words carried them back to the days when they had played about the Town Hill parsonage while editors, professors, pastors, and missionaries came in and out on errands of orthodoxy. When they heard Sprague's comment that Jedidiah's most remarkable quality was his versatility, Richard and Sidney may well have thought to themselves that fickle Finley had inherited most of his father's capacities. The two older brothers liked Sprague's work and made only minor suggestions, but Richard offered many corrections. Finley waited years for the biography, and never saw the printed volume. Eventually it appeared with one of Finley's portraits of his father as a frontispiece, a reminder of the astonishing force and intensity of the little pastor of Town Hill.

As befitted a son of Jedidiah, Finley contributed to Christian work at home and abroad. When some of the congregation with which he worshipped in Poughkeepsie began to talk of a new church, Finley offered $5,000 worth of telegraph stock, nearly one third of the sum needed. He contributed to Presbyterian, Baptist, and Methodist churches, and to the work of societies both denominational and undenominational, among them the American Tract Society, the American Temperance Union, the American and Foreign Christian Union, the American Bible Society, the City Mission Society in New York, the Union Theological Seminary in Virginia, and the American Chapel in Paris.

Morse the wealthy telegrapher found a peculiar joy in giving for the benefit of artists. Against stout opposition, but with the warm partisanship of his old associate Cummings,[12] he was reelected president of the National Academy for one year. He presented to the academy Charles Leslie's painting of their common mentor. "Allston was more than any other person my master in art," he wrote in making the gift. "Leslie was my life-long cherished friend and fellow-pupil, whom I loved as a brother. We all lived together for years in the closest intimacy and in the same house. Is there not, then, a fitness that the portrait of the master by one distinguished pupil should be presented by the surviving pupil to the Academy over which he presided in its infancy, as well as assisted in its birth?"[13] Soon afterward he gave Daniel Huntington, on behalf of the Artist Fund Society, stock worth $2,000 to aid poor artists. He reminded Huntington that as an artist, "although never for any length of time suffering from actual want," yet he had come so near to it that he could "readily sympathize with those whose lot it is to be at the bottom of the valley." He concluded by assuring Huntington that he still had "an Artist's heart, while deprived by long disuse of an Artist's skill."[14]

By the fall of 1866 the Morses, including the flying squirrel, were in Paris. On the avenue du Roi-de-Rome, conveniently near the Bois de Boulogne, the American Chapel, and the grounds where the great exposition was soon to open, Morse took a furnished apartment of eleven rooms. He took care that his lease stipulated that his rent of $280 a month should not rise during the time of the exhibition.

His household grew. Like many Southerners, Sarah's sister, Mrs. Goodrich of New Orleans, brought her family to France to escape the horrors of Reconstruction. Susan's son Charles came from Porto Rico to study painting. One of Sidney's sons, the "Turkeyfied"-

looking Livingston, and the Colgates, the New York soap-manufacturers who had married into Richard's family, came to visit the exposition. Samuel I. Prime of the *Observer,* Morse's future official biographer, a ponderous man known for his ponderous travelogues, dined with them now and then. The patriarch was happy. He believed in family anniversaries, in family worship, in family entertainments, charades, and garden parties. He had missed being with his own family for so much of his life, and he had such affectionate recollections of his parents' home, that he was delighted to preside over a household of eighteen. He thought that Sidney might wish to bring his family over too. "If in the changes of our Government at home," he wrote him, "from a *confederated* or rather *Federal* to a *consolidated* government, which is the next step of Radicalism towards military despotism . . . the condition of our home should be too unquiet for our advanced age, then you can join us here." [15] The United States under President Johnson was less congenial for Morse than France under the Emperor Napoleon III, the recent friend of the Confederacy.

Sometimes he wondered at himself, a republican, dressing in a blue coat embroidered with gold lace, a vest of cashmere with gilt buttons, pantaloons with a stripe of gold lace on the seam from hip to patent leather shoes, sword at his side, and decorations on his breast. Parisian ceremony seemed ridiculous to him, but if arbitrary government was necessary, he thought, then exclusiveness doubtless helped to bring the best people in touch with the government. Having properly reflected on the vanity of the world, he stepped cheerfully into society.

Sarah was more shy than her husband; she could hardly enter into conversation in English, much less in French or German. When first asked to a reception at the Tuileries, Sarah would not go; Morse and his brother-in-law Goodrich were presented to the Emperor Napoleon alone, and the Emperor spoke those words that had become so familiar: "Your name, sir, is well known here." [16]

The night that Paris gave its greeting to the sovereigns visiting the fair seemed to Morse a scene out of the *Arabian Nights.* The Hôtel de Ville was lighted by seventy thousand candles. Napoleon, the King of Prussia, and Czar Alexander moved about among ten thousand guests. When Napoleon passed in a formal procession through the throng, Morse and his wife, neither very tall, were standing on chairs to look over the heads in front of them. "The Emperor gave his usual bow on each side," Morse explained, "but, as he came near us, he gave an unusual and special bow to me, which I returned, and he then, with a smile, gave me a second bow so marked as to draw the attention of those around, who at once turned to see to whom this courtesy was shown. I should not mention this, but that Sarah and others observed it as an unusual mark of attention."[17] It seemed to him that he was seeing as much glory as had been in one spot since Solomon's time. "And after all of what account is it," he asked himself, "except to confirm the wisdom of Solomon in his utterance of 'All is vanity & vexation of spirit'? I make this reflection not in a cynical, or ascetic spirit, but in view of the better things laid up for those who love God, and whose crowns & treasures are not the perishing temporary baubles of earth."[17] The French Empire soon proved to be a bauble indeed.

Meanwhile Morse had been appointed a United States commissioner to the exposition with the particular duty of studying the telegraph exhibits. For days he regularly spent his afternoons in the exposition grounds. He would walk down the avenue du Roi-de-Rome into the place du Roi-de-Rome, and cross the Seine and the Quai d'Orsay, walk through the gardens and enter the colosseum-like exhibition palace by a huge arch, nearly as high as the palace itself.

Some of the exhibits must have thrown him abruptly into the past. The G. and C. Merriam Company of Springfield, Massachusetts, was displaying the latest edition of their dictionary with a frontispiece engraving of Morse's portrait of Webster; Dr. C. T. Jackson of Boston, specimens of his latest discoveries in stone. On the other hand, his brother Sidney's entries, a bathometer, an instrument to measure the depth of the ocean without a line, and a device for laying submarine cables, brought the future to Morse's mind. "Hare Morse," as Finley sometimes called himself, warned the Tortoise that he had better keep his inventions from the sight of John Bull to prevent his appropriating them. An Englishman meeting Morse by the telegraph booths remarked that it was a pity that he was exhibiting nothing. "Nothing," replied Morse, piqued, "why I can scarcely pass by the telegraph instruments whether in

Courtesy, Leila Livingston Morse

MORSE IN OLD AGE

the Exposition, or in all the Offices of the Continent, and in England too, that I do not hear the cry of *father* from almost every one of them."[18] When the exposition awarded prizes to Cyrus Field and David Hughes, some of his friends asked why he did not receive a prize also; he reminded them that he had already been decorated by many governments, and had been given a more glorious prize than any the exposition had to offer, the honorary gratuity conferred by the ten nations in concert.

All together the exhibition was glorious excitement. "It is the world in epitome," he explained. ". . . I believe my children will learn more of the condition of the arts, agriculture, customs, manufactures and mineral and vegetable products of the world in five weeks than they could by books at home in five years, and as many years' travel."[19]

The children liked Europe. After the death of her father, Leila refused an offer of marriage from Samuel J. Tilden, and to the distress of the family married, of all persons, an Englishman. While William and Arthur found satisfaction in America as sportsmen, "Sweet Eddie," as Morse called his ninth child, studied many years in Europe after his father's death. He became perhaps the most like his father of all the children; he followed his father's profession, painting; he edited his father's letters; and he was of admirably simple habits, the gentle host of delightful homes in Washington and the Berkshire Hills.

In the meantime Morse was worrying, with some justice, about the welfare of Lucretia's children, Fin, Charles, and Susan. Fin was safe enough with relatives at home. But Charles, spoiled when his uncle Charles Walker left him money, had lost the $37,000 more which Morse had given him several years before. Morse also made loans to Susan's husband, which he poured into his Porto Rico plantation to no avail. Fortunately Morse was spared knowledge of the sequel. When Susan's only child, Charles Lind, who went to Paris to study painting, died, Susan and her husband grew apart. Eventually a black mistress came into the household, and Susan and her husband sat at table with a screen between them. Finally the death of her husband shattered her faith in her future, and on her way back to America she was lost at sea, probably a suicide.

Morse presently realized that there were some things his children could learn better in America, even an America under Republican rule, than on the Continent. And Morse himself became weary. He suspected that his memory was failing. On the tours he made to the Isle of Wight, Germany, and Switzerland he found that he could not travel with the exhilaration he had once known. He noticed that only eight of his classmates at Yale were still living and wondered when it would be his turn to go. Against the advice of his brother Sidney and the Washington official in charge of printing the reports of the commissioners to the exposition,[20] he had determined to use his opportunity as commissioner to restate his claims to originality and to report on the extent to which his system of telegraphy was used in Europe. He had already begun to collect the necessary information and to write, staying up as late as midnight often enough to worry his Sarah. He was given to repeating his father's motto: "Better wear out than rust out," but he knew that he could proceed with his wearing out as effectively at home now as on the Continent. As he prepared to leave Europe he was sure that he would never see it again.

Soon after settling in the peace of his towered home on the Hudson death struck close to him. "And so the *triple cord is broken,*" he wrote Sidney, "and our dear brother Richard, the youngest, is the first of us to pass the dark valley. A happy Spirit now we have not a doubt, with his Savior and his friends that have preceded him."

Finley had less questioning about death now than when his Lucrece had died; it was less the fashion to wonder whether one's loved ones were among the elect; one simply assumed it.

"How the few weaknesses which may have given us uneasiness," he wrote on, "vanish in the light of his beautiful Christian character, which now shines out. These were more the product of physical infirmity than of the heart. He was an affectionate brother, a devoted son, and most devoted father, erring if at all, on the side of indulgence."

The brothers who had always been closest together remained. As he sought assurance for the difficult days to come, Finley recalled the expression they had learned together from their parents. He told Sidney: "I feel stirred to more diligent improvement."[21]

CHAPTER *xxviii*

Harvest

AROUND Delmonico's Fourteenth Street banquet room hung the coat of arms of the nations which had adopted the Morse telegraph. On the tables were statuettes of Jupiter tossing thunderbolts, Franklin with a kite, and Morse with a palette. The menu bore a likeness of Morse.

His memory plucked the strings of his years. The last time he had returned from Europe, Poughkeepsie had surprised him by closing its schools, ringing its bells, and escorting him from the station to Locust Grove. This time on his return from Europe, New York had chosen to entertain him. He was in the same restaurant in which he and his friends were first discovered by Bryant's *Evening Post* in a conspiracy. Many of his fellow conspirators were at the banquet table now, including James Brooks of the *Express,* recently a Congressman, and Samuel J. Tilden, now leader of New York Democracy. And Bryant himself was there. Looking around the room, Morse recognized some famous associates: Cyrus Field, Amos Kendall, Ezra Cornell, and his old painting pupil Huntington.

As they banqueted, Morse may have twitted the gentleman on one side, Her Majesty's Minister Edward Thornton, for Britain's refusal to grant him a patent, or have laughed with the gentleman on his other side, Chief Justice Chase, about his work as counsel in suits against the Morse patentees.

As the coffee was being served Field announced that he had received messages of congratulation from President Johnson, President-elect Grant, and Speaker Colfax. He read a message from

Governor Bullock of the state of Morse's birth: "Massachusetts honors her two sons – Franklin and Morse." The audience applauded. Then came a clumsy response by General Irvin McDowell to the toast to the army and navy of the United States. Whether the guest of the evening intended it or not, said the General, he with Fulton and Stephenson had contributed more to the engines of destruction than any other three men. To make his words seem more tactful the General tumbled into the same stupidity which had trapped Fulton: the more terrible the weapon, he said, the shorter the war.

Mr. Chase rose to introduce Morse. He chose words more carefully than most speakers on Morse then or since. He avoided calling Morse *the* inventor of *the* telegraph.

Many persons had made the discoveries which prepared the way for telegraphy, the Chief Justice said. But "it is the providential distinction and splendid honor of the eminent American who is our guest tonight that, happily prepared by previous acquirements and pursuits, he was quick to seize the opportunity and give to the world the first recording telegraph. Fortunate man! thus to link his name forever with the greatest wonder and the greatest benefit of the age!"

The banqueters cheered as Morse slowly rose to his feet – cheered again and again. He had always been dignified, and this evening he spoke more impressively than ever. He recalled his *Sully* voyage, his poverty, the early "stammering" of his "child," and the ridicule of Congress. Paying tribute to the scientists who had prepared the way for him, he mentioned Henry. But even now he declined to specify what Gale or Vail had contributed to his telegraph. Of Vail he merely said that with his father and brother he "furnished the means to give the child a decent dress." He praised Field. When he paid tribute to Kendall such a shout filled the hall that the peaked little man finally rose to acknowledge it.

"I trust it will not be considered irrelevant to this occasion," Morse went on, "if I allude to the movement just now making in Congress to attach the Telegraph to the Post Office Department. . . . It was first broached in my correspondence with the Treasury Department more than thirty years ago. . . . It was again proposed by Hon C. G. Ferris . . . and a remark from his [1842 Commerce Committee] Report is worthy of quotation: '. . . it is a matter of serious consideration whether the government should not . . . seize the present opportunity of securing to itself the regulation of a system which, if monopolized by a private company, might be used to the serious injury of the Post Office Department,' (and please note his remark which follows), '*which could not be prevented without such an interference with the rights of the inventor and of the stockholders as could not be sustained by justice or by public opinion.*' The far-seeing mind of Mr. Ferris comprehended the future of the telegraph."

He turned to the artists about the tables: "Brothers (for you are yet my brothers)," he said, "if I left your ranks, you well know it cost me many a pang. I did not leave you until I saw you well established and entering on that career of prosperity due to your own just appreciation of the important duties belonging to your profession. You have an Institution which now holds . . . a high position in the estimation of this appreciative community.

"If I have stepped aside from Art to tread what seems another path, there is good precedent for it in the lives of Artists. Science and Art are not opposed. *Leonardo da Vinci* could find congenial relaxation in scientific researches and invention, and our own *Fulton* was a painter, whose scientific studies resulted in steam navigation. It may not be generally known that the important invention of the *percussion cap* is due to the scientific recreations of the English painter *Shaw*. . . .

"If not a sparrow falls to the ground without a definite purpose in the plans of infinite wisdom, can the creation of an instrumentality, so vitally affecting the interests of the whole human race, have an origin less humble than the Father of every good and perfect gift? I am sure I have the sympathy of such an assembly as is here gathered, if in all humility and in the sincerity of a grateful heart, I use the words of inspiration in ascribing honor and praise to him to whom first of all and most of all it is pre-eminently due. 'Not unto us, not unto us, but to God be all the glory.' Not what hath man, but '*What hath God wrought!*'"

The banqueters cheered as the venerable gentleman found his chair.

Even then he could not rest. One after another speakers addressed him. William M. Evarts, Attorney General of the United States, reminded him that his painting of his father, Jeremiah Evarts, was the only likeness in existence. William E. Dodge accused him of disorganizing life so that a New York merchant's dinner might be interrupted at any time by reports of prices in London. The president of the Montreal Telegraph Company read a telegram of greeting from Ottawa, the capital of the new nation that the telegraph had helped to make possible by linking the Atlantic and Pacific. William Cullen Bryant thanked him for confirming his faith by presenting new evidence that matter could respond to intelligence. On the other hand, Bryant added that without an ordered press the telegraph would merely spread rumor. A. A. Low reminded him that the telegraph had helped to unite the South in rebellion, and Evarts declared that in an unmoral society the telegraph would do more harm than good. Evarts quarreled with President Orton of the Western Union Company as they vied in paying tribute to the inventor: the one insisted that the government keep its ugly claws off the telegraph, while the other urged government supervision of irresponsible private companies.

The last speech was a relief. It was the greeting of Daniel Huntington, now president of the National Academy, to his master.

"Morse, the painter, invented the electric telegraph," he said; "Fulton, the painter, discovered steam navigation; Daguerre, an artist, gave us the photographic process. . . . The studio of my beloved master, in whose honor we have met tonight, was indeed a laboratory. . . . I can never forget the occasion when he called his pupils together to witness one of the first, if not the first, successful experiment with the new electric telegraph. It was in the winter of 1835–6. I can see now that rude instrument, constructed with an old stretching frame, a wooden clock, a home-made battery, and the wire stretched many times around the walls of the studio. With eager interest we gathered about it, as our master explained its operation, while with a click, click, the pencil, by a succession of dots and lines, recorded the message in cypher. The idea was born. The words circled that upper chamber as they do now the globe."

The banqueters interrupted with applause.

"Yet the love of art still lives in some inner corner of his heart, and I know he can never enter the studio of a painter and see the artist silently bringing from the canvas forms of life and beauty, but he feels a tender twinge as one who catches a glimpse of the beautiful girl he loved in his youth whom another has snatched away."[1]

Despite the sparkle of the banquet, night was deepening about Morse. He knew it. He had lived his time – more than his time. He was of another generation, and could no longer be wholly understood. "His patriarchal beard – like Merlin's – is his chief sign of age," wrote a journalist. "Everything else about him – his twinkling eye, his sly humor, his vivacious talk, his steady hand, his elastic step – all indicate a man who might readily pass for ten or a dozen years younger. And yet, on the other hand, it must be honestly confessed that his manners, his spectacles, his red-silk handkerchief, and his dreadfully bad politics are the peculiar signs of a gentleman of the old rather than of the new school."[2]

He could hardly be understood or understand. The industrialism that the telegraph had helped to create was twisting society into distorted shapes. Unkempt cities were beginning to sprawl, dust farmers to be ground by Eastern money, factory hands to be bent by the whips of a new industrial aristocracy that lacked honesty, compassion, or taste. Rotten government in cities and even in Washington spread a stench across the land. If the war had not taught Morse that America had left behind the ideals of the merchants of the New York and Boston he had known, surely Gould's and Fisk's cornering of the gold market on "Black Friday," and the Tweed Ring's open looting of New York, must have told him so. He could hardly understand the new America except through the age that had gone, and the new America could hardly understand him except as a legend.

He knew the end was coming. Many of his early literary friends, like Halleck, Percival, Hillhouse, and Cooper, had died long before. Early artist friends had gone too, Allston, Dunlap, and Greenough among them. So had some of the great men of the Old World whom he had known – Lafayette, Humboldt, and Arago. Even his friend Leslie had gone, and Vail, and more recently his own younger brother Richard. Only since the last winter's snow, five of his eight remaining classmates at Yale had died. Then the transparently good Kendall was gone too. "I feel the loss of a *father*," Morse wrote on hearing the news, ". . . for he was one in whom I confided as a father, so sure was I of affectionate and sound advice." [3] Kendall's passing left him much alone.

He lived increasingly in his memories. After a lapse of nearly fifty years he corresponded with his Finley relatives in Carolina and remembered his gala days in the South. The death of a cousin reminded him of his painting excursions to Utica and Sconandoa when he teased his cousins and wrote poetry. Following the progress of his son Willie as a student at Phillips Andover, he remembered wistfully that he had entered the academy himself over seventy years before. After not having painted a picture for some thirty years,[4] he went one day to an exhibition at the National Academy and found one of his own portraits on show, painted forty-two years before. "The Artists are charmed with it," he said; "they say it proves that they have made no advances in portrait since that was painted. Looking at it with a fresh eye I am pleased with it myself." [5] Someone asked him for a picture of the *Sully* and he answered that he knew of none but imaginary ones in existence. Someone in Charlestown discovered an old painting with his name on it and asked him to explain. It was his *Landing of the Pilgrims,* he replied, painted at the age of eighteen, and approved by Stuart and Allston. Charlestown, the town that had once rejected his parents, hung it near where he was born below Breed's Hill and has kept it there ever since.

Those who honored him knew that he was soon to go and wished to give him yet one more token of their esteem. At first they questioned whether it was fitting to erect a statue to a living man, but they persuaded themselves that at the age of eighty he was so far removed from this earth as to be no longer subject to ordinary rules of propriety. Telegraphers organized a committee to collect contributions.

On the morning of June 10, 1871, two thousand of Morse's telegraph "children" boarded an excursion steamer in the North River and sailed around Governor's Island, where their "father" had once experimented with submarine telegraphy. Whistles blew on vessels in the harbor, a band played on board, and the telegraphers cheered for S. F. B. Morse.

In the afternoon, long before four o'clock, the telegraphers were strolling through the shady walks of Central Park toward the knoll where the Morse statue was waiting to be unveiled. About the statue they found two canopied grand-stands reserved for official guests, and rows of garden settees for the public. But the day was sunny, some of the ladies did not have their parasols, and many of the company chose to sit on the grass under the trees. Most of them were operators for the Western Union Company, come from all over the country to see the monument to which they had contributed their dollars and messenger boys their quarters. Some were from the few remaining independent lines. "Here is the opposition Telegraph purse," a Hartford independent operator had written. "It includes everyone in the office. Will make amount $100 if needed. It is given in honor of Prof. Morse, the 'Father of the Telegraph.' Hope we are welcome." The chairman of the fund, the telegraph historian Reid, had replied: "When we come to honor the 'Father,' there is but one family." [6] Canadian telegraphers were present too; they had done more than their share in contributing to the statue.

As the operators waited for the moment when the red, white, and blue would be taken from the statue, they watched the distinguished guests take their places in the grand-stand. They saw William Cullen Bryant, who, with Andrew Carnegie, once a telegraph boy, had contributed generously toward the construction of the monument. They saw Governor Hoffman of New York, Governor Claflin of Massachusetts, President Orton of the Western Union Company, Cyrus Field and several of his associates, and the sculptor of the monument, Byron Pickett. They looked for Morse. They had hoped he would come on the morning excursion. Now some thought they saw him, but perhaps they confused him with other bearded men; some were certain it would be unseemly for him to come. Those who knew Morse's family noticed that Theodore Roosevelt, Sr., drove up in a four-in-hand with pretty Leila Morse.

Governor Claflin and President Orton moved toward the statue. They pulled aside the flag, revealing the heroic figure of Morse in bronze, beside a telegraph instrument, one hand resting on it, the other holding a ribbon of paper marked in dots and dashes with "What hath God wrought!" * As the telegraphers applauded, the beloved poet Bryant stood before them to give expression to their emotion.

"We come together on the occasion of raising a statue," he said, "not to buried but to living merit. . . . Yet we cannot congratulate ourselves on having set an example of alacrity in this manifestation of the public gratitude. If our illustrious friend, to whom we now gladly pay these honors, had not lived beyond the common age of man we should have sorrowfully laid them on his grave."

Nearly fifty years before, Bryant recalled, even as a painter Morse's tendency to mechanical invention was conspicuous. "His mind, as I remember, was strongly impelled to analyze the processes of his art – to give them a certain scientific precision, to reduce them to fixed rules, to refer effects to clearly defined causes, so as to put it in the power of the artist to produce them at pleasure and with certainty, instead of blindly groping for them, and, in the end, owing them to some happy accident, or some instinctive effort, of which he could give no account. The mind of Morse was an organizing mind. He showed this in a remarkable manner, when he brought together the artists of New York, then a comparatively little band of mostly young men, whose profession was far from being honored as it now is, reconciled the disagreements which he found existing among them, and founded an association, to be managed solely by themselves – the Academy of the Arts of Design. . . .

"Long may we keep with us what is better than the statue – the noble original," he said in his peroration, and the telegraphers were delighted. The band played *Hail to the Chief* and Mayor Hall on behalf of the city promised to guard the bronze figure of Morse for the generations to come. The ceremony concluded as the gathering ascribed the accomplishment of Morse, just as he wished that it should always be, to God. They sang together: *Praise God from Whom All Blessings Flow.* The telegraphers milled about the statue and dispersed for supper. The *Times* summarized the ceremony as one of the most brilliant of its kind.[7]

* The statue still stands in Central Park near East Seventieth Street.

That night the telegraphers quickly filled Music Hall on Fourteenth Street, for they wished to see Morse do what they did every day, operate a telegraph key. On the stage were Morse, and among others Cyrus Field, Horace Greeley, and Henry Ward Beecher. Someone gave Morse a list more than nineteen feet long of the names of those who had contributed for the statue. At nine o'clock speechmaking was cut short, for, as President Orton announced, the time had come for Morse to send his farewell message. Morse was much moved to find on the stage one of the identical instruments used in transmitting his first message and to see that Annie Ellsworth herself was in the company. The telegraph wires were open to every city in the United States and Canada, Mr. Orton explained; a woman operator was to send Morse's message, and then Morse himself would add his signature.

A young lady swept to the table, fan in hand, and sat down to the key. A profound silence reigned throughout the hall. She moved her fingers, and the audience followed in the click, click of the Morse code the words Morse had chosen: "Greetings and thanks to the telegraph fraternity throughout the world. Glory to God in the highest, on earth peace, goodwill to men."

The young lady rose and stood by the table while Morse took her place. Bent over the instrument, he touched his finger to the key. A cheer burst through the hall. In a moment it died away, for the professor was moving his hand. Then the audience heard Morse's click, click, in his own code. He struck out the letters: "S. F. B. Morse." As he finished, by common impulse the gathering rose and shouted.

Morse returned to his chair, "visibly affected." He pressed his hand to his brow.

Mr. Orton said: "Thus the Father of the telegraph bids farewell to his children." [8]

As the telegraphers went out into the night they saw a rare sight for New York, the playing colors of the aurora borealis. It was as if the heavens themselves knew it was time for Morse's farewell.

The constant praise that he heard about him made him more tired than ever. "Bless the Lord, O my soul, and forget not all his benefits," he said over and over again to himself. "It is doubtless this continued referring all to Him," he wrote Susan, "that prevents this universal demonstration of kindly feeling from puffing me up with the false notion that I am anything but the feeblest of instruments. I cannot give you any idea of the peculiar feelings which gratify and yet oppress me."[9]

That summer he went to Locust Grove for the last summer of his life. Most of the time he was in his half-octagonal library, under the vine-covered porch. There he was surrounded by the many books and pamphlets that he had written himself, some thirty in all, on painting, poetry, politics, and telegraphy; there he had near him his portraits of the family and his early telegraph instruments. At his great oak desk he answered an inquiry about his painting in Portsmouth during his itinerant days; for someone who owned one of his paintings he explained how he had come to paint in upstate New York; for someone who had known him in Washington he recalled how the news of the death of Lucretia had come to him while he was painting Lafayette. As if to prove that he was still himself he bought a microscope and used it for the first time.

Soon after his return to New York in the fall his brother Sidney died. His two younger brothers had both gone now, and he was just waiting.

"I love to be studying the Guide-Book of the country to which I am going," he said to his friends.[10]

He continued to conduct family prayers with vigor, attend his business promptly, and answer Smith's chronic aspersions in pungent form. He continued to be concerned about public affairs. He served as chairman of a committee appointed at Cooper Institute for the purpose of persuading the American government to use the Chinese indemnity fund for the establishment of an American college in China. He gave $100 for the construction of a statue to Galvani in Italy. He spoke briefly at the unveiling of a statue of Franklin near the New York City Hall when he really was not well enough to do so. When he heard that Cyrus Field was about to leave for Rome to participate in a telegraph convention he wrote him earnestly what he wished the convention would do. The telegraph is an advocate of peace, he told Field. "Not that of itself it can command a 'Peace, be still!' to the angry waves of human passions, but that, by its rapid interchange of thought and opinion, it gives the opportunity of explanations to acts and to laws which, in their ordinary wording, often create doubt and suspicion." If the convention were to neutralize the telegraph during war-time, he thought, an instrument for peace negotiations would be available.[11]

During the last few weeks of his life there were jumbled together in his mind his childhood, painting days, family needs, early telegraph friends, and recent telegraph honors. In February 1872 Mrs. Vail came in from Morristown to call. At the request of Robert Donaldson he recalled the circumstances in which he had copied a Raphael for him in Rome forty years before. His loss of a large sum of money through a swindle into which Charles had drawn him reminded him that his brothers were right in believing he would never be a business man. Reading the article on telegraphy in a new survey of the industries of the United States, he concluded that it had been written under the influence of Smith and O'Reilly [12] and that it constituted the most outrageous attack upon him he had yet known.

Just as he was preparing to answer the article, neuralgic pains forced him to stop reading and writing. On March 14 his doctor permitted him to write the last letter which remains in his correspondence. It was an inquiry as to what position Joseph Henry was taking on Smith's latest "atrocious & absurd" attack.[13]

The pain slackened, but he grew weaker and kept his bed. He became periodically unconscious. His New York pastor called on him where he lay in his Twenty-second Street house, and the old man looked up from his bed to say: "The best is yet to come."

Pneumonia set in. A doctor tapped him on the chest, saying: "This is the way we doctors telegraph," and he found strength to whisper: "Very good." [14] These were his last words.

As he lay on his bed in fever, it seemed to his friends that he was handsome. They said the light of heaven was shining in his eyes.

On the 1st of April for a moment he recognized his Sarah. He could only smile. On the 2nd of April, 1872, he was quietly gone.

Around the world the telegraph flashed the news that its father was dead.

ACKNOWLEDGMENTS

AFTER those named in the Preface, those who have contributed most to this work are Samuel I. Prime and Edward L. Morse, the one the author of the official biography of Morse and the other the editor of his letters. Neither knew Morse during the years in which he was discovering himself. Prime first met him in 1840 and only some years later as editor of the *Observer* became intimately connected with the family; Edward L. Morse as the youngest son of Morse hardly knew him at all. Their studies lack the benefit of a variety of sources and are too uncritical, but on the other hand are affable in tone and generally accurate. They are indispensable to the student of Morse.

One of the pleasures of the preparation of this biography has been the discovery that goodwill is the daily armor of many of the librarians of the eastern seaboard. Since it is not possible to mention each one of them who has assisted this enterprise, I wish here and now to thank them all.

For commenting on certain chapters in manuscript I am indebted among others to Mrs. Henry Amsden, Concord, New Hampshire, who is preparing a new history of Concord (Ch. v); Anna Wells Rutledge, assistant, Carolina Art Association, Charleston, South Carolina (Ch. vi); Mabel A. Brown, Remsen, New York, a student of Morse's career especially in upstate New York (Ch. x); Professor Ray A. Billington, Smith College, an authority on American nativism (Ch. xv); Professor Robert Taft, University of Kansas, an authority on the history of American photography (Ch. xix); George Oslin, Western Union Telegraph Company, New York, Donald D. Millikin, Radio Corporation of America, New York, and Professor Robert L. Thompson, Hofstra College of New York University (chapters on early telegraph history), to the last of whom I am especially grateful for donations from his collection of materials for his forthcoming history of the American telegraph industry. For comments on the whole work in manuscript I am indebted to Professor Nevins, as I have already explained, and to my mother, Miriam Bentley Mabee.

To Mrs. Russell Colgate, West Orange, New Jersey, I wish to express my thanks for her and her late husband's courtesy in opening their home to me while I read letters in their possession; to Miss Leila Livingston Morse, among many other courtesies for which I am indebted to her, for her trust in lending me many of the letters in her hands; to C. G. Davis, of the Ship Studio, Cazenovia, New York, for information on the *Sully;* to Ernest C. Kyte, librarian, Queens University, Kingston, Ontario, for his kindness in guiding me through the McNicoll telegraph papers.

Others who have contributed to this undertaking in some way include Franklin B. Dwight, Ossining, New York; Mary Lydon, Petersham, Massachusetts; Webster D. Hasbrouck, Poughkeepsie, New York; Marguerite Cockett, Cooperstown, New York; H. C. Durston, Manlius, New York; Ruth B. Mabee, Jackson, Michigan; Mary Elliot, Hindman, Kentucky; Pauline Joy MacLean, New York; Howard Herwitz, New York; Florence Lerrigo, Claremont, California; Eunice Turner, Boston; Elizabeth Ring, research editor, Maine Historical Records Survey, Portland; Josephine Mayer, Teachers College, Columbia University; Professor William R. Whitehorne, Bates College; Laura Turnbull, reference librarian, Princeton University; Lawrence Floyd, assistant librarian, General Theological Seminary.

Still others whom I wish to thank are named here and there in the references where the information they gave is cited; to the many who have assisted in gathering information on Morse paintings I hope to give some acknowledgment when the painting list is issued.

Acknowledgments are due to several persons and companies for permission to quote from works to which they hold title: Clara Morse Watson and John P. Morse, *Samuel F. B. Morse: His Letters and Journals* (1914); Goodspeed's Book Shop, William Dunlap: *A History of the Rise and Progress of the Arts of Design in the United States* (1918); Essex Institute, William Bentley: *Diary,* III (1911); Yale University Press, *Correspondence of James Fenimore-Cooper* (1922); New York University Press, Theodore F. Jones: *New York*

University, 1832:1932 (1933); Macmillan Company, Robert Taft: *Photography and the American Scene* (1938); Dodd, Mead & Company, *The Diary of Philip Hone* (1927); New York Historical Socity, William Dunlap: *Diary* (1930); Columbia University Press, James K. Morse: *Jedidiah Morse* (1939); William A. Church Company, Albert W. Smith: *Ezra Cornell* (1934).

Finally, I wish to thank my family and friends for their forbearance in listening to my chatter about Morse and for their generous encouragement.

REFERENCES

In the use of quotations idiosyncrasies of spelling, punctuation, and grammar have been retained for the sake of their flavor, except where they interfere with clarity.

When no reference is cited for a letter quoted in the text, and the name of its addresser and addressee, and its date are there given, it may be understood that the original is in the Library of Congress.

The sources listed at the head of some chapter references are not general bibliographies on certain subjects but specific bibliographies on the relation of those subjects to Morse. When the sources listed in such a bibliography are cited in the references which immediately follow, they are cited by author or short title only.

References to the date, size, or present location of paintings have been omitted as they are expected to appear in the list of paintings to be separately issued.

For the sake of simplicity, symbols have been adopted for use in the references to represent members of the family, location or ownership of sources, and books which are frequently named:

MEMBERS OF THE FAMILY

SFBM	Samuel Finley Breese Morse	the hero
JM	Jedidiah Morse	his parents
Mrs. JM	Mrs. Jedidiah Morse	
SEM	Sidney Edwards Morse	his brothers
RCM	Richard Cary Morse	
LPW	Lucretia Pickering Walker	his wives
Mrs. SFBM	Sarah Ann Griswold	

LOCATION OR OWNERSHIP OF SOURCES

BPL	Boston Public Library
COLG	Mrs. Russell Colgate (A collection of Morse family papers, including especially the papers of RCM, to whom the Colgates are related.)

References

LC	Library of Congress (The largest collection of SFBM's papers, deposited for the most part by the family, is in this library.)
LLM	Leila Livingston Morse
MHS	Maine Historical Society (The person who came into the possession of the house of F. O. J. Smith after his death found Smith's papers and deposited them with this society.)
NYHS	New York Historical Society
NYPL	New York Public Library (A small collection of JM's papers is in this library.)
PENN	Pennsylvania Historical Society
SM	Smithsonian Institution (The Alfred Vail papers were given by the family to the American Historical Association, which deposited them with this institution.)
YC	Yale University library (A large collection of Morse family papers has been recently obtained by this library.)
YC – Rare Bk	Yale University library, Rare Book Room

BOOKS

Alfred Vail: *Telegraph* Alfred Vail: *The American Electro Magnetic Telegraph* (Philadelphia, 1845)

Dunlap, I, II, III William Dunlap: *A History of the Rise and Progress of the Arts of Design in the United States* (rev.) (Boston, 1918)

J. C. Vail J. C. Vail: *Early History of the Electro-Magnetic Telegraph* (New York, 1914)

J. K. Morse: *JM* James K. Morse: *Jedidiah Morse: A Champion of New England Orthodoxy* (New York, 1939)

Letters, I, II Edward L. Morse, ed.: *Samuel F. B. Morse: His Letters and Journals* (Boston, 1914)

Prime Samuel I. Prime: *The Life of Samuel F. B. Morse* (New York, 1875)

Reid James D. Reid: *The Telegraph in America, and In Memoriam Samuel F. B. Morse, and William Orton* (New York, 1879)

Sprague: *Life of JM* William B. Sprague: *The Life of Jedidiah Morse* (New York, 1874)

CHAPTER I

Below Breed's Hill

On Charlestown: William I. Budington: *The History of the First Church, Charlestown* (Boston, 1845); Richard Frothingham, Jr.: *The History of*

Charlestown (Boston and Charlestown, 1845–9); James F. Hunnewell: *A Century of Town Life* (Boston, 1888); Timothy T. Sawyer: *Old Charlestown* (Boston, 1902); Justin Winsor: *The Memorial History of Boston,* III (Boston, 1881).

[1] Ebenezer Hazard to JM, Jan. 28, 1792, NYPL.

[2] Mass. Hist. Soc. *Coll.,* Ser. 5, III, 30–1 (1877).

[3] Jeremy Belknap: *A Sermon Preached at the Installation of the Rev. Jedidiah Morse . . . on the 30th of April 1789* (Boston, 1789), p. 21.

[4] JM: *The American Gazetteer* (Charlestown and Boston, 1804), n. pa.

[5] Mass. Hist. Soc. *Coll.,* Ser. 5, III, 98 (1877). A varying version of this letter is in Sprague: *Life of JM,* p. 15.

[6] Mass. Hist. Soc. *Coll.,* Ser. 5, III, 101 (1877).

[7] Ibid., p. 127.

[8] JM to Mrs. JM, March 11, 1800, NYPL.

[9] Mrs. JM to JM, March 19 and 20, 1800, NYPL.

CHAPTER II

Hare and Tortoise

On Phillips Academy, Andover: *An Andover Primer* (Andover, 1928); Claude M. Fuess: *Men of Andover* (New Haven, 1928), chapter on SFBM, and *An Old New England School* (Boston and New York, 1917); William E. Park: *The Earlier Annals of Phillips Academy* (Andover, 1878).

On Yale College: Franklin B. Dexter: *Sketch of the History of Yale University* (New York, 1887), and "Student Life at Yale College under the First President Dwight," in Am. Antiq. Soc. *Proc.,* N.S., XXVII, 318–35 (1917).

[1] Prime, pp. 13–14, 628.

[2] *Letters,* I, 5.

[3] SFBM was already in Andover in Feb. 1799, according to the Rev. Mr. French to JM, Feb. 13, 1799, YC.

[4] William Foster, Jr.'s school. Oliver Brown to JM, June 15, 1799, YC; JM to SFBM, Sept. 30, 1799, YC.

[5] JM: *An Address to the Students at Phillips Academy, in Andover, Delivered July 9, 1799* (Charlestown, 1799), pref.

[6] Ibid., p. 11.

[7] Park, op. cit., p. 37.

[8] JM to SFBM, Aug. 23, 1799, library of Phillips Academy, Andover.

[9] Mrs. JM to SFBM, Dec. 25, 1799, YC.

[10] JM to SFBM, Feb. 4, March 7, 1801, YC.

[11] SFBM to JM, Aug. 2, 1799, National Museum, Washington.

[12] JM to Samuel Breese, March 15–16, 1800, NYPL.

[13] JM to Deacon Jedidiah Morse, Oct. 25, 1802, YC.

[14] Mrs. JM to SFBM, July 30, 1805, LC.

[15] SFBM to SEM and RCM, March 15, 1805, LC.

[16] J. K. Morse: *JM*, p. 87.

[17] William Bentley: *Diary*, III (Salem, 1911), 149.

[18] Leonard Woods: *History of the Andover Theological Seminary* (Boston, 1885), p. 597.

[19] Entry of Oct. 2 in "Journal of S. F. B. Morse for 1805," LC.

[20] Henry Davis to JM, Jan. 31, 1806, copy, YC.

[21] SFBM to JM and Mrs. JM, June 18, 1807, LC.

[22] JM to SFBM, June 27, 1807, YC.

[23] Mrs. JM to SFBM and SEM, March 29, 1808, YC.

[24] Prime, p. 19.

[25] SFBM to JM and Mrs. JM, Feb. 1809, LC.

[26] Smith v. Downing, New York, 1850, 68.

[27] The story appeared in Abner Morse: *Memorial of the Morses* (Boston, 1850), appendix to p. 125. The author acknowledged SFBM's denial of it in his letter to SFBM, Nov. 9, 1864, YC. The story reappeared as recently as in Mary Crawford: *The Romance of Old New England Rooftrees* (Boston, 1922), p. 269.

[28] Prime, p. 23.

[29] Mrs. JM to SFBM and SEM, July 26, 1808, YC.

[30] SFBM to JM and Mrs. JM, July 22, 1810, LC.

[31] JM to SFBM, July 26, 1810, LC.

[32] SFBM to Mrs. JM, Sept. 8, 1810, LC.

[33] Edward E. and E. M. Salisbury: *Family-Histories*, I, Pt. 1 ([New Haven], 1892), 91.

[34] *Phillips Bulletin*, XVIII, 6 (1924); cf. *An Andover Primer*, op. cit., n. pa.; Dexter: "Student Life," op. cit., p. 335.

CHAPTER III

Rebellious Son

On Allston's circle in London: Jared B. Flagg: *The Life and Letters of Washington Allston* (New York, 1892), a wholly satisfactory book; Leigh Hunt: *Autobiography*, I (New York, 1850); Charles R. Leslie: *Autobiographical Recollections* (Boston, 1860).

[1] SFBM to SEM and RCM, Dec. 8, 1810, LC.

[2] *Letters*, I, 32.

[3] SFBM to RCM and SEM, Jan. 15, 1811, LC.

[4] SFBM to unknown, Sept. 17, 1811, LC.

[5] *Letters*, I, 45–6.

[6] Prime, p. 31.

[7] Hunt, op. cit., p. 100.

[8] *Letters,* I, 46 and 55, seem to suggest that it was his gladiator thus commented upon; Prime, p. 40, however, seems to suggest it was his drawing of the Farnese Hercules.

[9] *Letters,* I, 56.

[10] Ibid., p. 49.

[11] Leslie, op. cit., p. 20.

[12] *Letters,* I, 74.

[13] Ibid., p. 75.

[14] James Wynne in *Harper's Magazine,* XXIV, 231 (1862).

[15] *Letters,* I, 77–8.

[16] Ibid., p. 118.

[17] Ibid., p. 49.

[18] SFBM to JM and Mrs. JM, Jan. 30, 1812, LC.

[19] SFBM to JM and Mrs. JM, April 21, 1812, LC.

[20] SFBM to Dr. Ezekiel Cushing, Sept. 24, 1812, YC – Rare Bk.

[21] *Letters,* I, 182.

[22] Ibid., p. 89.

[23] SFBM to JM and Mrs. JM, Nov. 1, 1812, LC.

[24] William Wilberforce to JM, March 17, 1814 [copy?], NYPL.

[25] William Wilberforce to JM, Aug. 19, 1814, NYPL.

[26] *Letters,* I, 140.

[27] SFBM to Dr. Ezekiel Cushing, n.d., 1812, YC – Rare Bk.

[28] SFBM to JM and Mrs. JM, Aug. 6, 1812, LC.

[29] Henry Bromfield to JM, June 16, 1815, YC.

[30] Mrs. JM to SFBM, Nov. 25, 1813, LC.

[31] JM to Deacon Jedidiah Morse, Oct. 19, 1814, YC. For SEM's views of the war see his articles in the Boston *Columbian Centinel,* Aug. 11, 1813 (signed "New-England"), and Nov. 24, 1813 (signed "A New-Englander").

CHAPTER IV

Painter to the Enemy

[1] Dunlap, III, 89–90.

[2] Ibid., p. 90.

[3] The medal is described in Timothy Alden: *A Collection of American Epitaphs,* II (New York, 1814), 224–5.

[4] *Letters,* I, 104.

[5] May 14, 1813. Dunlap, III, 91.

[6] May 4, 1813. Prime, p. 64.

[7] JM to Timothy Dwight, July 19, 1813, YC.

[8] *Letters,* I, 103, 105.

[9] Samuel Isham: *The History of American Painting* (New York, 1915),

p. 120. None of SFBM's eight brothers and sisters who died in infancy lived over eighteen months. Isham's error may have originated in the legend that Morse's great-uncle Jonathan Morse had read the Bible through twice before he died at the age of three years and four months. Prime, p. 2.

10 Dunlap, II, 332. Similarly, William Dunlap: *Diary* (New York, 1930), p. 742.

11 *Letters*, I, 180.

12 Sprague: *Life of JM*, p. 120, and J. K. Morse: *JM*, p. 144. Neither presents evidence. Sprague asserts that JM's son in England, who could only be SFBM, first called JM's attention to this book in the spring of 1815. But Sprague's date can be positively disproved. On Feb. 6, 1815 JM wrote RCM: "I have been to Cambridge to-day with Mr. Evarts – & called at the Library for Belsham's life of Lindsey – but it was not in." COLG. And still earlier, on Dec. 27, 1814, Dr. Nicholas Romayn, who had just returned from England, where he had seen SFBM, wrote JM from New York as if in answer to a request for the book: "I have not Belsham's life of Lindsey." LC. JM used the book as a bombshell in his pamphlet *American Unitarianism . . . extracted from . . . "Memoirs of the Life of the Rev. Theophilus Lindsey,"* (Boston, 1815), reviewed in the *Panoplist*, June 1815, pp. 241–72. That JM sent a copy of the pamphlet to SFBM without any comment would indicate that SFBM might not have been in any way connected with discovering the book. April 15, 1815, LC. On why JM opened the controversy, see Jacob C. Meyer: *Church and State in Massachusetts* (Cleveland, 1930), p. 169.

13 *Letters*, I, 137.

14 JM's notes for the service, Feb. 14, 1815, YC.

15 *Letters*, I, 184–5.

16 Ibid., p. 131.

17 Ibid., p. 132.

18 Ibid., p. 177.

19 Washington Allston to JM, Aug. 4, 1815, PENN.

20 Dunlap, III, 93.

21 *Letters*, I, 194–5.

CHAPTER V

Itinerant

On Concord: Morse supplied information about himself in 1854 for Nathaniel Bouton's *The History of Concord* (Concord, 1856). Mrs. Henry Amsden, who is preparing a needed new history of Concord, has generously given advice on this chapter.

1 Boston *Recorder*, Feb. 7, 1816, and occasionally until March 6. The 1816 *Boston Directory* lists SFBM as a "portrait painter," 3 Cornhill Square.

2 JM to James Lloyd, March 20, 1816, draft, YC.

[3] SFBM to JM and Mrs. JM, Sept. 7, 1816, YC.

[4] SFBM to JM and Mrs. JM, Aug. 20, 1816, LC.

[5] *Letters,* I, 180.

[6] Ibid., p. 206.

[7] SFBM to JM and Mrs. JM, Oct. 14, 1816, LC.

[8] Sprague: *Life of JM,* pp. 269–72; SEM: *Memorabilia in the Life of Jedidiah Morse* (Boston, 1867), pp. 5–7; *Semi-Centennial Celebrations of the First Sabbath School Society in Massachusetts* (Boston, 1867); "Semi-Centennial Celebration of the First Parish Sabbath School, Charlestown . . . 14 October, 1866" [broadside, BPL]. It was not the first Sunday-school in the state. Boston had such a school in the 1790's.

[9] Dec. 8, 1816; RCM and SEM joined Feb. 9, 1817, according to church records. James F. Hunnewell: *A Century of Town Life* (Boston, 1888), pp. 203–4.

[10] JM to RCM, Jan. 2, 1817, COLG.

[11] SFBM to LPW, Feb. 27, 1817, LLM.

[12] SFBM to LPW, July 3, 1817, LC.

[13] RCM to JM and Mrs. JM, July 11, 1817, COLG.

[14] Prime, p. 90, appears to suggest that the idea of the pump was conceived in 1816. *Letters,* I, 211, associates it with a letter of December 1816. SEM "has got a new machine in his head but has not made known to us what kind it is," wrote LPW to SFBM, Feb. 20, 1817, LC. "Your b.r wants your assistance now in making some imp.t philosophical experiments with him," wrote JM to SFBM, March 4, 1817, LC. SFBM may first have worked on the pump in late March 1817, for on April 8 Mrs. JM wrote RCM that his brothers had been engaged in engrossing "phylosophical experiments" for only two weeks, COLG. These three letters appear to be the first in existing correspondence which may be interpreted as referring to the pump.

They may also refer, however, to experiments in propelling steamboats by forcing water from the vessel. On the inside of the back cover of RCM's account book, NYHS, appears the following:

> Disclosed the project of propelling a vessel by action on a column of water to Cap.t Hull this day April 2.d 1817
>
> Sam.l F. B. Morse
>
> Charlestown April 2.d 1817
>
> Sidney E. Morse
>
> The above was written on the 2.d day of April
>
> Jed.h Morse
> Eliza. A. Morse
> Ann Shepard

Captain Isaac Hull, the husband of a sister of Jeannette Hart, was at this time commander of the Charlestown Navy Yard.

The date of the letter quoted on this subject in Prime, pp. 114–15, is patently wrong; the article therein referred to as describing a steamboat on a similar principle is in the Washington *National Intelligencer,* Jan. 28, 1819.

[15] Prime, p. 103.

[16] JM to J. S. V. Wilder, Aug. 5, 1817, YC; JM to Henry Bromfield, Dec. 15, 1817, YC; George M. Woolsey to JM, Sept. 13, 1817, NYPL. Bromfield entered a caveat for a patent in England, but on the advice of John Millington, then a professor at the Royal Institution, that the leather sphere would not long withstand the force of air and water that would have to be contained within it, declined to proceed with an application. Bromfield to JM, March 23, 1818, NYHS.

[17] SFBM said the patent was secured in his letter to Samuel Williams, Dec. 15, 1817, LC; JM said the same to DeWitt Clinton, Dec. 27, 1817, library of Columbia University. The United States Patent Office, however, now reports that it has no record of such a patent.

[18] SFBM to LPW, Nov. 27, 1817, "Miscellany" box, LC.

[19] SFBM to LPW, Sept. 13, 1817, LC.

[20] Prime, p. 106.

[21] Ibid., pp. 107–8.

CHAPTER VI

Winters at the South

On Charleston: Local histories hardly mention Morse. Aside from the correspondence the most useful source has been the Charleston *Courier.*

[1] Dunlap, III, 94.

[2] LPW to SFBM, March 20, 1818, LLM.

[3] 58 King St., Charleston *Courier,* Feb. 3, 1818.

[4] Prime, p. 112.

[5] SFBM to LPW, July 15, 1818, LLM.

[6] Prime, p. 104, quoting Concord *Patriot,* April 14, 1818. In March the town had voted one hundred dollars toward the purchase of a fire-engine. *Concord Town Records, 1732–1820* (Concord, 1894), p. 494.

[7] LPW to SFBM, July 10, 1818, LLM.

[8] Entry just after one dated Nov. 5, 1818, RCM's account book, NYHS.

[9] SFBM to LPW, Sept. 2, 1818, LLM.

[10] LPW to SFBM, Sept. 7, 1818, LLM.

[11] SFBM to LPW, Sept. 16, 1818, LLM.

[12] LPW to SFBM, Sept. 21, 1818, LLM.

[13] The wedding date is usually given as Oct. 1, the date mentioned in the correspondence previous to the wedding. The error apparently originates in Prime, p. 113, in the quotation of the marriage notice from the Concord *Patriot* of Oct. 6, 1818. Prime interpolates in the quotation: "October 1st." No date appeared in the original *Patriot* notice. *Letters,* I, 217, apparently follows Prime. On the same page appears a contradictory quotation from SFBM's letter of Oct. 5: "I was married . . . on Tuesday morning last." Oct. 1 was

Thursday; Sept. 29 was Tuesday. The date is given correctly in Joseph B. Walker's manuscript Life of the Rev. Timothy Walker (1902), II, 136, in the New Hampshire Historical Society library, and in a manuscript of SFBM, Feb. 1864, LC.

[14] Jane Keith to JM, Jan. 30, 1819, YC.

[15] SFBM to RCM, Jan. 19, 1819, COLG.

[16] Information on back of the drawing, owned by the Rev. Shiefe Walker, Concord.

[17] SFBM to JM and Mrs. JM, Dec. 22, 1818, LC.

[18] Charleston *Courier*, April 29, 1819.

[19] SFBM to RCM, Dec. 21, 1818, COLG. On Dec. 2, 1818 the Charleston *Courier* carried advertisements for portrait-painting by W. D. Parisen of New York, and C. Thompson.

[20] Timothy Dwight: *Travels in New-England and New-York* (London, 1823), I, 427.

[21] Sprague: *Life of JM*, p. 5.

[22] Mrs. JM to SEM, April, 1919, LC.

[23] SFBM to JM and Mrs. JM, March 26, 1819, LC. SFBM drew up a statement of the issues involved in JM's conflict with his church and read it to members of the church and Andover Seminary professors. Mrs. JM to RCM, Aug. 19, 1819, COLG.

[24] Mrs. JM to LPW, Feb. 3, 1820, LLM.

[25] SFBM to LPW, Jan. 1, 1820, LC.

[26] RCM to JM and Mrs. JM, Feb. 5, 1820, COLG.

[27] SFBM to LPW, Feb. 25, 1821, LLM.

[28] SFBM to LPW, Feb. 11, 1821, LLM.

[29] SFBM to LPW, Jan. 13–14; Jan. 20, 1821, LLM.

[30] SFBM to LPW, Jan. 28–Feb. 1, 1821, LLM.

[31] SFBM to Mrs. Caroline Ball, copy, with SFBM's comments, March 16 and 18, and Mrs. Ball to SFBM, March 29, 1821, LC.

[32] Charleston *Courier*, Feb. 17, 1821; Dunlap, III, 58–9.

CHAPTER VII

Congress Hall

[1] JM's inventory, Jan. 1, 1823, YC.

[2] Mrs. JM to SEM, June 16, 1820, LLM.

[3] JM to Mrs. JM, Oct. 2, 1822, YC.

[4] James L. Yvonnet to Percival, in Julius H. Ward: *Life and Letters of James Gates Percival* (Boston, 1866), p. 158.

[5] Frederick G. Cogswell: "James Gates Percival and His Friends," in *Publ. of the Conn. Soc. of the Order of the Founders and Patriots of Am.*, 1902, No. 6, p. 21. As so often happened with Percival, there was a misunderstanding

between him and his publisher, the engraving of SFBM's portrait was stopped, and in the confusion which followed SFBM indignantly ran to a lawyer to recover his portrait.

[6] Silliman wrote an account of a journey with SFBM in his *Journal*, IV, 40–50 (1822). He refers to SFBM as to a respected scientific colleague.

[7] It is Dunlap, III, 95, who attributes SFBM's idea of *Congress Hall* to Granet's success. *Godey's Magazine*, XXXIII, 213 (1846) (an article on SFBM which Tuckerman himself may have written), and Henry T. Tuckerman: *Book of the Artists* (New York, 1867), p. 168, also attribute it erroneously to SFBM's experience in painting the *Gallery of the Louvre*, which was not in fact painted until many years after *Congress Hall*.

[8] Prime, pp. 123–4.

[9] Ibid., p. 123.

[10] SFBM to LPW, Jan. 5, 1822, LC.

[11] JM to RCM and SEM, Jan. 30, 1822, YC.

[12] Mrs. JM to JM, Jan. 25, 1822, YC.

[13] JM to Mrs. JM, March 12, 1822, YC.

[14] See JM to SFBM, Dec. 1, 1822, YC; LPW to SFBM, Dec. 28, 1821, LLM; JM to Mrs. JM, March 12, 1822, YC; Washington *National Intelligencer*, Jan. 21, 1822; New Haven *Connecticut Journal*, June 25, 1822.

[15] Ibid., Jan. 22, Feb. 4, 1823.

[16] Similar notices appeared every few days through the period of exhibition in Boston in the *Columbian Centinel* and the *Commercial Gazette*.

[17] Abbreviated from *Key to Morse's Picture of the House of Representatives* [New Haven, 1823], pp. 2–4.

[18] Notice of the last day of exhibition appeared in the Boston *Columbian Centinel*, April 12, 1823.

[19] New York *Advertiser*, July 5 (*sic*), 1823.

[20] New York *Observer*, July 12, 1823.

[21] Julius H. Ward: *Life and Letters of James Gates Percival* (Boston, 1866), pp. 171–2.

[22] LPW to SFBM, Aug. 30, 1823, LLM.

CHAPTER VIII

Fulfillment Comes Late

[1] *Letters*, I, 251.

[2] *Minutes of the Common Council of the City of New York, 1784–1831* (New York, 1917), XIV, 53, 123; *Letters*, I, 261.

[3] SFBM to LPW, Dec. 24, 1824, LLM.

[4] Prime, p. 139.

[5] *Letters*, I, 261.

[6] RCM to JM and Mrs. JM, Oct. 18, 1824, COLG.

[7] JM to SFBM, Feb. 7, 1825, YC.

[8] An obituary of LPW appears in the New York *Observer*, Feb. 19, 1825. See also Emily E. F. Ford: *Notes on the Life of Noah Webster,* II (New York, 1912), 282.

[9] Prime, p. 140.

[10] SFBM to JM and Mrs. JM, Nov. 18, 1825, LC.

CHAPTER IX

Founding the National Academy

On founding the academy: The standard source is Thomas S. Cummings: *Historic Annals of the National Academy of Design* (Philadelphia, 1865). Benson J. Lossing, in "The National Academy of the Arts of Design, and Its Surviving Founders," in *Harper's*, LXVI, 852–63 (1883), adds doubtful but interesting detail, probably in part derived from *Godey's Magazine,* XXXIII, 212 (1846). SFBM gives his account in his *Fine Arts, A Reply to Article X, No. LVIII, in the North American Review* (New York, 1828) (reviewed in *Southern Review,* IV, 70–86 [1829], in an article that has been attributed to Allston), and his *Examination of Col. Trumbull's Address* (New York, 1833).

[1] Assuming SFBM's intentions for the use of his rooms as explained in his letter to JM and Mrs. JM, March 22, 1825, LC, were carried out. In this letter as in *Letters,* I, 274, the address is given as 20 Canal. In *Longworth's American Almanac, New York Register* (1825), it is given as 66 Canal.

[2] Cummings, op. cit., pp. 22–3.

[3] The chairman of the American Academy committee, Jeremiah Van Rensselaer, reported to the academy that the committee was unwilling to accept recommendations for candidates from those outside the academy. Statement dated Dec. 24, 1825, records of the American Academy, NYHS.

[4] Cummings, op. cit., p. 25.

[5] *Letter from Joe Strickland* [pseud.] *to Samuel F. B. Morse,* "Memphremagog" (1828), p. 9. SFBM identified the author as Dr. James E. De Kay, a college friend, in his letter to C. H. Hart, Feb. 17, 1871, LC. De Kay was active in the American Academy.

[6] New York *Evening Post,* n.d., in Cummings, op. cit., p. 101.

[7] Ibid., p. 29.

[8] Address of Trumbull, appended to SFBM: *Examination of Col. Trumbull's Address,* op. cit., p. 19.

[9] *Letter from Joe Strickland* [pseud.] *to Samuel F. B. Morse,* "Memphremagog" (1828), p. 16.

[10] New York *Evening Post,* May 17, 1828.

[11] Ibid., May 31, 1828.

[12] "Trumbull's Answer," quoted from ibid., n.d., in Cummings, op. cit., p. 103.

[13] SFBM to Mrs. JM, May 6, 1828, LC.

[14] SFBM to DeWitt Bloodgood, Dec. 26, 1828, PENN.

CHAPTER X

Discovering Versatility

On the founding of the New York *Journal of Commerce:* Its association with the New York *Observer* is described in [William H. Hallock:] *Life of Gerard Hallock* (New York, 1869), pp. 61–9, and in the *Journal of Commerce,* Sept. 27, 1927 (centennial number). Its association with SFBM is revealed only in the files of the *Observer* and in correspondence.

[1] *Correspondence of James Fenimore-Cooper* (New Haven, 1922), p. 358.

[2] SFBM to Mrs. JM, May 11, 1828, LC. One of the words crossed out seems to be "Albany."

[3] RCM to SEM [May 15? 1828], COLG.

[4] SFBM to DeWitt Bloodgood, Dec. 26, 1828, PENN.

[5] SFBM to DeWitt Bloodgood, Dec. 29, 1833, PENN.

[6] SEM to RCM, Dec. 25, 1825, LC.

[7] Mrs. JM to RCM, July 7, 1827, COLG.

[8] "Madame Hutin – The Bowery Theatre," signed "A Father," in New York *Observer,* March 3, 1827.

[9] The 1827 correspondence shows SFBM to be the author of the following *Observer* articles: the article cited in reference 8; the article signed "A Father," March 17, 1827; "The Moral Interests of Our City," editorial, March 24, 1827. The following is also so identified in Hallock, op. cit., pp. 66–7: "To the Ladies of New-York City," April 14, 1827.

[10] Ibid.

[11] RCM to SEM, March 17, 1827, COLG.

[12] RCM to SEM, March 19, 1827, COLG.

[13] SFBM to SEM, March 20, 1827, LLM.

[14] SFBM to editors of the New York *Herald* [*ca.* Jan. 1866], filed undated, LC.

[15] New York *Observer,* March 24, 1827.

[16] Reference 14. Roger M. Sherman wrote SFBM, March 28, 1827, declining the editorship. NYHS.

[17] Una Pope-Hennessy, ed.: *The Aristocratic Journey, Being the Outspoken Letters of Mrs. Basil Hall* (New York and London, 1931), p. 69.

[18] Moss Kent to SFBM, May 2, 1829, LC.

[19] London *Quarterly Review,* XLI, 301 (1829).

[20] James Kent to Moss Kent, Jan. 2, 1830, James Kent papers, LC.

[21] Jared Sparks, ed.: *The Library of American Biography,* VII (Boston and London, 1837), 221; Catharine M. Sedgwick: *Poetical Remains of the Late Lucretia Maria Davidson* (Philadelphia, 1841).

[22] Edgar Allan Poe: *Works,* VI (New York, 1884), 150, 162–3.

[23] *Personal Reminiscences of the Late Sarah Breese Walker* ([Utica?], 1884), pp. 46–8.

[24] SFBM to JM and Mrs. JM, Aug. 10, 1824, LC.

[25] Morgan Dix: *Memoirs of John Adams Dix,* I (New York, 1883), 89.

[26] When SFBM entertained Governor Clinton and others at a breakfast he called the affair a "Clintonian party." SFBM to JM and Mrs. JM, Dec. 1, 1825, LC. Charles Walker was a minor political lieutenant of Clinton at this period. See Clinton's manuscript diary, NYHS.

[27] SFBM to Mrs. JM, Nov. 9, 1826, LC.

[28] Records of the New York Athenæum, NYHS.

[29] In 1826 SFBM lectured for the Athenæum in the chapel of Columbia College on March 20 and 27 and April 3 and 12. In 1827 Dana lectured for the Athenæum on electricity on Jan. 11, 15, 18, and 22 and Feb. 1, 5, and 8. He died in April and Morse was one of his pall-bearers. Undated manuscript of SFBM, LC; cf. Prime, pp. 162–9. On SFBM's lectures see Winifred E. Howe: *A History of the Metropolitan Museum of Art* (New York, 1913), pp. 53–4.

[30] SFBM: *Academies of Arts* (New York, 1827), p. 23.

[31] *Penn. Mag. of Hist. and Biog.,* XXIX, 135 (1905).

CHAPTER XI

Puritan Seeking Beauty

[1] SFBM to Margaret Roby, Jan. 1830, draft, LC.

[2] *Letters,* I, 324.

[3] Ibid., p. 333.

[4] Dunlap, III, 99–100.

[5] Prime, p. 188.

[6] *Letters,* I, 349–50.

[7] Ibid., p. 348.

[8] Ibid., p. 371.

[9] Allan Nevins, ed.: *The Diary of Philip Hone* (New York, 1927), p. 93.

[10] *Letters,* I, 375.

[11] James E. Freeman: *Gatherings from an Artist's Portfolio* (New York, 1877), p. 11.

[12] Louisa Dresser: "*The Chapel of the Virgin at Subiaco* by Samuel F. B. Morse," in Worcester Art Museum *Annual,* 1941, pp. 65–71.

[13] *Letters,* I, 343.

[14] Francis J. Connors: "Samuel Finley Breese Morse and the Anti-Catholic

Political Movements in the United States," in *Illinois Catholic Hist. Rev.*, X, 99 (1927).

[15] Prime, p. 728.

[16] *Letters,* I, 385.

[17] Ibid., pp. 377–8.

[18] Prime, p. 196.

[19] *Letters,* I, 363.

[20] Ibid., p. 369.

[21] Notebook, dated May 14, 1830, LC.

[22] *Letters,* I, 353; a clipping in SFBM's scrapbook, Western Union Library, New York, indicates that he retold the story in 1836.

[23] *Letters,* I, 398–9.

[24] Ibid., p. 382. In a letter delivered to an American to carry home, SFBM wrote that in letters mailed by usual methods he did not dare explain his political views. New York *Observer,* Nov. 27, 1830.

[25] SFBM told the story of his journey in ibid., May 28, 1831, and in a letter to John C. S. Abbott, March 4, 1867, letter-book, LC.

[26] New York *Observer,* April 20, 1831.

[27] *Letters,* I, 401–2.

CHAPTER XII
Lafayette Liberal

On the American Polish Committee in Paris: There is nothing of significance on SFBM in the notes by various committee secretaries, now in the New York State Library, Albany. There is background and brief mention of his role in Robert E. Spiller: "Fenimore Cooper and Lafayette: Friends of Polish Freedom, 1830–1832," in *American Literature,* VII, 56–75 (1935), and Laura E. Richards, ed.: *Letters and Journals of Samuel Gridley Howe: The Greek Revolution* (London, 1906), pp. 411–14.

On Lafayette's anti-Catholicism: Michael de la Bedoyere: "Lafayette and the Church," in the *Catholic World,* CXXXIX, 166–70 (1934) is useful. SFBM's controversy with Bishop Spalding of Kentucky on what Lafayette said on the influence of Catholicism is summarized by SFBM in the New York *Herald,* Feb. 18, 1872, and by a Catholic writer in "Lafayette and Professor Morse," in *Metropolitan,* N.S., I, 144–55 (1858). The controversy began in the anti-Know-Nothing Cincinnati *Enquirer* in 1854 (see *Enquirer* of May 17, 1855), and took the form of a series of letters in the Louisville *Courier* from the winter through the summer of 1855. Letters and clippings about the controversy are at LC.

[1] New York *Observer,* Nov. 19, 1831.

[2] Prime, p. 213.

[3] SFBM to DeWitt Bloodgood, draft [Dec. 1831?], LC.

[4] SFBM to SEM and RCM, July 18, 1832, LC.

[5] William Dunlap: *Diary* (New York, 1930), p. 608.

[6] Prime, p. 214.

[7] See Charlotte P. Browning: *Full Harvest* (Philadelphia, 1932), pp. 30–1, 102; *Correspondence of James Fenimore-Cooper* (New Haven, 1922), pp. 314, 365.

[8] Prime, p. 223.

[9] Signed statement of R. W. Habersham, n.d., filed 1832, LC. Part of it is in *Letters,* I, 417–18. A slightly different version is in Prime, pp. 229–31. Cooper's statement for Lafayette has been republished as Robert E. Spiller, ed., James Fenimore Cooper: *Letter to Gen. Lafayette* (New York, 1931).

[10] SFBM to Benjamin Silliman, July 12, 1832, Cooper papers, YC.

[11] SFBM to SEM and RCM, Oct. 2, 1831, COLG.

[12] Bernard Sarrans: *Memoirs of General Lafayette and the French Revolution of 1830,* II (London, 1832), 293. The sentence is omitted from some reprints of the speech.

[13] As in SFBM's letters in the Louisville *Courier,* Aug. 11, 1855, and the New York *Herald,* Feb. 18, 1872.

[14] New York *Observer,* Aug. 27, 1831.

[15] SFBM, ed.: *Confessions of a French Catholic Priest* (New York, 1837), p. ix.

[16] Bedoyere, op. cit. Lafayette, on his last visit to America, when SFBM first made his acquaintance, divided his church attendance between Protestant and Catholic services. In Boston he attended Brattle Street Meeting, in New York Trinity Church, in Philadelphia St. Augustine's Catholic Church, and in Baltimore the Catholic Cathedral. J. B. Nolan: *Lafayette in America Day by Day* (Baltimore, 1934), pp. 245, 249, 252–3. Lafayette seems to have been a Mason in France before coming to America at all; on his last visit he was often entertained by Masons. André Lebey: *La Fayette ou le Militant Franc-Maçon,* I (Paris, 1937), pp. 47–8; Louis Gottschalk: *Lafayette Joins the American Army* (Chicago, 1937), pp. 337–8.

[17] Bedoyere, op. cit., p. 170, apparently unaware of the quotation publicized by Morse, called this phrase the nearest approach to an anti-Catholic expression of Lafayette he could find.

[18] "Lafayette and Professor Morse," op. cit., pp. 150–1.

[19] The alleged book was Jeane Bap. Marchand: *Essai sur la République des États Unis d'Amérique* (Paris, 1835), 12 mo., 245 pp. SFBM could not discover that any such book had been published and neither can I.

[20] Horatio Greenough to SFBM, April 23, 1832, LC.

[21] LC.

[22] Prime, p. 217.

[23] Statement of R. W. Habersham. See reference 9.

[24] Ibid.; James F. Cooper: *The Sea-Lions* (New York, 1873), pp. 161–2; *Letters,* I, 418–21; *Correspondence of James Fenimore-Cooper* (New Haven,

1922), pp. 620, 633–5; Prime, pp. 231–2. Professor James Renwick testified that SFBM was already in search of a scheme for an electric telegraph before going to Europe. French v. Rogers (Compls'. Ev.), Philadelphia, 1851, 497–8.

[25] Cf. reference 24 with SFBM to R. W. Habersham, April 3, 1858, LC.

[26] New York *Observer*, June 23, 1832.

CHAPTER XIII
Sully *Voyage*

[1] J. F. Cooper to SFBM, Sept. 21, 1832, copy, LC.

[2] SFBM to J. F. Cooper, Oct. 2, 1832, copy, LC.

[3] SFBM gave the day of his conception of his telegraph as Oct. 19, 1832, in an undated letter to Alfred Vail, in Alfred Vail: *Telegraph*, p. 154. Usually, however, he said it was several days out of Havre.

[4] SFBM to C. T. Jackson, Sept. 18, 1837, draft, LC; similarly to Levi Woodbury, Sept. 27, 1837, in Alfred Vail: *Telegraph*, p. 152.

[5] William Pell to SFBM, Sept. 27, 1837, in ibid., p. 153.

[6] SFBM to C. T. Jackson, Sept. 18, 1837, draft, LC.

[7] Statement of J. F. Fisher, *Letters*, II, 11.

[8] The original notebook was used as evidence in a telegraph suit in Kentucky in 1848; after the suit was appealed to the United States Supreme Court, the notebook was burned in a mysterious fire in April 1852, in the office of the clerk of the Supreme Court. Fortunately a certified copy was in the possession of F. O. J. Smith. From that copy was made a copy, the accuracy of which was attested by E. Fitch Smith in 1853, which is now in the National Museum, Washington. It seems to be the only copy in existence.

CHAPTER XIV
Born Too Soon

[1] *Letters*, II, 25–6. When SFBM read in Lawrence Turnbull and Edward Highton: *History of the Invention of the Electric Telegraph* (abridged) (New York, 1853), p. 38, that it was strange that there was no record of his telegraphic activity for several years after 1832, he wrote in his copy of the book, now at LC: "Is this a fair statement? What becomes of the successful operating of my recording telegraph in Nov. 1835, and onward in 1836 & 1837?" He commented similarly in the margin of his copy, now in the possession of LLM, of George B. Prescott: *History, Theory, and Practice of the Electric Telegraph* (Boston, 1860), p. 58. It is significant that he could refer to nothing showing his telegraphic activity before 1835.

[2] Clipping, marked *Tribune*, Dec. 5, 1865, LC.

[3] SFBM to J. F. Cooper, Feb. 21, 1833, filed 1839, LC.

[4] Theodore F. Jones: *New York University, 1832:1932* (New York and London, 1933), p. 38.

[5] C. R. Leslie to SFBM, Oct. 25, 1833, filed 1839, LC.

[6] New York *Evening Star,* Oct. 15, 1833.

[7] Jared B. Flagg: *The Life and Letters of Washington Allston* (New York, 1892), p. 345.

[8] *Letters,* II, 24.

[9] William Dunlap: *Diary* (New York, 1930), p. 659.

[10] Thomas S. Cummings: *Historic Annals of the National Academy of Design* (Philadelphia, 1865), p. 151.

[11] William Dunlap: *Diary* (New York, 1930), p. 723.

[12] "Our Legation to France," in the New York *Commercial Advertiser,* March 5, 1833, is identified as by SFBM in his letter to Lafayette, March 5, 1833, draft, LC.

[13] SFBM to DeWitt Bloodgood, Dec. 29, 1833, PENN.

[14] George P. A. Healy: *Reminiscences of a Portrait Painter* (Chicago, 1894), p. 34.

[15] *Letters,* II, 27.

[16] Horatio Greenough to SFBM, Aug. 24, 1834, LC.

[17] DeWitt Bloodgood to SFBM, Aug. 9, 1834, LC.

[18] Dunlap, III, 97.

[19] Ibid., p. 99.

CHAPTER XV

Native American

On SFBM as a nativist: Louis D. Scisco: *Political Nativism in New York State* (New York, 1901), and Ray A. Billington: *The Protestant Crusade, 1800–1860, A Study of the Origins of American Nativism* (New York, 1938), both of which give attention to SFBM in a scholarly manner; SFBM: *Foreign Conspiracy* (New York and Boston, 1835), *Imminent Dangers* (New York, 1835), and *Our Liberties Defended* (New York and Boston, 1841); SFBM, ed.: *The Proscribed German Student* (New York, 1836), and *Confessions of a French Catholic Priest* (New York, 1837); Peter Guilday: *The Life and Times of John England,* II (New York, 1927), 195–210. See also references for Chapters XI and XII.

[1] SFBM to Lafayette, March 5, 1833, draft, LC.

[2] Richardson L. Wright: *Forgotten Ladies* (Philadelphia and London, 1928), pp. 131–2. A recent student of nativism, Carroll J. Noonan, in *Nativism in Connecticut* (Washington, 1938), p. 96, remarks that SFBM's work was of more effect than the fire in stirring nativist opinion.

[3] SFBM's scrapbook, Western Union Library, New York.

[4] Theodore Dwight translated works in the romance languages and wrote occasionally for the *American Protestant Vindicator*, and for the paper his father had founded, the New York *Commercial Advertiser*. His *Open Convents,* depending for its evidence on Rebecca Reed's and Maria Monk's descriptions of convent life, was introduced by letters from W. C. Brownlee of the *Vindicator* and SFBM, the latter describing the book as "showing . . . the hollowness, and the depravity and danger of the Convent system." *Open Convents* was issued in 1836 by Van Nostrand and Dwight, the firm of David Van Nostrand and William R. Dwight, Theodore's brother.

[5] *Correspondence of James Fenimore-Cooper* (New Haven, 1922), pp. 354–5.

[6] Ibid., p. 358.

[7] *American Protestant Vindicator,* Aug. 17, Sept. 21, 1836.

[8] [Laughton Osborn]: *The Vision of Rubeta . . . with Illustrations, Done on Stone* (Boston, 1838), p. 162. Osborn was an erratic poet of promise. His poem was largely an attack on editor Stone, who, though friendly to nativism, had been instrumental in exposing Maria Monk.

[9] Billington, op. cit., pp. 101–2.

[10] Ibid., p. 123.

[11] *American Protestant Vindicator,* Sept. 3, 1834.

[12] SFBM: *Foreign Conspiracy,* op. cit., p. 3.

[13] Ibid., p. 118–19.

[14] SFBM's church affiliation at this period is obscure. According to records of the Center Church, New Haven, he was dismissed to an unnamed church in New York in 1836. According to records of the First Presbyterian Church, Poughkeepsie, however, he became a member of that church soon after moving there in 1847, by letter directly from New Haven.

Be that as it may, the Morse family joined Presbyterian and Congregational churches indiscriminately. Mrs. JM had been originally Presbyterian. JM had candidated in the First Presbyterian Church in New York, of which one of Mrs. JM's forebears was an early pastor, before becoming pastor of the Congregational church of Charlestown. As a youth RCM preached in a Presbyterian church in Johns Island while SFBM was attending the Congregational church in Charleston. During the period in which the family belonged to the Center Church, New Haven, it was called indifferently Congregational or Presbyterian, a situation peculiar to Connecticut at the time. In New York RCM's and SEM's *Observer* was regarded as semi-Presbyterian; RCM's daughter Louisa was baptized in the Brick Presbyterian Church in 1837; RCM later became a member of the Madison Square Presbyterian Church, where SFBM also attended when he spent his winters in his house on Twenty-second Street, but in 1864 RCM retired to New Haven and rejoined the Center Church, which by this time, since Congregationalists and Presbyterians had terminated their *ad hoc* union for Western mission work, had become wholly Congregational.

According to records at the First Presbyterian Church, New York, with which the Mercer Street Church eventually united, SFBM's daughter Susan joined the latter church on confession of faith, March 7, 1839, but SFBM is not listed as a member.

[15] SFBM: *Imminent Dangers,* p. 11.

[16] *American Protestant Vindicator,* March 18, 1835.

[17] Billington, op. cit., pp. 60, 78.

[18] Allan Nevins, ed.: *The Diary of Philip Hone* (New York, 1927), p. 205.

[19] New York *Morning Courier and Enquirer,* April 11, 1836.

[20] Ibid., April 9, 1836.

[21] Theodore F. Jones: *New York University, 1832:1932* (New York, 1933), p. 43.

[22] New York *Morning Courier and Enquirer,* April 14, 1836.

[23] New York *Observer,* April 23, 1836.

[24] SFBM, ed.: *The Proscribed German Student,* p. 11.

[25] Now at LC.

[26] SFBM, ed.: *The Proscribed German Student,* p. 19.

[27] *Correspondence of James Fenimore-Cooper* (New Haven, 1922), p. 365.

[28] *Downfall of Babylon,* July 23, 1836, cited Billington, op. cit., pp. 125, 137; New York *Journal of Commerce,* July 6; New York *Observer,* July 23; *American Protestant Vindicator,* July 13, 1836.

[29] Clipping, Darien *Telegraph,* n.d., SFBM's scrapbook, Western Union Library, New York.

[30] Charles Beck to SFBM, July 15, 1836, LC; Charles Follen to SFBM, July 30, 1836, LC.

[31] Brooklyn *Advocate,* Dec. 30, New York *New Era,* Dec. 22, 24, 1836, and other clippings, SFBM's scrapbook, Western Union Library, New York.

[32] New York *Morning Courier and Enquirer,* April 12; New York *Express,* April 13; and see ibid., April 12, 1841.

[33] New York *Evening Post,* New York *American,* April 12, New York *Express,* April 13, 1841.

[34] New York *Evening Post,* April 14, 1841.

[35] New York *Tribune,* April 13, 1841.

[36] New York *Morning Courier and Enquirer,* April 13, 1841.

[37] New York *Commercial Advertiser,* April 13, 1841.

[38] Scisco, op. cit., p. 34. See New York *Observer,* June 12, 1841, cited in Billington, op. cit., pp. 168, 186.

[39] New York *Evening Post,* New York *Tribune,* Oct. 30, 1841.

[40] Scisco, op. cit., p. 35.

[41] L. D. Chapin to SFBM, April 26, 1844, LC. SFBM may have attempted to run for office again as a nativist as late as 1845. A petition on his behalf, for an unknown purpose, was circulated by L. D. Gale, Mr. Dudley of the firm of Dudley and Hinman, and Chapin, a nativist leader whom SFBM distrusted; nativist Mayor Harper supported it. L. D. Gale to SFBM, Jan. 24, 1845, LC.

[42] Rough draft of the address, dated Oct. 1840, LC.

[43] R. S. Cook to SFBM, Feb. 14, 1849, LC; SFBM to SEM, Oct. 29, 1846, LC.

[44] Herman Norton to SFBM, July 1, 1848, LC.

CHAPTER XVI

Painting Bows to Telegraphy

[1] SFBM to Absalam Peters, April 6, 1838, draft, LC; cf. Theodore F. Jones: *New York University, 1832:1932* (New York, 1933), p. 394.

[2] *New-York Mirror,* March 25, 1837.

[3] Statement of Robert Dodge, 1851, LC.

[4] Rankin's account of the interview, Prime, pp. 304–7.

[5] Prime, pp. 308–9, 311.

[6] SFBM to Mrs. F. E. H. (Cooper) Haines, April 24, 1864, letter-book, LC.

[7] O'Rielly v. Morse (Ev.), Washington [1851?], 142–6.

[8] Prime, pp. 292–4.

[9] Ibid., p. 293.

[10] SFBM to Absalam Peters, April 6, 1838, draft, LC.

[11] Deposition of SFBM, French v. Rogers (Compls'. Ev.), Philadelphia, 1851, 169.

[12] Extract from an address by L. P. Clover, a former National Academy student, filed Oct. 16, 1856, LC; Prime, p. 310.

[13] *Journal* of the H. of R., 24 Cong., 1 Sess., 1108, 1112.

[14] Jared B. Flagg: *The Life and Letters of Washington Allston* (New York, 1892), pp. 228, 238; *New-York Mirror,* July 16, 1836; SFBM to Washington Allston, March 21, 1837, draft, LC.

[15] For the Committee report see H. of R. Rep. No. 294, 24 Cong., 2 Sess.

[16] Washington *National Intelligencer,* Feb. 19, 1846; *Petition of A. B. Durand and Others,* Sen. Doc. No. 380, 29 Cong., 1 Sess.

[17] See reference 19 and *New-York Mirror,* March 4, 1837, Oct. 16, 1841; New York *Evening Star,* May 3, 1837.

[18] SFBM to RCM, Feb. 24, 1848, COLG.

[19] Prime, p. 290. I have found no support for this story in SFBM's correspondence or congressional documents. The story is told, however, by James Wynne in *Harper's Magazine,* XXIV, 224–5 (1862), in an article which SFBM said was accurate.

[20] *Letters,* II, 33.

[21] Prime, p. 290.

[22] SFBM to Thomas Cole, March 20, 1837, New York State Library, Albany.

[23] Prime, p. 291, quoting Cummings.

[24] Statement of the "Association" to SFBM, n.d., filed 1841, LC. A record of the meeting at Cummings's house, March 17, 1837, at which the "Association" was organized, is at NYHS.

[25] SFBM to *New-York Mirror,* n.d., draft, filed 1841, LC.

[26] SFBM to J. F. Cooper, Nov. 20, 1849, copy, LC. Even a year before his death SFBM told an interviewer: "This opposition of Mr. Adams is what ruined me as an artist." *The Golden Age,* April 15, 1871.

[27] SFBM to T. S. Cummings, March 15, 1838, draft, LC.

CHAPTER XVII

Partners Gale, Vail and "Fog" Smith

On Henry's contributions to telegraphy: The most useful document, William B. Taylor: "Henry and the Telegraph," in Smithsonian Institution *Annual Report* for 1878, pp. 262–360; SFBM: *The Electro-Magnetic Telegraph. A Defence against the Injurious Deductions Drawn from the Deposition of Prof. Joseph Henry* [Paris, 1867?], reprinted from Shaffner's *Telegraph Companion,* Jan. 1855; Smithsonian Institution *Miscellaneous Coll.,* II, article 2 (1862).

On Jackson's contributions to telegraphy: Amos Kendall: *Morse's Patent. Full Exposure of Dr. Chas. T. Jackson's Pretensions* (Washington, 1852).

On Vail's contributions to telegraphy: Alfred Vail: *Telegraph;* J. C. Vail; Frank L. Pope: "The American Inventors of the Telegraph," in *Century,* XXXV, 924–44 (1888); Frank L. Pope: "The Genesis of the American Electric Telegraph," in *Electrical Engineer,* XIX, 444–6 (1895); Edward L. Morse: "The Dot-and-Dash Alphabet," in *Century,* LXXXIII, 695–706 (1912); Vail's manuscript account of his connection with telegraphy, 1848, "Miscellaneous telegraph papers" volume, SM.

A useful summary of all contributions to telegraphy is the series of articles by Frank L. Pope, Edward L. Morse, Mary A. Henry, Stephen Vail, J. J. Fahie, and others, in *Electrical World,* XXVI, 71–686, *passim* (1895).

[1] New York *Observer,* April 15, 1837. SEM deposed that he mentioned twenty-four wires because it was simpler so to explain the telegraph, and because he himself believed it wiser to use twenty-four wires. Smith v. Downing (Ev.), New York, 1850, 149; same in French v. Rogers (Compls'. Ev.), Philadelphia, 1851, 23.

[2] Smith v. Downing (Ev.), New York, 1850, 51. SFBM seems not to have made a formal agreement with Gale until March 1838. See Alfred Vail to George Vail, Jan. 22, 1838, in J. C. Vail, p. 14.

[3] Smith v. Downing (Ev.), New York, 1850, 123; similarly, French v. Rogers (Compls'. Ev.), Philadelphia, 1851, 433.

[4] Smith v. Downing (Ev.), New York, 1850, 123.

[5] The relay was not mentioned in SFBM's first documentary description of his invention, his caveat of September 1837, contrary to the statement in the generally excellent article on SFBM in the *Dictionary of American Biography* (see reference 11). The first direct evidence that SFBM contemplated

the use of the relay is his reference to it in his revised specifications of his invention filed with the Patent Office, April 7, 1838 (see reference 53). By this time, according to Joseph Henry, he and SFBM had met. There is evidence, on the other hand, to show that SFBM did not know its importance and was not sure of the necessity of using it even then. Henry afterward said that he did not hear of the relay as part of the Morse system until 1839 (Smith v. Downing [Ev.], New York, 1850, 90); Henry's testimony is weakened by the fact that he became estranged from SFBM and himself claimed an independent discovery of the relay. In the summer of 1838 after SFBM had consulted the British Solicitor General, that gentleman told Edward Davy, another person to whom the independent discovery of the relay principle has been conceded, that SFBM had no idea of the relay at all (J. J. Fahie: *A History of Electric Telegraphy, to the Year 1837* [London and New York, 1884], p. 359); what the Solicitor General said, however, is also to be discounted, because he was unfriendly to SFBM. More damaging to SFBM's claim to credit for the discovery are the facts that a committee of the Franklin Institute examining his invention early in 1838 did not report on the relay but only anticipated "no serious difficulty" in sending signals to a distance (Alfred Vail: *Telegraph*, pp. 79–80); that when SFBM was later confronted with a description of his invention written in the fall of 1838, he explained that the description did not include the relay, "the utility of which was then unknown" (Smith v. Downing [Ev.], New York, 1850, 52); that in an estimate which he submitted to a prospective telegraph builder in 1839, costs for relays were only provisionally included: "Relays," he wrote, "(perhaps 4 perhaps none) an instrument to propagate a fresh impulse (if necessary) of the Galvanic fluid £2.0.0. each" (SFBM to Baron Meyendorf, Feb. 20, 1839, draft, LC).

6 Smith v. Downing (Ev.), New York, 1850, 94 A.

7 SFBM to William Pell, C. T. Jackson, and others, in ibid., 70. The New York *Journal of Commerce*, Aug. 28, 1837, mentions the telegraph projects of Barlow, Wheatstone, Alexander, and the five needle telegraphs of an "eminent gentleman" of London.

8 SFBM to Catherine Pattison, Aug. 27, 1837, "copy" in SFBM's hand, LC.

9 The demonstration is described in an article in Silliman's *Journal*, XXXIII, 185–7 (1838) [*sic*], reprinted in *Journal of the Franklin Institute* N.S., XX, 323–5 (1837) [*sic*]. For SFBM's comment: his letter to the editors in the New York *Journal of Commerce*, Sept. 7, 1837, reprinted in Alfred Vail: *Telegraph*, pp. 74–6. For Vail's comment: Vail's manuscript account, op. cit.

10 One of the original copies of the agreement is preserved at LC. The text is printed in *Electrical World*, XXVI, 471 (1895).

11 The caveat is printed in Prime, pp. 320–4, and in O'Rielly v. Morse [Washington, 1851?], 48–52. The Patent Office now reports that the original has been destroyed.

12 Undated fragment, LC.

[13] *Letter from the Secretary of the Treasury upon . . . Telegraphs,* H. of R. Doc. No. 15, 25 Cong., 2 Sess.

[14] Kendall: *Morse's Patent,* op. cit., p. 48.

[15] Ibid., pp. 49–51.

[16] Ibid., p. 15.

[17] Ibid., pp. 19–25; Smith v. Downing (Ev.), New York, 1850, 70–76.

[18] Prime, p. 324.

[19] Recollection of William Baxter, then fifteen years of age, in Pope: "The American Inventors," op. cit., pp. 934–5.

[20] Morristown *Jerseyman,* Jan. 17, 1838. Prime, p. 330, mistakenly cites the report as from the Morristown *Journal.*

[21] Alfred Vail to George Vail, Jan. 22, 1838, in J. C. Vail, p. 14. For one of the invitations addressed to Cummings see Thomas S. Cummings: *Historic Annals of the National Academy of Design* (Philadelphia, 1865), p. 152. In Cummings the note is dated June 22, 1838. Elsewhere, as in Prime, p. 331, it is dated January 22, 1838. Because SFBM was not in the United States in June, and because in January he was preparing to go to Washington as the note states, and because " June " and " Jan." look alike in manuscript, I accept Prime's rendering as probably correct, in spite of the fact that the earlier source is Cummings's own work.

[22] *Letters,* II, 77–8.

[23] Pope, in *Electrical World,* op. cit., p. 155.

[24] SFBM to F. O. J. Smith, April 13, 1838, in J. C. Vail, pp. 16–17.

[25] Information supplied by C. P. Lenart, director, personnel bureau, Adjutant General's office, Albany.

[26] New York *Journal of Commerce,* Jan. 29, 1838.

[27] Edward L. Morse: "The Dot-and-Dash Alphabet," op. cit., p. 700. In 1848 the commissioner of patents certified that the drawings attached to SFBM's caveat had been mislaid. His statement opened the way for claims that the Morse alphabet appeared in those drawings. The drawing in SFBM's hand, purporting to show the alphabet of the caveat drawings, reproduced opposite page 66 in *Letters,* II, cannot be accepted on its face as it is undated, was certainly written as late as 1844, and may have been written long afterward when SFBM could not be expected to have remembered accurately. Vail partisans admit that a drawing of an alphabet was once found in the same envelope with the caveat in the Patent Office, but insist that it was originally attached to later documents, and the statement of the commissioner of patents makes this assertion plausible. Edward L. Morse in *Letters,* II, 66, bases his claim that the alphabet drawing was attached to the caveat on the wording of the caveat itself. But I believe that a candid reading of the caveat leads to the assumption that only twelve different pieces of type were used to make marks, all dots or all dashes or all punctures; and that these twelve different marks stood for numbers, which in turn stood for words or the letters of the alphabet, except only when these twelve different marks were intended to stand for numbers, in which case a special sign preceded them. No

provision was made for a special sign to precede the marks when these same types were to stand for the letters of the alphabet.

28 Edward L. Morse: "The Dot-and-Dash Alphabet," op. cit., pp. 700–4.

29 Alfred Vail to S. Vail and son, Feb. 7, 1838, in J. C. Vail, p. 15.

30 Alfred Vail: *Telegraph,* p. 30.

31 J. C. Vail, pp. 35–6.

32 See reference 19, and *Electrical World,* editorial, op. cit., 686.

33 Newark *Evening News,* Nov. 25, 1913.

34 J. C. Vail, p. 10. See also Alfred Vail's full statement, *Electrical World,* op. cit., 181.

35 J. C. Vail, p. 25. See also *Electrical World,* op. cit., 183.

36 J. C. Vail, p. 25.

37 Alfred Vail to George Vail, Jan. 23, 1838, in J. C. Vail, p. 14.

38 Alfred Vail: *Telegraph,* pp. 79–80.

39 A. B. Durand to Thomas Cole, Feb. 7, 1838, Durand papers, NYPL.

40 Alfred Vail to Stephen Vail, Feb. 17, 1838, in Pope: "The American Inventors," op. cit., pp. 935–6.

41 H. of R. Rep. No. 753, 25 Cong., 2 Sess.

42 Civis [pseud. for F. O. J. Smith]: *A Dissertation on the Nature and Effects of Lottery Systems* (Portland, 1827), p. 35; *Letters,* II, 131.

43 John Chandler to Martin Van Buren, Sept. 14, 1835, Van Buren papers, LC.

44 B. B. French to Henry French, June 16, 1843, French papers, LC.

45 Washington *Globe,* Feb. 10, 1838.

46 Information on Smith's career apart from the telegraph is not easily available. The sketches of him in *Appleton's Cyclopædia of American Biography,* the *Biographical Dictionary of the American Congress,* and *Sprague's Journal of Maine History,* XI, 151–2, are inaccurate. This sketch is based on the Smith papers, MHS; newspaper clippings filed at MHS; the French papers, LC; H. W. Greene: *Letters Addressed to Francis O. J. Smith* [Portland?], 1839; Levi Bartlett: *Genealogical and Biographical Sketches of the Bartlett Family* (Lawrence, Mass., 1876), pp. 44, 57; Louis C. Hatch: *Maine: A History,* I (New York, 1919), *passim.*

47 French v. Rogers (Compls'. Ev.), Philadelphia, 1851, 170.

48 Reid, p. 352.

49 *Congressional Globe,* 6, 25 Cong., 2 Sess., 285; the text of the report is in H. of R. Rep. No. 753, 25 Cong., 2 Sess. SFBM seems to have been already confident that Smith would become a partner when he wrote Vail, March 15, 1838, in Prime, p. 345.

50 *Journal* of the H. of R., 25 Cong., 2 Sess., 751, 808.

51 F. O. J. Smith to Alfred Vail, Jan. 20, 1839, SM.

52 An original copy of the agreement is at LC. Texas was specially excepted from its terms; SFBM soon offered telegraph rights gratuitously to the new Republic, but when the offer was still unaccepted in 1860, withdrew it. *Telegraph and Telephone Age,* Feb. 16, 1914, p. 103.

[53] The April 7, 1838 specifications are printed in full in *Telegraph Age,* XXIV, 623–8 (1906), and in French v. Rogers (Compls'. Ev.), Philadelphia, 1851, 148–58. Smith assisted in preparing this document.

[54] SFBM's deposition, in ibid., 170.

[55] The wording and punctuation here used follows that of the draft at LC. One of the printed forms is also at LC.

CHAPTER XVIII

Bureaucracy Abroad

[1] *Letters,* II, 100.

[2] J. J. Fahie: *A History of Electric Telegraphy, to the Year 1837* (London and New York, 1884), pp. 431–2.

[3] The article described the results but not the mechanism of SFBM's telegraph. It was copied from Silliman's *Journal* and the *Journal of the Franklin Institute.* See Ch. XVII, reference 9.

[4] SFBM to RCM, July 15, 1838, COLG.

[5] *Letters,* II, 102; Prime, p. 358.

[6] At LC. Printed in Prime, pp. 349–52.

[7] SFBM: *Lord Campbell and Professor Morse* (Poughkeepsie [1848?]), p. 6.

[8] SFBM to Edward Salisbury, Aug. 27, 1838, LC.

[9] For accounts of the academy exhibition see Prime, pp. 364–9; New York *Observer,* Nov. 10, 1838, Jan. 5, 1839; Paris *Courier Français,* Sept. 13, 1838, LC scrapbook; French v. Rogers (Compls'. Ev.), Philadelphia, 1851, 208–10.

[10] SFBM to F. O. J. Smith, Oct. 9, 1838, MHS.

[11] The application for this patent is printed in *Electrical World,* XXVI, 320 (1895).

[12] SFBM to F. O. J. Smith, Jan. 21, 1839, MHS.

[13] SFBM to F. O. J. Smith, March 2, 1839, MHS.

[14] SFBM to F. O. J. Smith, Feb. 13, 1839, MHS.

[15] Prime, pp. 383–7; SFBM to Baron Meyendorf, draft, Feb. 20, 1839, LC; tentative agreement, dated March 1, 1839, LC, for the revised terms of which see Prime, pp. 394–5.

[16] *Letters,* II, 116.

[17] Ibid., pp. 115–16.

[18] Ibid., p. 110.

[19] SFBM to F. O. J. Smith, July 29, 1839, MHS; New York *Commercial Advertiser,* July 25, 1839; New York *Observer,* Aug. 10, 1839.

[20] The cause of the Czar's refusal, SFBM said in a letter to C. G. Ferris, Dec. 6, 1842, in H. of R. Rep. No. 17, 27 Cong., 2 Sess., was not satisfactorily

explained. For the possible cause here given, see *Annales télégraphiques,* IV, 671 (1861).

CHAPTER XIX

Daguerreotypist

On SFBM as a daguerreotypist: Robert Taft: *Photography and the American Scene* (New York, 1938); Marcus A. Root: *The Camera and the Pencil* (Philadelphia, 1864).

On Gouraud: *Description of the Daguerreotype Process, or A Summary of M. Gouraud's Public Lectures, According to the Principles of M. Daguerre* (Boston, 1840); Francis Fauvel-Gouraud (i.e., François Gouraud): *Phreno-Mnemotechny; or, the Art of Memory* (New York and London, 1845); Francis Fauvel-Gouraud: *Practical Cosmophonography; a System of . . . Phonetic Alphabet* (New York, 1850); S. H. Branch: *A Brief History of Francis Fauvel Gouraud, Who Is About to Bamboozle the* (*Verdant?*) *Bostonians with an Exploded System of Artificial Memory* (Boston, 1845); *Philadelphia Photographer,* VIII, 316 (1871); *McClure's Magazine,* VIII, 8–10 (1896); Julius (?) Rockwell, manuscript sketch of Gouraud, NYPL. Gouraud died about 1848.

Extant daguerreotypes by SFBM: A very poor facsimile of what is said to be the first daguerreotype of the face made in America, and said to be by SFBM, is in *Scribner's Monthly,* V, 584 (1873). SFBM gave the original and some other of his early daguerreotypes to Vassar College; its authorities now decline, for fear of damaging, to restore them. The claim of the donor of two identical daguerreotypes to NYHS, that they are the first daguerreotypes by SFBM is rendered inadmissible by the facts that the process of producing identical daguerreotypes was not used in 1839, and that one of the subjects is SFBM's second wife, whom he did not marry until 1848. The daguerreotype of Jacob Gebhard, listed by Harry B. Wehle: *Samuel F. B. Morse* (New York, 1932), p. 48, as taken by SFBM in 1839, is now in the possession of Mrs. Russell Colgate.

1 On Nov. 24, 1821 LPW wrote from New Haven to SFBM in Washington that she would send him " the Camera-obscura," LC.

2 On July 6, 1839 the New York *Observer* quoted the New York *Journal of Commerce* as saying that some artists and connoisseurs were experimenting in the effort to discover Daguerre's process. On Sept. 21, 1839 the *Observer* noted that the secret was already in the possession " of a gentleman of high chemical attainments in the city." Cf. Taft, op. cit., note 13.

3 " In hundreds of journals," SFBM told Daguerre, *Letters,* II, 142. In Boston alone, for example, it was published in the *Daily Advertiser,* April 22, and the *Courier,* April 27, 1839.

4 Prime, p. 405. Cf. reference 11.

[5] Prime, pp. 406–7.

[6] The letter is dated Sept. 18 as first printed. Obvious internal evidence justifies changing it to Sept. 28.

[7] SFBM to Edward L. Wilson, Nov. 18, 1871 in *Philadelphia Photographer,* IX, 3–4 (1872). A hint as to the maker of SFBM's early instruments appeared in his brothers' New York *Observer,* which had been following the advent of the daguerreotype with interest ever since SFBM first wrote of it from Paris, and was one of the first journals to publish a full account of Daguerre's process (Nov. 2, 1839; cf. Taft, op. cit., note 53). On Oct. 19, 1839 it announced that G. W. Prosch was making daguerrean instruments. On Nov. 4 SFBM wrote Alfred Vail that Prosch was making perfect daguerrean instruments for $40. SM. This same year Prosch was making telegraph instruments for SFBM.

[8] Philadelphia *Dollar Newspaper,* July 25, 1855. These reminiscences of SFBM were reprinted in the *Photographic Art Journal,* Sept., 1855, and often since.

[9] The address in part is in Root, op. cit., pp. 390–2.

[10] *Letters,* II, 160.

[11] SFBM to Senator T. H. Benton, Feb. 5, 1855, LC.

[12] Mathew B. Brady to SFBM, Feb. 15, 1855, LC.

[13] Taft, op. cit., p. 28.

[14] Prime, pp. 407–8. Robert Taft wrote on the manuscript of this chapter at this point: "It seems to me that if Morse had made a portrait in any degree successful, he would have mentioned the unusual event in this letter."

[15] The notebook is at LC, filed in a box labeled "Miscellaneous Printed." An entry ostensibly for Nov. 1839 has been disregarded because of apparent tampering with the date.

[16] Identical letters, dated Nov. 29, 1839: François Gouraud to A. B. Durand, Durand papers, NYPL, and to Thomas S. Cummings in his *Historic Annals of the National Academy of Design* (Philadelphia, 1865), p. 158 (with inexplicable error in signature).

[17] *Description of the Daguerreotype Process,* op. cit., pp. 14–16.

[18] Georges Potonniée: *Histoire de la découverte de la photographie* (Paris, 1925), p. 230; Taft, op. cit., note 30 (in which read "Susse" for "Lusse").

[19] New York *Evening Star,* Feb. 21, 1840.

[20] Ibid., Feb. 24, 1840.

[21] Ibid., March 3, 1840.

[22] New York *Observer,* Nov. 30, 1839.

[23] Ibid., Dec. 14, 1839, quoting the announcement of Giroux and Co. from the Paris *Journal des Débats,* Nov. 10, 1839.

[24] Taft, op. cit., p. 43.

[25] New York *Commercial Advertiser,* New York *Evening Signal,* June 24, 1840; Boston *Daily Advertiser,* June 26, 1840.

[26] Ibid., July 2, 1840, quoting New York *Evening Signal,* probably June 26, 1840.

[27] Boston *Daily Advertiser*, July 2, 11, 1840.
[28] Abel Rendu to SFBM, July 22, 1840, LC.
[29] SFBM to Nathan Hale [Oct. 1840?], LC.
[30] SFBM to SEM, June 26, 1841, NYHS.
[31] Taft, op. cit., p. 23.
[32] *Personal Reminiscences of the late Mrs. Sarah Breese Walker* ([Utica?], 1884), p. 49. She placed the date in the fall of 1844, but it is unlikely that Morse had a studio at that time.
[33] *Niles' Register*, April 17, 1841.
[34] In July 1842 SFBM wrote that he had devoted all his time for nearly a year to the telegraph. Prime, p. 436.
[35] Taft, op. cit., pp. 87–92. There are more than a dozen letters between Hill and SFBM in 1852 alone at LC.

CHAPTER XX

Congressional Blessing

[1] *New-York Mirror*, Oct. 16, 1841.
[2] SFBM to *New-York Mirror* [*ca.* Oct. 1841], draft, LC.
[3] Circular dated Nov. 30, 1841, LC.
[4] R. V. DeWitt to SFBM, Dec. 13, 1841, LC.
[5] Statement of Strother, *Letters,* II, 162–3.
[6] Ibid., pp. 163–4.
[7] W. F. Cooke to SFBM, Jan. 17, 1840, LC.
[8] F. O. J. Smith to SFBM, Dec. 6, 1841, LC.
[9] SFBM to F. O. J. Smith, Sept. 19, 1842, MHS.
[10] *Letters,* II, 140–1.
[11] H. of R. Rep. No. 17, 27 Cong., 3 Sess.
[12] Prime, p. 434.
[13] *Letters,* II, 154.
[14] Edward B. Bright and Charles Bright: *The Life Story of the Late Sir Charles Tilston Bright,* I (Westminster [Eng.], [1899?]), pp. 93–4. SFBM believed his was "probably the first submarine telegraph line." SFBM to Michael Faraday, Sept. 30, 1854, draft, LC. The conception of submarine telegraphy has often been attributed to John W. Brett, but he wrote SFBM, Oct. 13, 1856, LC, stating that his conception was in 1845 after Wheatstone's.
[15] The account in Prime, pp. 441–3, is substantially confirmed by SFBM in H. of R. Doc. No. 24, 28 Cong., 2 Sess.
[16] Prime, p. 441.
[17] Washington *National Intelligencer,* quoted in New York *Observer,* Dec. 24, 1842.
[18] Clipping, correspondence of the *Times,* dated Washington, Dec. 27, 1842, LC.

the experiment see Silliman's *Journal,* XLV, 390–4 (1843), and Washington *National Intelligencer,* Oct. 18, 1843.

[11] Tatham brothers contract, dated Oct. 30, 1843, copy, LC; memorandum of F. O. J. Smith, Nov. 25, 1843, copy, LC.

[12] *Letters,* II, 212–13.

[13] Ezra Cornell to S. I. Prime, April 28, 1873, LC.

[14] J. C. Fisher to SFBM, Dec. 9, 1843, LC.

[15] [A. B. Cornell:] *Biography of Ezra Cornell* (New York, 1884), pp. 79–80.

[16] SFBM to J. C. Fisher, Dec. 29, 1843, draft, LC.

[17] SFBM to L. S. Bartlett by F. O. J. Smith, Dec. 18, 1843, MHS.

[18] L. S. Bartlett to SFBM, Dec. 18, 1843, draft, MHS. Part of the letter is apparently in F. O. J. Smith's hand.

[19] SFBM to F. O. J. Smith, Dec. 21, 1843, MHS.

[20] F. O. J. Smith to SFBM, Dec. 21, 1843, draft, MHS.

[21] *Letters,* II, 212.

[22] Entry of Jan. 11, 1844, in a journal of Alfred Vail, SM. By June 10, 1844 Vail's salary was $1,500 a year; by March 20, 1845 it was $1,400. Account of SFBM, LLM.

[23] *Letters,* II, 233.

[24] New York *Journal of Commerce,* Dec. 27, 1843.

[25] J. C. Spencer to SFBM, Dec. 29, 1843, LC.

[26] SFBM to F. O. J. Smith, May 17, 1844, draft, LC.

[27] Cf. Ezra Cornell to S. I. Prime, April 28, 1873, LC, and [A. B. Cornell:] *Biography of Ezra Cornell* (New York, 1884), pp. 87–9.

[28] Washington *National Intelligencer,* April 10, 1844.

[29] Ibid., April 19, 1844.

[30] J. W. Kirk in *Scribner's Magazine,* XI, 654–5 (1892). For a curious rewriting of this incident with the quotations changed to magnify the role of Alfred Vail, see the account attributed to Stephen Vail, son of Alfred, in *Graded Literature Readers,* VI (New York, 1901), 83–7, there used "by permission of *Truth.*" Aside from the direct quotations the circumstances of the incident are substantially confirmed in Prime, p. 491 (though the dates there are confused); *Letters,* II, 219; Washington *National Intelligencer,* May 8, 1844; and SFBM to J. B. Aycrigg, May 8, 1844, LC.

[31] Alfred Vail to unknown, in Stephen Vail: "Early Days of the First Telegraph Line," in *New England Magazine,* N.S., IV, 458 (1891).

[32] Entry of May 6, 1844, in a journal of Alfred Vail, SM.

[33] SFBM to SEM, LLM. SFBM dated the letter May 24, 1844. In part of the letter not quoted here, however, he mentions events which he dates May 25.

[34] Entry of May 29, 1844, in a journal of Alfred Vail, SM.

[35] Recollection of Ezra Cornell in 1864, in Albert W. Smith: *Ezra Cornell* (Ithaca, 1934), pp. 42–4.

[36] *Letters,* II, 225.
[37] New York *American Republican,* June 13, 1844, clipping, LC.
[38] New York *Herald,* May 30–1, 1844.
[39] Utica *Daily Gazette,* June 5, 1844, clipping, LC.
[40] Washington *National Intelligencer,* May 29, 1844.
[41] *Letters,* II, 223–5.

CHAPTER XXII

In the Fire of Fame

[1] Alfred Vail to George Vail, Sept. 1, 1844, in J. C. Vail, p. 19.
[2] Entry of Sept. 13, 1844, in a journal of Alfred Vail, SM.
[3] Entry of Aug. 17, 1844, in ibid.
[4] George Vail to David Burbank, Aug. 26, 1844, SM.
[5] George Vail to Alfred Vail, Aug. 17, 1844, SM.
[6] George Vail to Alfred Vail, Aug. 22, 1844, SM.
[7] SFBM, Alfred Vail, and SFBM as attorney for L. D. Gale to F. O. J. Smith, June 5, 1844, LC.
[8] F. O. J. Smith to SFBM, June 11, 1844, copy, LC.
[9] *Maine Farmer,* April 8, 1843.
[10] SFBM to Alfred Vail, June 11, 1844, copy, LC.
[11] SFBM to F. O. J. Smith, July 10, 1844, LC. SFBM said in an address in 1868, in *Journal of the Telegraph,* Jan. 1, 1869, that at this time the whole patent was offered to the government for $100,000; Prime, p. 510, and *Letters,* II, 232, probably follow this statement, neither offering evidence. It is unlikely, however, that SFBM would have accepted $100,000 for the whole sum when he was offering his share alone for the same price. In a letter to F. O. J. Smith, Dec. 20, 1844, MHS, SFBM recommended selling the whole for $250,000; in a letter to SEM, Oct. 1, 1838, SM, he had recommended selling for $322,000.
[12] SFBM to Zadock Pratt, Feb. 13, 1845, draft, LC, printed in H. of R. Rep. No. 184, 28 Cong., 2 Sess. The *Telegrapher,* Jan. 30, 1865, called "novel" a proposal for a similar machine invented by F. J. Grace.
[13] SFBM to L. D. Gale, March 11, 1845, LC.
[14] *Articles of Association . . . of the Magnetic Telegraph Company* (New York, 1847), p. 23.
[15] F. O. J. Smith offered this sum to SFBM in his letter of July 5, 1845, MHS. In reply, July 16, 1845, LC, SFBM reiterated his willingness to sell for cash or good notes at $100,000, but only if Kendall agreed. For some reason the transaction was not completed.
[16] SFBM to F. O. J. Smith, July 16, 1845, draft, LC. Alfred Vail invented the first printing telegraph in 1837, but did not promote its use, believing it impractical.

[17] *Letters,* II, 250.

[18] SFBM to D. F. Arago, Nov. 1, 1845, PENN.

[19] Prime, p. 537.

[20] SFBM to SEM, Nov. 1, 1845, LC.

[21] *Letters,* II, 256.

[22] SFBM to Alfred Vail, Jan. 17, 1846, SM.

[23] *Scientific American,* Nov. 20, 1845.

[24] SFBM does not refer to Audubon in available letters. SFBM and A. S. Doane, treasurer of the company, were commissioned to effect the river crossing. The wires on the New York side of the river terminated near what is now Riverside Drive and 155th Street, where Audubon's house then was. Doane reported to the company on July 7, 1846, a bill: "Audabon [*sic*] for Rent $20.00." In 1923 it was said that within the memory of men then living telegraph wires had been picked up from the floor of the laundry of the house; in 1931 when the demolition of the house was threatened, the story of Morse's association with it had become the legend that he did much of his experimental work on the telegraph there. *Articles of Association . . . of the Magnetic Telegraph Company* (New York, 1847), p. 37; Reid, pp. 120, 128; *Telegraph and Telephone Age,* Sept. 16, 1923; New York *Herald Tribune,* Oct. 2, 1931.

[25] Page testified that he did not charge SFBM for the privilege of using his magnets: French v. Rogers (Compls'. Ev.), Philadelphia, 1851, 405. SFBM wrote Alfred Vail, July 26, 1845, SM, however, that he had just sent Page $20 for the right to make two of his magnets.

[26] SFBM to Charles Page, April 1860, draft, LC; SFBM to Alfred Vail, Jan. 3, 1846, SM.

[27] SFBM to D. F. Arago [1846?], in Prime, p. 550.

[28] For example, F. O. J. Smith so threatened Davis and Co. of Boston for advertising to make telegraph instruments in a letter apparently to the company's lawyers, Messrs. Rantoul and Woodbury, April 28, 1846, BPL.

[29] Prime, p. 467.

[30] Prime, p. 471. Cf. Charles Francis Adams: *Richard Henry Dana,* I (Boston and New York, 1890), 80–1.

[31] SFBM to RCM, Feb. 20, 1846, COLG. A long anonymous letter in favor of SFBM had appeared in the Washington *National Intelligencer* of the previous day.

[32] *Letters,* II, 267.

[33] Washington *National Intelligencer,* Jan. 31, 1845; Baltimore *Sun,* Feb. 5, 1845; Baltimore *Republican and Daily Argus,* Feb. 8, 1845.

[34] *Petition of A. B. Durand and Others,* Sen. Doc. No. 380, 29 Cong., 1 Sess.; Washington *Union,* July 17, 1846, clipping, scrapbook of Alfred Vail, I, 73, SM.

[35] Ernest Green: "Canada's First Electric Telegraph," in Ontario Hist. Soc. *Papers and Records,* XXIV, 369 (1927). The Kingston, Canada West, *Chronicle* explained the rapid spread of telegraph lines across the border as

preparation for war with Canada. Quoted in Washington *Union,* Dec. 1, 1845, clipping, scrapbook of Alfred Vail, I, 135, SM.

[36] Clipping, dated Sept. 9, 1846, LC.

[37] *Letters,* II, 267–8.

CHAPTER XXIII

A Victorian Takes a Wife

On Locust Grove: Helen W. Reynolds: "The Story of Locust Grove," in Dutchess County Hist. Soc. *Year Book,* 1932, pp. 21–8; Lewis C. Carman: "Morse, the Poughkeepsian," in the Poughkeepsie *Thrift Messenger,* Sept. 1932.

[1] O'Rielly v. Morse (Ev.) [Washington, 1851?], 90–1. Though O'Rielly's name often appears as O'Reilly, it is here spelled as he preferred it.

[2] SFBM to Amos Kendall, Feb. 16, 1847, draft, LC.

[3] SFBM to Amos Kendall, Feb. 24, 1847, draft, LC.

[4] SFBM to SEM, Oct. 12, 1847, LC.

[5] SFBM to RCM, March 13, 1848, COLG.

[6] SFBM to SEM, Nov. 27, 1847, LC.

[7] SFBM to T. S. Faxton, March 15, 1848 [copy?], LC. Similarly, SFBM to F. O. J. Smith, April 18, 1848, MHS: "There has not been an improvement to the value of a pin's head on my invention since it went first into operation." At this same period SFBM was berated for claiming that he invented his alphabet on the *Sully* in 1832. Clippings from the Louisville *Journal,* Feb. 1848, in the scrapbook of Alfred Vail, II, 15–16, SM. SFBM's claim was in answer to the current charge that he stole his code from Steinheil.

[8] Agreement between William Gintl and SFBM, Feb. 28, 1856, LC.

[9] T. P. Shaffner to SFBM, Jan. 9, 1848, LC.

[10] *Letters,* II, 287–8.

[11] Reid, p. 198.

[12] *Letters,* II, 289.

[13] SEM to RCM and SFBM [?], July 3, 1847, LC.

[14] SFBM to SEM, Aug. 7, 1848, LLM.

[15] SFBM to RCM, July 29, 1848, COLG.

[16] SFBM to RCM, Aug. 27, 1848, COLG.

CHAPTER XXIV

On Trial

The important evidence in the telegraph suits is in the following: Morse v. O'Rielly (Dec. of Monroe), Frankfort, 1848; O'Rielly v. Morse (Ev.) [Washington, 1851?]; O'Rielly v. Morse (Dec. of Sup. Ct.), in *Reports of Cases Argued and Adjudged in the Supreme Court,* XV, (New York, 1884), in *Patent-*

Copyright-Trade Mark Cases, I, (New York, 1929), and in large part in Prime, pp. 565–79; Bain v. Morse (Ev. and Dec. of Cranch), Washington, 1849; Smith v. Downing (Ev.), New York, 1850; Smith v. Downing (Dec. of Woodbury), New York, 1852; French v. Rogers (Compls'. Ev.), Philadelphia, 1851; French v. Rogers (Respts'. Ev.), Philadelphia, 1851; French v. Rogers (Dec. of Grier and Kane), Philadelphia, 1851. These reports are not generally available in such libraries as BPL, NYPL, or LC; most are available, however, in the collection of telegraph papers which O'Rielly gave to NYHS.

[1] Philadelphia *American*, quoted in the Utica *Daily Gazette*, Sept. 1, 1848.

[2] New York *Tribune*, Sept. 18, 1848. Similarly, New York *Herald*, Sept. 13, 1848, clipping, scrapbook of Alfred Vail, II, 49, SM; *Scientific American*, Oct. 14, 1848.

[3] George E. Ellis to SFBM, June 3, 1839, LC, referring to *Paradise Lost*, Book vi, lines 498–501.

[4] Alfred Vail to Joseph Henry, marked about July 22, 1846, draft, LC. The letter is in SFBM's hand. In SFBM to Joseph Henry, Oct. 15, 1846, LC, SFBM admitted that he had drafted Alfred Vail's letter.

[5] Deposition of Henry, in Smith v. Downing (Ev.), op. cit., pp. 90–2.

[6] *Letters*, II, 263.

[7] SFBM: *The Electro-Magnetic Telegraph. A Defence* (Paris, [1867?]), p. 9.

[8] On Dyar see Alfred Monroe: *Concord and the Telegraph* (Concord, Mass., 1902); French v. Rogers (Respts'. Ev.), op. cit., pp. 13–18.

[9] Attributed by the Boston *Post* to "Randall" according to an undated clipping at LC. The author may be John Witt Randall, Boston poet and naturalist.

While their suit was pending, the Morse patentees and O'Rielly had effected a working agreement. O'Rielly issued to the patentees one fourth of the stock on his lines, less a small portion to be returned to O'Rielly in consideration of their having interfered with his contract. *American Telegraph Magazine*, I, appendix to issue of Dec. 15, 1852.

[10] Draft of an artitcle written by SFBM for the New York *Observer*, dated Jan. 7, 1851, LC.

[11] *Before the Commissioner of Patents . . . Application of Samuel F. B. Morse, for an Extension for Seven Years of Letters Patent Granted to Him June 20th, 1840 . . . Argument in Favor of the Extension* (Washington, 1854), pp. 32–6.

[12] Certified copy of the decision of Charles Mason, June 23, 1854, LC.

[13] *Electrical World*, XXVI, 184 (1895). See also *Decision of Hon. Philip F. Thomas, Commissioner of Patents, on the Application of Samuel F. B. Morse, for an Extension of His Patent . . . Patented April, 1846. Patent Extended for Seven Years from the 11th Day of April, 1860* (Washington, 1860). SFBM also attempted to have his 1840 patent again extended so as to expire at the same time as his 1846 patent; that is, in 1867. To do so he applied to

Congress for a special act. See Sen. Rep. No. 310, 36 Cong., 2 Sess. His request was not granted. By this time SFBM had sold his rights, and the attempts were being made for him.

[14] Printed report, "Dinner to Professor Morse of the United States," Oct. 9, 1856, approved by the presiding officers, and sent to SFBM by W. F. Cooke, LC.

CHAPTER XXV

Atlantic Cable

On telegraphy and the development of journalism: Oliver Gramling: *AP: the Story of News* (New York and Toronto, 1940); Frederic Hudson: *Journalism in the United States* (New York, 1873); Victor Rosewater: *History of Coöperative News-Gathering in the United States* (New York and London, 1930).

On the Atlantic cable: Charles F. Briggs and Augustus Maverick: *The Story of the Telegraph and . . . Atlantic Cable* (New York, 1858); Edward B. Bright and Charles Bright: *The Life Story of the Late Sir Charles Tilston Bright* (Westminster [Eng.], [1899?]); Henry M. Field: *History of the Atlantic Telegraph* (New York, 1869); Isabella Field Judson: *Cyrus W. Field* (New York, 1896); Allan Nevins: *Abram S. Hewitt with Some Account of Peter Cooper* (New York and London, 1935); Philip McDonald: *A Saga of the Seas* (New York, 1937); John Mullaly: *The Laying of the Cable* (New York, 1858); John W. Wayland: *The Pathfinder of the Seas: The Life of Matthew Fontaine Maury* (Richmond, 1930); William W. Wheidon scrapbook on the Atlantic cable, BPL.

[1] New York *Herald,* April 13, 1850. Cf. Reid, pp. 362–9; Daniel H. Craig: *A Review of "an Exposition"* (Halifax, 1850).

[2] SFBM to [Amos Kendall], Nov. 4, 1852, draft, LC.

[3] *Proceedings of the American Telegraph Convention* (Philadelphia, 1853).

[4] Prime, p. 615.

[5] SFBM to editor of the *Scientific American,* April 23, 1864, draft, LC.

[6] Prime, p. 614.

[7] M. F. Maury to SFBM, Feb. 23, 1854, LC.

[8] SFBM to Cyrus Field, March 11, 1854, LC.

[9] Prime, p. 637.

[10] James Wynne in *Harper's Magazine,* XXIV, 228 (1862).

[11] Prime, p. 645.

[12] Printed report, "Dinner to Professor Morse of the United States," Oct. 9, 1856, LC.

[13] C. R. Leslie to SFBM, Oct. 10, 1856, LC.

[14] J. W. Brett to SFBM, Oct. 13, 1856, LC.

[15] Amos Kendall to SFBM, Dec. 7, 1855, LC.

[16] T. R. Walker to SFBM, March 6, 1856, LC.
[17] Amos Kendall to SFBM, Feb. 22, 1857, LC.
[18] Peter Cooper to SFBM, March 10, 1857, LC.
[19] *Letters,* II, 374.
[20] SFBM: *A Memoir Showing the Grounds of My Claim on . . . the European States* (Paris, 1857).
[21] SFBM's notebook, containing a record of the April 1857 *Niagara* voyage from New York to England and a few subsequent entries, LLM.
[22] *Letters,* II, 378.
[23] Briggs and Maverick, op. cit., p. 97.
[24] *Letters,* II, 380.
[25] Ibid., p. 382.
[26] SFBM to Mrs. SFBM, Aug. 12, 1857, draft, LC.
[27] Field, op. cit., p. 161; Mullaly, op. cit., pp. 150–1.
[28] Briggs and Maverick, op. cit., pp. 108–9, 113–14.
[29] SFBM to RCM, Oct. 15, 1857, COLC.
[30] SFBM to Mrs. Mary S. Field, Feb. 27, 1858, copy, LC.
[31] SFBM to Cyrus Field, March 12, 1858, copy, LC.
[32] Clipping, Wheidon scrapbook, op. cit.
[33] Reid, pp. 141, 418–20. As the Western Union Company gradually supplanted the American Company as the controlling interest in all telegraph lines on the continent, SFBM exchanged American Company stock for its stock. In June 1866 he received for himself, his wife, and his daughter 2,369 shares. SFBM to SEM, May 27, 1867, LLM.
[34] Reid, pp. 421–2; cf. Ch. XXIV, reference 13.
[35] A copy of the statement sent to SFBM, dated May 30, 1860, LC.
[36] SFBM to Amos Kendall, June 8, 1860, LC.
[37] See *The Telegraph and the Press* (New York, 1860); *The American Telegraph Company . . . Remarks of R. W. Russell . . . in Reply to the Statements of Messrs. Abram S. Hewitt . . . and Others . . . on June 29th, 1860* (New York, 1860); Daniel H. Craig: *The American Telegraph Company and the Press* (New York, 1860).
[38] Hudson, op. cit., p. 615.

CHAPTER XXVI

Copperhead

[1] Signed statement of R. W. Habersham, filed 1832, LC.
[2] Sprague: *Life of JM,* p. 141.
[3] Undated fragment, filed 1854, LC.
[4] SFBM's "Notes on Social Compact, Rousseau," in possession of the present author.
[5] SFBM to SEM, Oct. 29, 1846, LC.

[6] Poughkeepsie *Dutchess Democrat,* Oct. 26, 1854.

[7] His statement is in part in ibid.

[8] New York *Tribune,* Nov. 2, 1854.

[9] SFBM to SEM, Feb. 27, 1854, LC. The Whig Poughkeepsie *Daily Eagle,* Nov. 4, 1854, guessed correctly that he favored the Nebraska bill.

[10] Poughkeepsie *Dutchess Democrat,* Nov. 23, 1854.

[11] SFBM to W. S. Tisdale, in the New York *Observer,* August 16, 1855.

[12] SFBM to B. J. Lossing, May 2, letter-book, 1864, LC; Benson J. Lossing: *Pictorial History of the Civil War,* I (Philadelphia, 1866), 245–7, including illustrations of the proposed flags, from drawings by SFBM.

[13] SFBM to J. D. Caton, Feb. 18, 1863, draft, LC.

[14] On the telegraph in the Civil War, see William R. Plum: *The Military Telegraph during the Civil War* (Chicago, 1882), and David H. Bates: *Lincoln in the Telegraph Office* (New York, 1907).

[15] Benson J. Lossing: *History of New York City* (New York, 1884), p. 716. Cf. Horace Greeley: *The American Conflict,* I (Hartford, 1864), 439–40.

[16] *Letters,* II, 416.

[17] New York *Evening Post,* Feb. 7, 1863.

[18] Ibid., Feb. 14, 1863.

[19] New York *Observer,* Feb. 19, 1863.

[20] Poughkeepsie *Daily Eagle,* Feb. 10, 1863.

[21] *The Writings and Speeches of Samuel J. Tilden,* I (New York, 1885), 335.

[22] New York *Evening Post,* Feb. 9, 1863.

[23] Ibid., Feb. 12, 1863.

[24] Ibid., Feb. 19, 1863.

[25] *The Constitution, An Argument on the Ethical Position of Slavery, The Letter of a Republican . . . and Prof. Morse's Reply* (Papers from the Society for the Diffusion of Political Knowledge) (New York, 1863).

[26] Ibid., 6. The New York *World* reprinted a large part of ibid., March 24, 1863.

[27] SFBM to J. H. Agnew, Sept. 9, 1864, letter-book, LC.

[28] New York *World,* Aug. 11, 1864.

[29] SFBM to Abner Morse, Nov. 1, 1864, letter-book, LC.

[30] New York *Evening Express,* Nov. 5, 1864.

[31] SFBM to RCM, Nov. 9, 1864, letter-book, LC.

CHAPTER XXVII

Patriarch

[1] SFBM's honors are detailed in Prime, pp. 603–13.

[2] Minutes of the proceedings of the Congress, filed Nov. 3, 1858, LC; Paris *Moniteur Universel,* April 29, 1858.

[3] These figures are based on the $5,105.60 which SFBM wrote Mrs. Alfred Vail, Nov. 17, 1862, SM, that he was giving her as Vail's share of two sixteenths.

[4] SFBM to F. O. J. Smith, May 24, 1860, draft, LC.

[5] According to SFBM's income-tax statement, filed 1863, LC.

[6] Alexander J. Davis, manuscript diary, Metropolitan Museum of Art, New York.

[7] Prime, p. 597.

[8] *Telegraph Age*, XVI, 224 (1895).

[9] *The Charter of Smith's Home for Aged Indigent Mothers* (Portland, 1865); *The Last Will and Testament of Francis O. J. Smith* [Portland, 1877]; Westbrook and Portland scrapbooks, MHS; F. O. J. Smith papers, MHS.

[10] Minutes of the trustees, typed copy, at Vassar College, Poughkeepsie.

[11] SFBM to RCM, June 6, 1865, letter-book, LC; records of the gift are in the minute book of the Board of Directors at Union Theological Seminary, New York.

[12] T. S. Cummings to A. B. Durand [1861?], Durand papers, NYPL.

[13] Prime, p. 708.

[14] SFBM to Daniel Huntington, Dec. 26, 1864, letter-book, LC.

[15] SFBM to SEM, Oct. 1, 1866, LLM.

[16] *Letters*, II, 449.

[17] SFBM to SEM, June 8–11, 1867, LLM.

[18] Fragment in SFBM's hand, filed 1867, LC.

[19] *Letters*, II, 453.

[20] SEM to SFBM, Jan. 25, 1867, LLM; William P. Blake to SFBM, Aug. 5, 1869, LC. SFBM's report was printed as *Examination of the Telegraphic Apparatus and the Processes in Telegraphy* (Washington, 1869).

[21] SFBM to SEM, Sept. 26, 1868, LLM.

CHAPTER XXVIII

Harvest

Memorials of SFBM: *A Memorial of Samuel F. B. Morse, from the City of Boston. Printed by Order of the City Council* ([Boston], 1872); *Memorial of Samuel Finley Breese Morse, Including Appropriate Ceremonies of Respect at the National Capitol, and Elsewhere. Published by Order of Congress* (Washington, 1875); Edward G. Porter: *Remarks Suggested by a Tablet at Rome Commemorative of S. F. B. Morse* (Cambridge, 1897); "Sesión Solemne Celebrada por las Sociedad, Mexicana de Geografía y Estadística . . . en Honor del . . . Samuel Morse," in *Sociedad de Geografía y Estadística, Boletín*, Ser. 3, I, 27–67 (1873); Reid.

[1] New York *Times*, Dec. 30, 1868; *Journal of the Telegraph*, Jan. 1, 1869; *Letters*, II, 467–75; menu of the dinner, NYHS.

[2] *The Golden Age,* April 15, 1871.

[3] Amos Kendall: *Autobiography* (Boston and New York, 1872), pp. 691–2.

[4] SFBM to Hesse E. Finley, April 16, 1869, letter-book, LC.

[5] SFBM to Susan Morse Lind, April 21, 1870, letter-book, LC.

[6] *Journal of the Telegraph,* Jan. 1, 1871.

[7] New York *Times,* June 11; New York *World,* June 10, 11; *Journal of the Telegraph,* June 15; *Hearth and Home,* July 1, 1871; typed article on Cornelia Morse Rummel, undated, LLM. There were other proposals to erect monuments to SFBM during his lifetime, one in New York by the city, and another in Washington by the National Monument Society. New York *Times,* Dec. 15, 1865; *Letters,* II, 442, 498–502.

[8] New York *Times,* New York *World,* June 11; *Journal of the Telegraph,* June 15, 1871.

[9] *Letters,* II, 493.

[10] *Memorial of . . . Morse . . . Published by Order of Congress,* op. cit., p. 27.

[11] *Letters,* II, 497–8.

[12] The book was Horace Greeley (and others): *The Great Industries of the United States* (Hartford, Chicago, and Cincinnati, 1872). The article on telegraphy, unsigned, pp. 1233–49, referred to the persons participating in the June 10, 1871, celebrations as "beguiled." Apparently SFBM was correct in assuming that Smith and O'Rielly were behind the move. See *Electrical World,* XXVI, 522–3 (1895), and *The Telegrapher,* Feb. 10, 1872.

[13] SFBM to F. J. Mead, March 14, 1872, letter-book, LC.

[14] *Letters,* II, 506–7.

INDEX

Index

Index

Index

Index

A NOTE ON THE TYPE

The text of this book is set in Caledonia, a Linotype face designed by W. A. Dwiggins. Caledonia belongs to the family of printing types called "modern face" by printers — a term used to mark the change in style of type-letters that occurred about 1800. Caledonia is in the general neighborhood of Scotch Modern in design, but is more freely drawn than that letter.

The book was composed, printed, and bound by The Plimpton Press, Norwood, Massachusetts.

VITA

Born in Shanghai, China, Dec. 25, 1914; Harrisonburg (Va.) and Lewiston (Me.) High Schools; Bates College, A.B., 1936; Columbia University, A.M., 1938; Delta Sigma Rho, Phi Beta Kappa